Kiln Sites of Ancient China

Kiln Sites of Ancient China

An exhibition lent by the People's Republic of China

Compiled by Penelope Hughes-Stanton and Rose Kerr

ORIENTAL CERAMIC SOCIETY

Compilers' note

The dates and details of excavation of the sherds in
this catalogue were supplied by the Chinese
authorities.
The sherds, except where explicitly stated to be
earthenware or porcelain, are presumed to be
stoneware.
The numbers of this catalogue do not exactly
correspond with those of the British Museum
handlist.

ISBN 0 903421 19 4
Typography and design by Dick Tyler of Balding + Mansell
Phototypeset in Photina on 'Monotype' 400/8
Printed and bound in Great Britain by
Balding + Mansell, London and Wisbech

Contents

Foreword

An exhibition of recent finds from kiln sites of China was first proposed by Sir John Addis, on behalf of the Oriental Ceramic Society, to the State Administrative Bureau for Museums and Archaeological Data, Peking in 1978. When the Chinese authorities agreed to this proposal the British Museum was consulted, and the Department of Oriental Antiquities of the museum most generously and enthusiastically supported the idea and eventually carried through the negotiations with the officials of the State Administrative Bureau and the Palace Museum, Peking. The Cultural Relations Department of the Foreign and Commonwealth Office and H.B.M. Embassy, Peking gave further indispensable help. As the result of these combined efforts, the exhibition was able to open in the British Museum, London on March 26 until May 9, 1980. Subsequently the same exhibition was shown at the Ashmolean Museum, Oxford from June 9 to July 19, 1980 by courtesy of the Department of Arts and Libraries. The Oriental Ceramic Society was able to offer assistance in transport costs of the exhibition and is now happy to offer a fully illustrated catalogue which, for practical reasons, could not be published before the exhibition was held.

The organisation of the exhibition was a joint enterprise of scholarship between Chinese scholars and the staff of the British Museum. We are glad that as a result of our study of the exhibition and further work by Penelope Hughes-Stanton and Rose Kerr, it has been possible to extend and emend the handlist produced at the time of the exhibition. By courtesy of the Chinese authorities we can now add a complete photographic coverage of the material shown.

For students of Chinese ceramics, study of such material is invaluable in the further understanding of the elaborate network of ceramic styles and types in China over many centuries. The use of sherd material enables a wider variety of exhibit than could be contemplated using whole specimens and is some small compensation for our distance from the sources of our study. In expressing our keen appreciation to the State Administrative Bureau for Museums and Archaeological Data and to the Palace Museum, Peking of the loan of such a carefully chosen and instructive collection the Oriental Ceramic Society, representing many serious students of Chinese ceramics in many countries as well as Great Britain, would also wish to record a hope that co-operation of this sort with our Chinese colleagues may grow and find further opportunities of similar activities.

We would also like to express our appreciation of the help which all enthusiasts and scholars receive from the British Museum and indeed all other museums concerned with the study of Chinese ceramics. The fine display of the exhibition mounted by the British Museum was but one example of this service.

We would acknowledge with thanks the assistance in the preparation of the manuscript most ably given by Kevin Ames and Nigel Wright and also by Sheila Nightingale who undertook the typing of the manuscript. Finally we are indebted to the British Museum authorities and to Mrs Jessica Rawson in particular for the preparation of the original handlist and for permission to use much material from both the handlist and the display in the compilation of this catalogue. The Society thanks the compilers for patient and expert work undertaken under pressure of time.

M. Tregear
President
Oriental Ceramic Society
London

Introduction

With a tradition of ceramic manufacture going back as much as eight thousand years, and as the country that invented porcelain, China occupies a pre-eminent position in the history of ceramics. In the last 30 years Chinese archaeologists working in 19 provinces, cities, and autonomous regions have discovered thousands of kilns of different periods located within the areas of 76 counties and towns. Tens of thousands of pots of all dates have also been excavated from ancient tombs. The large scale of these finds has created excellent conditions for systematic study of the history of Chinese ceramics.

Among the representative kilns chosen for this exhibition are kilns from 44 counties and towns situated in 13 provinces. The 500 exhibits range in date from the Eastern Han to the Yuan dynasty. The exhibition provides a survey of the development of Chinese ceramics, and includes green and black glazed wares of the Eastern Han (AD 25 – 220), green wares of the Southern Dynasties (AD 420 – 580), and the famous ceramics of the Tang (AD 618 – 906) and Song periods (AD 960 – 1279), all from the province of Zhejiang. Further, the products of eight northern and southern kilns are systematically examined, together with the export porcelains of the Song and Yuan periods from the south-east coastal region. Over a third of the exhibits are recent discoveries.

The exhibition of 'Archaeological Treasures Excavated in the People's Republic of China' held in London in the Autumn of 1973, attracted several hundreds of thousands of visitors, thereby increasing friendship and mutual understanding between Britain and China. Britain has long been noted for its collections of Chinese porcelain, and for the number of famous scholars known for their study in the field of Chinese ceramics. We hope that this exhibition will promote closer ties of friendship and academic co-operation between the two countries.

The State Administrative Bureau for Museums and Archaeological Data

Kiln Sites represented in the Exhibition

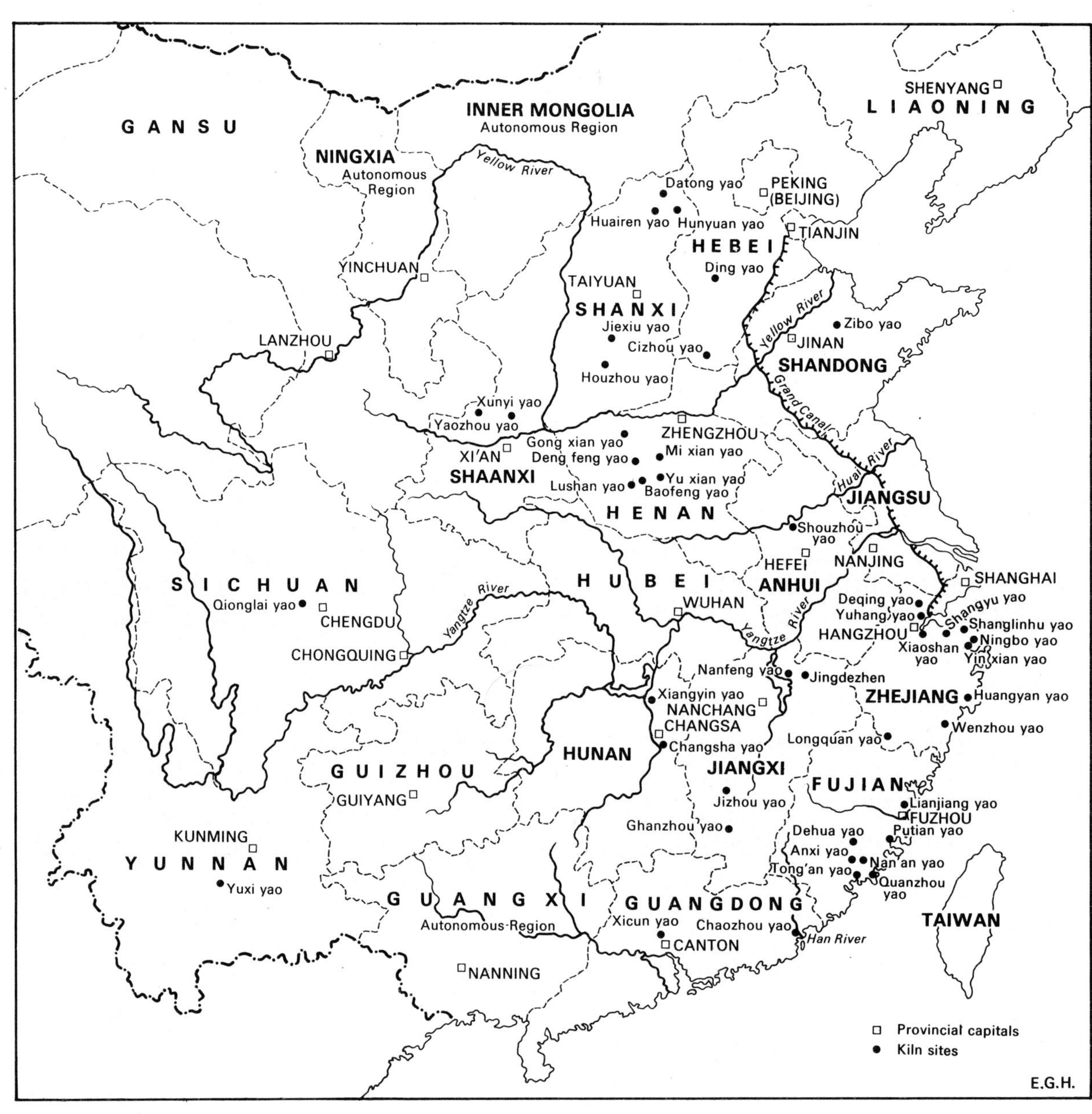

Zhejiang nos. 1–100

The kilns in this east coast province range in date from Eastern Han to the Yuan dynasty and mark the long development of green glazed stoneware in the region. The earlier kilns show the emergence of this influential ware and the later group the very fine Longquan wares of Song and Yuan.

Shangyu	nos. 1–24, 64–72
Ningbo	nos. 25–29, 73–81
Yuhang	nos. 30–39
Deqing	nos. 40–41
Xiaoshan	nos. 42–46
Yueyao	nos. 47–63
Wenzhou	nos. 82–88
Huangyan	nos. 89–92
Longquan	nos. 93–100

Shangyu   nos. 1–24, 64–72

Kilns of Eastern Han date, manufacturing green glazed wares, have been discovered in Shangyu xian in the past few years. The excavated sherds have been examined by a research team which has concluded that Shangyu was one of the earliest sources of Chinese greenwares. Many remains of the kilns of the Six Dynasties period, whose products were sold in the Yangtze valley, have also been discovered.

Tribute wares of the Five Dynasties and early Song periods (nos. 64–72) made for the Qian family, the ruling house in the small kingdom of Wu-Yue in the Jiangsu-Zhejiang region, have been excavated at a large number of kiln sites. At least 350 kiln sites have been found in Shangyu xian, illustrating its importance as a major centre of ceramic production in the province of Zhejiang.

1

Fragment of a jar with impressed decoration under a green glaze
From Zhejiang Shangyu (1979:7)
Eastern Han dynasty (2nd–3rd century AD)

This flat fragment from the wall of a jar is decorated with a repeated impressed comb-like design. The fine buff-grey body is glazed with a thin, even, pale olive glaze on both sides. The force of the impressions has gone through and made the inside wall uneven.

Dimensions: 8 × 5 cm. Body: 0.6–0.9 cm.

2

Fragment of a jar with impressed decoration under a green glaze
From Zhejiang Shangyu (1979:7)
Eastern Han dynasty (2nd–3rd century AD)

Also from the wall of a jar, this sherd is stamped with a repeated rectangle divided by double diagonal lines into four triangles filled with vertical and horizontal lines. The light grey, rather fine body is uneven on the inside where the stamp impressions have gone through. The pale olive glaze is crazed where deeper in the impressions, and only partially covers the inside of the fragment.

Dimensions: 8.6 × 5.2 cm. Body: 0.7–0.8 cm.

3

Fragment of a jar with an impressed decoration under a green glaze
From Zhejiang Shangyu (1979:7)
Eastern Han dynasty (2nd–3rd century AD)

This sherd from the wall of a jar is decorated on the outside with a repeated stamped basketwork design. The fine buff-grey body is glazed on the outside with a thin olive glaze.

Dimensions: 6.4 × 4.4 cm. Body: 0.4–0.5 cm.

4

Fragment of a jar with impressed designs under a green glaze
From Zhejiang Shangyu (1979:7)
Eastern Han dynasty (2nd–3rd century AD)

From the rounded wall of a jar, this sherd is decorated with a repeated stamped triangular design infilled with horizontal and criss-cross patterns. The unglazed inside shows the pressure of the stamps. The fine buff-grey body is glazed on the outside with a thin olive glaze which runs thick in the impressions.

Dimensions: 9.5 × 6.7 cm. Body: 0.4 cm.

5
Fragment of a jar with stamped decoration under a
green glaze
From Zhejiang Shangyu (1979:7)
Eastern Han dynasty (2nd–3rd century AD)

This sherd from the rounded wall of a jar is decorated
with a repeated stamped triangular design filled with
vertical lines. The triangles appear to be part of a
larger stamped rectangular motif. The fine grey body
is uneven on the unglazed inside which shows the
pressure of the stamps. The outside is glazed with a
thin, even, olive glaze which contains small dark
specks.

Dimensions: 12.4 × 8.2 cm. Body: 0.5–0.7 cm.
Published: GGBWYYK 1980 (1) pp. 3–27, Fig. 1

6
Fragment of a jar with stamped decoration under a
green glaze
From Zhejiang Shangyu (1979:7)
Eastern Han dynasty (2nd–3rd century AD)

A sherd from the wall of a jar, this is decorated with
repeated stamped rectangular designs filled in with a
mesh pattern. The inside shows the pressure marks
of the stamps. The fine buff-grey body is glazed inside
and out with an olive glaze, which is crazed
especially where deep in the impressions.

Dimensions: 16.3 × 6.6 cm. Body: 0.6 cm.
Published: GGBWYYK 1980 (1) pp. 3–27, Fig. 1

7
Fragment with handle from the wall of a jar with a
green glaze
From Zhejiang Shangyu (1979:7)
Eastern Han dynasty (2nd–3rd century AD)

From the wall of a jar this sherd has a sprigged lug
handle. The strip of clay for the handle was
impressed with a net pattern before application to
the piece. The buff-grey body is fine grained, and the
sherd is glazed on the outside with a thin olive glaze,
which runs thick in the depressions.

Dimensions: 8 × 7 cm. Body: 0.7 cm.
Published: GGBWYYK 1980 (1) pp. 3–27, Fig. 1

8
Fragment of a jar with a lug handle and a green
glaze
From Zhejiang Shangyu (1979:7)
Eastern Han dynasty (2nd–3rd century AD)

This sherd, from the wall of a thick jar, has a
sprigged lug handle with impressed decoration
similar to that of no. 7. The wall of the jar is stamped
with a repeated comb-like design. The fine grey body
is glazed on the outside with a thin olive glaze.

Dimensions: 9.3 × 6.3 cm. Body: 0.9 cm.
Published: GGBWYYK 1980 (1) pp. 3–27, Fig. 1

9
Fragment of a jar with a green glaze
From Zhejiang Shangyu (1979:7)
Eastern Han dynasty (2nd–3rd century AD)

A rim sherd of a thick-walled jar, this fragment has a
high rounded shoulder and an everted rim, square
cut at the lip, and is decorated with three incised
bands round the rim. The sherd has a fine, grey body
and is unglazed on the inside, while the outside and
the top of the rim are glazed with a thin, olive glaze.

Dimensions: 10 × 7 cm. Body: 1.1–1.8 cm.
Published: GGBWYYK 1980 (1) pp. 3–27, Fig. 1

10
Fragment of a jar with incised decoration under a
green glaze
From Zhejiang Shangyu (1979:7)
Eastern Han dynasty (2nd–3rd century AD)

This fragment from a jar, with a high rounded
shoulder and flaring everted rim, is decorated on the
shoulder with a freely incised wavy line beneath
which is a band of incised lines. The thick wall has a
fine, grey body, and is glazed on the outside with a
thin green glaze which is crazed where thick. The
inside of the rim is glazed but the rest of the inside is
unglazed.

Dimensions: 6 × 5 cm. Body: 0.7 cm.
Published: GGBWYYK 1980 (1) pp. 3–27, Fig. 1

11
Fragment of a jar with impressed decoration under a
dark brown glaze
From Zhejiang Shangyu (1979:7)
Eastern Han dynasty (2nd–3rd century AD)

This sherd from the rounded wall of a jar is decorated
on the outside with a repeated stamped design of a
square with a net infill. The medium-coarse, grey-
buff body is glazed on the outside with an olive
brown glaze, which appears almost black where it
runs thick. The inside is unglazed except for streaks
of glaze.

Dimensions: 9.5 × 4.6 cm. Body: 0.6 cm.

12
Fragment of a jar with an impressed design under a
dark brown glaze
From Zhejiang Shangyu (1979:7)
Eastern Han dynasty (2nd–3rd century AD)

From the wall of a jar, this sherd is decorated on the
outside with a repeated diamond shaped, stamped
design, filled with diamond shapes diminishing
towards the centre. Some of the stamps overlap. The
medium-coarse, dark grey body has a dark brown
glaze on the outside. The glaze is thin and matt
except for a greenish shiny spot. The inside is glazed
with a dark olive glaze which has crawled.

Dimensions: 7 × 6.5 cm. Body: 0.9 cm.

13

Fragment with handle from a jar with stamped
designs under a dark brown glaze
From Zhejiang Shangyu (1979:7)
Eastern Han dynasty (2nd–3rd century AD)

From the wall of a jar, this fragment is decorated
with repeated stamped comb-like designs on the
body, and on the lug handle with an impressed
linear pattern. Unglazed on the inside, the sherd has
a medium-coarse, dark grey body with a green glaze,
which appears dark brown in the impressions.

Length: 10.5 cm. Body: 0.4–0.6 cm.

14

Part of a bowl with a band of impressed design under
a green glaze
From Zhejiang Shangyu (1979:7)
Western Jin dynasty (AD 265–316)

This fragment is part of a bowl with a thick flat base,
rounded sides, constricted at the neck and at the
everted rim. It is decorated with a rouletted band of
net pattern and incised bands around the sides. The
fairly coarse, grey body shows small air bubbles and
the light olive, slightly crazed glaze runs thick in the
incised lines. The base is unglazed, and where the
glaze was wiped away on the outside wall there is
red oxidisation, perhaps indicating excess iron in
either slip or body.

Height: 11.5 cm. Width: 17 cm.
Body: 0.5 (rim) – 1.4 cm. (base)

15

Part of a bowl with bands of impressed decoration
under a green glaze
From Zhejiang Shangyu (1979:7)
Western Jin dynasty (AD 265–316)

Part of a bowl, decorated with a band of rouletted
mesh pattern enclosed by two bands of stamped
rosettes around the sides and with incised rings
round the neck. The fragment has a thick, flat base,
rounded sides and a straight mouth rim. The grey,
coarse body, which contains air bubbles, is glazed
inside and out with a light olive, slightly crazed glaze
which runs thick in the depressions. Where the glaze
is trimmed above the foot and on the unglazed base
the body appears reddish brown.

Height: 12 cm. Available diameter: 21 cm.
Body: 0.6 (rim)–2.5 cm. (base)

16

Fragment of a bowl with bands of impressed
decoration under a green glaze
From Zhejiang Shangyu (1979:7)
Western Jin dynasty (AD 265–316)

This fragment is part of a bowl with a rounded wall,
sharply everted and flattened rim. It is decorated
round the sides with a band of rouletted net pattern
between two bands of roulette-stamped rosettes, and
on top of the rim with a band of net pattern, with a
band of rosettes on the inside edge. The medium-
coarse, grey body is glazed inside and out with a thin
green glaze.

Dimensions: 13 × 6 cm. Width of rim: 2.8 cm.
Body: 0.6 cm.

17

Part of an ink slab, glazed on the outside with a
green glaze
From Zhejiang Shangyu (1979:7)
Western Jin dynasty (AD 265–316)

This part of an ink slab for grinding ink has a flat
base which is glazed and decorated with a double
band of triple incised lines. The sides spread from the
base, are flattened and rise again towards the
grooved rim, forming a stepped profile. The coarse,
grey body has oxidised slightly on the unglazed
inside, where three spur marks are visible. The glaze
is green.

Dimensions: 15 × 10.5 cm. Body: 1–1.2 cm.

18

Part of a bowl with a band of rouletted design under
a green glaze
From Zhejiang Shangyu (1979:7)
Western Jin dynasty (AD 265–316)

Part of a bowl with rounded sides, slightly
constricted and everted rim and a flat base, this
fragment is decorated with a band of rouletted
scrolling pattern round the sides beneath the rim.
The medium-coarse, grey body is glazed inside, and
outside down to the unglazed base, with a green
glaze which is thin and slightly degraded. Kiln debris
adheres to the inside.

Height: 6.5 cm. Width of available base: 5 cm.
Body: 0.3–1 cm.

19
Part of a jar with impressed decoration and a mask
motif under a green glaze
From Zhejiang Shangyu (1979:7)
Western Jin dynasty (AD 265–316)

This sherd from a high shouldered jar with a
straight, squared mouth rim, is decorated with a
band of rouletted net pattern between two bands of
stamped rosettes, and with two incised rings around
the neck. Over the rouletted bands is an applied
feline mask with a ring in its mouth. The medium-
coarse, grey body is glazed on the outside, and to just
below the neck on the inside, with a thin, crazed
grey-olive glaze.

Dimensions: 7 × 7 cm. Body: 0.6–0.9 cm.

20
Part of a jar with a lug handle and impressed
decoration under a green glaze
From Zhejiang Shangyu (1979:7)
Western Jin dynasty (AD 265–316)

This fragment from the rounded shoulder of a jar is
decorated with a band of rouletted net pattern
between two bands of stamped roulettes. A sprigged
lug handle, and the remains of another, are applied
over the bands of design. The medium-coarse, grey
body is glazed with a lustrous green glaze inside and
out.

Dimensions: 10.5 × 6.5 cm. Body: 0.5–1 cm.

21
Fragment of a jar with a lug handle under a green
glaze
From Zhejiang Shangyu (1979:7)
Western Jin dynasty (AD 265–316)

This rim sherd, from a jar with a high rounded
shoulder and straight, rounded rim, is decorated
with a lug handle with an impressed design. There
are incised grooves around the shoulder and neck.
The medium-coarse grey body is glazed on the
outside and to just below the neck on the inside with
a thin olive glaze.

Dimensions: 10 × 9.5 cm. Body: 0.7–1 cm.

22
Part of a dish with an incised lotus decoration under
a brown glaze
From Zhejiang Shangyu (1979:7)
Southern Dynasties (AD 420–589)

This sherd, from the thick rounded wall of a dish, is
decorated on the inside with a lotus petal pattern in
fine incised line and two bands of triple incised line.
The coarse buff-grey body is glazed with a runny,
brown glaze which ranges from yellowish to black
where thick. The body is exposed and oxidised in
places.

Dimensions: 14.8 × 9.5 cm. Body: 0.3 (rim)–1.7 cm.

23
Fragment of a dish with lotus leaves incised under
the green glaze
From Zhejiang Shangyu (1979:7)
Southern Dynasties (AD 420–589)

This fragment is part of a dish with a rounded wall
and thick flat base. The inside walls are decorated
with lotus petals in multiple incised line. The coarse
grey body is glazed all over with a shiny green glaze.
Kiln grit adheres to the glaze on the base and two
spur marks are visible on the inside.

Dimensions: 10.5 × 10.2 cm. Body: 1–2.2 cm.

24
Part of a dish with incised lotus decoration under a
green glaze
From Zhejiang Shangyu (1979:7)
Southern Dynasties (AD 420–589)

This fragment of a dish with a rounded wall and a
flat, unglazed base, is decorated on the outside with
incised lotus petals rising from the base. Two spur
marks are visible on the inside. The medium-coarse,
grey body contains large air bubbles and is glazed
with a green, shiny, viscous glaze.

Height: 8 cm. Width: 10.5 cm.
Width of available base: 3 cm.
Body: 0.5 (wall)–1.8 cm. (base)

Ningbo   nos. 25–29, 73–81

The kilns at Ningbo and the related kilns in Yin xian (see below nos. 73–81) had a history largely similar to those of Shangyu, production again beginning in the Eastern Han. Greenwares, blackwares and high fired earthenwares with impressed designs were all made at the same kiln. Kiln remains have been discovered on the banks of the Dongqian Lake dating to the Five Dynasties and Song periods. The form and decoration of the pots from these kilns have exact counterparts among those from the Yuyao and Shangyu kilns, demonstrating that Ningbo yao was, like them, one of the group of kilns producing tribute wares for the Qian family, the ruling house in Wu-Yue.

25
Fragment of a jar with impressed decoration under a green glaze
From Zhejiang Ningbo (1979:7)
Eastern Han dynasty (2nd–3rd century AD)

From the shoulder of a jar with an everted neck this sherd is decorated with a repeated stamped rectangular design infilled with a net pattern. The fine grey body contains small air bubbles and is glazed on the outside with a thin, runny, light olive glaze, which appears darker where deep in the impressions, and which has crawled slightly around the neck. The unglazed interior has oxidised to a tan colour.

Dimensions: 14.5 × 10.8 cm. Body: 0.4–1 cm.
Published: GGBWYYK 1980 (1) pp. 3–27, Fig. 2

26
Fragment of a jar with impressed decoration under a green glaze
From Zhejiang Ningbo (1979:7)
Eastern Han dynasty (2nd–3rd century AD)

This sherd from the high, rounded shoulder of a jar has a broad, flattened rim with an obliquely cut outside edge and a raised, rounded inside edge. The wall is decorated with a repeated stamped comb-like design which gives the impression of basketwork. The fine, grey body is glazed on the outside with a thin, runny, light olive glaze, and has oxidised on the unglazed inside to a light tan colour.

Dimensions: 15 × 9.8 cm. Body: 0.3–0.5 cm.
Published: GGBWYYK 1980 (1) pp. 3–27, Fig. 2

27
Fragment of a jar with incised and combed designs under a dark brown glaze
From Zhejiang Ningbo (1979:7)
Eastern Han dynasty (2nd–3rd century AD)

This sherd from the rounded wall of a jar is decorated round the sides with a combed wave design superimposed on incised bands. The fine grey body, which appears buff where exposed, is glazed outside, and partially inside, with a thin brown glaze which runs from yellow to black where it gathers. The sherd appears to come from the same vessel as no. 29.

Dimensions: 9.8 × 7 cm. Body: 0.5–0.8 cm.

28
Part of a jar with impressed decoration under a dark brown glaze
From Zhejiang Ningbo (1979:7)
Eastern Han dynasty (2nd–3rd century AD)

The sherd is part of a jar with a high shoulder and thick flattened rim. The rim has a raised and rounded outside lip and inside edge. The wall is decorated with a repeated stamped rectangular design infilled with a net pattern. The fine grey body appears buff where exposed and is glazed with a thick, runny, iron oxide glaze which appears black where deep in the impressions and rich olive where thin.

Height to neck: 4.5 cm. Width: 11.2 cm.
Width of rim: 4 cm. Body: 0.6–0.8 cm.

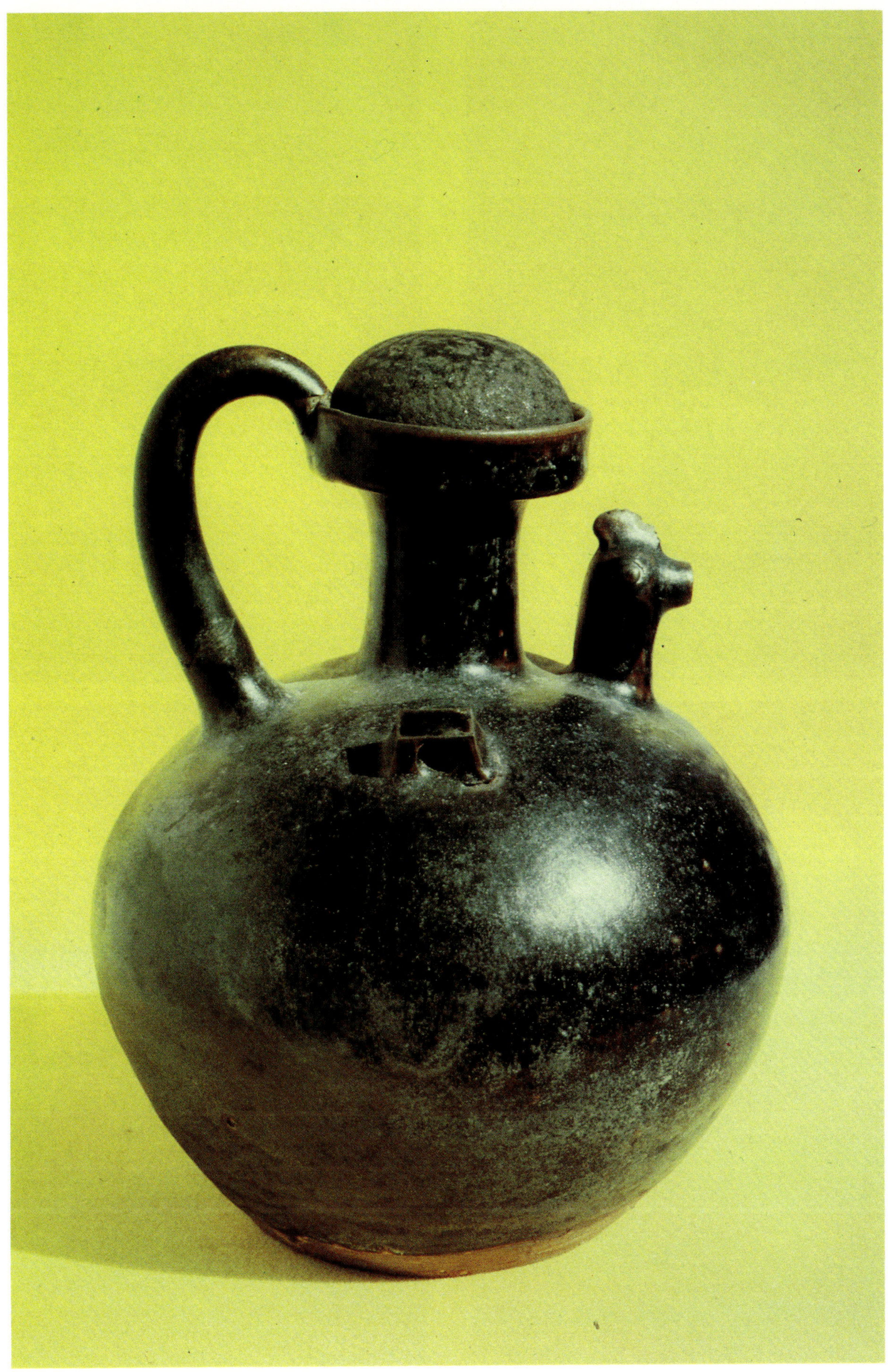

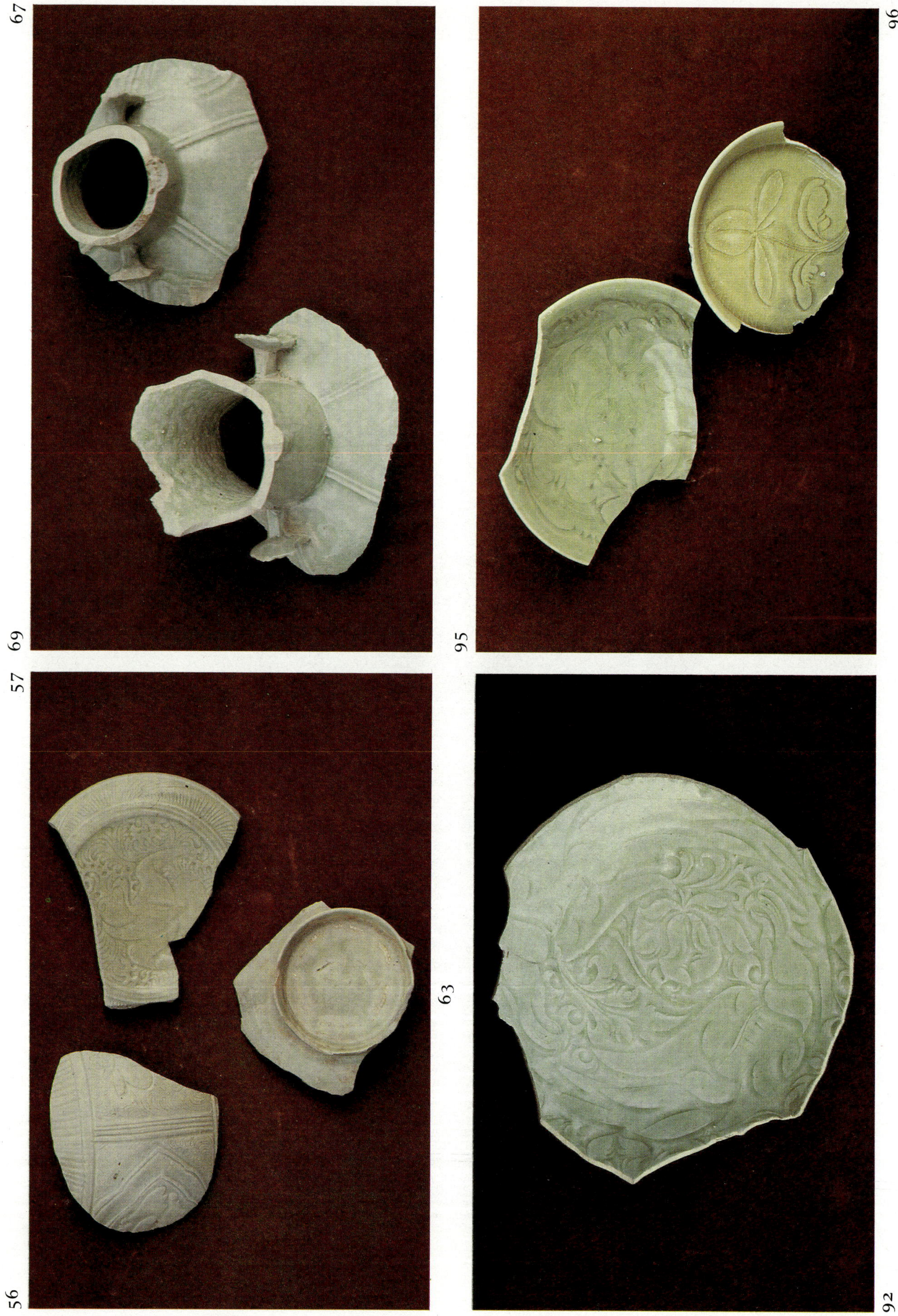

29
Fragment from a jar with combed, incised and
impressed decoration under a dark brown glaze
From Zhejiang Ningbo (1979:7)
Eastern Han dynasty (2nd–3rd century AD)

From the high, rounded shoulder of a jar with a
straight, upright neck this sherd is decorated with
bands of combed wave pattern and bands of incised
line. The sprigged lug handle is decorated with an
impressed linear design and is attached to the
shoulder. The fine, grey body appears buff where
exposed; and the predominantly brown glaze ranges
from a thin yellow to black where thick. The sherd is
glazed outside and partially inside. It appears to
come from the same vessel as no. 27.

Dimensions: 14 × 7 cm. Body: 0.4–0.8 cm.

Yuhang   nos. 30–39

Yuhang, another kiln site producing black wares, was discovered in recent
years. It adjoins Deqing xian and started production in the Eastern Jin, ceasing
again in the Southern Dynasties period. Both greenwares and blackwares were
made. At the two kiln sites discovered at Yuhang, the remains of black glazed
chicken-headed vases of large, medium and small sizes are fairly numerous.
Dishes, bowls, jars and inkstones were also produced.

30
Parts of three bowls stuck together during firing
From Zhejiang Yuhang (1979:7)
Eastern Jin dynasty (AD 317–419)

The outer bowl of these three stacked bowls stuck
together during firing has a flat base and rounded
wall. The dark grey coarse body is covered with the
remains of a slip and a green glaze. The inside bowl is
smaller, also with a flat base and rounded wall, but is
slipped, then glazed with a black-brown iron oxide
glaze. The remains of a coarse firing saggar adheres
beneath and between the bowls.

Height of outer bowl: 5.8 cm.
Diameter: 11 cm. (approx.)
Height of inner bowl: 4.8 cm. Diameter: 10.7 cm.
Diameter of base: 6 cm.

31
Part of a bowl with a black glaze
From Zhejiang Yuhang (1979:7)
Eastern Jin dynasty (AD 317–419)

This fragment is part of a bowl with a rounded wall,
rolled rim, and flat base. The charcoal grey, medium-
coarse body is glazed inside and out with a black iron
oxide glaze, which appears brown where thin and is
lightly crazed. The glaze runs short of the unglazed
base on the outside.

Height: 6 cm. Width: 2.7 cm.
Body: 0.4 (rim)–0.9 cm.

32

Part of a bowl with a green glaze with brown
markings
From Zhejiang Yuhang (1979:7)
Eastern Jin dynasty (AD 317–419)

Part of a bowl with rounded sides and a flat,
unglazed base, this fragment is glazed with a thin,
greyish green glaze with brown spots at the rim. The
dark grey, coarse-grained body appears coated with
a thin wash of slip under the glaze. Five spur marks
and kiln debris are apparent on the inside base. Kiln
grit also adheres to the foot.

Height: 8.8 cm. Diameter of base: 10.5 cm.
Body: 0.5 (rim)–1.4 cm. (base)

33

Fragment of a jar with a green glaze
From Zhejiang Yuhang (1979:7)
Eastern Jin dynasty (AD 317–419)

This fragment of a jar with a high, rounded shoulder,
and a short upright neck squared across the lip, has
a square lug handle high on the shoulder. The grey,
medium-coarse body is glazed on the outside with a
lustrous, green glaze which has a tinge of blue, and is
crazed. The inside is unglazed except for the neck
and the glaze is chipped off along the rim.

Dimensions: 7.3 × 4.5 cm. Body: 0.7 cm.

34

Part of a dish with a black glaze
From Zhejiang Yuhang (1979:7)
Eastern Jin dynasty (AD 317–419)

The fragment is part of a dish with a flat base,
rounded sides and a flattened, everted rim turned up
at the edge. The charcoal grey body is medium-
coarse. The black iron oxide glaze appears brown
where thin, and is crazed. The dish is glazed inside
and out, but the glaze on the outside runs short of
the base which is unglazed.

Height: 3.5 cm. Width: 10.3 cm. Body: 0.5–0.9 cm.

35

Fragment with handle from a black glazed jar
From Zhejiang Yuhang (1979:7)
Eastern Jin dynasty (AD 317–419)

This small sherd from the wall of a jar has a square
sprigged lug handle and is glazed on the outside with
a black matt glaze. The inside is unglazed, and the
fine grey body appears buff where exposed.

Length: 6.5 cm. Height: 2 cm. Body: 0.5 cm.

36

Fragment of an ink slab with a black glaze
From Zhejiang Yuhang (1979:7)
Eastern Jin dynasty (AD 317–419)

This fragment of an ink slab has a flat base with an
obliquely cut flange below the straight sides, and a
small cabriole leg. The fine, grey body appears buff
where exposed on the inside. The black glaze runs
thin to a yellowish colour on the outside, leg and
base.

Height: 4 cm. Width: 6 cm.
Body: 0.4 (side)–1.1 cm. (base)

37

Part of a black glazed vessel
From Zhejiang Yuhang (1979:7)
Eastern Jin dynasty (AD 317–419)

This fragment is part of a candlestick-like vessel. The
outside bowl has a flat base, spreading sides and an
everted, flattened rim. From the centre of the pierced
base rises a straight neck with a dished mouth,
whose edges are raised and rounded. The dark grey,
fairly fine body appears buff where exposed on the
unglazed base and the underside of the neck's
mouth. The black glaze runs thin to a yellowish
colour on the outside and inside the neck.

Height: 5.5 cm. Width: 14 cm. Body: 0.5–1.5 cm.

38

Spout of a chicken headed ewer with a black glaze
From Zhejiang Yuhang (1979:7)
Eastern Jin dynasty (AD 317–419)

This sherd is the chicken head spout from a ewer.
The body is dark grey, medium-coarse and is glazed
on the outside with a black glaze which appears
yellow where thin.

Height: 7 cm. Body: 0.6 cm.

39

Fragment from a chicken headed ewer with a black
glaze
From Zhejiang Yuhang (1979:7)
Eastern Jin dynasty (AD 317–419)

The chicken head spout of this ewer fragment sits
high on the shoulder of the vessel. The columnar
neck spreads to a dished mouth. The dark grey body
is medium-coarse. The matt black glaze runs yellow
where thin on the outside, and inside the neck. The
ewer is unglazed inside.

Height: 3.6 cm. Diameter of mouth: 7 cm.
Body: 0.2 (dish)–0.4 cm. (body)

Deqing   nos. 40–41

Deqing was the first group of kilns producing blackwares to be discovered in Zhejiang; four kilns have so far been uncovered. To the east of the *xian* lies Jiaoshan, to the south west lie Daijiashan, Chenshan and Dingshan. The specimens excavated from Deqing are basically similar to the vessels excavated from the tomb in Hangzhou, dated in accordance with AD 364 in the Eastern Jin period. Production started under the Eastern Jin and continued until the Southern Dynasties period.

40
Black glazed chicken head ewer
From a tomb at Zhejiang Hangzhou (1960:11)
Eastern Jin dynasty, dated to the year equivalent to AD 364

A ewer with globular body, flat base, tall neck with dished mouth, two square lug handles and a chicken head spout on the shoulder and another handle linking shoulder to mouth. The domed lid is stepped to fit into the neck and has a small dent to accommodate the handle. The grey, medium-coarse body is burnt brownish with red spots and has large air bubbles visible on the base. The underside of the lid is also red where unglazed. The thick black glaze is iridescent in places and stops short of the foot. The glaze on the lid has crawled.

Height including lid: 21.2 cm.
Height to rim: 19.2 cm. Diameter of rim: 6.7 cm.
Diameter of base: 9.3 cm.

41
Black glazed chicken head ewer
From Zhejiang Deqing (1959:3)
Eastern Jin dynasty (AD 317–419)

This chicken head ewer is similar to the previous example, no. 40. The light grey, medium-coarse body is burnt red where exposed on the slightly concave base. The glaze is dark brown rather than black and appears yellow where thin. It is crazed and runs short of the base. A hole has been knocked through the side where there was originally a welt of glaze.

Height to rim: 18.5 cm. Diameter of base: 10.8 cm. Diameter of rim: 8 cm.
Published: WWCKZL 1959 (12) pp. 51–52, Pl. opp. p. 51: no. 2

Xiaoshan   nos. 42–46

Three greenware kiln sites were discovered in Xiaoshan xian. One, in the Jinhua district, started ceramic production at a fairly early date, the specimens being similar to objects excavated from tombs of the Warring States and Western Han period in the Zhejiang area. At another kiln, at Shangdongcun, in the Daicun district, all the excavated pieces are of Eastern Jin or Southern Dynasties date; among them are four-handled flasks with a green glaze mottled with brown, and decoration of lotus petal designs executed in incised parallel lines; while at Shigaicun were found remains typical of the Eastern Jin period, similar to those from Shangdong.

42

Fragment of a jar with green glaze with touches of
brown
From Zhejiang Xiaoshan (1954:11)
Eastern Jin dynasty (AD 317–419)

This fragment of a jar with a rounded wall, a straight
sloping shoulder and an everted rim, is glazed with
an even, smooth, grey-green glaze with touches of
brown on the rim and the square lug handle. The
glaze runs in tear drops down the inside of the
shoulder. The body is dark grey and medium-coarse.

Dimensions: 8 × 7 cm. Body: 0.6 cm.

43

Neck of a ewer with a green glaze
From Zhejiang Xiaoshan (1954:11)
Southern Dynasties (AD 420–589)

This waisted neck with a dished mouth comes from a
ewer with a lotus petal decoration and a green glaze.
The grey, medium-coarse body appears buff where
exposed and is glazed outside and down inside the
neck with a thin, runny, green glaze which is crazed.

Height: 10 cm. Diameter of mouth: 7.4 cm.
Body: 0.5 (dish)–1.5 cm. (neck)

44

Part of a dish with incised decoration under a green
glaze
From Zhejiang Xiaoshan (1954:11)
Southern Dynasties (AD 420–589)

The fragment is part of a dish with a flat, unglazed
base and a rounded wall, decorated on the inside
with incised lotus petals in quintuple parallel lines
radiating from around the inside base. The grey,
medium-coarse body appears buff where exposed,
and the runny, olive glaze stops short of the base.
Marks of spurs are visible inside and out.

Dimensions: 9 cm. Body: 0.6 cm.

45

Part of a bowl with incised decoration under a green
glaze
From Zhejiang Xiaoshan (1954:11)
Southern Dynasties (AD 420–589)

This is part of a bowl with a thick, flat base, rounded
sides and a straight rim. It is decorated on the outside
with lotus petals incised in quintuple parallel lines
rising from the base. The thick, dark grey, medium-
coarse body appears buff where exposed on the
unglazed base. The dark olive glaze runs in tear
drops down the inside. Five spur marks are visible on
the inside and outside bases.

Height: 8 cm. Approx. diameter: 16 cm.
Diameter of base: 6 cm. Body: 0.7 cm.

46

Fragment of a bowl with incised decoration under a
green glaze
From Zhejiang Xiaoshan (1979:7)
Southern Dynasties (AD 420–589)

This fragment of a bowl, with a flat base, straight
foot and rounded walls, is decorated on the outside
with coarsely incised lotus petals rising from the foot.
The remains of spurs and kiln debris are visible inside
and outside the base. The thick, medium-coarse body
appears buff where exposed on the base, and is
glazed with an olive glaze.

Height: 5.5 cm. Diameter of base: 6 cm.
Body: 0.6–1 cm.

Yue yao   nos. 47–63

Yue yao in Yuyao xian was one of the four great kiln complexes making green-wares in Zhejiang. Production started in the Eastern Jin, flourished in the Tang and Five Dynasties, and was discontinued in the Song. Over twenty kiln sites have been discovered, mostly in the area of Shanglinhu and Binhu, and finds made there are extremely rich. Vessels made in the Tang period had a rather thick body and from the middle and later Tang were decorated with incised and moulded designs, while in the Five Dynasties carved decoration was current. Human figures, landscapes, flowers and birds, animals, grasses, and insects were all taken as the subjects of the ornament. This was the main kiln producing tribute wares for the Qian ruling family of the Wu-Yue Kingdom. At the beginning of the Song the volume of production was very large, but when Wu-Yue fell to the Song production of Yue yao abated and subsequently gradually declined.

47
Part of a bowl with incised decoration under a green glaze
From a Zhejiang Yue yao kiln site (1979:7)
Tang dynasty (AD 618–906)

Thick walled and solid, this part of a bowl has a tall foot inclined on the inside, a recessed base and rounded, lobed walls spreading to an everted rim. On the inside base is a sketchily incised flower decoration. The light grey, fine grained body is glazed with a thin, even, yellowish olive glaze all over except for the foot ring.

Height: 5.5 cm.

48
Part of an oval cup with a green glaze
From a Zhejiang Yue yao kiln site (1979:7)
Tang dynasty (AD 618–906)

From an oval bowl with a high spreading foot and a slightly recessed base, this fragment is undecorated, and is glazed with a light, even, yellowish olive glaze. The light grey body is fine grained. The bowl is glazed all over except for the foot ring.

Height: 5.8 cm. Length: 12 cm.
Maximum diameter of foot ring: 5.8 cm.
Body: 0.4 cm.

49
Part of a lobed water pot with a green glaze
From a Zhejiang Yue yao kiln site (1979:7)
Tang dynasty (AD 618–906)

This is part of a five-lobed water pot. The fine, grey body is glazed with a smooth, yellowish olive glaze which stops short of the flat unglazed base, which is oxidised red.

Height: 4.2 cm. Diameter of base: 4.8 cm.
Body: 0.5 cm.

50
Lid of a box with carved and incised decoration under a green glaze
From a Zhejiang Yue yao kiln site (1954:11)
Tang dynasty (AD 618–906)

The box lid is decorated on the top with an incised and carved quatrefoliate floral motif. It was fired on the box rim where seven spur marks are visible and which is partially unglazed. The very fine body appears buff where exposed and is glazed with a thin, even, yellowish olive glaze.

Height: 1 cm. Diameter: 6.1 cm. Body: 0.3 cm.

51

Fragment of a bowl with a green glaze
From a Zhejiang Yue yao kiln site (1979:7)
Tang dynasty (AD 618–906)

The undecorated bowl of which this fragment was a part was fired on its base on eight spurs. The broad foot ring is unglazed while the circular, recessed base is glazed with a greyish green glaze that covers the light grey, fine body.

Diameter of body: 6.5 cm. Body: 0.6 cm.

52

Part of a bowl with incised decoration under a green glaze
From a Zhejiang Yue yao kiln site (1954:11)
Five Dynasties (AD 907–960)

The inside of this bowl fragment is decorated with an incised design of two parrots. The small foot ring and the base, where seven spur marks are visible, are glazed with the olive glaze, which is even on the inside, but shows tear marks on the outside. The fine body is pale grey.

Diameter of foot: 9.2 cm. Dimensions: 13.8 × 13 cm. Body: 0.2–0.5 cm.

53

Part of a dish with an incised and carved decoration under a green glaze
From a Zhejiang Yue yao kiln site (1954:11)
Five Dynasties (AD 907–960)

From a dish with a small, straight foot, flat base, rounded sides, this fragment is carved with lotus petals on the outside walls, and decorated with an incised design of two phoenixes on the inside. The character *xin* or 'bitter' is incised on the base under the even olive glaze. The dish is glazed all over and fired on five spurs on the base. The fine body is light grey.

Height: 7 cm. Diameter of base: 8.5 cm.
Body: 0.4–0.7 cm. (base)

54

Fragment of a bowl with incised decoration under a green glaze
From a Zhejiang Yue yao kiln site (1979:7)
Five Dynasties (AD 907–960)

On the inside this bowl fragment is decorated with incised phoenixes. Over the decoration a broken piece of another pot adheres. On the underside there is a ridge of spur marks inside the warped foot ring. The thick, fine, grey body is glazed with an even, light green-blue glaze, which is slightly crazed.

Length: 14 cm. Width: 11 cm. Body: 0.5–0.7 cm.

55

Part of a box with incised decoration under a green glaze
From a Zhejiang Yue yao kiln site (1979:7)
Five Dynasties (AD 907–960)

This fragment consists of parts of the top and bottom of a box stuck together during firing. The sides of each part are decorated with incised floral panels on a scale-like ring-matted ground. Above the base is a band of peony scroll. The light grey, coarse body is glazed with a light grey-green glaze which is even on the outside but has crawled extensively on the inside.

Height: 8 cm. Length: 15 cm. Body: 0.8 cm.

Part of a ewer with carved and incised decoration under a green glaze
From a Zhejiang Yue yao kiln site (1979:7)
Five Dynasties (AD 907–960)

This fragment from the wall of a ewer is decorated with two carved panels, one floral ogival, and the other a plain peony, both on a sketchily incised ground, and separated by ribbed bands which also decorate the shoulder. The grey, fine body is glazed inside and out with a thin, even, grey-green glaze.

Dimensions: 9 × 9 cm. Body: 0.5 cm.

57

Lid of a box with carved and incised decoration under a green glaze
From a Zhejiang Yue yao kiln site (1954:11)
Five Dynasties (AD 907–960)

This fragment from the lid of a box is decorated on the top with a carved decoration of a fabulous bird among waves within a border of incised lines, and round the sides with an incised petal band. The rim is unglazed and shows the remains of three spur marks. The grey, medium-coarse body is glazed with a thin, green glaze which has crawled on the inside.

Dimensions: 11.5 × 10 cm. Body: 0.5 cm.

58

Part of a jar with a green glaze
From a Zhejiang Yue yao kiln site (1954:11)
Five Dynasties (AD 907–960)

This fragment of a wide mouthed jar has a high, rounded shoulder and a small, constricted mouth rim. Two incised rings form a rib around the shoulder. The light grey, fine body is glazed, including the mouth rim, with a thin, runny, light green glaze.

Dimensions: 9 × 7 cm. Body: 0.5 cm.

59
Part of a bowl with incised decoration under a green glaze
From a Zhejiang Yue yao kiln site (1954:11)
Five Dynasties (AD 907–960)

Part of a bowl with a flat base and a straight foot, this fragment is decorated on the inside with an incised design of cranes amid scrolls. Five spur marks are visible on the base which is glazed, as is the foot. The light grey, fine body appears brown where exposed. The even glaze is olive tending to a yellow.

Diameter of foot: 8.4 cm.
Available diameter: 13.4 cm. Height of foot: 1.2 cm.
Body: 0.4 cm.

60
Fragment of a bowl with incised decoration under a green glaze
From a Zhejiang Yue yao kiln site (1954:11)
Five dynasties (AD 907–960)

The flat base of this bowl with everted foot has on the inside an incised design of a bird amid flowers and foliage. A single spur mark is visible on the glazed base inside the foot ring. The grey, medium-coarse body is glazed with a thin, even, grey-green glaze.

Diameter of foot: 11.5 cm.
Body: 0.4 (side)–0.8 cm. (foot)

61
Base of a bowl with decoration incised through the green glaze
From a Zhejiang Yue yao kiln site (1979:7)
Five Dynasties (AD 907–960)

This base fragment is decorated on the inside with a design similar to that of no. 60, but the bird is facing the opposite direction and this time the design appears incised through the glaze. There are six spur marks on the flat base, which, like the foot ring, is glazed. The fine, light grey body is glazed with a thin, even, yellow-olive glaze.

Available diameter: 14.5 cm.
Diameter of base: 10.6 cm. Body: 0.6 cm.

62
Fragment of a dish with incised decoration under a green glaze
From a Zhejiang Yue yao kiln site (1979:7)
Five Dynasties (AD 907–960)

This fragment of a dish with a flat base and a slightly everted foot ring is decorated on the inside with an incised design of a pair of butterflies. The body is light grey and medium-coarse. The glaze is thin and a grey-green colour. The dish was fired on six spurs on the base which is glazed.

Diameter: 13.3 cm. Diameter of foot ring: 10.2 cm.
Body: 0.4–0.8 cm.

63
Base of a dated dish with incised decoration under a green glaze
From a Zhejiang Yue yao kiln site (1954:11)
Northern Song dynasty, dated in accordance with AD 978

This fragment, with a flat base and thin, everted foot, both glazed, has on the inside an incised decoration of a tortoise on a lotus leaf. The base is inscribed: *Taiping wuyin*, the cyclical date equivalent to AD 978. There are six spur-marks on the base where the shiny green glaze has crawled. The grey, fine body is thin.

Diameter: 10 cm. Diameter of foot: 7 cm.
Body: 0.3 cm.

Shangyu nos. 64–72

64

Part of a ewer with carved decoration under a green glaze
From Zhejiang Shangyu (1979:7)
Northern Song dynasty (AD 960–1126)

From the rounded wall of a ewer, this fragment is decorated with carved chrysanthemum petals in a band around the shoulder, which is separated from the neck by a raised rib. Carved vertical ribs also divide panels of floral motifs around the body. The thick body is light grey, medium-coarse and shows buff where exposed. The light green, crackled glaze is slightly degraded.

Dimensions: 9.5 × 8 cm. Body: 0.6–1 cm.

65

Part of the lid of a box with a carved decoration under a green glaze
From Zhejiang Shangyu (1979:7)
Five Dynasties (AD 907–960)

This fragment of the domed lid of a box is decorated with a carved design of a peony spray within a border of thumbnail-like marks. The lid was fired on its rim on several spurs, of which five are visible here. The light grey, fine body is glazed with a thin, green glaze.

Height: 1.2 cm. Length: 9.2 cm. Body: 0.6 cm.

66

Fragment of a bowl with carved and incised decoration under a green glaze
From Zhejiang Shangyu (1956:5)
Five Dynasties (AD 907–960)

This bowl fragment has a flat base and an everted foot, both glazed, and was fired on five spurs on the base. The inside is decorated with a single carved lotus flower with incised details. The light grey, fine body is glazed with a thin, even, olive glaze

Dimensions: 12 × 11 cm. Body: 0.4–0.9 cm. (base)
*Drawing published: WW 1963 (1) pp. 43–49,
Fig. 1:10*

67

Fragment of a ewer with carved decoration under a green glaze
From Zhejiang Shangyu (1979:7)
Northern Song dynasty (AD 960–1126)

This ewer fragment has a straight neck with the beginning of a spout, and a high rounded shoulder with five carved ribs and the remnants of two carved foliated panels with a floral design. Two tablet shaped handles are attached to the neck and shoulder. The thick, fine, grey body is glazed with a thin, green glaze, which has oxidised to yellow inside.

Height: 9.9 cm. Diameter of neck: 4.6 cm.
Body: 0.6 cm.

68

Part of a bowl with incised decoration under a green glaze
From Zhejiang Shangyu (1956:5)
Northern Song dynasty (AD 960–1126)

From the base of a bowl with a high, straight foot, this fragment is decorated on the inside base with a sketchily incised lotus scroll. There are three spurs on the base. The light grey, fine body is glazed with a shiny green glaze that runs in tears.

Length: 12.4 cm. Diameter of base: 7 cm.
Height of foot: 1.5 cm. Body: 0.3–0.8 cm.

69

Fragment of a ewer with carved decoration under a green glaze
From Zhejiang Shangyu (1979:7)
Five Dynasties (AD 907–960)

This fragment from the neck and shoulder of a ewer has a straight neck, slightly everted towards the rim and carved ribs on the shoulders forming divisions for six panels containing sketchy floral designs. There are the beginnings of a spout, and the two tablet shaped handles with moulded feather designs connecting the neck and the body. The light grey, medium-coarse body is glazed with a thin, runny light green glaze, which is iridescent in places and has crawled on the inside.

Height: 10 cm. Diameter of neck: 4.6 cm.
Body: 0.4 cm.

70
Fragment of a bowl with a carved decoration under a
green glaze
From Zhejiang Shangyu (1979:7)
Northern Song dynasty (AD 960–1126)

From the base of a bowl with a tall everted foot this
fragment is carved with lotus petals on the outside.
There are four spur marks on the base and turning
marks on the inside of the bowl. The light grey, fine
body is glazed with a thin, runny, olive glaze.

Height: 9.8 cm. Diameter of foot ring: 4.7 cm.
Body: 0.3–0.4 cm.

71
Part of the lid of an incense burner with pierced
decoration and a green glaze
From Zhejiang Shangyu (1956:5)
Northern Song dynasty (AD 960–1126)

This lid from an incense burner is pierced with a
petal-like decoration around a central knob and
glazed on both sides with an even, light olive glaze
over the fine, grey body.

Length: 9.1 cm. Body: 0.4 cm.

72
Fragment of a bowl with carved and incised
decoration under a green glaze
From Zhejiang Shangyu (1979:7)
Northern Song dynasty (AD 960–1126)

This fragment from the lobed wall of a bowl is
decorated with sketchy incised floral motifs in a band
round the inside of the foliated rim, and with deeply
carved floral roundels interspersed with carved and
incised sprays. The light grey, fine body is glazed
with a thin, runny, olive glaze.

Dimensions: 11 × 6.6 cm. Body: 0.3–0.6 cm.

Ningbo   nos. 73–81

73
Part of a vessel with carved decoration under a green
glaze
From Zhejiang Yin xian (1979:7)
Five Dynasties (AD 907–960)

This fragment from the rounded wall of a vessel is
deeply carved round the outside with a meander
pattern. The vessel was fired on the base ring. The
fine body which appears buff where exposed is glazed
with a thin olive glaze.

Height: 4.8 cm. Length: 11.6 cm. Body: 0.3–0.5 cm.
Published: WW 1973 (5) pp. 30–40, Fig. 16:13

74
Part of a bowl with carved decoration under a green
glaze
From Zhejiang Yin xian (1979:7)
Five Dynasties (AD 907–960)

This fragment from the rounded wall of a deep bowl
with an everted rim is decorated on the outside with
a deeply carved and incised lotus petal pattern. The
fine body shows buff where exposed and the thin
olive glaze gathers in the deep crevices.

Height: 11 cm. Width: 11 cm. Body: 0.2–1 cm.
Published: WW 1973 (5) pp. 30–40, Fig. 17:2

75
Fragment of a bowl with carved and incised
decoration under a green glaze
From Zhejiang Yin xian (1963:9)
Five Dynasties (AD 907–960)

From the base of a bowl with a tall, everted foot, this
fragment is decorated on the outside with a carved
decoration of lotus petals with incised details. The
bowl was fired on three spurs on the base. The light
grey, fine body is glazed with a thin, runny, green
glaze.

Dimensions: 8 × 7.3 cm.
Body: 0.3 (foot ring)–0.4 cm.
Published: WW 1973 (5) pp. 30–40, Fig. 16:4

76
Fragment of a wide mouthed jar with a green glaze
From Zhejiang Yin xian (1963:9)
Five Dynasties (AD 907–960)

From the rounded wall of a wide mouthed jar with a
constricted and flattened rim, this sherd has a fine,
light grey body and is glazed inside and out with a
lustrous, celadon glaze.

Dimensions: 15 × 8 cm. Body: 0.45 cm.
Published: WW 1973 (5) pp. 30–40, Fig. 17:1

77
Part of a bowl with carved decoration under a green
glaze
From Zhejiang Yin xian (1963:10)
Five Dynasties (AD 907–960)

This fragment of a bowl with a flat, slightly recessed
base where three spur-marks are visible, is carved on
the outside of the rounded wall with lotus petals, and
is incised on the inside base with a wave pattern. The
fine grey body is glazed with a green glaze which is
slightly overfired.

Dimensions: 11.2 × 5.5 cm. Body: 0.3 cm.
Published: WW 1973 (5) pp. 30–40, Fig. 16:3

78
Fragment of a bowl with carved decoration under a
green glaze
From Zhejiang Yin xian (1979:7)
Five Dynasties (AD 907–960)

From the straight wall of a bowl, which is rounded at
the bottom and has a straight rim, this sherd is
decorated with deeply carved roundels of scrolling
peony with incised detail. The grey, coarse body
appears brown where exposed and the green glaze
has crawled inside and out.

Dimensions: 10.5 × 9.6 cm. Body: 0.5 cm.
Published: WW 1973 (5) pp. 30–40, Fig. 16:6

79
Part of a dish with incised decoration under a green
glaze
From Zhejiang Yin xian (1963:10)
Five Dynasties (AD 907–960)

This fragment from a dish with a flat base, an everted
foot and rounded sides is decorated on the inside
with an incised design of two parrots. The light grey,
medium-coarse body is glazed with a thin green-grey
glaze. There are six spurs on the base.

Dimensions: 16.3 × 14 cm.
Diameter of foot-ring: 10.4 cm. Body: 0.5 cm.
Published: WW 1973 (5) pp. 30–40, Fig. 16:1

80
Fragment of a dish with incised decoration under a
green glaze
From Zhejiang Yin xian (1963:10)
Five Dynasties (AD 907–960)

This fragment of a dish with a flat base, a fine,
everted foot and rounded walls, is decorated on the
inside with a pair of incised butterflies. The light
grey, medium-coarse body is glazed with a thin, olive
glaze.

Dimensions: 12.2 × 6 cm. Height of foot: 0.9 cm.
Body: 0.3–1 cm. (base)
Published: WW 1973 (5) pp. 30–40, Fig. 5:5

81
Fragment of a ewer with carved and incised
decoration under a green glaze
From Zhejiang Yin xian (1979:7)
Northern Song dynasty (AD 907–960)

From a ewer with a thick, flat base and a straight
foot, on which it was fired and to which kiln grit
adheres, this fragment is decorated on the outside
with carved ribs and petal panels with incised details.
The turning marks on the inside culminate in a peak
of clay in the centre of the inside base. The coarse
grey body is glazed with a thin, olive-brown glaze.

Available diameter: 10.5 cm.
Diameter of foot: 7.2 cm. Body: 0.3–1.3 cm. (base)

Wenzhou   nos. 82–88

Wenzhou belonged to the Ou yao complex of kilns. Production started here in
the Tang dynasty and ended in the Song. In the Tang period the methods of
firing on spurs, and the use of decoration in boldly incised line, were similar to
Yue yao practices. During the Song period a particular type of bowl was made
that was decorated inside and out with incised designs. The clay used for the
pots made at Wenzhou has a relatively low content of iron, with the result that
the bodies are a greyish white and the glaze a pale green colour. All the vessels
from this area have particular quality.

82

Part of a green glazed box stuck inside a bowl during firing
From Zhejiang Wenzhou (1954:11)
Tang dynasty (AD 618–906)

The box involved in the kiln accident has rounded sides and a glazed stepped rim to take a lid. The bowl has a thick, flat base, slightly recessed in the centre and shows eight spur marks. The glaze stops short of the base on the short, flaring sides. The fine, light grey body material is glazed with a thin, even, light olive glaze which is crazed.

Height of bowl: 4.6 cm. Diameter of bowl: 14.5 cm. Diameter of foot: 6.8 cm. Diameter of box: 10 cm.

83

Fragment of a bowl with incised decoration under a green glaze
From Zhejiang Wenzhou (1954:11)
Tang dynasty (AD 618–906)

This fragment of a bowl with incised decoration inside, has a shallow foot ring and a wide flat base with a deeper, gouged ring inside the foot ring. The thin, green glaze stops short of the foot and the fine, grey body appears buff where exposed on the unglazed foot and base. There are nine (out of 16) spur marks visible on the foot ring and the remains of a circle of spurs on the inside.

Dimensions: 13.5 × 8 cm. Diameter of foot: 9.7 cm. Body: 0.5–0.8 cm.

84

Part of a bowl with incised decoration under a green glaze
From Zhejiang Wenzhou (1954:11)
Five Dynasties (AD 907–960)

Part of a bowl with rounded sides and high, everted and rolled foot recessed in the centre, this fragment is decorated on the inside with an incised lotus design with seven stamped seeds inside a double ring in the centre. The very fine, light grey body is covered all over with a grey-olive crazed glaze. Four spurs are visible on the base.

Height: 4.5 cm. Diameter of foot: 4.8 cm. Body: 0.4–0.5 cm.

85

Fragment of a cup with carved decoration under a green glaze
From Zhejiang Wenzhou (1954:11)
Five Dynasties (AD 907–960)

A fragment of a cup with deeply carved lotus petals on the outside of the walls, which are rounded at the bottom, then rise straight up to the rim. The remains of the high, straight foot and the flat base, which has four spurs, are glazed. The fine, grey body is covered with a crackled, green glaze, which runs thick in the deep carving.

Height: 11.5 cm. Diameter of foot: 6.7 cm. Body: 0.4–0.9 cm.

86

Fragment of a bowl with carved decoration under a green glaze
From Zhejiang Wenzhou (1954:11)
Western Song dynasty (AD 960–1126)

From a bowl with a shallow foot and a wide, flat, thick base, this fragment is decorated on the outside with carved vertical ribs and on the inside with carved peony designs around a single rosette in the centre. The fine, grey body is glazed overall with the green glaze and was fired on a spur ring on the base.

Dimensions: 10.5 × 10 cm. Diameter of foot: 5.5 cm. Body: 0.3–0.9 cm.

87

Fragment of a bowl with carved decoration under an olive brown glaze
From Zhejiang Wenzhou (1954:11)
Northern Song dynasty (AD 960–1126)

This bowl fragment has a straight foot, and a solid round spur adhering to the base. The thick walls are carved on the outside with vertical ribs, and the inside is decorated with a single carved rosette. The light grey, fine porcellanous body is glazed with a thin, olive brown glaze.

Dimensions: 11.5 × 8.5 cm. Diameter of base: 5.8 cm. Body: 0.4–0.8 cm.

88

Part of a brush washer with a green glaze
From Zhejiang Wenzhou (1954:11)
Northern Song dynasty (AD 960–1126)

This fragment is part of a brush washer with a small, straight foot, a wide, flat base and a short, rounded well with an inclined rim, rolled on the outside edge. The fine, light grey body is glazed overall with a thin, even, grey-olive glaze with a slight crackle. Three spurs are visible on the inside, and spur marks are apparent around the inside of the foot.

Height: 3.1 cm. Dimensions: 12 × 7 cm. Body: 0.4–0.6 cm.

Huangyan   nos. 89–92

In the area of Shabujie a group of eight kilns was discovered, the largest in area being that at Zhujialing. Many varieties of pot were made, including dishes decorated with carved designs of parrots, or paired parrots under a green glaze. These patterns are different in character from those on wares from Yuyao, Yin xian, and Shangyu. Among the coarser wares made for popular use there are many decorated with lively carved and combed designs.

89
Sherd of a dish with carved decoration under a green glaze
From Zhejiang Huangyan (1957:11)
Northern Song dynasty (AD 960–1126)

This sherd from a dish with a thick base and a small, slightly inverted foot, is carved with a decoration of chrysanthemum heads on the inside. The fine, grey body is darker than that of the pale Wenzhou wares. The thick, green-olive glaze is crazed and covers the whole piece. Three spur marks are visible on the base.

Dimensions: 13 × 12.5 cm. Body: 0.5–0.6 cm.
Published: KGTX 1958 (8) pp. 44–47, pl. 5:5

90
Fragment of a lid with carved decoration under a green glaze
From Zhejiang Huangyan (1957:11)
Northern Song dynasty (AD 960–1126)

From a lid with domed sides and the remains of a knob set on a raised, central roundel, this fragment is decorated on the outside with a carved lotus scroll with combed details. There is the mark of a round spur on the centre of the inside. The fine, grey body is glazed with a brown-olive glaze.

Dimensions: 10.5 × 9.5 cm. Body: 0.5 cm.
Published: KGTX 1958 (8) pp. 44–47, Pl. 6:4

91
Part of a bowl with carved and combed decoration under a green glaze
From Zhejiang Huangyan (1957:11)
Northern Song dynasty (AD 960–1126)

This fragment is part of a bowl with spreading sides and a high, straight foot. It is decorated on the inside with carved and combed flower scrolls around a single floret in the centre. The yellow-olive glaze covers the foot and base where a circular spur is visible. Kiln grit adheres to the glaze on the inside. The fine, dark grey body is very thick.

Dimensions: 16 × 15.5 cm.
Diameter of foot ring: 6.4 cm.
Body: 0.3 cm. to very thick at base.
Published: KGTX 1958 (8) pp. 44–47, Pl. 5:6

92
Part of a dish with carved and combed decoration under a green glaze
From Zhejiang Huangyan (1957:11)
Northern Song dynasty (AD 960–1126)

This fragment is part of a dish with a shallow, flat foot, a thick, flat, recessed base and flaring sides. The inside is decorated with a carved and combed design of parrots amid scrolling lotus. The bluish grey, fine body is glazed overall with a greyish green glaze. A single round spur mark is visible on the base.

Dimensions: 19 × 18 cm. Diameter of foot: 8 cm.
Body: 0.3 cm. to very thick at base

Longquan   nos. 93–100

Longquan is one of the areas famous for the manufacture of greenwares; production started in the early Song, and flourished in the Southern Song. In the Yuan dynasty the technique of firing large pieces was successfully mastered, but by the middle of the Ming the kilns were gradually declining in importance. The eight hundred years of ceramic manufacture at these kilns started, in the Northern Song, with wares decorated with carved and combed decoration. In the Southern Song, of the wares now produced for use at the imperial court, many were made in shapes imitating archaic bronze and jade vessels. The bodies were pure white and the glaze a greenish blue. In the Yuan dynasty advances were made in moulded decoration, with sunken designs being more common than raised. Longquan yao's powerful influence in the Linjin area encouraged many kilns to start up, forming what is known as the 'Longquan kiln complex'.

93
Part of a dish with carved and combed decoration under a green glaze
From Zhejiang Longquan (1979:7)
Northern Song dynasty (AD 960–1126)

This fragment is part of a dish with a small, slightly inclined foot. The outside of the spreading walls is decorated with carved, vertical lines and the inside with a carved and combed design of fish among waves around a central roundel. The light grey body, which is very thick at the base is glazed to the foot with a thick, glassy, grey-olive glaze.

Dimensions: 16 × 14 cm.
Diameter of foot ring: 6.5 cm. Body: 0.5 cm.

94
Dish with carved decoration under a green glaze
Longquan type, from the Gugong, Peking
Northern Song dynasty (AD 960–1126)

The dish has a small, slightly concave base and spreading sides which are angled towards the straight rim. It is decorated on the inside with a sketchy carved lotus. The fine, grey body has oxidised red on the unglazed base and is glazed with a glossy, green glaze.

Diameter of dish: 12.8 cm. Diameter of base: 3.8 cm.

95
Part of a bowl with carved and combed decoration under a green glaze
From Zhejiang Longquan (1979:7)
Northern Song dynasty (AD 960–1126)

Part of a bowl with rounded sides, an everted rim and a short foot, this fragment is decorated on the inside with a freely carved and combed decoration of waves. The fine, grey body is glazed overall with a pale greyish olive glaze. A lump of kiln support adheres to the base and grit is stuck to the underside of the walls.

Diameter: 16.3 cm. Height: 4 cm.
Diameter of foot ring: 5.2 cm. Body: 0.5 cm.

96
Part of a dish with carved decoration under a green glaze
From Zhejiang Longquan (1979:7)
Northern Song dynasty (AD 960–1126)

From a dish with a small unglazed base, spreading walls which are sharply angled and inclined towards the straight rim, the fragment is decorated on the inside with a carved and combed design of a lotus. The fine, grey body is glazed with a lustrous, olive, crackled glaze down to the foot which has been trimmed off.

Dimensions: 3 × 3.6 cm. Body: 0.3–1.5 cm.

97

Part of an incense burner with a bluish green glaze
From Zhejiang Longquan (1960)
Southern Song dynasty (AD 1127–1279)

From the side of an incense burner, this fragment
has a rounded wall, a short, straight neck and a
flattened, everted rim. The greyish white body is
glazed with a smooth, top quality, pale greenish blue,
rather matt glaze.

Inside diameter of neck: 15 cm. Body: 0.7 cm.

98

Fragment of a basin with applied moulded
decoration under the green glaze
From Zhejiang Longquan (1960)
Southern Song dynasty (AD 1127–1279)

The basin of which this is a fragment, has a rounded
wall, carved in relief on the outside with petals, and a
flattened, everted rim. Two moulded fish are sprigged
on to the inside under the thick, glossy, green-blue
glaze, which has a wide crackle. Spur marks are
visible on the unglazed foot ring, where the light
greyish white body has burnt red. The base is glazed.

Height: 7 cm. Diameter of foot ring: 12 cm.
Body: 0.3–0.7 cm.

99

Base fragment of a dish with stamped decoration
under a green glaze
From Zhejiang Longquan (1979:7)
Yuan dynasty (AD 1280–1368)

This sherd from the very thick base of a dish is
decorated with a stamped design of two phoenixes.
The thin, green glaze stops short of the foot on the
outside, but there is a circle of glaze on the base. A
firing ring adheres to an unglazed band on the base.
The body material is grey and fine.

Dimensions: 15 × 7.5 cm. Body: 1.5 cm.

100

Base sherd of a bowl with stamped and carved
decoration under a green glaze
From Zhejiang Longquan (1979:7)
Yuan dynasty (AD 1280–1368)

This base sherd of a bowl is decorated with a
stamped design of two fish in the centre and with the
remains of carved scrolls around the well. The glassy
blue-green glaze has a broad crackle and runs in a
thick tear over the foot to the base, to which the
remains of a kiln support adhere. The fine body is
pale grey.

Dimensions: 13.5 × 9 cm. Body: 0.7–1 cm.

Fujian   nos. 101–193

This province to the south of Zhejiang has long been associated with the black glazed wares made in the central and northern part of the province. The kilns represented in this exhibition are situated further south, and many of them made white wares in the Song and Yuan dynasties.

Dehua	nos. 101–114
Anxi	nos. 115–129
Tongan	nos. 130–143
Nan'an	nos. 144–158
Quanzhou	nos. 159–175
Putian	nos. 176–187
Lianjiang	nos. 188–193

Dehua nos. 101–114

Dehua xian, where 180 kiln sites dating from the Song to the Qing dynasty have been discovered, has yielded more kiln sites than any other *xian* in Fujian province. In 1976 the kiln site at Qudougong was excavated, and the six thousand specimens found reveal that it began production in the late Song period and ended in the Yuan. The kiln at Gaide started up rather earlier in the Northern Song, but also ceased production in the Yuan dynasty. All the products of both kilns were made for export, and, over many years now, Dehua ceramics of the Song to the Ming dynasties have been excavated at ancient sites in several Asian countries.

101
Fragment of a jar with a carved design under a *qingbai* glaze
From Fujian Dehua (1979:6)
Song dynasty (AD 960–1279)

From a jar, with a lug handle ridged with three incised lines, this fragment is decorated on the outside with a freely carved and combed design. The white, glassy body is glazed outside, and patchily inside, with a pale whitish-grey *qingbai* glaze.

Dimensions: 13.4 × 11.2 cm. Body: 0.5–0.8 cm.

102
Part of a large bowl with combed decoration under a *qingbai* glaze
From Fujian Dehua (1979:6)
Song dynasty (AD 960–1279)

This fragment of a very large bowl, with rounded, spreading sides and an everted rim, a short, broad foot and a convex base, is decorated inside with swirling combed designs. A round kiln support (or trimmed foot of another vessel) adheres at six points to the inside and is surrounded by kiln grit. The base and foot ring are unglazed. The body and glaze are similar to those of no. 101.

Diameter: 26 cm. Height: 6.6 cm.
Diameter of foot ring: 9.3 cm. Body: 0.2–0.6 cm.

103
Fragment of a bowl with carved and combed decoration under a *qingbai* glaze
From Fujian Dehua (1979:6)
Song dynasty (AD 960–1279)

This fragment of a bowl, with rounded sides and an everted rim, is decorated on the inside with a carved and combed design of leaf sprays around a central medallion of carved rings, which are filled with the *qingbai* glaze. The glaze covers the foot ring but the convex base, the inside of the foot, and the mouth rim are unglazed. The body and glaze are as for no. 101.

Height: 6.5 cm. Diameter of foot: 5.5 cm.
Body: 0.2–0.6 cm.

104
Sherd from a jar with carved and combed designs under a *qingbai* glaze
From Fujian Dehua (1979:6)
Song dynasty (AD 960–1279)

This sherd, from the rounded wall of a jar, is decorated on the outside with a carved and combed design under the pale whitish-grey *qingbai* glaze. There are odd splashes of glaze on the inside. The body, again, is hard, white and glassy.

Dimensions: 9.5 × 7.9 cm. Body: 0.3 cm.

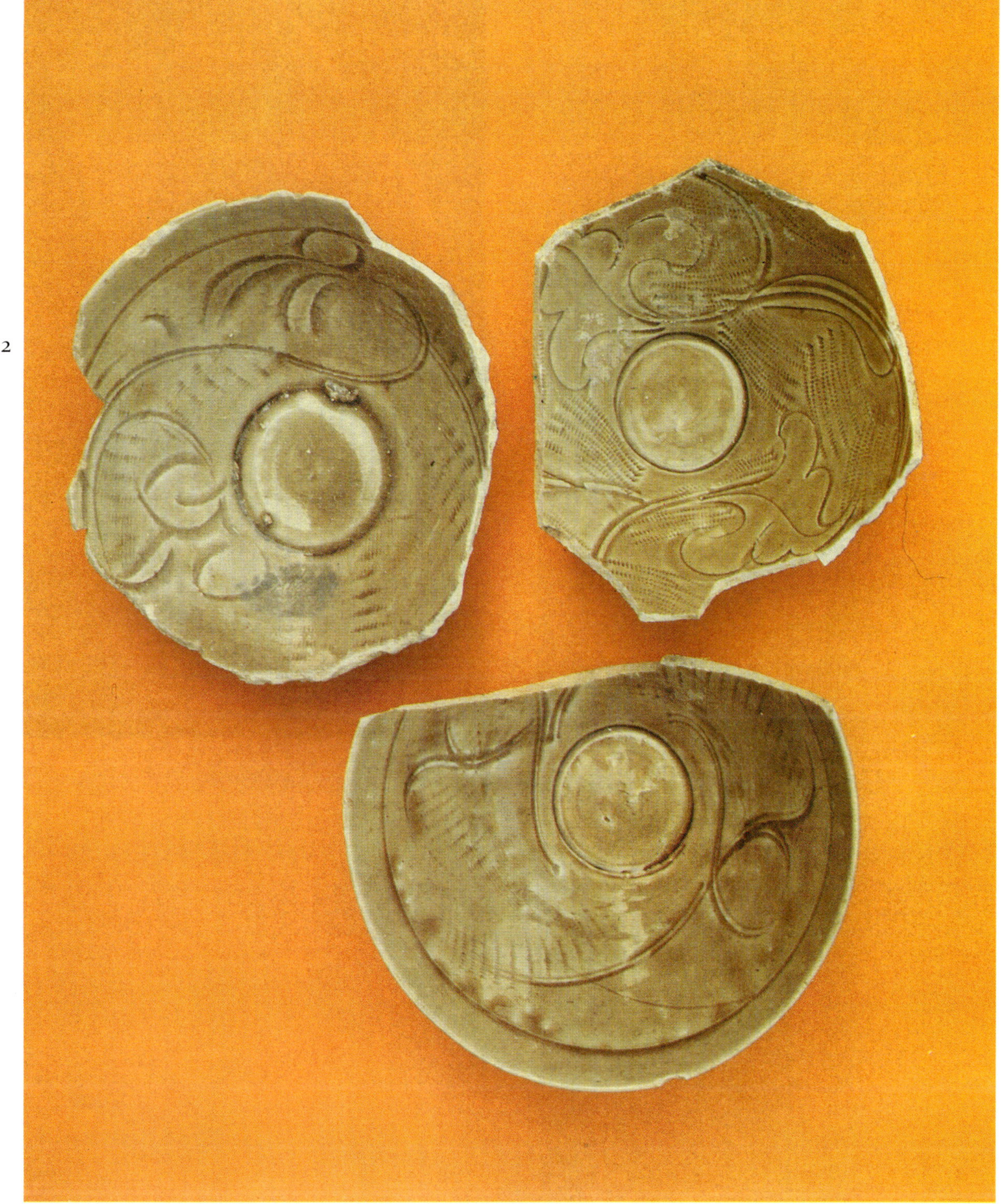

132
130
131

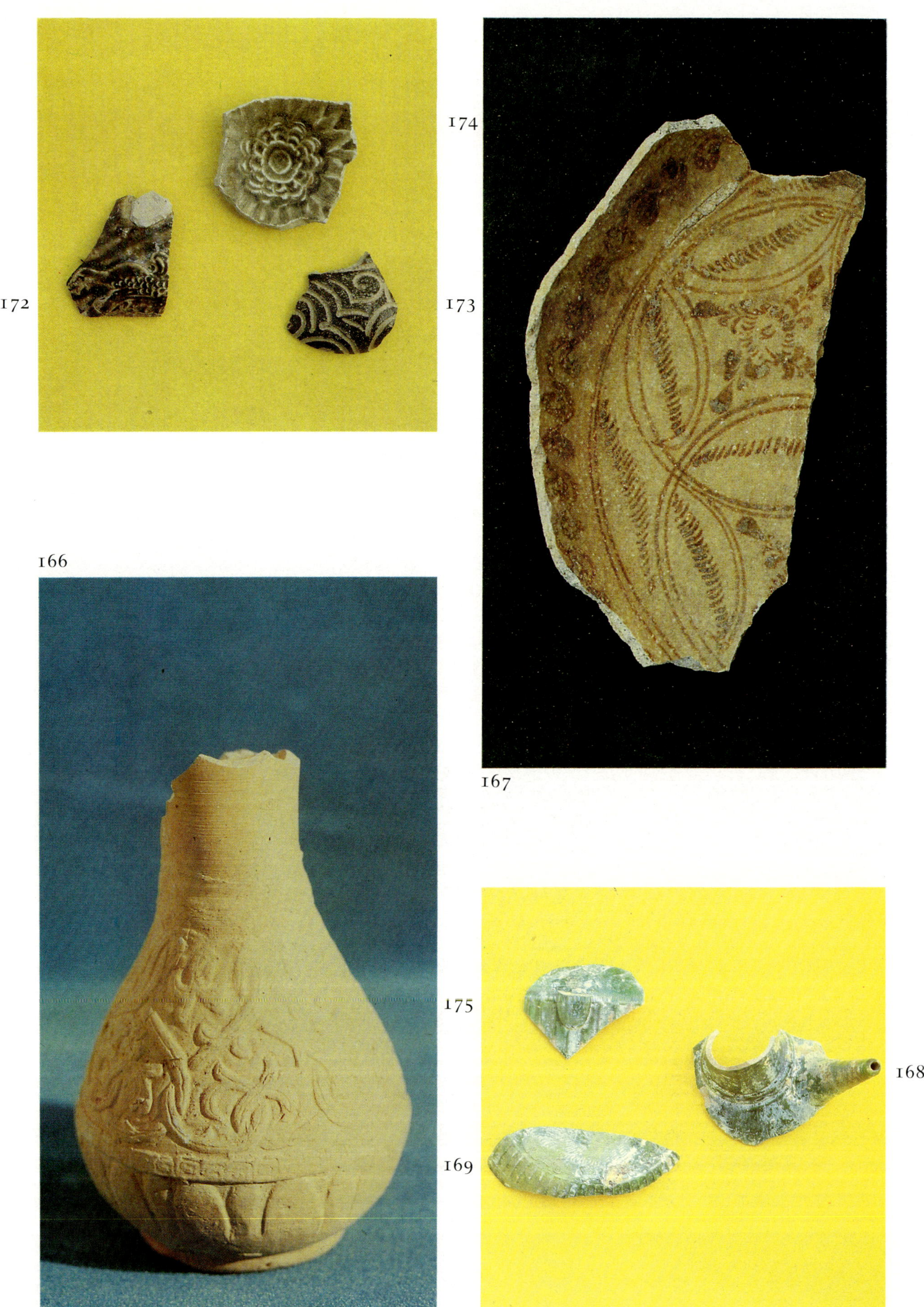

172
174
173
166
167
175
168
169

105
Base sherd of a dish with carved and combed
decoration under a *qingbai* glaze
From Fujian Dehua (1979:6)
Song dynasty (AD 960–1279)

From the base of a dish which appears to have
collapsed during firing, this sherd is decorated with a
carved and combed design of fish among waves on
the inside, and with a petal design (or chatter marks)
on one side of the outside. The short foot and
recessed base are unglazed. The body and *qingbai*
glaze are the same as for no. 101.

Dimensions: 18 × 16 cm.
Diameter of foot ring: 8 cm. Body: 0.3–0.6 cm.

106
Fragment of a box lid with moulded decoration
under a *qingbai* glaze
From Fujian Dehua (1979:6)
Song dynasty (AD 960–1279)

This fragment, from the moulded lid of a box, has
short, straight sides decorated with a band of wave
pattern. The domed top is lobed around the sides,
and decorated with a lobed panel containing a lotus
design in the centre. The character *you*, 'have', also
appears in the panel. The white glassy body is glazed
with a thin, greyish glaze which has crawled where
overfired. The mouth rim and a band inside the
mouth rim are unglazed.

Dimensions: 11.8 × 10.7 cm. Body: 0.3–0.5 cm.

107
Part of a box lid with moulded decoration under a
qingbai glaze
From Fujian Dehua (1979:6)
Song dynasty (AD 960–1279)

This lid fragment is decorated on the top with a
moulded lotus pattern surrounded by a band of
alternating flowers and scroll motifs. The lid would
have originally had eight sides. The white, glassy
body is partially glazed inside the top with the thin
greyish glaze to which kiln grit adheres on the
outside.

Diameter: 10.6 cm. Body: 0.2 cm.

108
Fragment of a box lid with moulded decoration
under a *qingbai* glaze
From Fujian Dehua (1979:6)
Song dynasty (AD 960–1279)

From an eight-lobed box lid, this fragment is
decorated on the top with a moulded flower spray. It
is glazed outside, and partially inside, with a thin
greyish *qingbai* glaze to which kiln debris adheres on
the top. The body is glassy and white.

Dimensions: 14.2 × 7.5 cm. Body: 0.3 cm.

109
Part of a box lid with moulded decoration under a
qingbai glaze
From Fujian Dehua (1979:6)
Song dynasty (AD 960–1279)

Part of a multi-lobed box lid, this fragment is
decorated on the top with a moulded peony design
and what appear to be Chinese characters. The
outside is glazed with the thin, greyish *qingbai* glaze
which also covers the inside of the top. The body is
glassy and white.

Dimensions: 12 × 9.5 cm. Body: 0.4 cm.

110
Fragment of a moulded bowl with a *qingbai* glaze
From Fujian Dehua (1979:6)
Song dynasty (AD 960–1279)

This fragment is from a bowl with rounded sides
ribbed on the inside to form chrysanthemum petals,
and with an everted foliated rim. The thin, greyish
qingbai glaze stops short of the foot which is straight
and inclined on the inside. Kiln grit adheres in a
thick blob of clay on the inside. The body is glassy
and white.

Dimensions: 8.7 × 6.1 cm. Body: 0.3 cm.

111
Rim sherd of a moulded, foliated dish with a *qingbai*
glaze
From Fujian Dehua (1979:6)
Song dynasty (AD 960–1279)

This rim sherd of a dish with rounded, ribbed sides
and an everted, flattened, foliated rim gives the
overall impression of a chrysanthemum. A band of
key-fret pattern decorates the rim. The glassy white
body is glazed with a thin, greyish *qingbai* glaze
which stops short of the foot on the underside.

Dimensions: 10 × 3.9 cm. Body: 0.2 cm.

112
Fragment of a moulded, foliated dish with a *qingbai*
glaze
From Fujian Dehua (1979:6)
Song dynasty (AD 960–1279)

From a moulded dish with shallow, rounded, ribbed
sides and a flattened, everted, foliated rim, giving the
overall effect of a chrysanthemum, this fragment is
decorated in the centre of the inside with two petals
of a lotus design. The thin, greyish *qingbai* glaze stops
short of the small, straight foot, which is inclined on
the inside. The glassy body is white.

Dimensions: 10.5 × 5 cm. Body: 0.3–0.6 cm. (base)

113
Part of a stem cup with a *qingbai* glaze
From Fujian Dehua (1979:6)
Yuan dynasty (AD 1280–1368)

This piece is part of a stem cup on a high, flaring foot.
The bowl has rounded sides and an everted rim. The
white, glassy body is glazed on the outside down to
the foot ring with a whitish-grey, viscous and rather
dull *qingbai* glaze. The foot ring and the inside of the
stem are unglazed.

Height: 7.7 cm. Height of stem: 3.3 cm.
Diameter of foot ring: 3.7 cm. Body: 0.2–0.5 cm.

114
Part of a moulded dish with a *qingbai* glaze
From Fujian Dehua (1979:6)
Yuan dynasty (AD 960–1279)

From a shallow dish, with a flattened, everted rim
raised at the outer edge, this fragment is decorated
on the inside with a moulded lotus design. The
glassy, white body has burnt yellowish where
exposed as the thick, whitish-blue, shiny, viscous
glaze stops short of the fine, straight foot and the
base.

Diameter: 17.5 cm. Diameter of foot ring: 5.2 cm.
Body: 0.2–0.3 cm.

Anxi   nos. 115–129

One hundred and twenty-eight kilns were discovered at Anxi, 23 of which date
to the Song and Yuan dynasties. The main production consisted of *qingbai*
wares, and these are generally similar in form and decoration to those from
Dehua. Large numbers of pieces have been found at the extensive kiln site at
Anyuan; these include some rather rare wares decorated with brown. Many
boxes of different shapes and sizes were discovered, on which the moulded
decoration in relief is rather coarser than the fine line designs of Dehua yao.

115
Fragment of a moulded bowl with a *qingbai* glaze
From Fujian Anxi (1979:6)
Song dynasty (AD 960–1279)

This fragment is part of a bowl with rounded sides
and an everted rim, decorated on the outside with a
moulded design of lotus petals. The greyish-white
fine body burns buff where exposed. The greyish-
blue, shiny, *qingbai* glaze stops short of the mouth
rim and the minimal, straight foot which is inclined
on the inside towards the flat, slightly recessed base
to which kiln grit adheres.

Height: 5.8 cm. Diameter of foot: 6.8 cm.
Body: 0.3–0.4 cm.

116
Part of a moulded box lid with a *qingbai* glaze
From Fujian Anxi (1979:6)
Song dynasty (AD 960–1279)

This fragment is part of a moulded box lid with
ribbed sides and is decorated on the top with various
flowers, including a lotus. The greyish-white, fine
body burns buff where exposed. The greyish-blue
qingbai glaze covers the outside, and the underside of
the top, leaving the rim and inside walls unglazed.

Dimensions: 13.3 × 9.1 cm. Body: 0.3–0.4 cm.

117

Fragment of a moulded box lid with a *qingbai* glaze
From Fujian Anxi (1979:6)
Song dynasty (AD 960–1279)

This box lid fragment has rounded, ribbed sides and is decorated on the top with a moulded lotus design within a border of two bands of double incised lines. The greyish-white, fine body burns buff where exposed. The greyish-blue, shiny *qingbai* glaze covers the outside and only the underside of the top on the inside.

Dimensions: 11.5 × 7.4 cm. Body: 0.3 cm.

118

Parts of a kendi with an applied tortoise motif and iron brown splashing under the *qingbai* glaze
From Fujian Anxi (1979:6)
Song dynasty (AD 960–1279)

This fragment consists of two pieces of a kendi luted together under the pale blue *qingbai* glaze, which is splashed with iron brown. The lower part is decorated with petals, and the upper part with an applied model of a tortoise. The bluish-white fine body is unglazed on the inside.

Dimensions: 11.6 × 7.3 cm.
Length of tortoise: 6.5 cm. Body: 0.3–0.4 cm.

119

Part of a jar with brown splashing under the *qingbai* glaze
From Fujian Anxi (1979:6)
Song dynasty (AD 960–1279)

This fragment is part of a jar with a flat base and decorated with fluid, linear designs in brown iron pigment under the pale blue, crackled *qingbai* glaze which runs short of the base. The inside, where turning marks are visible, is glazed. The bluish-white, fine body burns buff where exposed.

Height: 7.5 cm. Width: 9.5 cm.
Body: 0.3–0.5 cm. (base)

120

Part of a brush washer with moulded decoration under a *qingbai* glaze
From Fujian Anxi (1979:6)
Song dynasty (AD 960–1279)

Part of a brush washer with spreading sides, this piece is decorated on the inside with a moulded floral roundel. The greyish-white, fine body burns buff where exposed inside the mouth rim and on the concave base. The greyish-blue *qingbai* glaze runs down to the minimal foot.

Diameter: 13.6 cm. Height: 2.1 cm. Body: 0.3 cm.

121

Fragment of a bowl with incised and combed decoration under a *qingbai* glaze
From Fujian Anxi (1979:6)
Song dynasty (AD 960–1279)

This is part of a bowl with spreading sides, a small, straight foot and a slightly recessed flat base, where the greyish-white body has burnt orange. The inside is decorated with incised and combed designs under the whitish-blue *qingbai* glaze.

Dimensions: 15.5 × 12.4 cm. Body: 0.3 cm.

122

Part of a bowl with incised and combed decoration under a *qingbai* glaze
From Fujian Anxi (1979:6)
Song dynasty (AD 960–1279)

A fragment of a bowl with spreading sides and a foliated rim, a fairly tall incised foot and a convex base, this piece is decorated with an incised and combed wave pattern on the inside. The greyish-white, fine body is glazed with a greyish-blue *qingbai* glaze which runs in tears to the foot ring.

Height: 6.8 cm. Diameter of foot: 5.6 cm.
Body: 0.3–0.6 cm. (base)

123

Part of a bowl with combed decoration under a grey-green glaze
From Fujian Anxi (1979:6)
Song dynasty (AD 960–1279)

This fragment of a conical bowl with a straight, thick foot and a small, thick, round base, is decorated on the inside with a combed design of a lotus flower around a central button of clay. The pale grey, fine body is covered with a grey-green shiny glaze, which stops short of the foot on the outside.

Height: 7.9 cm. Diameter: 13.2 cm.
Diameter of foot: 3.8 cm. Body: 0.2–0.8 cm.

124

Part of a bowl with chrysanthemum foliations under a *qingbai* glaze

Part of a bowl with rounded sides spreading to the multi-foliate rim. The inside walls are ribbed in line with the foliations and give an overall chrysanthemum effect. The slightly convex base and the small foot are unglazed, and the greyish-white, fine body appears buff where exposed. The *qingbai* glaze is whitish-grey.

Height: 4.6 cm. Diameter: 11.5 cm.
Diameter of foot ring: 4.6 cm. Body: 0.3–0.5 cm.

125
Sherd of a moulded box lid with a *qingbai* glaze
From Fujian Anxi (1979:6)
Yuan dynasty (AD 1280–1368)

This sherd from the lid of a moulded box is decorated with raised scrolling in panels round the sides and with continuous scrolling on the top. The rim and a strip inside the rim are unglazed. Otherwise the bluish-white, fine body is glazed with a watery blue *qingbai* glaze.

Dimensions: 5.8 × 5.8 cm. Body: 0.4 cm.

126
Fragment of a moulded box lid with a *qingbai* glaze
From Fujian Anxi (1979:6)
Yuan dynasty (AD 1280–1368)

The warped fragment of a moulded box lid with foliated sides is decorated on the sides and the top with foliated panels containing scroll patterns. The bluish-white, fine body is glazed inside and out with a watery blue *qingbai* glaze.

Dimensions: 16 × 6.8 cm. Body: 0.3 cm.

127
Part of the moulded lid of a box with a *qingbai* glaze
From Fujian Anxi (1979:6)
Yuan dynasty (AD 1280–1368)

This box lid fragment is decorated on the domed top and sides with a moulded scroll decoration. Spots of kiln grit adhere to the watery blue *qingbai* glaze on the outside. The bluish-white, fine body is glazed also on the underside of the top.

Height: 4 cm. Body: 0.2–0.3 cm.

128
Sherd from the base of a moulded box with a *qingbai* glaze
From Fujian Anxi (1979:6)
Yuan dynasty (AD 1280–1368)

This sherd from the bottom of a box is decorated round the sides with a moulded scroll pattern. The watery blue *qingbai* glaze stops well short of the slightly concave base. The mouth rim is unglazed and is deeply grooved to accommodate a lid. There is an unglazed band on the inside just below the rim. The body is whitish-blue, and fine. Kiln grit adheres to the inside.

Dimensions: 14 × 6.4 cm. Body: 0.5 cm.

129
Part of the bottom of a moulded box with a *qingbai* glaze
From Fujian Anxi (1979:6)
Yuan dynasty (AD 1280–1368)

From the bottom of a box, this sherd is decorated with a moulded floral design on the slightly concave, unglazed base, a moulded scroll design around the walls, and a triple ribbed band above the minimal foot. The greyish-blue *qingbai* glaze covers the outside down to the foot, and the base of the inside. The mouth rim, which is grooved to accommodate a lid, is unglazed, and the bluish-white, fine body appears buff were exposed.

Dimensions: 12.5 × 8 cm. Body: 0.2–1.4 cm.

Tong'an   nos. 130–143

In 1956 three kiln sites were discovered, and these have now been investigated several times. Tong'an produced both green wares and *qingbai* wares. The glaze colour of the greenwares tends towards yellow, the insides of bowls often being embellished with carved decoration together with stippled designs or comb marks. On the outside, the bowls were decorated with carved lines. The decoration of *qingbai* wares was similar to that of the green wares, except that the lines tended to be finer. Lamps, flasks and jars, lightly carved on the outside with lotus petal panels, were often also decorated with obliquely crossed lines. Most of the wares of the Song and Yuan periods were made for export, the number excavated in Japan being particularly large.

130

Part of a bowl with carved and combed decoration
under an olive glaze
From Fujian Tong'an (1979:6)
Song dynasty (AD 960–1279)

This piece is part of a bowl with a thick, straight foot,
inclined on the inside towards the thick, slightly
convex base. The spreading walls are decorated on
the outside with vertical combed striations, and on
the inside with a carved leaf scroll on a ground of zig-
zags of dotted combing. The grey, coarse body burns
buff were exposed. The olive, crackled glaze stops
short of the foot on the outside.

Dimensions: 14.8 × 14.8 cm.
Diameter of foot ring: 5.3 cm. Body: 0.4–0.7 cm.

131

Part of a bowl with carved and combed decoration
under an olive glaze
From Fujian Tong'an (1979:6)
Song dynasty (AD 960–1279)

Part of a bowl with a straight foot, roughly cut base
and spreading sides rising towards the straight rim,
this piece is decorated on the outside with vertical
bands of combing and on the inside with a carved
scroll and lines of dotted combing within a line
border beneath the rim. The grey, coarse body burns
buff where exposed on the foot and base. The olive
glaze is crackled.

Height: 7.8 cm. Diameter: 6.7 cm.
Diameter of foot ring: 5.5 cm. Body: 0.3–0.6 cm.

132

Part of a bowl with carved and combed decoration
under an olive glaze
From Fujian Tong'an (1979:6)
Song dynasty (AD 960–1279)

Part of a bowl with a straight foot, a convex base and
spreading sides rising to the straight rim, this
fragment is decorated on the outside with bands of
vertical combing, and on the inside with a lotus
scroll and lines of dotted combing. The olive,
crackled glaze runs to the foot ring on the outside,
leaving the base and foot ring unglazed. The grey,
coarse body burns buff where exposed. Kiln grit
adheres to the glaze on the inside.

Height: 7 cm. Diameter of foot: 5.9 cm.
Body: 0.3–0.5 cm.

133

Part of a bowl with carved and combed designs
under an olive glaze
From Fujian Tong'an (1979:6)
Song dynasty (AD 960–1279)

This fragment is part of a bowl similar to the
previous three, but smaller and shallower. The
outside is decorated with random bands of combing
and the inside with carved scrolling lines and lines of
dotted combing. The grey, coarse body burns reddish
where exposed on the straight foot and convex base.
It is glazed with an olive, crackled glaze.

Height: 4.8 cm. Diameter: 13.3 cm.
Diameter of foot: 4.6 cm. Body: 0.3–0.9 cm. (base)

134

Part of a bowl with combed decoration under an
olive glaze
From Fujian Tong'an (1956:10)
Song dynasty (AD 960–1279)

This fragment of a bowl, with spreading sides rising
towards the straight rim, is decorated on the outside
with six bands of vertical combing, and on the inside
with radial lines of dotted combing. The olive,
crackled glaze stops short of the straight foot on the
outside. The grey, coarse body burns buff where
exposed and rust coloured marks are visible on the
unglazed convex base and the foot ring.

Height: 4.5 cm. Diameter of foot ring: 4.3 cm.
Body: 0.3–0.5 cm.

135

Fragment of a dish with carved and combed
decoration under an olive glaze
From Fujian Tong'an (1979:6)
Song dynasty (AD 960–1279)

This fragment is part of a dish with gently rounded
walls, decorated on the outside with carved lotus
petals and on the inside with a sketchily carved lotus
scroll on a ground of zig-zags of dotted combing. The
olive, crackled glaze runs to the rounded foot ring
leaving the thick, flat base and the inside of the
straight foot unglazed. The grey, coarse body shows
buff where exposed. Kiln grit adheres to the glaze on
the outside.

Dimensions: 5.5 × 3.5 cm. Body: 0.5–0.8 cm.

136

Part of a bowl with carved and stamped designs
under an olive glaze
From Fujian Tong'an (1956:10)
Song dynasty (AD 960–1279)

From a bowl with spreading walls, a straight foot
and a convex base, this fragment is decorated with
vertical bands of combing on the outside, and with a
carved lotus scroll round the inside walls and a
stamped motif of a deer in the centre. The grey,
coarse body burns buff where exposed on the foot
and base. The olive glaze is paler and less crackled
than that of the other Tong'an pieces.

Dimensions: 11.7 × 10.1 cm.
Diameter of foot ring: 6.2 cm. Body: 0.3–0.5 cm.

137

Fragment of a bowl with carved, combed and
stamped decoration under an olive glaze
From Fujian Tong'an (1979:6)
Song dynasty (AD 960–1279)

This fragment of a bowl with spreading sides, a foot
inclined slightly on both sides and a convex base, is
decorated in the centre of the inside with a stamped
motif of a deer, and round the walls with a sketchily
carved scroll and zig-zags of dotted combing. The
grey, coarse body appears buff where exposed on the
foot and base. The olive, crackled glaze stops just
short of the foot ring on the outside.

Dimensions: 10.7 × 9.2 cm.
Diameter of foot ring: 5.8 cm. Body: 0.4–0.6 cm.
*Drawing published: WW 1974 (11) pp. 80–84, Fig. 3
Also: GGBWYYK (2) p. 128, Fig. 10*

138

Part of a dish with carved and combed decoration
under an olive glaze
From Fujian Tong'an (1979:6)
Song dynasty (AD 960–1279)

Part of a shallow dish with spreading sides and an
everted rim, this fragment is decorated on the outside
with seven bands of vertical combing, and on the
inside with sketchily carved scrolls and wavy
combed lines within an incised line border. The grey,
coarse body appears buff where exposed on the
straight foot and the roughly cut base. The olive
glaze is crazed.

Height: 3.9 cm. Diameter: 15.7 cm.
Body: 0.2–0.3 cm.

139

Part of a bowl with carved and combed decoration
under a *qingbai* glaze
From Fujian Tong'an (1979:6)
Song dynasty (AD 960–1279)

Part of a conical bowl with a thick, straight foot and
a thick, convex base, this piece is decorated on the
inside with a carved and combed wave pattern
radiating from the centre. The greyish-white, fine
body burns buff where exposed. The greyish *qingbai*
glaze stops short of the foot on the outside.

Height: 8.9 cm. Diameter: 7.3 cm.
Diameter of foot ring: 5.2 cm. Body: 0.2–0.4 cm.

140

Fragment of a bowl with combed designs under a
qingbai glaze
From Fujian Tong'an (1956:10)
Song dynasty (AD 960–1279)

This fragment is part of a bowl with spreading sides,
a straight foot inclined on the inside, and a convex
base. The inside is decorated with free combed
designs under the greyish *qingbai* glaze, which stops
short of the foot on the outside. The greyish-white,
fine body has burnt orange where exposed.

Dimensions: 13 × 9.5 cm.
Diameter of foot ring: 5.4 cm. Body: 0.4–0.5 cm.

141

Part of an incense burner with carved decoration
under a *qingbai* glaze
From Fujian Tong'an (1979:6)
Song dynasty (AD 960–1279)

This sherd from an incense burner with a rounded
wall and an everted rim is decorated on the outside
with lotus petals carved in high relief. The greyish-
white, fine body is glazed with a greyish *qingbai* glaze
which is trimmed short of the base on the inside.

Height: 7.5 cm. Body: 0.4–0.8 cm. (base)

142

Part of a dish with incised and combed decoration
under a *qingbai* glaze
From Fujian Tong'an (1979:6)
Song dynasty (AD 960–1279)

Part of a dish with spreading walls, angled on the
outside towards the tapering rim, this fragment is
decorated on the inside with a sketchily incised and
combed design within a grooved line border beneath
the rim. The greyish-white body is burnt buff where
exposed on the flat base. The greyish *qingbai* glaze
runs to the base on the outside.

Dimensions: 12.5 × 9.8 cm.
Diameter of base: 4.6 cm. Body: 0.3–0.4 cm.

143
Fragment of a dish with stamped decoration under a
qingbai glaze
From Fujian Tong'an (1979:6)
Yuan dynasty (AD 1280–1368)

This fragment of a dish with a rounded well and a
flattened, everted rim with an upturned rounded
edge, is decorated in the centre of the inside with a
stamped design of two fish. The grey, medium-coarse
body is glazed with a greenish-grey *qingbai* glaze
which is crackled and stops short of the thick foot
and the thick, roughly cut base.

Height: 4.8 cm. Diameter of foot ring: 5.9 cm.
Body: 0.4 –1.5 cm. (base)

Nan'an   nos. 144–158

Nan'an xian was one of the areas in the Jinjiang region producing ceramics.
Forty kilns of Song date have been discovered, principally on the north-east and
south-west borders of the *xian*. Both greenwares and *qingbai* wares were made,
with greenwares predominating. These were similar in form and design to the
products of Tong'an. The *qingbai* wares have, in the main, carved decoration,
and include a large number of boxes with rather tall, thick bodies, unlike the
form of the thinner, flatter bodies of the boxes known from other kilns in the
Jinliang area.

144
Part of a bowl with combed decoration under a grey-
green glaze
From Fujian Nan'an (1979:6)
Song dynasty (AD 960–1279)

From a bowl with rounded walls and a slightly
everted rim, a straight foot and a convex base, this
piece is decorated on the inside with combed zig-
zags. The pale grey, fine body is glazed with a pale
grey-green glaze, and is burnt orange where exposed
on the foot and base.

Height: 8 cm. Diameter of foot: 5.3 cm.
Body: 0.3 –1.0 cm. (base)

145
Fragment of a bowl with carved and combed designs
under a grey-green glaze
From Fujian Nan'an (1979:6)
Song dynasty (AD 960–1279)

From a bowl, similar to those from Tong'an, with
spreading walls rising towards the rim, a straight,
thick foot and a recessed thick base rising to a pimple
of clay in the centre. The fragment is decorated on
the outside with broad vertical bands of combing and
on the inside with a sketchily carved scroll design
and combed zig-zag lines. The pale body is burnt
orange-buff where exposed and is glazed with a
crazed pale grey-green glaze.

Height: 7.5 cm. Diameter of foot ring: 5.4 cm.
Body: 0.2 –0.7 cm.

146

Part of a bowl with carved decoration under an olive glaze
From Fujian Nan'an (1979:6)
Song dynasty (AD 960–1279)

Part of a bowl, with a rounded wall and slightly everted rim and the remains of a straight foot, this fragment is decorated on the inside with a carved scrolling lotus. The very fine, whitish-grey body is glazed with a pale olive glaze which runs unevenly to the foot on the outside.

Height: 7.3 cm. Dimensions: 13.5 × 7 cm.
Body: 0.3–0.7 cm.

147

Fragment of a bowl with carved and combed decoration under an olive glaze
From Fujian Nan'an (1979:6)
Song dynasty (AD 960–1279)

This fragment of a bowl with spreading sides is decorated on the outside with bands of vertical combing, and on the inside with a carved scrolling lotus design and with zig-zags of dotted combing within a border of incised lines below the rim. The fine, whitish-grey body is burnt buff where exposed and appears orange on the recessed base and the foot ring. The pale olive glaze stops short of the foot on the outside.

Dimensions: 10 × 9.2 cm.
Diameter of foot ring: 4.9 cm. Body: 0.3–0.5 cm.

148

Sherd from a bowl with carved and combed decoration under an olive glaze
From Fujian Nan'an (AD 960–1279)

The sherd from a bowl with spreading sides rising towards the rim is decorated on the inside with a carved and combed scrolling design with an incised line border beneath the rim. The pale olive glaze stops short of the thick, slightly inclined foot on the outside, leaving the fine, whitish-grey body exposed and burnt buff on the foot and the roughly cut convex base. Kiln grit adheres to the glaze inside and out.

Dimensions: 12 × 7 cm.
Body: 0.4–0.9 cm. (base)

149

Fragment of a bowl with incised decoration under a *qingbai* glaze
From Fujian Nan'an (1979:6)
Song dynasty (AD 960–1279)

From a bowl, with rounded sides, an inclined foot and a flat base rising to a nipple of clay in the centre, this fragment is decorated on the inside with an incised scrolling lotus design. The greyish-white, fine body is visible in the large chip on the inside base but has burnt orange where exposed on the foot ring and base. The pale greyish-blue glaze runs unevenly to the foot on the outside.

Dimensions: 13 × 11.2 cm.
Diameter of base: 6.2 cm.
Body: 0.3–0.6 cm.

150

Part of a bowl with incised decoration under a *qingbai* glaze
From Fujian Nan'an (1979:6)
Song dynasty (AD 960–1279)

From a bowl with rounded sides, an everted rim, a short, straight foot and a flat base, this piece is decorated on the inside with an incised leafy scroll. The greyish-white body has burnt orange where exposed on the foot ring and base. The pale greyish-blue *qingbai* glaze has deteriorated on the outside.

Height: 6.8 cm. Diameter of foot: 5.8 cm.
Body: 0.3–0.4 cm.

151

Part of a bowl with incised and combed designs under a *qingbai* glaze
From Fujian Nan'an (1979:6)
Song dynasty (AD 960–1279)

This part of a bowl with spreading sides rising towards the rim is decorated on the inside with sketchily combed designs within an incised line border beneath the rim. The pale greyish-blue *qingbai* glaze stops short of the thick, straight foot which is inclined on the inside. The greyish-white, fine body is burnt orange where exposed on the foot and the roughly turned convex base.

Height: 6.6 cm. Diameter of foot ring: 6.1 cm.
Body: 0.4 cm.

152

Sherd from a foliated bowl with incised decoration under a *qingbai* glaze
From Fujian Nan'an (1979:6)
Song dynasty (AD 960–1279)

This sherd is part of a bowl with rounded sides and a foliated rim, decorated on the inside with sketchily incised designs. The greyish-blue *qingbai* glaze runs in tears down the outside to the foot. The fine body is greyish-white.

Dimensions: 8.5 × 3.5 cm. Body: 0.3 cm.

153
Sherd of a bowl with carved and combed decoration under a *qingbai* glaze
From Fujian Nan'an (1979:6)
Song dynasty (AD 960–1279)

This sherd from a bowl with spreading sides and an inverted rim is decorated on the outside with carved lotus petals with combed details. The body is fine and almost white, and the *qingbai* glaze a clear glassy blue. There seems to be an unglazed ring on the inside base.

Dimensions: 8.6 × 8 cm. Body: 0.4 cm.

154
Part of a lidded box with carved decoration under a *qingbai* glaze
From Fujian Nan'an (1979:6)
Song dynasty (AD 960–1279)

This piece consists of the bottom of a box and part of its lid stuck together during firing. The side walls are incised with matching lines and the lid is domed and fluted with a flat, undecorated top. The greyish *qingbai* glaze stops short where the wall inclines towards the flat, unglazed base. The inside of the top and the rim of the bottom, which has a very tall ridge to accommodate the lid, are unglazed. The greyish-white, fine body is burnt orange where exposed.

Height: 10.5 cm. Diameter: 9 cm.
Diameter of base: 6.7 cm. Body: 0.6–0.7 cm.

155
Fragment of the lid of a box with incised decoration under a *qingbai* glaze
From Fujian Nan'an (1979:6)
Song dynasty (AD 960–1279)

The fragment from the lid of a box is decorated round the sides with incised oblique lines, and on the top with a faintly incised design within a carved, double ribbed border. The outside and the underside of the top are glazed with a pale grey-blue *qingbai* glaze. The greyish-white, fine body is burnt orange where exposed.

Dimensions: 5.8–4.7 cm. Body: 0.5 cm.
Published: GGBWYYK 1980 (1) pp. 3–27, Fig. 7

156
Part of the lid of a box with combed decoration under a *qingbai* glaze
From Fujian Nan'an (1979:6)
Song dynasty (AD 960–1279)

This fragment of a box lid is decorated on the sides with deeply combed vertical lines. The sides are stepped with a groove half way up to the flat, undecorated top. The inside of the lid and the rim are unglazed. The greyish-white fine body is glazed with a pale grey-blue *qingbai* glaze.

Height: 5.5 cm. Body: 0.4 cm.
Published: GGBWYYK 1980 (1) pp. 3–27, Fig. 7

157
Part of the lid of a box with a *qingbai* glaze
From Fujian Nan'an (1979:6)
Song dynasty (AD 960–1279)

This lid fragment in the form of a gourd has six incised lines radiating from a central button. The unglazed inside shows the turning with a pimple of clay in the centre. The greyish-white, fine body is glazed on the outside with a pale grey-blue *qingbai* glaze which is crazed.

Height: 4 cm. Diameter: 7.4 cm. Body: 0.6 cm.
Published: GGBWYYK 1980 (1) pp. 3–27, Fig. 7

158
Fragment of the lid of a box with combed decoration under a *qingbai* glaze
From Fujian Nan'an (1979:6)
Song dynasty (AD 960–1279)

This box lid fragment is decorated with vertical combed lines up the sides, which are stepped with a groove half way up the flat top, to which kiln grit adheres. The greyish-white, fine body is glazed with an almost ivory coloured *qingbai* glaze with a very slight trace of green in it. The inside and the rim are unglazed.

Height: 5 cm. Diameter of top: 8 cm.
Body: 0.4–0.6 cm.
Published: GGBWYYK 1980 (1) pp. 3–27, Fig. 7

Quanzhou   nos. 159–175

Quanzhou was a most important port in China during the Song and Yuan dynasties; from there were exported all the wares from the Jinjiang area. A Song kiln producing *qingbai* wares was found outside the eastern gate of Quanzhou. Eleven Song and Yuan kilns making stonewares have been discovered, but as well as the greenwares and blackwares a large quantity of low fired pottery was also manufactured. The decoration was usually moulded and the glaze added after an initial firing. The Tongzishan kiln specialised in large dishes with a green-yellow glaze and coarsely painted decoration. Some are inscribed with poems. Quanzhou wares have been excavated at sites in the Philippines, Japan and other countries.

159
Part of a dish with stamped decoration under a
qingbai glaze
From Fujian Quanzhou (1956:10)
Song dynasty (AD 960–1279)

This fragment is part of a dish that appears to have warped during firing. The shallow, rounded walls have a slightly everted rim which is unglazed. The inside is decorated with an impressed lotus motif in the centre. Apart from the rim the dish is glazed inside and out with a greyish *qingbai* glaze, which is badly burnt on the underside. The fine body is greyish-white.

Height: 3 cm. Approximate diameter: 12.5 cm.
Body: 0.2–0.3 cm.

160
Fragment of an incense burner with carved and combed decoration under a *qingbai* glaze
From Fujian Quanzhou (1956:10)
Song dynasty (AD 960–1279)

This fragment is part of an incense burner with straight sides and a flat base, with a straight foot inclined on the inside. The sides are decorated with carved lotus petals with combed details. The greyish-white, fine body is burnt orange-buff where exposed on the foot and on the base inside the foot ring. On the outside the pale blue *qingbai* glaze runs unevenly to the foot and is trimmed half way down the inside.

Height: 9.3 cm. Width: 13.3 cm.
Body: 1.3–1.4 cm. (base)

161
Sherd from a bottle with an incised and combed design under a *qingbai* glaze
From Fujian Quanzhou (1956:10)
Song dynasty (AD 960–1279)

This sherd from the wall of a bottle is decorated on the outside with vertical panels of incised and combed wave pattern, separated by raised, double ribbed borders. The greyish-white, fine body is glazed on the outside with a pale grey-blue *qingbai* glaze.

Dimensions: 8.6 × 6.6 cm. Body: 0.4 cm.

162
Fragment of a moulded box lid with a *qingbai* glaze
From Fujian Quanzhou (1979:6)
Song dynasty (AD 960–1279)

From the lid of a box, this fragment has moulded, ribbed sides and on the top a moulded design of a peony. The greyish-white, fine body is burnt orange where exposed on the rim and the inside walls. The outside and the underside of the top are glazed with a pale blue *qingbai* glaze.

Height: 3.2 cm. Dimensions: 10.5 × 7.5 cm.
Body: 0.4 cm.

163
Neck fragment of a flask with brown iron pigment painting under the *qingbai* glaze
From Fujian Quanzhou (1979:6)
Song dynasty (AD 960–1279)

The fragment from the straight neck of a flask is stepped where the neck joins the shoulder, and has a spot of brown iron pigment under the pale blue *qingbai* glaze. The neck is unglazed inside, revealing the greyish-white, fine body.

Height: 3.5 cm. Available diameter: 6 cm.
Body: 0.9–1.2 cm.

164

Sherd of a foliated dish with a *qingbai* glaze
From Fujian Quanzhou (1979:6)
Song dynasty (AD 960–1279)

This thin sherd is from the wall of a moulded dish, fluted on the inside and with a foliated rim, giving the overall effect of a chrysanthemum. The greyish-white, fine body is glazed with a pale blue *qingbai* glaze which runs deep in the grooves.

Dimensions: 6.1 × 4.9 cm. Body: 0.2–0.3 cm.

165

Kendi with a black glaze
From Fujian Quanzhou (1979:6)
Song dynasty (AD 960–1279)

The kendi has a flat base, a flattened globular body and an uneven tapering spout. The neck is ribbed where it broadens towards the body and it spreads to the everted rim, which has a raised inside edge and an unglazed step to accommodate a lid. The putty grey, medium-coarse, sandy body is glazed with a black glaze which has deteriorated in places on the outside. The glaze stops short of the base, and runs unevenly down the inside of the neck. The rim is also unglazed on the underside.

Height: 13 cm. Diameter of base: 7.2 cm.
Diameter of rim: 8.2 cm.

166

Unglazed flask with moulded decoration
From Fujian Quanzhou (1979:6)
Song dynasty (AD 960–1279)

The flask has a straight foot, a slightly recessed flat base, a rounded body with moulded bands of intertwining tendrils, key-fret and petal decoration, and the remains of a turned neck luted on to the moulded body. The unglazed earthenware body is fired to an orange-buff colour.

Height: 14 cm. Diameter of base: 5.8 cm.

167

Fragment of a dish with brown painted decoration under a greenish glaze
From Fujian Quanzhou (1979:6)
Song dynasty (AD 960–1279)

This fragment of a large dish with a flat base and slightly rounded sides is painted on the inside in brown over a pale slip with leaf and floral patterns and with a sketchy scroll around the well. The greyish-green transparent glaze covers the inside and stops short of the base on the unslipped outside, leaving the grey-buff, coarse, sandy body exposed.

Height: 6.6 cm. Dimensions: 24 × 10 cm.
Body: 0.5–0.8 cm.
Published: GGBWYYK 1980 (1) pp. 3–27, Fig. 5

168

Part of a kendi with a green glaze
From Fujian Quanzhou (1979:6)
Song dynasty (AD 960–1279)

From a kendi with a flattened globular body, a long, almost conical spout and a raised rib where the body is joined to the neck. A rough hole is cut through the body for the spout. The inside is unglazed and the pale grey, medium-coarse earthenware body appears orange on one side and dark grey on the other. The outside is glazed with a green glaze which is iridescent and milky-blue in places, and which has decayed around the spout.

Height: 7.5 cm. Length of spout: 7 cm.
Body: 0.2–0.4 cm.

169

Fragment of a moulded box lid with a green glaze
From Fujian Quanzhou (1979:6)
Song dynasty (AD 960–1279)

This fragment of a moulded box lid has rounded, fluted sides and a decoration on the top of a phoenix within a border of clouds. The pale grey, medium-coarse earthenware body is glazed on the outside with a green lead glaze which is degraded in some places and iridised to a silvery blue in others. The body has burnt orange on the inside, where the glaze shows just over the rim.

Dimensions: 12.8 × 4.5 cm. Body: 0.3 cm.

170

Part of an unglazed kendi with moulded decoration
From Fujian Quanzhou (1979:6)
Song dynasty (AD 960–1279)

This piece is from a kendi with a sloping shoulder decorated with a moulded band of peony scroll. The neck is ribbed where it is luted to the shoulder. The bottom half of the ewer inclines sharply inward towards the foot, from the point where it is luted to the shoulder. The unglazed grey high-fired earthenware body is burnt buff on the outside.

Diameter of neck: 3 cm. Diameter of body: 11.5 cm.
Body: 0.3–0.4 cm.

171

Unglazed fragment of a flask with a moulded dragon decoration
From Fujian Quanzhou (1979:6)
Song dynasty (AD 960–1279)

The sherd from the wall of an unglazed flask is decorated on the outside with a moulded decoration of a dragon on a striated ground, and its mirror image. Finger prints are visible in the clay on the inside. The earthenware body is pinkish buff.

Dimensions: 5.4 × 4.5 cm. Body: 0.3–0.5 cm.

172
Brown glazed sherd with a moulded dragon
decoration
From Fujian Quanzhou (1979:6)
Song dynasty (AD 960–1279)

This sherd is moulded with a dragon decoration on
the outside. The outside is glazed with a brown glaze
which appears yellow where thin. The putty
coloured body is fairly fine grained high fired
earthenware. An unglazed piece of kiln debris
adheres to the outside.

Dimensions: 6 × 5.6 cm. Body: 0.2 cm.

173
Fragment of a jar with decoration carved through
the black glaze
From Fujian Quanzhou (1979:6)
Song dynasty (AD 960–1279)

From the rounded wall of a jar, this fragment is
decorated on the outside with a pattern carved
through the black-brown glaze to reveal the putty
coloured, medium-coarse body beneath. The body
appears grey towards the outside and buff towards
the unglazed inside.

Dimensions: 5.3 × 4.5 cm. Body: 0.3–0.4 cm.

174
Bowl fragment with moulded decoration under a
brown-olive glaze
From Fujian Quanzhou (1979:6)
Song dynasty (AD 960–1279)

From the base of a bowl with a straight foot and a
flat, recessed base with an incised ring in the centre,
this fragment is decorated on the inside with a
moulded flower design. The putty coloured, fairly
fine grained body is burnt orange where exposed on
the foot, and reddish brown on the base. The olive
brown glaze stops short of the foot on the outside.

Dimensions: 7.4 × 6.9 cm. Body: 0.5 cm.

175
Sherd from a kendi with a green lead glaze
From Fujian Quanzhou (1979:6)
Song dynasty (AD 960–1279)

This sherd from a kendi is decorated on the sloping
shoulder with moulded leaf and petal designs. On the
upright fluted sides are the remains of a handle. The
pale grey, medium-coarse earthenware body is burnt
buff and orange on the unglazed inside. The green
lead glaze is iridescent and degraded.

Dimensions: 8 × 6.5 cm. Body: 0.2–0.3 cm.

Putian   nos. 176–187

In the past few years many Song and Yuan kilns have been found within the
borders of Putian xian. Investigation has been concentrated at Lingchuan and
Zhuangbian. Lingchuan specialised in *qingbai* wares, the shape and method of
manufacture of the bowls, dishes, and brush washers being very similar to those
of Dehua. Zhuangbian greenwares generally imitated Longquan wares; for
example the bowls and brush washers, decorated with two fish, show the
influence of Yuan wares from Longquan.

176

Part of a bowl with combed decoration under a green glaze
From Fujian Putian (1979:6)
Song dynasty (AD 960–1279)

This fragment is part of a bowl with a straight foot and spreading sides. The base is obscured by a large lump of coarse-bodied kiln support. Kiln debris also adheres to the olive glaze on the inside, which is decorated with combed lines and zig-zags. There are six bands of combing up the outside walls where the glaze runs short of the foot. The pale grey, fine body appears buff where exposed.

Dimensions: 13.8 × 12.2 cm.
Body: 0.2–0.5 cm.
Published: WW 1979 (12) pp. 37–42, Fig. 9:4 and Pl. 6:18

177

Sherd from a saucer with incised and combed decoration under a greyish green glaze
From Fujian Putian (1979:6)
Song dynasty (AD 960–1279)

From a saucer with a flat base and shallow sides angled over a mould and spreading to an everted rim, this sherd is decorated on the inside with an incised lotus design on a background of combing. The fine grey body is exposed where the dark greyish blue-green glaze stops short of the base. The glaze is pitted on the outside and kiln grit adheres.

Height: 3.4 cm. Available diameter: 13.5 cm.
Body: 0.3–0.7 cm.
Published: WW 1979 (12) pp. 37–42, Fig. 9:1 and Pl. 6:23

178

Dish fragment with combed decoration under a grey-green glaze
From Fujian Putian (1979:6)
Song dynasty (AD 960–1279)

This fragment is part of a dish with rounded walls and an everted rim, a straight foot inclined on the inside, and a roughly turned convex base. The inside is decorated in the centre with a free design of combed lines and zig-zags of dotted combing. The fine, grey body is glazed with a dark greyish blue-green glaze which runs well short of the foot on the outside.

Dimensions: 12.1 × 7.1 cm.
Diameter of base: 5.2 cm.
Body: 0.4–0.8 cm. (base)
Published: WW 1979 (12) pp. 37–42, Fig. 9:4

179

Part of a bowl with moulded decoration under a *qingbai* glaze
From Fujian Putian (1979:6)
Song dynasty (AD 960–1279)

This is part of a bowl with a rounded wall, an everted rim, a minimal foot and a flat recessed base. The inside is decorated with moulded lotus designs round a recessed circle in the centre. The pale grey, fine body appears to have cracked under the pale greyish-blue *qingbai* glaze. The glaze stops short of the foot on the outside and is trimmed below the lip on the inside, leaving the rim unglazed.

Height: 6.1 cm. Diameter of foot ring: 6.6 cm.
Dimensions: 14.5 × 9.6 cm. Body: 0.1–0.4 cm.
Published: GGBWYYK 1980 (1) pp. 3–27, Fig. 8
Also: WW 1979 (12) pp. 37–42, Fig. 11:7

180

Fragment of a bowl with moulded decoration under a *qingbai* glaze
From Fujian Putian (1979:6)
Song dynasty (AD 960–1279)

This fragment is part of a bowl with rounded sides, decorated on the inside with moulded lotus designs. The pale grey, fine body is exposed where the pale blue *qingbai* glaze stops on the outside and where the glaze is trimmed on the inside just below the lip, leaving the rim unglazed. Again, like no. 179, cracks are visible in the body under the glaze.

Dimensions: 17 × 17.5 cm. Body: 0.3 cm.
Published: GGBWYYK 1980 (1) pp. 3–27, Fig. 8
Also: WW 1979 (12) pp. 37–42, Fig. 11:8

181

Part of a bowl with stamped decoration under a blue-green glaze
From Fujian Putian (1979:6)
Yuan dynasty (AD 1280–1368)

Part of a bowl with a thick, straight foot inclined on the inside and a convex base, this sherd is decorated on the inside with an impressed peony design in the centre. The fine, grey body is burnt orange on the foot, and the bluish-green glaze stops short of the foot on the outside.

Dimensions: 12 × 8.6 cm.
Diameter of base: 6.7 cm.
Body: 0.4–1.1 cm.
Published: WW 1979 (12) pp. 37–42, Fig. 4:5

182

Part of a dish with impressed decoration under a
grey-green glaze
From Fujian Putian (1979:6)
Yuan dynasty (AD 1280–1368)

Part of a dish with rounded sides, a flattened and
everted rim, a broad, rounded foot and a flat base,
tooled to leave a nipple of clay in the centre.
Decorated with an impressed design of two fish in the
centre of the inside. The motif is surrounded by an
unglazed firing ring, where traces of kiln material are
apparent. The fine, grey body is glazed with a pale
green glaze which stops short of the foot on the
outside.

Height: 4.6 cm. Approximate diameter: 18 cm.
Diameter of foot ring: 8.5 cm.
Body: 0.2–0.9 cm. (base)
Published: WW 1979 (12) pp. 37–42, Fig. 6
Also: Fig. 5:4 (drawing)

183

Fragment of a small jar with two handles and a
qingbai glaze
From Fujian Putian (1979:6)
Yuan dynasty (AD 1280–1368)

This is part of a small jar with rounded walls, a small
concave base and an everted rim, constricted on the
outside and with a small lug handle attached. The
fine, grey body is glazed on the outside to just short of
the base with a grey *qingbai* glaze. The inside, which
is turned with a small peak in the centre, is fully
glazed.

Height: 3.9 cm. Diameter of mouth: 6.7 cm.
Body: 0.3–0.9 cm.

184

Fragment of a dish with carved and impressed
decoration under a *qingbai* glaze
From Fujian Putian (1979:6)
Yuan dynasty (AD 1280–1368)

This fragment is part of a dish with a large, flat base,
a straight foot chamfered on the outside and shallow,
rounded walls with a straight rim. The outside is
decorated with carved petals with lightly combed
details. On the inside round the well is a band of
carved scrolls and an impressed fungus spray in the
centre. The unglazed firing ring round the fungus
motif has a circle of spurs adhering. The grey body is
pale and fine and the *qingbai* glaze a greyish green
and crazed.

Height: 3.7 cm. Diameter of foot ring: 10 cm.
Dimensions: 13 × 8.3 cm. Body: 0.3–0.9 cm. (base)

185

Part of a bowl with moulded decoration under a
qingbai glaze
From Fujian Putian (1979:6)
Yuan dynasty (AD 1280–1368)

This fragment is part of a bowl with a rounded wall,
an inclined, rounded foot and a slightly recessed, flat
base. The outside is decorated with a moulded design
of lotus petals. The pale grey, fine body appears
cracked under the very pale blue *qingbai* glaze and is
exposed on the base just above the foot, and where
the glaze is trimmed short of the mouth rim inside
and out.

Height: 4.5 cm. Diameter of foot ring: 5.1 cm.
Body: 0.2–0.3 cm.
Published: WW 1979 (12) pp. 37–42, Fig. 11:5

186

Part of a bowl with moulded decoration under a
qingbai glaze
From Fujian Putian (1979:6)
Yuan dynasty (AD 1280–1368)

This fragment of a small bowl with a rounded wall,
minimal foot and flat, slightly recessed base, is
decorated on the outside with a crudely moulded
design of petals. The pale grey, fine body is burnt buff
where the very pale blue *qingbai* glaze stops short of
the foot on the outside, where it is trimmed on the
outside of the unglazed rim and on what appears to
be an unglazed firing ring on the inside.

Height: 6 cm. Dimensions: 9.5 × 7 cm. Body: 0.5 cm.
Published: WW 1979 (12) pp. 37–42, Fig. 11:3

187

Sherd from a bowl with incised and combed
decoration under a *qingbai* glaze
From Fujian Putian (1979:6)
Yuan dynasty (AD 1280–1368)

This sherd from a bowl with a rounded wall and a
flattened, protruding rim, is decorated on the outside
with incised lotus petals with combed details. The
pale grey, fine body is glazed on the outside and just
over the rim with a greyish-green *qingbai* glaze
which is crazed.

Dimensions: 9.6 × 6.5 cm. Body: 0.5–0.7 cm.
Width of rim: 1.4 cm.

Lianjiang   nos. 188–193

Lianjiang is situated at Pukouzhen on the northern bank of the Dai River. Sites of extensive Song and Yuan kilns have been found with rich remains. Both greenwares and *qingbai* wares were made, mostly in the form of bowls decorated with incised lotus decoration. In the Yuan dynasty bowls might be decorated in the centre with impressed flowers or with the character *ji*, 'auspicious'.

188

Bowl fragment with incised designs under a grey-olive glaze
From Fujian Lianjiang (1979:6)
Song dynasty (AD 960–1279)

This fragment is part of a bowl with rounded sides, an everted, foliated rim, a thin, straight foot and a flat base tooled to leave a pimple of clay in the centre. The inside is decorated with a sketchily incised lotus petal design around the walls. The pale grey, fine body has burnt putty coloured where exposed on the base and appears pitted and split beneath the thin, pale greyish-olive glaze, which has deteriorated on the outside.

Height: 6 cm. Diameter of foot ring: 5.6 cm.
Body: 0.3–1.2 cm. (base)

189

Bowl fragment with carved and combed waves under a *qingbai* glaze
From Fujian Lianjiang (1979:6)
Song dynasty (AD 960–1279)

This bowl fragment has rounded, spreading sides, a slightly inclined foot and a flat, recessed base. The inside is decorated with a carved and combed, formalised wave pattern. The greyish-white, hard, fine body is glazed inside and down to the foot with a greyish-blue *qingbai* glaze, which has deteriorated on the outside and is crazed in places.

Dimensions: 14.2 × 11.2 cm.
Diameter of foot ring: 5.9 cm. Body: 0.15–0.5 cm.

190

Sherd from a bowl with carved and combed decoration under a *qingbai* glaze
From Fujian Lianjiang (1979:6)
Song dynasty (AD 960–1279)

This sherd is part of a dish with an everted, lobed rim and a rounded wall which thickens towards the base. On the inside incised lines match the foliations, between which carved and combed designs decorate the walls. The pale bluish-grey body is glazed inside and out with a *qingbai* glaze with a slight greyish tinge.

Dimensions: 13 × 5.6 cm. Body: 0.2–0.8 cm.

191

Fragment of a dish with carved and combed decoration under a *qingbai* glaze
From Fujian Lianjiang (1979:6)
Song dynasty (AD 960–1279)

From a dish with spreading sides angled over a mould towards the everted rim, this fragment is decorated on the inside with a carved and combed lotus design and with an incised line up the wall to what was presumably a lobed rim. The pale bluish-grey body is glazed inside and down to the foot with a slightly greyish-blue *qingbai* glaze. A piece of kiln grit adheres to the inside.

Height: 3.5 cm. Dimensions: 8.5 × 7.5 cm.
Body: 0.2–0.8 cm. (base)

192
Bowl fragment with impressed decoration under a
greyish-olive glaze
From Fujian Lianjiang (1979:6)
Yuan dynasty (AD 1280–1368)

This bowl fragment with rounded spreading sides, a
slightly inclined foot and a rough, convex base, is
decorated on the inside with a stamped lotus motif in
the central medallion. The pale grey, fine body is
burnt buff on the base which is unglazed. Otherwise
the bowl is glazed inside and out with a light greyish-
olive glaze. An accidental splash of glaze and the
remains of a kiln support adhere to the base, while
specks of kiln grit adhere to the inside.

Dimensions: 13 × 10 cm.
Diameter of foot ring: 6.4 cm. Body: 0.4–0.7 cm.

193
Bowl fragment with stamped decoration and
inscription under a greyish-olive glaze
From Fujian Lianjiang (1979:6)
Yuan dynasty (AD 1280–1368)

This fragment is part of a bowl with rounded,
spreading sides, a slightly inclined foot and a convex
base. It is decorated in the centre of the inside with a
stamped lotus design, over which the Chinese
character *ji*, 'auspicious', has been impressed. The
fine, pale grey body is burnt buff on the unglazed
base. The greyish-olive glaze stops short of the foot
on the outside.

Dimensions: 11.5 × 7.5 cm.
Diameter of foot ring: 6.1 cm. Body: 0.4–0.5 cm.

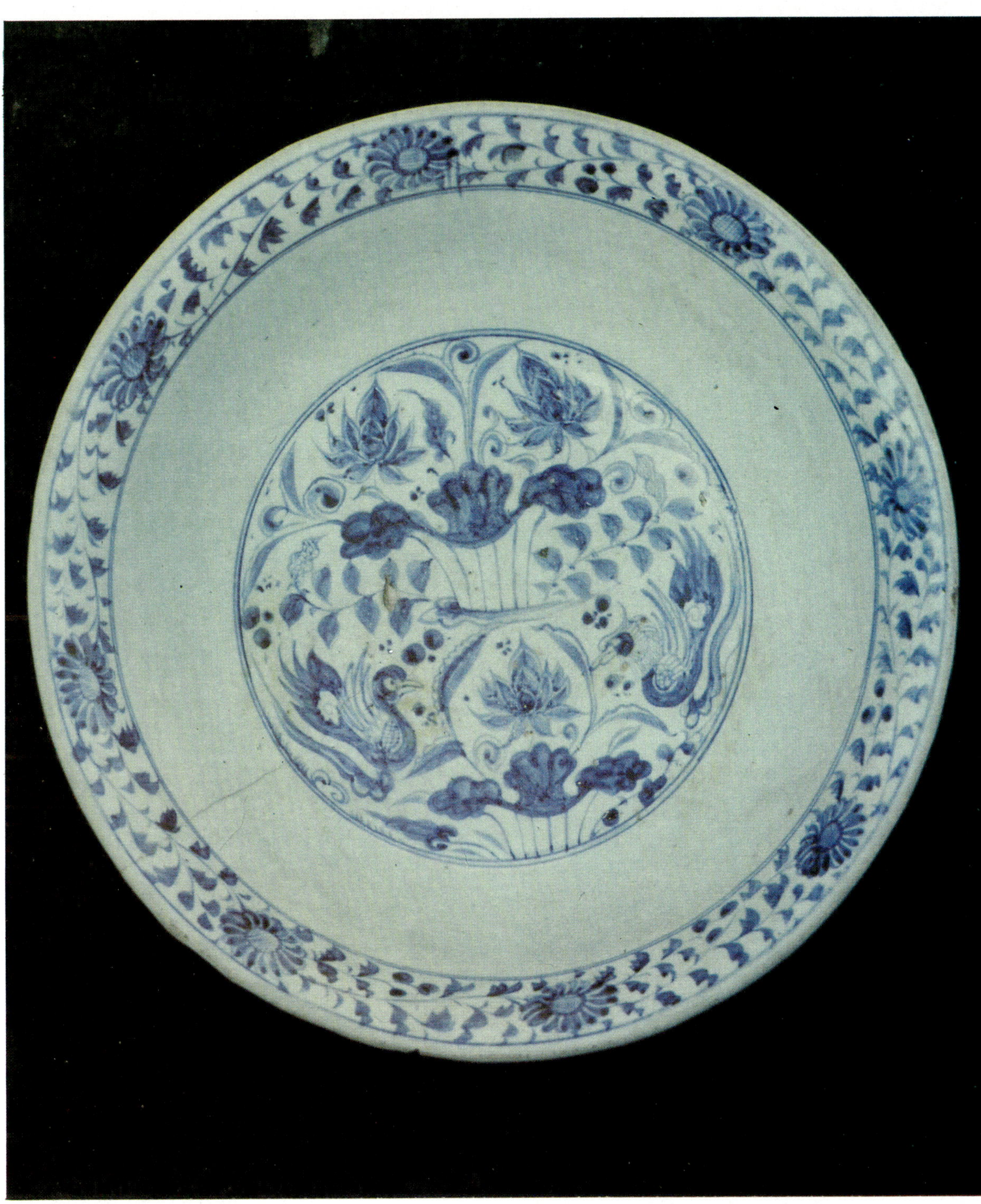

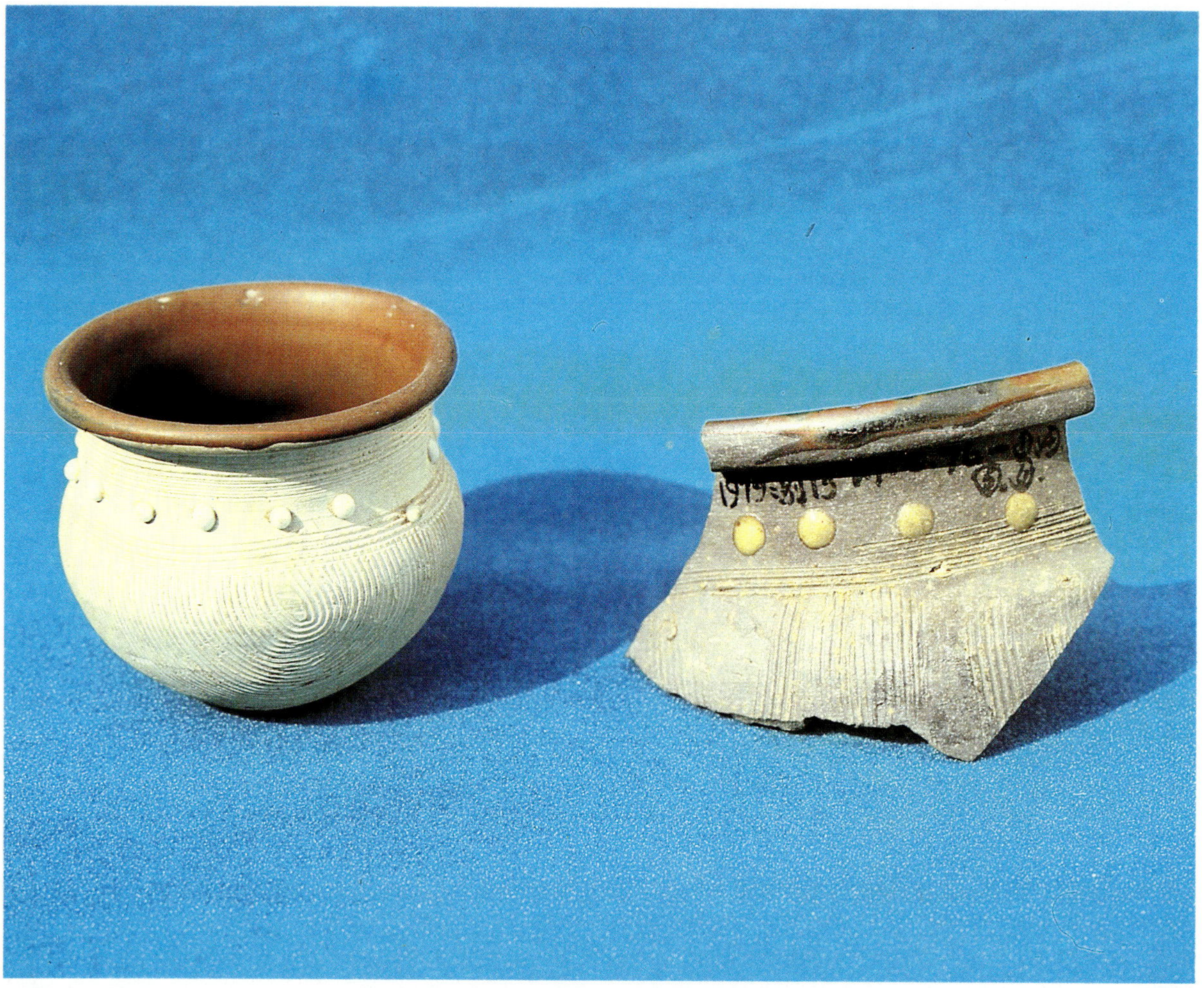

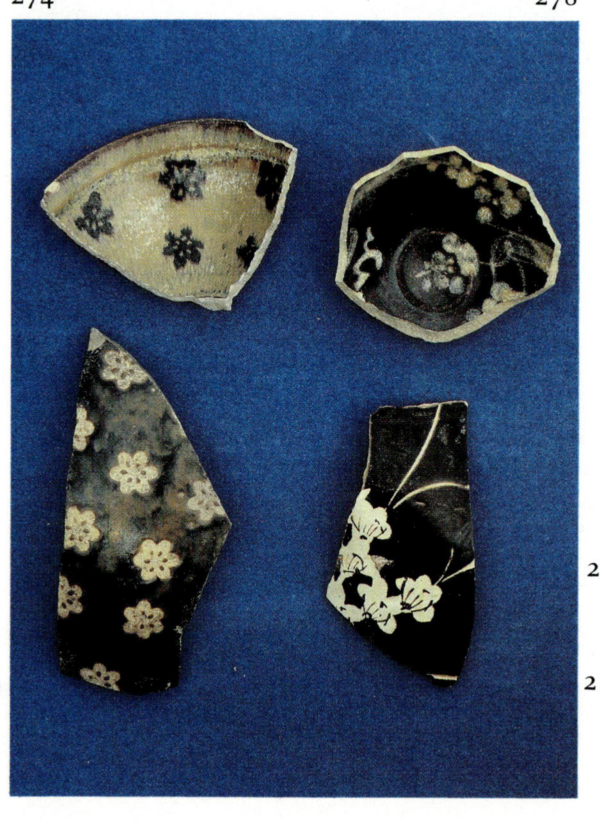

251

252

274 278 269 265

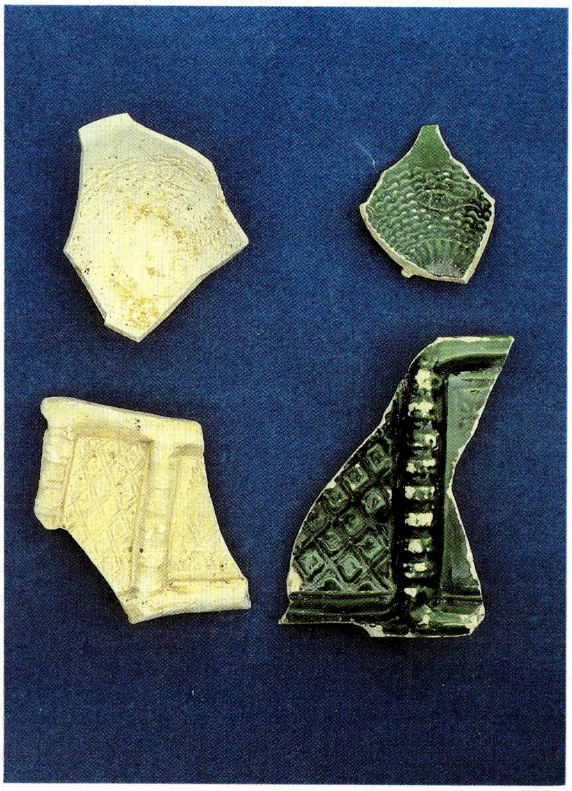

270

279 277 267

Guangdong   nos. 194–213

Both the kilns of this province which have been investigated and are
represented here were active during the Song dynasty and were important in
the Canton trade.

Chaozhou	nos. 194–203
Xicun	nos. 204–213

Chaozhou nos. 194–203

Many kiln sites have been found at Chaozhou dating from the Tang, Song and Yuan dynasties. For Song wares the kiln at Bijiashan is representative. *Qingbai* wares were the main product, with forms including flasks, jars, lamps, cups, bowls and dishes, generally decorated with fluently incised decoration. In the Song dynasty Canton was one of the important ports for foreign trade, and it was through Canton that most of the products of Chaozhou were exported.

194
Fragment of a bowl with a *qingbai* glaze
From Guangdong Chaozhou (1955:4)
Song dynasty (AD 960–1279)

This fragment is from the base of a bowl with a high, straight foot and an unglazed flat base. The inside is decorated with a carved and combed design of a peony flower among foliage. The bowl has a light grey, fine body and is glazed down to the foot with a greyish-blue *qingbai* glaze.

Dimensions: 12 × 12 cm.
Diameter of foot ring: 6.7 cm. Body: 0.3–0.7 cm.

195
Fragment of a jar with a moulded lotus petal design under a *qingbai* glaze
From Guangdong Chaozhou (1955:4)
Song dynasty (AD 960–1279)

This sherd from a jar is decorated on the shoulder with a moulded design of overlapping lotus petals, and beneath with an incised groove on the body with a vertical band of combed lines. The white, fine body is glazed with a greyish-blue *qingbai* glaze on the outside and half way down the inside.

Dimensions: 9.7 × 5 cm. Body: 0.4–0.5 cm.

196
Fragment of a two-handled jar with a *qingbai* glaze
From Guangdong Chaozhou (1955:4)
Song dynasty (AD 960–1279)

This fragment from the shoulder of a jar is carved with a band of oblique hatching beneath which the lobed and ribbed sides are decorated with carved designs. The upstanding neck has a deeply carved horizontal flange and rising ribs. A small lug handle is attached to the shoulder at the base of the neck. The pale greenish-grey *qingbai* glaze runs thick in the carved areas. The pale grey fine body is exposed on the unglazed interior.

Dimensions: 15.4 × 11.3 cm. Body: 0.3–0.6 cm.

197
Part of a dish with incised decoration under a *qingbai* glaze
From Guangdong Chaozhou (1955:4)
Song dynasty (AD 960–1279)

This piece is part of a dish with a small, uneven, bevelled foot and a flat base. The inside is decorated with a five-petalled flower in double incised line, surrounded by leaves and ribs also in double line radiating up the walls to the single line border beneath the straight rim. The white, fine body has burnt reddish where exposed on the base. The *qingbai* glaze, which stops short of the foot on the outside, is a pale greyish blue.

Height: 3.6 cm. Diameter of foot ring: 5.2 cm.
Body: 0.2–0.7 cm. (base)

198
Fragment of a lid of a box with a *qingbai* glaze
From Guangdong Chaozhou (1955:4)
Song dynasty (AD 960–1279)

This sherd is part of the lid of a box with a domed top and rounded, ribbed sides. The inside is unglazed and the outside is glazed with a bluish-grey *qingbai* glaze.

Dimensions: 6.9 × 6.3 cm. Body: 0.4–0.7 cm.

199
Part of a cup with an incised design under a *qingbai* glaze
From Guangdong Chaozhou (1955:4)
Song dynasty (AD 960–1279)

This fragment is part of a cup with an everted rim, a small, thick round base and a minimal foot ring. Round the well is an incised sketchy floral design. The pale greyish-white body is glazed to the foot with a whitish-grey *qingbai* glaze. The base of the cup is unglazed.

Height: 4.6 cm. Diameter of base: 3.8 cm.
Body: 0.3–0.4 cm.

200
Fragment with incised and combed decoration under
a *qingbai* glaze
From Guangdong Chaozhou (1955:4)
Song dynasty (AD 960–1279)

This sherd, part of the wall of a lobed jar or flask, is
decorated on the outside with an incised and combed
repeated design of waves. The white, fine body is
fully glazed on the outside and partially glazed on the
inside with the greyish-blue *qingbai* glaze.

Dimensions: 9.5 × 5 cm. Body: 0.4–0.5 cm.

201
Fragment of a stem cup with a *qingbai* glaze
From Guangdong Chaozhou (1955:4)
Song dynasty (AD 960–1279)

This fragment is part of a stem cup with a bulb
shaped bowl with inverted rim, and a high ridged
and everted foot. The whitish-grey fine body, burnt
to a buff colour where exposed on the conical interior
of the foot, is glazed with a light greenish-blue glassy
qingbai glaze to which kiln grit adheres. The mouth
rim is unglazed.

Height: 5.6 cm. Diameter of foot: 3.8 cm.
Body: 0.2–0.5 cm.

202
Fragment of a cup with a moulded design under a
qingbai glaze
From Guangdong Chaozhou (1955:4)
Song dynasty (AD 960–1279)

This sherd from the base of a cup with a high,
straight foot is decorated on the inside with a
moulded chrysanthemum design. The pale grey, fine
body is burnt to a pinkish colour where exposed on
the base and inside the foot. The greyish *qingbai* glaze
is crackled.

Dimensions: 5.6 × 5.4 cm.
Diameter of foot ring: 3.6 cm. Body: 0.3 cm.

203
Whistle in the shape of a bird with a *qingbai* glaze
From Guangdong Chaozhou (1955:4)
Song dynasty (AD 960–1279)

The whistle in the form of a bird is pierced with three
holes in the top of the body. The fine body is burnt to
a reddish buff where exposed on the underside. The
light blue *qingbai* glaze has kiln grit adhering all over.

Height: 3.3 cm. Length: 9.3 cm.

Xicun   nos. 204–213

Xicun is situated to the north-west of Canton, five kilometres from the city
centre. Greenwares, *qingbai* wares and blackwares were produced, in the shape
of dishes, bowls, cups, bottles, basins, boxes and toys, and with moulded, incised
or painted decoration. Xicun worked under the influence of other kilns, and
moulded bowls were, for example, made in imitation of Yaozhou greenwares.
The products of Xicun were mostly made for export, and were shipped through
Canton from the Song dynasty onwards.

204
Remains of a cupstand with a black glaze
From Guangdong Xicun (1955:4)
Song dynasty (AD 960–1279)

This piece consists of the remains of a small bulb-
shaped cup and a spreading, slightly upturned
saucer with a high everted foot. The light grey, fine,
sugary body appears buff where exposed inside the
foot. The rest of the object is glazed with a black glaze
which shows patches of brown.

Overall height: 8.3 cm. Height of cup: 4.8 cm.
Diameter of foot: 4 cm.
Body: 0.3 (cup)–0.5 cm. (stand)

205
Fragment of a cup with a *qingbai* glaze
From Guangdong Xicun (1955:4)
Song dynasty (AD 960–1279)

This piece is part of a cup with a thick, flat, unglazed
base and a minimal foot. The sides rise to a straight
rim and are decorated on the outside with lotus
petals in double incised line. Three spur marks are
visible on the inside base. The slightly coarse, sugary
body is light grey, and the pale bluish-grey *qingbai*
glaze is crazed and stops short of the foot.

Height: 8.2 cm. Diameter of rim: 6.8 cm.
Diameter of foot: 4.4 cm. Body: 0.3 cm.

206

Part of a bowl with incised and combed decoration
under a *qingbai* glaze
From Guangdong Xicun (1955:4)
Song dynasty (AD 960–1279)

This fragment is part of a bowl with a rounded wall,
an everted rim and a small straight foot. The inside is
decorated with an incised and combed design of a
peony spray. The fine, sugary body is light grey. The
blue glossy *qingbai* glaze stops short of the foot on the
outside where kiln grit adheres.

Height: 6 cm. Diameter of foot: 4.7 cm.
Body: 0.3–0.7 cm.

207

Part of a bowl with carved and combed decoration
under a *qingbai* glaze
From Guangdong Xicun (1955:4)
Song dynasty (AD 960–1279)

This piece is part of a conical bowl with a small,
thick, flat base and a minimal foot ring, both
unglazed. The inside is decorated with a carved and
combed lotus design and has a thick button of clay in
the centre. The light grey fine sugary body is glazed
with a blue glossy *qingbai* glaze, which is crazed and
dotted with kiln grit on the outside wall.

Dimensions: 10.7 × 10.7 cm.
Diameter of foot: 4 cm. Body: 0.2 cm.

208

Part of a bowl with carved and combed decoration
under a *qingbai* glaze
From Guangdong Xicun (1955:4)
Song dynasty (AD 960–1279)

This fragment is part of a bowl with a thick, straight
foot and a flat base, which is tooled to leave a nipple
of clay in the centre. The outside of the rounded wall
is decorated with oblique carved panels and the
inside base with a carved chrysanthemum
surrounded by carved and combed floral designs
around the inside walls. The grey, slightly coarse,
sugary body is glazed with a pale greyish *qingbai*
glaze with a crackle, which is burnt to a reddish
colour. The foot and base are unglazed.

Dimensions: 11.5 × 9.2 cm.
Diameter of foot: 5.9 cm. Body: 0.3–0.6 cm.

209

Fragment of a bowl with a grey-olive glaze
From Guangdong Xicun (1955:4)
Song dynasty (AD 960–1279)

This fragment is part of a small bowl, or cup, with a
fine foot and small round base turned to leave a
nipple of clay in the centre. The rounded sides are
decorated on the inside with a carved flower. The
fine, sugary body is grey. The grey-olive glaze stops
short of the foot.

Height: 4.2 cm. Diameter: 9.7 cm.
Diameter of foot: 3.7 cm. Body: 0.2–0.3 cm.

210

Part of a bowl with carved and combed designs
under a grey-olive glaze
From Guangdong Xicun (1955:4)
Song dynasty (AD 960–1279)

This fragment is part of a bowl with rounded sides
and a slightly everted rim, a small foot and a thick
round base. On the centre of the inside base is a thick
button of clay which is surrounded with carved and
combed floral designs. The pale grey *qingbai* glaze
stops short of the foot and the base on the outside,
revealing the fine, grey, sugary body.

Height: 5.3 cm. Diameter of foot: 4.4 cm.
Body: 0.2–0.8 cm. (base)

211

Miniature model of a dog
From Guangdong Xicun (1955:4)
Song dynasty (AD 960–1279)

This hand-pinched model of a dog has a medium-
coarse, grey body which is burnt reddish where
exposed. The glassy glaze is a greyish-green colour.

Height: 6.3 cm. Length: 5.8 cm.

212

Part of a lid in the shape of a gourd with a black glaze
From Guangdong Xicun (1955:4)
Song dynasty (AD 960–1279)

This fragment is part of a lid in the form of a gourd.
The rim around the domed lobed sides is everted and
the knob on top is in the form of a twig. The greyish-
white, medium-coarse body is visible on the unglazed
inside, while the outside of the lid is glazed with a
black glaze, mottled with brown.

Dimensions: 6.2 × 5.3 cm. Body: 0.4 cm.

213

Part of a large dish with decoration painted in brown
under a greenish glaze
From Guangdong Xicun (1955:4)
Song dynasty (AD 960–1279)

This fragment comes from the thick, flat base of a
large dish with an everted, rolled foot. The inside
base is decorated with sketchy and free scrolling
designs painted in brown under the greenish
transparent glaze on the light grey, medium-coarse
body. The foot and base are partially glazed and have
kiln grit adhering.

Diameter of foot: 15.2 cm. Body: 1.4 cm.

A distinctive *qingbai* ware has been found a Nanfeng bearing some relation to
Ding ware and distinguishing it from wares produced at Jingdezhen. The
complex of kilns at Jingdezhen is under continuing study and individual kilns
gradually take on individuality to the extent that dating of wares and kilns alike
is becoming a possibility. The present exhibits are of the 10th–14th centuries
and show the early cobalt underglaze decorated wares. Wares from Ganzhou
and Jizhou mark the breadth of style in this province, each is related to kilns
further north and to the south.

Nanfeng	nos. 214–223
Jingdezhen	nos. 224–250
Ganzhou	nos. 251, 252
Jizhou	nos. 253–279

Nanfeng   nos. 214–223

Nanfeng yao was first discovered in 1960, and investigated again in August 1979. The kiln site lies in the Baishe commune, 30 kilometres to the south-west of the city. Nanfeng specialised in *qingbai* wares with a thin white body and a clear glaze. Dishes and bowls were the main shapes produced, and were decorated with incised or combed patterns. Similar bowls with a bare rim and carved decoration are not found at Jingdezhen or other Jiangxi kilns. No *fushao* kiln furnishings have as yet been found at Nanfeng. All the wares were fired over kiln supports. The spur marks are clearly different from the dark coloured marks on Jingdezhen wares.

214
Bowl with a carved and combed design under a
qingbai glaze and a brown rim
From Jiangxi Nanfeng (1979:7)
Song dynasty (AD 960–1279)

This bowl, with spreading sides, a straight rim, a neat tapering foot and a slightly recessed base, is decorated on the inside with a carved and combed design of waves. A narrow band of brown glaze, imitating a metal binder, decorates the inside of the mouth rim. Otherwise the bowl is glazed with a pale blue *qingbai* glaze down to the foot ring. The fine greyish-white body is burnt reddish buff where exposed on the unglazed base and inside of the foot.

Height: 4.5 cm. Diameter: 15.8 cm.
Diameter of foot: 4.6 cm.

215
Fragment of a bowl with carved and combed design
under a *qingbai* glaze with a brown band
From Jiangxi Nanfeng (1979:7)
Song dynasty (AD 960–1279)

This rim sherd is part of a bowl, similar to no. 214, with a carved and combed wave decoration on the inside wall under a pale blue *qingbai* glaze which is crazed. A band of brown glaze runs round the inside of the mouth rim. The fine body is greyish white.

Dimensions: 6.4 × 5.2 cm. Body: 0.1–0.5 cm.

216
Part of a bowl with carved and combed decoration
under a *qingbai* glaze
From Jiangxi Nanfeng (1979:7)
Song dynasty (AD 960–1279)

This fragment is part of a bowl with spreading sides, a small, neat foot inclined on the outside and straight on the inside and a small, flat base. The inside is decorated with a carved and combed design. The body is fine and greyish white and the *qingbai* glaze a clear blue. There is a thick welt of glaze inside the rim. The bowl is unglazed on the inside of the foot and on the base where a circle of kiln support is visible. Grit adheres to the glaze on the outside wall.

Diameter of foot: 4.7 cm. Body: 0.1–0.5 cm. (base)

217
Part of a bowl with carved and combed designs
under a *qingbai* glaze
From Jiangxi Nanfeng (1979:7)
Song dynasty (AD 960–1279)

This fragment is part of a bowl similar to no. 216. The bowl has sides spreading from a small base and a small, inverted foot. The inside of the walls is decorated with carved and combed designs. The clear blue *qingbai* glaze covers the inside and the outside down to the foot ring. It is slightly degraded on the outside. The fine body is greyish white.

Dimensions: 12.5 × 10.3 cm. Body: 0.2–0.3 cm.
Published: GGBWYYK 1980 (1) pp. 3–27, Fig. 9

218

Part of a bowl with a carved and combed design
under a *qingbai* glaze
From Jiangxi Nanfeng (1979:7)
Song dynasty (AD 960–1279)

This fragment is part of a bowl with a fairly high V-
shaped foot and a flat, recessed base which is tooled
to leave a nipple of clay in the centre. The inside of
the bowl is decorated with a carved and combed
peony scroll. The greyish-blue *qingbai* glaze covers
the bowl inside and outside down to the foot ring.
The fine, greyish-white body is exposed on the
unglazed base.

Dimensions: 12.8 × 9.1 cm. Body: 0.2–0.4 cm.

219

Part of a bowl with incised decoration under a
qingbai glaze
From Jiangxi Nanfeng (1979:7)
Song dynasty (AD 960–1279)

This fragment is part of a bowl with an everted
foliated rim and a small V-shaped foot. The inside is
decorated with an incised design within a line border
beneath the lip. The fine, greyish-white body is
glazed inside and down to the foot ring on the
outside. The base and the inside of the foot are
unglazed and there are unglazed patches on the
inside where something has fallen on to the bowl.
The glaze is crazed and has deteriorated on the
outside.

Dimensions: 14.4 × 10.8 cm. Height: 3.9 cm.
Body: 0.3–0.4 cm.

220

Part of a small dish with a *qingbai* glaze
From Jiangxi Nanfeng (1979:7)
Song dynasty (AD 960–1279)

This sherd is part of a small dish with rounded walls
and an everted foliated rim. Incised lines on the
underside and the small ribs on the inside match the
foliation notches of the rim. The minimal foot ring is
glazed with a very pale blue *qingbai* glaze. The inside
of the foot and the base are unglazed and reveal the
fine, greyish-white body.

Dimensions: 8.6 × 5.4 cm. Body: 0.2–0.4 cm.
Published: GGBWYYK 1980 (1) pp. 3–27, Fig. 9

221

Fragment of a pillow with incised decoration under a
qingbai glaze
From Jiangxi Nanfeng (1979:7)
Song dynasty (AD 960–1279)

This sherd is part of a small dish with rounded walls
and an everted foliated rim. Incised lines on the
underside and the small ribs on the inside match the
foliation notches of the rim. The minimal foot ring is
glazed with a very pale blue *qingbai* glaze. The inside
of the foot and the base are unglazed and reveal the
fine, greyish-white body.

Dimensions: 5.9 × 3.8 cm. Height: 2.9 cm.
Body: 0.4 cm.
Published: GGBWYYK 1980 (1) pp. 3–27, Fig. 9

222

Part of a bowl with a carved decoration through a
qingbai glaze
From Jiangxi Nanfeng (1979:7)
Song dynasty (AD 960–1279)

This is part of a bowl with spreading sides and a
constricted rim, with a minimal foot ring and a
small, thick, slightly recessed base. The inside walls
are decorated with plum blossom and crescent moon
carved through the greyish-blue *qingbai* glaze to
reveal the whitish-grey, fine body. There is also a
band of brown glaze round the inside of the mouth
rim. The glaze is much deteriorated on the inside.

Height: 4.7 cm. Diameter of foot: 3.6 cm.
Dimensions: 11 × 10 cm. Body: 0.2 cm.
Published: GGBWYYK 1980 (1) pp. 3–27, Fig. 9

223

Part of a lobed ewer with a *qingbai* glaze
From Jiangxi Nanfeng (1979:7)
Song dynasty (AD 960–1279)

This fragment of a lobed ewer has vertical incised
ribs between the lobes and a triple band of ribs round
the body beneath the shoulder and round the base of
the neck. The fine, greyish-white body is glazed, on
the outside only, with an almost colourless *qingbai*
glaze.

Dimensions: 12.3 × 7 cm. Body: 0.2–0.5 cm.
Published: GGBWYYK 1980 (1) pp. 3–27, Fig. 9

Jingdezhen   nos. 224–250

From the Five Dynasties period, green and white wares were made at such kilns as Shihuwan, Shengmeiting, and Huangnitou. In the Song dynasty there was a great expansion in production, and *qingbai* wares of white translucent body and of the colour and quality of jade have been discovered at Hutian, Liujiawan, Nanshije, Niupiling and Shengmeiting. In the Yuan dynasty Hutian became the centre of production, making the most famous underglaze blue wares, as well as a large quantity of wares with an egg white glaze and moulded decoration. The bowl in the exhibition, decorated in underglaze blue with mandarin ducks and lotus plants, is similar to specimens collected at Hutian, and can be considered to be a product of Hutian. It was excavated in Nanking from the tomb of one of Song Sheng's wives, dated AD 1418.

224
Part of a bowl with a white glaze
From Jiangxi Jingdezhen Yangmeiting (1958:10)
Five Dynasties (AD 907–960)

This fragment is part of a bowl with rounded sides and a rounded, thickened rim. Five spur marks are visible on the straight, unglazed foot ring, and there are the remains of five spurs on the undecorated inside of the bowl. The bowl is glazed with an ivory white glaze which appears bright white in places on the inside, outside and the recessed base. The body is a fine, dry, white material.

Dimensions: 10.5 × 10.5 cm. Body: 0.3–0.5 cm.

225
Part of a foliated bowl with a white glaze
From Jiangxi Jingdezhen Yangmeiting (1958:10)
Five Dynasties (AD 907–960)

This sherd is part of a bowl with lobed sides and foliated rim. It appears to have been pressed over a mould. The base and the inside of the foot, which is inclined on the inside, are unglazed. The fine, dry, white body appears reddish buff where exposed and is glazed with a creamy white glaze inside and outside down to the foot ring.

Height: 3.5 cm. Diameter: 10.5 cm.
Diameter of foot ring: 5.2 cm.
Body: 0.2–0.4 cm. (base)

226
Part of a bowl with a greyish olive glaze
From Jiangxi Jingdezhen Yangmeiting (1958:10)
Five Dynasties (AD 906–960)

This fragment is part of a bowl with rounded sides and an everted, rounded rim, a broad foot ring inclined on the inside and a recessed base tooled to leave a nipple of clay in the centre. The whole bowl is glazed with a greyish-olive glaze, except on the foot ring where nine faint spur marks are visible. The body is fine and grey. Kiln grit adheres to the inside of the bowl which is undecorated.

Height: 4.5 cm. Diameter: 12.5 cm.
Diameter of foot ring: 5.2 cm. Body: 0.2–0.3 cm.

227
Part of a bowl with a carved and combed design under a *qingbai* glaze
From Jiangxi Jingdezhen Nanshijie (1979:8)
Song dynasty (AD 960–1279)

This fragment from the base of a bowl with spreading sides and a small neat foot is decorated on the inside base with a carved and combed lotus design. The body is fine and white, and the *qingbai* glaze a clear pale blue. The base is unglazed.

Dimensions: 10.2 × 7.4 cm. Diameter of foot 4.5 cm.
Body: 0.3–0.6 cm.

228

Part of a bowl with a carved and combed design
under a *qingbai* glaze
From Jiangxi Jingdezhen Nanshijie (1979:8)
Song dynasty (AD 960–1279)

This fragment is part of a bowl with sides spreading
from the thick, low, tapering foot and the thick base
and angled towards the rim. The inside is decorated
with a carved and combed decoration of a peony.
The fine, white body is glazed with a clear pale blue
qingbai glaze on the inside, and on the outside down
to the foot ring.

Dimensions: 12 × 10 cm. Diameter of foot: 4.2 cm.
Body: 0.2–0.4 cm.

229

Fragment from a dish with carved and combed
decoration under a *qingbai* glaze
From Jiangxi Jingdezhen Nanshijie (1979:8)
Song dynasty (AD 960–1279)

This fragment is part of a bowl with ribs of white slip
down the interior wall, which has been shaped over
a mould. The mouth rim is slightly everted and
foliated. The inside base is decorated with a carved
and combed lotus design under a clear pale blue
qingbai glaze which covers the inside and the outside
down to the fine inclined foot. The base is unglazed.
The body is fine and white.

Dimensions: 10.6 × 6.6 cm. Body: 0.1–0.5 cm.

230

Part of a bowl with a carved and combed decoration
under a *qingbai* glaze
From Jiangxi Jingdezhen Liujiawan (1979:8)
Song dynasty (AD 960–1279)

This fragment of a conical bowl with a slightly
everted mouth rim, a minimal foot and a small,
unglazed base, is decorated on the inside with a
carved and combed floral design. It is glazed inside
and out with a greyish-blue *qingbai* glaze which pools
in the deep hollow in the centre. The body is fine and
white.

Height: 5.3 cm. Diameter of foot: 3.3 cm.
Body: 0.1–0.3 cm.

231

Fragment of a dish with carved and combed designs
under a *qingbai* glaze
From Jiangxi Jingdezhen Liujiawan (1979:8)
Song dynasty (AD 960–1279)

This fragment is part of a dish with sides which have
been angled over a mould. It has a low foot and a
small, round, unglazed base. The base is very thick in
relation to the walls. The inside is decorated with
carved and combed designs on the base and walls.
The fine, white body is glazed with a greyish-blue
qingbai glaze.

Height: 3.5 cm. Diameter of inside base: 7.4 cm.
Diameter of foot ring: 4.2 cm. Body: 0.1–0.3 cm.

232

Fragment of a bowl with carved and combed designs
under a *qingbai* glaze
From Jiangxi Jingdezhen Liujiawan (1979:8)
Song dynasty (AD 960–1279)

This fragment is part of a bowl with sides which are
angled over a mould, a small neat foot and a thick,
unglazed base. The inside is decorated with slip-
ribbed divisions around the well and with a carved
and combed peony design on the base. The fine white
body is glazed with a blue glassy crackled *qingbai*
glaze which pools on the inside.

Dimensions: 13 × 12.5 cm.
Diameter of inside base: 8.5 cm.
Diameter of foot ring: 4.3 cm.

233

Part of a lid with a *qingbai* glaze
From Jiangxi Jingdezhen Hutian (1979:8)
Song dynasty (AD 960–1279)

This sherd is part of a lid with a domed top and a flat
rim. The white porcelain body is glazed inside the
dome and on the outside of the lid with a pale blue
qingbai glaze, which runs to a clear blue around the
base of the dome.

Length: 9.8 cm. Depth of rim: 2.2 cm. Body: 0.3 cm.

234

Part of a brush washer with a *qingbai* glaze
From Jiangxi Jingdezhen Hutian (1979:8)
Song dynasty (AD 960–1279)

This fragment is part of a brush washer with shallow
rounded sides. The base of the vessel has sagged in
the firing to give a convex curve in the basin. The
piece has no foot and was fired on the mouth rim
where the *qingbai* glaze is trimmed away from the
rim. The fine body is white.

Height: 3 cm. Length: 8 cm. Body: 0.3 cm.

235

Part of a bowl with incised decoration under a
qingbai glaze
From Jiangxi Jingdezhen Hutian (1979:8)
Song dynasty (AD 960–1279)

This fragment is part of a conical bowl with a thin,
high, straight foot. The inside is incised with a floral
decoration and random dotted combing. The white,
fine body is glazed a pale *qingbai* inside, and outside
down to the foot ring. The base is glazed and has a
ring of kiln support and other kiln material adhering
to it.

Dimensions: 10.1 × 6.3 cm.
Diameter of base: 3.8 cm. Body: 0.1–0.3 cm.

236

Fragments of two dishes with moulded decoration
under a clear glaze
From Jiangxi Jingdezhen Hutian (1979:8)
Song dynasty (AD 960–1279)

These fragments of two dishes stuck together during
the firing were evidently fired on the mouth rim, in
the same way as wares from Ding yao. The small
neat foot is glazed. On the inside of the dishes is a
moulded design of phoenixes among lotus plants.
The fine, white body is glazed with an ivory white
thin glaze.

Dimensions: 13 × 10 cm. Diameter of foot: 5.2 cm.
Body: 0.1–0.3 cm.

237

Part of a dish with carved and moulded decoration
under a clear glaze
From Jiangxi Jingdezhen Hutian (1979:8)
Song dynasty (AD 960–1279)

This piece is part of a small dish with a small, neat
foot and a flat base. The shallow sides are carved on
the outside with petals and on the inside base is a
moulded decoration of two fish among waves. The
dish was presumably fired on the mouth rim as the
foot and base are completely glazed with an ivory
white clear glaze, like Ding ware. The body is again
fine, white porcelain.

Overall maximum width: 10.6 cm.
Diameter of base: 5.8 cm. Body: 0.25 cm.

238

Fragment of a dish with a moulded decoration under
a clear glaze
From Jiangxi Jingdezhen Hutian (1979:8)
Song dynasty (AD 960–1279)

This fragment is part of the base of a dish with a
high, straight foot and a slightly convex base. The
rounded sides are carved on the outside with petals
and are decorated on the inside with a moulded band
of peony scroll around a flower scroll in the central
medallion. The foot and base are glazed with an
ivory clear glaze which runs thick in the carved
grooves on the outside. The body is fine and white.

Dimensions: 9.2 × 8.1 cm. Diameter of base: 6 cm.
Body: 0.2–0.4 cm.

239

Part of a bowl with an incised decoration under a
qingbai glaze
From Jiangxi Jingdezhen Hutian (1979:8)
Song dynasty (AD 960–1279)

This fragment of a conical bowl has a straight foot
with a narrow, neat foot ring on which it was fired.
The inside is decorated with a scrolling peony under
the *qingbai* glaze which gathers in deep pools. The
body is fine white porcelain.

Dimensions: 10.2 × 10 cm.
Diameter of base: 4.5 cm. Body: 0.2–0.3 cm.

240

Part of a bowl with incised decoration under a
qingbai glaze
From Jiangxi Jingdezhen Hutian (1979:8)
Song dynasty (AD 960–1279)

This fragment is part of a bowl similar to the
preceding one, no. 239. It has a straight foot, with a
narrow, neat foot ring on which it was fired. The
inside is decorated with a design of scrolling peony. It
is glazed over the white porcelain body with a *qingbai*
glaze.

Dimensions: 10.8 × 9.6 cm. Diameter of base: 6 cm.
Body: 0.25–0.5 cm.

241

Fragment of a bowl with carved and combed
decoration under a *qingbai* glaze
From Jiangxi Jingdezhen Hutian (1979:8)
Song dynasty (AD 960–1279)

This fragment is part of a rounded bowl with an
everted rim, a straight foot and a narrow, neat foot
ring. The inside is decorated with a carved and
combed decoration under a *qingbai* glaze. Kiln grit
adheres to the unglazed base. The body is white
porcelain.

Dimensions: 11.2 × 10 cm.
Diameter of base: 5.2 cm. Body: 0.3 cm.

242

Fragment from the base of a bowl decorated in
underglaze blue
From Jiangxi Jingdezhen Hutian (1958:10)
Yuan dynasty (AD 1280–1368)

Fragment from the base of a bowl decorated on the
inside with mandarin ducks in a lotus pond painted
in underglaze blue. The body is white porcelain and
the glaze is transparent, reduced with a bluish tinge.
The base and foot ring are unglazed.

Dimensions: 10.5 × 7.6 cm.
Diameter of foot ring: 10.8 cm. Body: 0.9 cm.
Published: WW 1965 (9) pp. 26–56, Pl. 3:2

243
Bowl decorated in underglaze blue
Jiangxi Jingdezhen Hutian type (Excavated in
Nanking)
From the tomb of Madame Ye, dated 1418 (1959:7)
Yuan dynasty (AD 1280–1368)

This deep bowl with rounded sides and an everted
rim, straight foot and flat base which is turned to
leave a pimple of clay in the centre, is decorated on
the inside with ducks in a lotus pond in the main
zone, and round the lip with a band of chrysanthemum scroll. The outside is decorated with a band
of lotus scroll above a band of petal panels. The
decoration is painted in underglaze blue on the white
porcelain body under a clear glaze with a bluish
tinge which stops just short of the foot ring.

Height: 13.4 cm. Diameter: 30.2 cm.
Diameter of base: 9.1 cm.
Published: KG 1962 (9) pp. 474–478, Pl. 6:3,4
See also: *Addis J M: Chinese Ceramics from Datable
Tombs, London and New York, 1978. p. 118, Pl. 39 u,v*

244
Part of a dish with underglaze blue decoration
From Jiangxi Jingdezhen Hutian (1958:10)
Yuan dynasty (AD 1280–1368)

This fragment from a dish has a flattened, foliated
rim decorated in underglaze blue with a classic
scroll. The inside of the cavetto is decorated with a
flower scroll, and the outside with a lotus scroll.
Body and glaze are the same as no. 243.

Dimensions: 10.5 × 7.5 cm. Body: 0.6–0.7 cm.

245
Part of the rim of a bowl with underglaze blue
decoration
From Jiangxi Jingdezhen Hutian (1958:10)
Yuan dynasty (AD 1280–1368)

This rim sherd comes from a bowl with a rounded
wall and straight rim. It is decorated on the inside
with a chrysanthemum scroll in underglaze blue and
on the outside with petal panels. The body and glaze
are the same as for no. 243.

Dimensions: 9.5 × 4.4 cm. Body: 0.4 cm.

246
Part of a bowl with underglaze blue decoration
From Jiangxi Jingdezhen Hutian (1958:10)
Yuan dynasty (AD 1280–1368)

This sherd is part of the base and wall of a bowl,
painted in underglaze blue on the outside with a
band of petal panels and inside the cavetto with a
chrysanthemum scroll. In the centre is a scrolling
lotus. The body and glaze are the same as no. 243.
The base and foot ring are unglazed.

Dimensions: 10.6 × 9 cm. Body: 0.5–1.0 cm.

247
Part of a bowl with underglaze blue decoration
From Jiangxi Jingdezhen Hutian (1958:10)
Yuan dynasty (AD 1280–1368)

This fragment from the rounded wall of a bowl with
an everted rim is painted in underglaze blue with a
lotus scroll round the outside and two bands of leaf
scroll separated by two double bands of blue round
the inside of the cavetto. The body and glaze are the
same as no. 243.

Dimensions: 9.7 × 8.3 cm. Body: 0.6–0.9 cm.

248
Qingbai stem cup and saggar
From Jiangxi Jingdezhen Hutian (1979:8)
Yuan dynasty (AD 1280–1368)

This stem cup with an everted mouth rim and
spreading foot is decorated on the inside with a
moulded decoration of two dragons. The foot ring
and the inside of the foot are unglazed. Kiln grit
adheres to the underside of the cup as well as inside
the foot. The white porcelain body is glazed with a
white *qingbai* glaze.

Height: 8.8 cm. Diameter: 11.2 cm.
Diameter of foot ring: 3.9 cm.

The saggar is made of very coarse reddish clay. It is
waisted and tapers at the bottom towards the small
flat base, on which the stem cup stands. There is a
removable support for the cup inside the saggar.

Diameter of rim: 14.7 cm. Diameter of base: 5 cm.
Body: 0.9 cm.

249
Part of a dish with a moulded decoration under a
qingbai glaze
From Jiangxi Jingdezhen Hutian (1979:8)
Yuan dynasty (AD 1280–1368)

Part of a dish, this fragment has rounded sides with a
straight rim, a straight foot and a flat base which is
turned with a nipple of clay in the centre. The inside
base and the cavetto are decorated with a moulded
leaf scroll. The white porcelain body is glazed with a
qingbai glaze to the foot ring but the base and inside
of the foot are unglazed.

Height: 4.9 cm. Diameter: 13.8 cm.
Diameter of base: 4.3 cm. Body: 0.3 cm.

250
Part of a dish with a moulded decoration under a
qingbai glaze
From Jiangxi Jingdezhen Hutian (1979:8)
Yuan dynasty (AD 1280–1368)

The sherd, which is part of a moulded dish, has
rounded sides, a straight rim, and a straight foot
undercut on the base which is domed in the centre
with a nipple of clay. The decoration inside is a
moulded leaf scroll. The white porcelain body is
glazed with a *qingbai* glaze to the foot ring. The base
and foot ring are unglazed and have kiln grit
adhering.

Height: 3.9 cm. Diameter: 17 cm. (approx.)
Body: 0.4–0.5 cm.

Ganzhou   nos. 251, 252

The kiln is situated at Qilizhen on the east bank of the Gan River. Black and
qingbai types have been discovered. The kiln site also yielded examples of jars
decorated with bosses, whose form and method of manufacture were similar to
those of the Yuan dynasty jars with bosses found in 1976 in the ship wrecked
off the coast of Korea. From this it can be argued that these jars with nipple-like
bosses are products of the Gangzhou kiln in Qilizhen, Jiangxi province.

251
Jar, outside unglazed with striated pattern, inside
with brown glaze
From Jiangxi Ganzhou (1979:7)
Yuan dynasty (AD 1280–1368)

This globular jar with a short, constricted neck and
an everted, rolled rim is decorated on the unglazed
outside walls with two sets of concentric, semi-
circular incised lines, the longest of which run over
the small, flattened base. Around the neck is a band
of horizontally incised lines and a row of 16 small
dots of white glaze. The buff body is glazed on the
inside and over the rim with a brown glaze.

Height: 5.9 cm. Diameter of mouth: 7.1 cm.
Diameter of base: 2.4 cm.
Published: GGBWYYK 1980 (1) pp. 3–27, Fig. 11

252
Sherd from a jar, the unglazed outside decorated
with striations
From Jiangxi Ganzhou (1979:7)
Yuan dynasty (AD 1280–1368)

The fragment, which is part of a jar similar to, but
larger than, no. 251, has rounded sides, a straight
neck and a rolled lip. The inside and the lip are glazed
with a shiny, iridescent black and rust glaze. The
outside of the grey, almost black, body is unglazed
and decorated with a row of dots of yellowish green
glaze around the neck above a band of fine, incised
lines and with vertical lines down the globular body.

Dimensions: 9 × 6 cm. Body: 0.4 cm.
Published: GGBWYYK 1980 (1) pp. 3–27, Fig. 11

Jizhou nos. 253–279

Jizhou is situated at Yonghezhen, seven kilometres south of Ji'an city. It reached the peak of its production in the Southern Song. The range of wares produced at Jizhou is very rich, with the main types of decoration including cut black glaze, hare's fur, tortoise shell and oil spot glazes, and the use of papercut motifs. Apart from these, white wares with moulded decoration were also made, as were pots with brown designs on a white ground related to Ding wares and Cizhou wares in the north.

253

Fragment of a large dish decorated with brown painting
From Jiangxi Jizhou (1955:4)
Song dynasty (AD 960–1279)

Two fish among waves are painted in brown on the inside base of this fragment of a dish. A band of leaf scroll decorates the well above a band of multiple lines. The base of the dish is flat and it was fired on its V-shaped small foot. The decoration is painted on to the putty-coloured, fine body and glazed with a thin, transparent glaze.

Dimensions: 14 × 12.2 cm. Body: 0.6–0.8 cm.
Published: WW 1965 (9) pp. 26–56, Pl. III:13

254

Fragment of a censer with brown painted decoration
From Jiangxi Jizhou (1979:7)
Song dynasty (AD 960–1279)

Part of a rectangular censer with spreading sides and a corner foot on which it was fired. The base is unglazed. The sides are decorated with the remains of a lobed panel containing a wave pattern on the corner against a ground of basketwork pattern. A meandering key-fret pattern runs along the bottom. The whole decoration is painted in brown on the putty-coloured body under a thin, transparent glaze.

Height: 6.8 cm. Length: 9.3 cm. Body: 0.6 cm.

255

Part of a large bowl with brown painted decoration
From Jiangxi Jizhou (1979:7)
Song dynasty (AD 960–1279)

This fragment of a bowl with rounded sides, square cut rim and flat foot is decorated on the inside with fish painted in brown, and round the well with a scrolling lotus reserved on a brown ground. Round the outside walls is a knobbed classic scroll and bands of brown, all painted on to the putty-coloured fine body, which is extremely thick and glazed with a transparent glaze.

Height: 10.5 cm. Dimensions: 13.5 × 11 cm.
Body: 0.8–2.1 cm.
Published: WW 1965 (9) pp. 25–56, Pl. III:12
Also: *WW 1973 (7) pp. 20–27, Fig. 5*

256

Part of a dish with brown painted decoration
From Jiangxi Jizhou (1979:7)
Song dynasty (AD 960–1279)

This piece is part of a dish with a rounded well, an everted rim and a flat base. The inside is decorated with a sketchily painted design in brown of a flower and a butterfly, with detail incised through the brown to reveal the putty-coloured fine body. Inside the rim is a band of brown. The whole of the inside is glazed with a thin transparent glaze while the outside, below the rim, is unglazed.

Height: 2.6 cm. Diameter: 13 cm. (approx.)
Body: 0.2–0.8 cm.

257
Fragment of a bottle with brown painted decoration
From Jiangxi Jizhou (1955:4)
Song dynasty (AD 960–1279)

This sherd from the side of a bottle is sharply inverted at the foot and decorated in brown with a lobed panel, containing ducks among lotus plants, on an interlocking triangular key-fret ground, and with a thin brown band at the base. The brown painted decoration on the putty coloured fine body is covered with a transparent glaze on the outside. The inside, where turning marks are visible, is unglazed.

Height: 7.3 cm. Width: 7 cm. Body: 0.5 cm.
Published: WW 1965 (9) pp. 26–56, Pl. III:10

258
Fragment of a small jar with brown painted decoration
From Jiangxi Jizhou (1979:7)
Song dynasty (AD 960–1279)

The body of this fragment from a small jar is slightly coarser than the previous pieces from the Jizhou kiln site, but still has the same putty colour. The everted and flattened rim is decorated with a meander scroll between two bands, the neck with broad and narrow bands and the rounded walls with the remains of a panel on a ground of regularly spaced florets. The decoration is painted in brown on the body and glazed, on the outside only, with a transparent glaze.

Height: 7 cm. Width: 8 cm. Body: 0.5 cm.

259
Fragment of a bottle with lotus decoration in reserve on a brown painted ground
From Jiangxi Jizhou (1979:7)
Song dynasty (AD 960–1279)

The sherd from the wall of a bottle is decorated on the outside with a scrolling lotus reserved on a brown ground. The brown is painted on to the putty-coloured, fine body under a transparent glaze. The inside which is unglazed is ribbed with turning marks.

Dimensions: 8.4 × 6 cm. Body: 0.5–0.7 cm.

260
Neck fragment of a bottle with golden brown painting
From Jiangxi Jizhou (1979:7)
Song dynasty (AD 960–1279)

From the neck of a bottle this sherd is decorated in golden brown with two bands enclosing a meander scroll below a band consisting of two butterflies. The decoration is painted on the putty-coloured, fine body and glazed with a transparent glaze. The inside is unglazed.

Dimensions: 5.2 × 5.2 cm. Body: 0.5 cm.

261
Fragment of a bottle with painted decoration and incised detail
From Jiangxi Jizhou (1979:7)
Song dynasty (AD 960–1279)

This sherd from the wall of a bottle is decorated on the outside with a knobbed scrolling pattern painted in brown, the details incised through the pigment to reveal the putty-coloured, fine body. The outside is glazed with a transparent glaze, while the unglazed inside shows turning marks.

Dimensions: 10.5 × 6 cm. Body: 0.3–0.5 cm.

262
Shoulder fragment of a jar with painting in golden brown
From Jiangxi Jizhou (1979:7)
Song dynasty (AD 960–1279)

This sherd from the shoulder of a jar is decorated with bands enclosing a row of overlapping petal panels containing a knobbed scroll, above a band of a feather-like scroll. The decoration is painted in golden brown on the putty-coloured fine body under a thin, transparent glaze.

Diameter of neck: 5.3 cm. Length: 10.4 cm.
Body: 0.2–0.3 cm.
Published: WW 1965 (9) pp. 26–56, Pl. III:11

263
Miniature model of a buffalo with a brown glaze
From Jiangxi Jizhou (1979:7)
Song dynasty (AD 960–1279)

This buffalo with a child on its back has a buff body glazed, except for the feet and belly, with a brown glaze.

Height: 5 cm. Length: 8 cm.

264
Miniature model of a man
From Jiangxi Jizhou (1979:7)
Song dynasty (AD 960–1279)

This hand-modelled figure of a man with brown painted hat, facial features and details of clothing, is made of a buff body material and is unevenly glazed with the transparent glaze.

Height: 7 cm.

265
Part of a moulded, unglazed bowl
From Jiangxi Jizhou (1979:7)
Song dynasty (AD 960–1279)

From a conical bowl with everted rim and small,
shallow, spreading foot, this unglazed fragment is
decorated with a moulded pattern of fish among
waves around a central medallion of radiating wavy
lines. The pinkish-buff body may have been biscuit
fired for glazing with a green glaze like that of
no. 269 which has a similar decoration.

Height: 4.5 cm. Length: 9 cm. Body: 0.2–0.3 cm.
Published: GGBWYYK 1980 (1) pp. 3–27, Fig. 10

266
Unglazed sherd from a bowl with moulded
decoration
From Jiangxi Jizhou (1979:7)
Song dynasty (AD 960–1279)

From the base of a bowl with a high, slightly inclined
foot, this sherd is decorated on the inside with a
moulded design of a flower and leaf scroll around a
central medallion of radiating wavy lines. The
pinkish-buff body is unglazed. For a green glazed
similar example, see no. 268.

Dimensions: 10.7 × 8 cm. Height of foot: 1.2 cm.
Diameter of foot: 5.2 cm. Body: 0.2–0.4 cm.

267
Unglazed fragment of a pillow
From Jiangxi Jizhou (1979:7)
Song dynasty (AD 960–1279)

This fragment of a pillow is decorated on the sides
with a moulded trellis pattern with stamped rosettes
in the diamonds, and on the corners with bamboo-
like columns. On the inside extra clay is pressed in to
reinforce the joints of the sides, top and base. The
piece, which has a pinkish-buff body, is unglazed.
For a green glazed similar piece, see no. 270.

Height: 7.8 cm. Body: 0.4 cm.
Published: GGBWYYK 1980 (1) pp. 3–27, Fig. 10

268
Rim sherd from a bowl with a green glaze and
moulded decoration
From Jiangxi Jizhou (1979:7)
Song dynasty (AD 960–1279)

This rim sherd of a bowl with an everted rim is
decorated with a moulded decoration of a flower and
leaf scroll under a green glaze. For a similar,
unglazed piece, see no. 266. The body, in each case,
is a pinkish buff.

Dimensions: 5 × 5 cm. Body: 0.3 cm.

269
Sherd from a green glazed bowl with moulded
decoration
From Jiangxi Jizhou (1979:7)
Song dynasty (AD 960–1279)

Similar to no. 265 with its pinkish-buff body, conical
shape with everted rim and small, spreading foot,
this sherd is likewise decorated with a moulded
design of fish among waves around a central floral
medallion. This sherd, however, has a green glaze.

Height: 3 cm. Dimensions: 6.5 × 5.4 cm.
Body: 0.25 cm.
Published: GGBWYYK 1980 (1) pp. 3–27, Fig. 10

270
Fragment of a moulded pillow with a green glaze
From Jiangxi Jizhou (1979:7)
Song dynasty (AD 960–1279)

Slightly larger than the unglazed similar fragment,
no. 267, this green glazed pillow sherd is decorated
on the sides with a moulded diamond trellis pattern
with central florets. The sides join at the corners with
bamboo-like columns which are reinforced inside
with extra cylinders of clay. The flat top is
undecorated. The body is the same pinkish buff.

Height: 12 cm. Body: 0.4 cm.
Published: GGBWYYK 1980 (1) pp. 3–27, Fig. 10

271
Fragment of a jar with carved decoration under a
green glaze
From Jiangxi Jizhou (1979:7)
Southern Song dynasty (AD 1128–1279)

This sherd is part of a small jar with an inverted
mouth rim. The rounded wall is decorated with a
crudely carved petal band consisting of triangles and
diamonds and, below a ridge, another, broader band
of lotus petals. The outside is glazed with a green lead
glaze and drips of glaze adhere to the pinkish-buff
fine body on the inside. The glaze is crazed.

Dimensions: 8.3 × 5.9 cm. Body: 0.5 cm.
Published: GGBWYYK 1980 (1) pp. 3–27, Fig. 10

272
Fragment from a bowl with a carved decoration
under a green glaze
From Jiangxi Jizhou (1979:7)
Southern Song dynasty (AD 1128–1279)

From the base of a bowl, this sherd has a straight
foot, inclined on the inside. The inside is decorated
with a carved and combed floral design under the
green lead glaze, which covers the piece inside and
out and which is iridescent in places. The body is
grey, hard and medium-coarse, while the remains of
a firing support under the base consist of red pottery.

Dimensions: 6.3 × 5.9 cm. Body: 0.3–0.7 cm.

273
Part of a bowl with paper-cut designs in the 'tortoise shell' glaze
From Jiangxi Jizhou (1979:7)
Southern Song dynasty (AD 1128–1279)

Part of a tea bowl, this fragment is decorated on the outside with a 'tortoise shell' yellow and brown glaze which has deteriorated slightly. The inside is decorated with paper-cut designs of foliated floral panels within a floral band beneath the rim. The glaze on the inside is a yellow and brown 'hare's fur' glaze. On the outside the glaze is trimmed short of the low, rounded foot. The slightly recessed flat base is also unglazed, revealing the fine, buff body.

Height: 7 cm. Width: 12.3 cm.
Body: 0.3–1.1 cm. (base)

274
Part of a tea bowl with paper-cut designs in the 'hare's fur' glaze
From Jiangxi Jizhou (1979:7)
Southern Song dynasty (AD 1128–1279)

This tea bowl fragment is decorated on the outside with a brown iron dressing and a dark brown 'hare's fur' glaze. On the inside in the yellowish 'hare's fur' glaze is a decoration of paper-cut plum blossom florets in dark brown. The brown iron dressing is visible where the glaze stops short of the foot on the outside. The fine body is putty-coloured. Below the rim on the inside is a small undercut ridge.

Dimensions: 10.5 × 7.3 cm. Body: 0.4–0.5 cm.

275
Part of a bowl with a brown 'hare's fur' glaze
From Jiangxi Jizhou (1979:7)
Southern Song dynasty (AD 1128–1279)

Part of a bowl with thick spreading sides angled towards the mouth rim at the point where there is a slight ridge around the inside. The brown 'hare's fur' glaze is streaked with blue. On the outside the glaze is trimmed where the sides are undercut to meet the low foot. The flat, slightly recessed base shows the fine, putty-coloured body.

Height: 6 cm. Width: 10.5 cm. Body: 0.3–0.9 cm.

276
Part of a brush washer with a 'hare's fur' streaked glaze
From Jiangxi Jizhou (1955:4)
Southern Song dynasty (AD 1128–1279)

This segment of a brush washer with rounded sides, a rounded rib round the inside base and a flattened, everted rim with a pie frill edge, is covered with a brown glaze on the inside and the outside walls. The glaze is heavily streaked with blue and yellow, and stops short of the flat base, where the fine, putty-coloured body is revealed and where the remains of kiln grit appear to have been trimmed off.

Dimensions: 12.8 × 6 cm. Body: 0.4–0.7 cm.

277
Fragment of a bottle with plum blossom carved through the black slip
From Jiangxi Jizhou (1955:4)
Southern Song dynasty (AD 1128–1279)

Part of the warped wall of a bottle, this fragment is decorated on the outside with a design of plum blossom carved through the black slip to reveal a white slip. The details of the blossoms are painted in brown. The branches of the prunus spray are cut right through to the putty-coloured, fine body. A brown iron kiln gloss covers the inside, and a transparent glaze the outside.

Dimensions: 12 × 6.2 cm. Body: 0.3–0.5 cm.

278
Part of a tea bowl with decoration in cream slip on a brown ground
From Jiangxi Jizhou (1979:7)
Southern Song dynasty (AD 1128–1279)

The base fragment of a tea bowl with spreading sides, small convex base and small V-shaped foot is decorated on the inside with a design of plum blossom painted in cream slip over a brown slip ground under a clear glaze. On the outside the slip and glaze run short of the foot, where the putty-coloured, fine body is revealed.

Dimensions: 10.5 × 8.7 cm.
Diameter of foot: 3.8 cm. Body: 0.2–0.8 cm.

279
Sherd from a jar with a black glaze and resist decoration of plum blossom
From Jiangxi Jizhou (1979:7)
Southern Song dynasty (AD 1128–1279)

From the wall of a jar, this sherd is decorated with a plum blossom design in resist against the black glaze ground. The glaze is tinged with rust and the stamens of the blossoms appear rust coloured. The inside shows the remains of an iron wash and kiln grit over the putty-coloured, fine body.

Dimensions: 14.7 × 6.6 cm. Body: 0.7–1.2 cm.

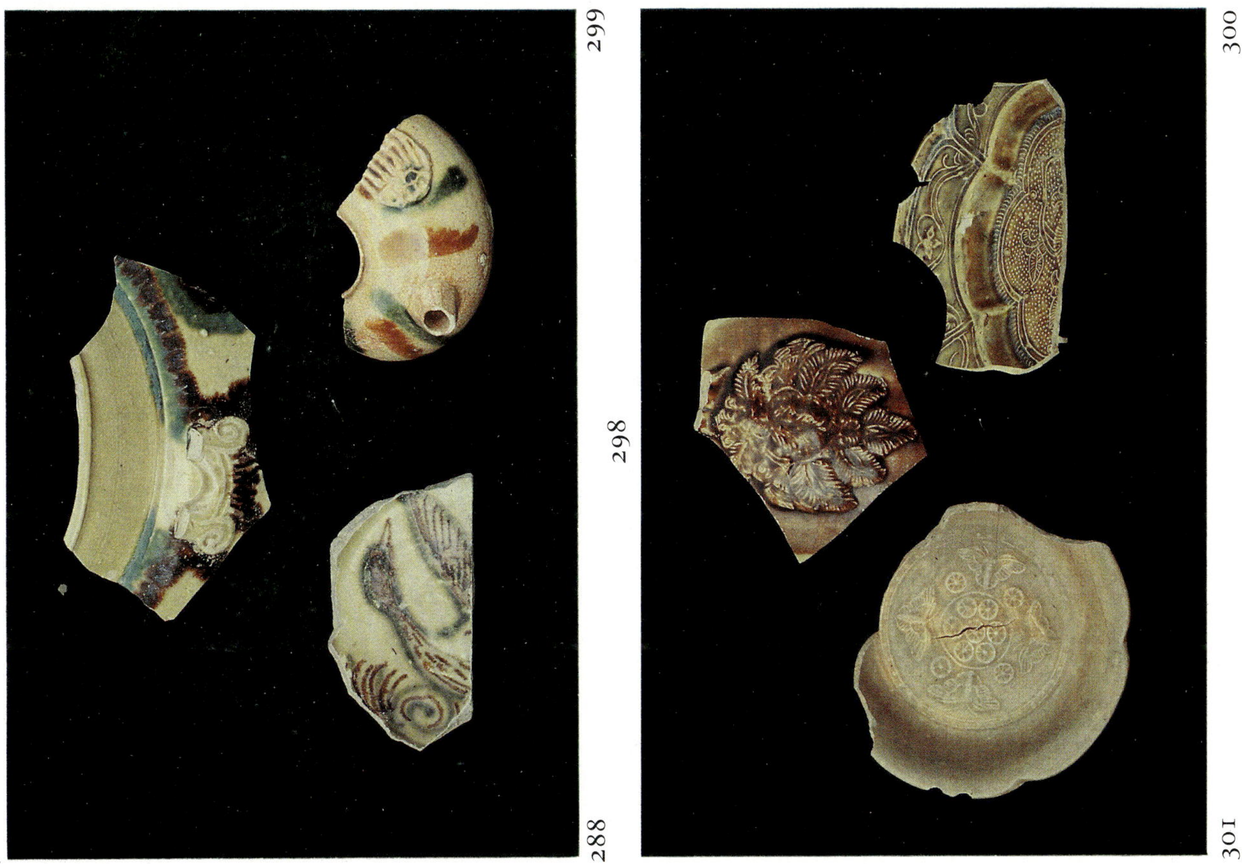

295
292
293
280
283
282
297
299
288
298
300
301

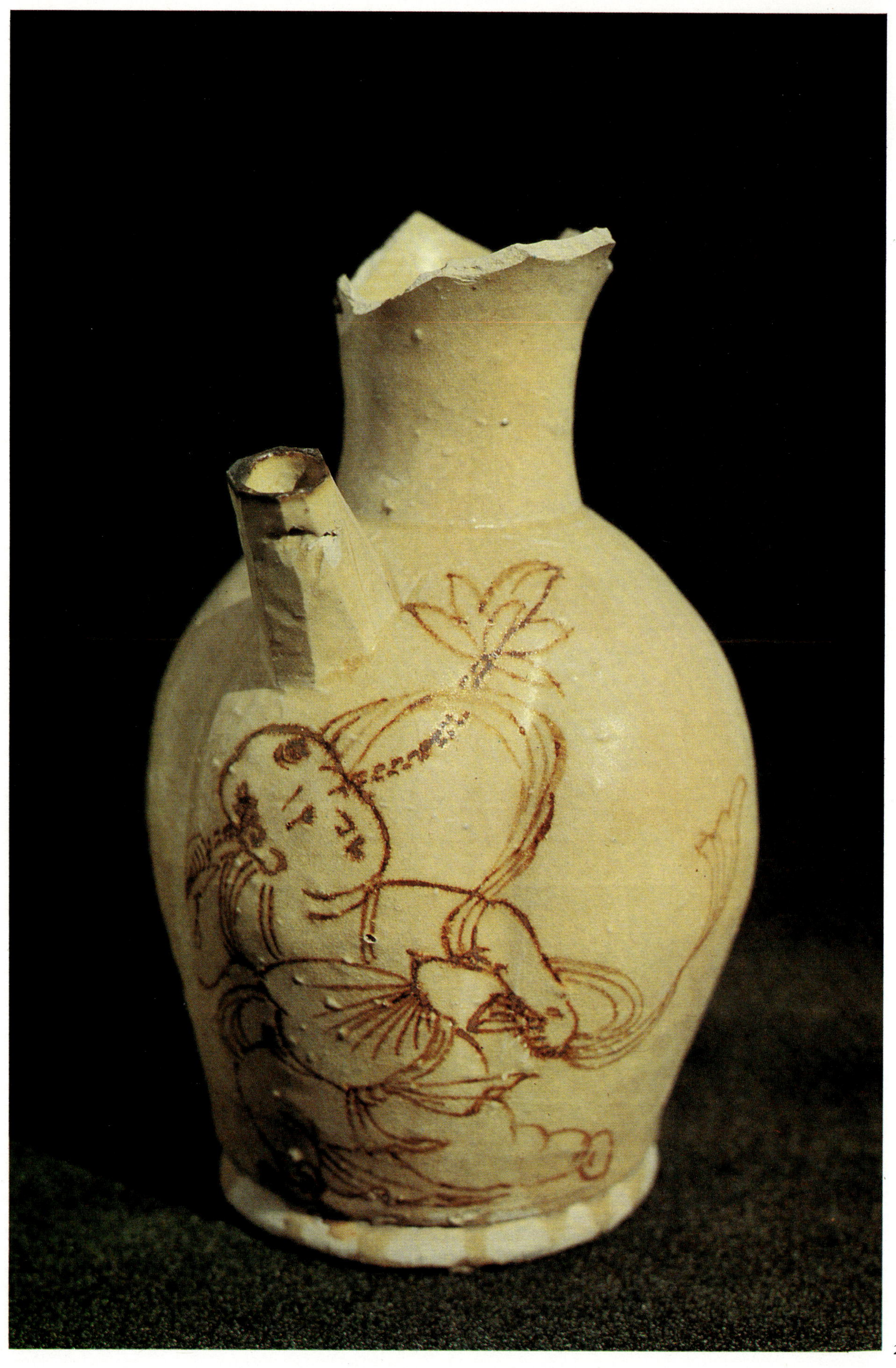

Hunan   nos. 280–301

Two kilns represent this province, both of the 6th–10th century. Xiangyin greenwares link with the contemporary Zhejiang wares and the underglaze painting of Tongguanzhen and Wazhaping, Changsha group are exceptional with a beauty which is not shown in a photograph. The significance of underglaze painting in iron and copper is evident in a consideration of the development of that technique in China.

Xiangyin   nos. 280–283
Changsha   nos. 284–301

Xiangyin nos. 280–283

In 1975 the Xiangyin kiln site was partially excavated. Production here started in the Eastern Jin, and was developed to a high level in the Sui dynasty. Dishes on high feet with impressed decoration, as well as four-handled jars with stamped motifs, both common types in the Sui dynasty, have been found in large numbers at the kiln site. Characteristic wares of Xiangyin are vessels decorated by small stamps placed within two or three concentric bands. Sui tombs, excavated in the area of Changsha, have yielded many greenwares, some of which were made at Xiangyin.

280

Part of a high-footed dish with impressed decoration under a green glaze
From Hunan Xiangyin (1973:3)
Sui dynasty (AD 581–618)

The inside of this fragment of a tall-footed dish is decorated with impressed designs of three chrysanthemum rosettes alternating with three leaf motifs around a central rosette, and between borders of incised lines. The outside walls spread from the small, thick base which appears concave under the mass of kiln grit adhering to the whole of the underside. The pale grey, fairly coarse body is glazed with an olive glassy glaze which wells thick in the stamped impressions.

Diameter of inside base: 10 cm.
Diameter of base: 4 cm. Body: 0.6 cm.
Published: WW 1978 (1) pp. 69–80, Fig. 12

281

Part of a high-footed dish with impressed decoration under a green glaze
From Hunan Xiangyin (1973:3)
Sui dynasty (AD 581–618)

This fragment is part of a dish with spreading sides, angled then curving inwards and then out towards the everted rim. The remains of the tall foot are visible. The inside is decorated with rings of impressed design around a central floret: a triple ring, two rows of circles, a triple ring, a band of florets separated by rectangles of lines, all within a final triple ring. The green glaze runs thick and crazed in the depressions and runs in tear drops on the outside walls. Where it stops short of the foot, the pale grey medium-coarse body has a shiny, brown kiln gloss.

Diameter: 19 cm.
Body: 0.4 cm. (side) – 2.2 cm. (base)
Published: WW 1978 (1) pp. 69–80, Fig. 12:14

282

Part of a high-footed dish with impressed decoration under a green glaze
From Hunan Xiangyin (1973:3)
Sui dynasty (AD 581–618)

Part of a dish on a high, spreading foot with an everted, rolled foot ring, this fragment is decorated on the inside with impressed florets and leaf sprays around a central floret within a chrysanthemum which is bordered by rings of multiple line. The pale, grey, medium-coarse body is glazed with a pale green glaze.

Height: 5.2 cm. Diameter: 16.5 cm.
Diameter of foot: 9.9 cm. Body: 0.8 cm.
Published: WW 1978 (1) pp. 69–80, Fig. 12:14

283

Part of a bowl with impressed decoration under a green glaze
From Hunan Xiangyin (1973:3)
Sui dynasty (AD 581–618)

Part of a hemispherical bowl with a flattened base, this piece is decorated on the inside with an impressed design of a central treble ring, surrounded by an eight-petalled 'flower', and round the walls with alternating petal shapes and striated rectangles. The pale olive glaze covers the inside of the bowl and half way down the outside, where the pale grey, fairly coarse body is revealed.

Diameter: 10.8 cm. Height: 3.5 cm.
Body: 0.3 – 0.4 cm.

Changsha   nos. 284–301

In 1956, at Tongguanzhen and Wazhaping, kiln sites of the Tang and Five dynasties were discovered. The decoration of the wares is richly varied. Painting under the glaze was the kiln's most notable achievement; over a thousand years ago potters were creating different colours from metal oxides, thus breaking the tradition of monochrome glazes, and initiating a new approach to the decoration of ceramics. The design on the flask, showing the boy playing, is painted with a finesse rarely seen on Tang ceramics.

284
Part of a lid with impressed decoration and a green glaze
From Hunan Xiangyin (1973:3)
Sui dynasty (AD 581–618)

This part of a domed lid has a wide, rounded groove on the underside of the rim for fitting to a vessel. The top is decorated around the central, hand-pinched handle with vague stamped impressions of florets and leaf sprays. The pale grey, fairly coarse body is glazed on the top with a pale green glaze. The underside is unglazed except for accidental splashes.

Height: 2.6 cm. Diameter: 13 cm.
Inside diameter: 9 cm. Body: 0.5–0.9 cm.
Published: WW 1978 (1) pp. 69–80, Fig. 12:8

285
Part of a ewer with underglaze decoration painted in brown
From Hunan Changsha (1978:3)
Tang dynasty (AD 618–906)

This four-lobed ewer, with an eight-faceted spout, has a tall flaring neck and the remains of a handle attached to the neck and body. It is decorated with a boy holding a lotus and a swirling scarf painted in iron brown on the off-white fine body under the transparent greenish glaze. The rim of the spout and the remains of the handle are touched with brown. The flat base is unglazed.

Height: 19.5 cm. Diameter: 8.8 cm. Body: 0.4 cm.
Published: KGXB 1980 (1) pp. 67–96, Pl. 3:1

286
Dish decorated with a flower painted in iron brown pigment
From Hunan Changsha (1978:3)
Tang dynasty (AD 618–906)

The dish with shallow sides and everted rim, short rounded foot ring and small base is decorated on the inside base with a flower painted in iron brown on a circle of cream slip. This central area is unglazed. The walls are glazed with a thin, brownish-green, transparent glaze, which is trimmed short of the foot, where the grey medium-fine body has burnt buff. There are dots of the brown pigment under the glaze around the rim.

Height: 4 cm. Diameter: 15.4 cm. Body: 0.3 cm.
Published: KGXB 1980 (1) pp. 67–96, Pl. 2:12 and Pl. 5:4

287
Part of a ewer with a duck in underglaze green and brown painting
From Hunan Changsha (1978:3)
Tang dynasty (AD 618–906)

Part of the lobed wall of a ewer this fragment is decorated with a flying duck and a lotus leaf painted in iron brown and copper green under the glaze. The transparent, slightly greenish glaze has deteriorated and appears matt on the outside. The off-white, fine body is partially glazed from the top on the inside.

Dimensions: 12.6 × 10 cm. Body: 0.45 cm.
Published: GGBWYYK 1980 (1) pp. 3–27, Fig. 12

288
Fragment of a bowl with a duck painted in
underglaze green and brown
From Hunan Changsha (1978:3)
Tang dynasty (AD 618–906)

This fragment from a bowl has a broad foot ring on
which it was fired. The shallow foot is inclined on the
inside and the base is convex. The inside is decorated
with a duck with outspread wings painted in copper
green and iron brown on the off-white, fine body
under a transparent, greenish glaze.

Dimensions: 9.7 × 5.1 cm.
Diameter of foot ring: 5.6 cm. Body: 0.5 cm.
Published: GGBWYYK 1980 (1) pp. 3–27, Fig. 12

289
Fragment of a flask decorated in underglaze green
and brown
From Hunan Changsha (1978:3)
Tang dynasty (AD 618–906)

This piece of a flask is decorated with a fish-dragon
and waves painted in copper green and iron brown
on the off-white, fine body under the transparent,
greenish glaze. The glaze is trimmed short of the flat
base.

Height: 9.6 cm. Width: 11 cm. Body: 0.4 cm.
Published: GGBWYYK 1980 (1) pp. 3–27, Fig. 12

290
Part of a ewer with painted decoration in blue and
brown under the glaze
From Hunan Changsha (1978:3)
Tang dynasty (AD 618–906)

This sherd, from the wall of a lobed ewer, is
decorated with a bird on a branch painted in copper
blue-green and iron brown on the off-white, fine
body. The glaze has deteriorated to such a degree
that the piece appears unglazed.

Dimensions: 11 × 9.5 cm. Body: 0.5 cm.

291
Part of a ewer with an underglaze brown painted
decoration
From Hunan Changsha (1978:3)
Tang dynasty (AD 618–906)

Part of a lobed ewer with a tall neck and an everted
rim, this fragment is decorated with a mythical
creature painted in iron brown on the off-white, fine
body under the transparent, greenish glaze. The
inside of the neck is also glazed.

Height: 16 cm. Width: 11.6 cm. Body: 0.5 cm.
Published: GGBWYYK 1980 (1) pp. 3–27, Fig. 12

292
Fragment of a pillow decorated in blue and brown
painting under the glaze
From Hunan Changsha (1978:3)
Tang dynasty (AD 618–906)

This section from the top of a pillow is decorated with
a loose, net-like pattern outlined in iron brown and
filled in with copper blue-green painting and with
brown dots in the mesh spaces. The body is an off-
white, fine material and the glaze is transparent and
slightly greenish in colour. A small fragment of the
side is attached to the top.

Dimensions: 10.8 × 9.7 cm. Body: 0.35–0.5 cm.

293
Fragment from a pillow decorated in blue and brown
painting under the glaze
From Hunan Changsha (1978:3)
Tang dynasty (AD 618–906)

This sherd from the top of a pillow is decorated with
a sketchy floral spray painted in copper blue-green
and iron brown on the off-white, fine body under the
transparent, greenish glaze.

Dimensions: 9.5 × 9.3 cm. Body: 0.5 cm.

294
Part of the top of a pillow with painted decoration
under the glaze
From Hunan Changsha (1978:3)
Tang dynasty (AD 618–906)

From the top of a pillow this fragment is decorated
with a sketchy floral design painted in copper green
and iron brown on the off-white, fine body under the
greenish, transparent glaze.

Dimensions: 13.5 × 9.3 cm. Body: 0.6 cm.

295
Top of a pillow decorated with a bird painted under
the glaze
From Hunan Changsha (1978:3)
Tang dynasty (AD 618–906)

The decoration on this top of a pillow is a bird among
foliage painted in copper blue-green and iron brown
on the off-white, fine body under the greenish,
transparent glaze.

Dimensions: 14.5 × 9.5 cm. Body: 0.5 cm.

296
Part of the top of a pillow with decoration painted
under the glaze
From Hunan Changsha (1978:3)
Tang dynasty (AD 618–906)

The sketchy floral motifs decorating this fragment
from the top of a pillow are painted in copper green
and iron brown on the off-white body, under the
greenish, transparent glaze to which kiln debris
adheres.

Dimensions: 14.5 × 9.3 cm. Body: 0.4 cm.

297
Fragment of a jar with designs painted under the glaze
From Hunan Changsha (1978:3)
Tang dynasty (AD 618–906)

This sherd is from a jar with a high rounded shoulder, tall, slanting neck with constricted rim, and the remains of an applied relief handle on the shoulder beneath a raised horizontal rib. It is decorated with copper bluish-green and iron brown designs painted under the greenish, transparent glaze on the off-white, fine body. The glaze stops short at the neck on the inside.

Dimensions: 13.5 × 7.7 cm. Body: 0.2–0.4 cm.

298
Sherd from a flask with moulded and painted decoration
From Hunan Changsha (1978:3)
Tang dynasty (AD 618–906)

This sherd from the rounded walls of a flask is unglazed inside, where turning marks are visible. The outside shows the remains of a sprigged handle consisting of three cylinders of clay above an elaborately moulded leaf design, which is painted brown under the thin, brownish, transparent glaze. The fine body is an off-white colour.

Dimensions: 10 × 9.5 cm. Body: 0.5 cm.

299
Part of a water pot with moulded and painted decoration
From Hunan Changsha (1978:3)
Tang dynasty (AD 618–906)

This is part of a water pot with rounded walls, a short, upstanding neck with a rolled rim, a 10-faceted spout and a moulded motif on the side. The off-white, fine body is glazed inside and out with copper green and iron brown painting and bluish streaking under the glaze.

Height: 6 cm. Length: 8.5 cm. Body: 0.35 cm.

300
Part of a dish with moulded decoration under an olive glaze
From Hunan Changsha (1978:3)
Tang dynasty (AD 618–906)

This fragment of a dish with a high, everted foot, flat base, lobed cavetto and broad, flattened rim turned up at the foliated edge, is decorated with a moulded design of scrolling floral sprays in panels on the rim and flowers on a dotted ground within a swagged and striated border on the inside base. The off-white, fine, thin body is glazed with a thin, olive glaze. The piece was fired on the foot ring, which was subsequently trimmed.

Dimensions: 11 × 8 cm. Height: 4 cm. Body: 0.3 cm.

301
Part of a dish with moulded decoration under a green glaze
From Hunan Changsha (1978:3)
Tang dynasty (AD 618–906)

Part of a dish with a high straight foot, rounded five-lobed walls and a flattened, everted and foliated rim, this sherd is decorated with a moulded design of four butterflies and roundels with radial segments surrounded by a double line border with dots. The off-white, fine, thick body is glazed with a thin, olive, slightly over fired glaze, and the dish was fired on the foot ring, which was trimmed clean afterwards.

Height: 3.5 cm. Diameter: 13 cm.
Diameter of foot ring: 7.2 cm. Body: 0.2 cm.
Published: WW 1960 (3) pp. 67–74, p. 72, Fig. 2

Sichuan   nos. 302–305

A group of later kilns is reported from Sichuan chiefly of greenwares but also
showing some decoration

Qionglai   nos. 302–305

Qionglai nos. 302–305

Four kiln sites were discovered at Qionglai. Production was begun in the Southern Dynasties and expanded greatly in the Tang dynasty. The vessels from the kiln site at Shifangtang are characteristic of the Tang period. The types of wares include some with designs in blue and green glaze, and others with underglaze painting; these resemble the decoration of vessels from Changsha in Hunan. At Shifangtang, apart from utensils for everyday use, the potters also made large quantities of lively little sculptures of fat babies, acrobats, birds and animals.

302
Base of a large dish
From Sichuan Qionglai (1957:7)
Tang dynasty (AD 618–906)

This base fragment of a very large dish is decorated on the inside with a quatrefoliate floral motif surrounded by floral sprays painted in yellow, green and brown over a cream slip. The greenish, transparent glaze runs short of the foot on the undecorated outside walls which are cut with a prominent horizontal ridge. The body material is very coarse and of a greyish-brown colour. The dish has rounded sides, a broad foot ring, and a slightly recessed convex base.

Dimensions: 28 × 25 cm. Diameter of foot: 12.5 cm. Body: 0.6 cm.
Published: WW 1965 (9), pp. 26–56, Pl. 1:1

303
Fragment from the rim of a bowl
From Sichuan Qionglai (1957:7)
Tang dynasty (AD 618–906)

This sherd from a bowl with a rounded wall and an everted rim is decorated inside and outside with blue-green and brown splashing over a white slip under a transparent, crazed glaze. The body material is a greyish buff and medium-coarse.

Dimensions: 5.5 × 4.8 cm. Body: 0.3–0.6 cm.
Published: WW 1965 (9), pp. 26–56, Pl. 1:7

304
Fragment of a wide mouthed jar with green and brown glazes
From Sichuan Qionglai (1957:7)
Tang dynasty (AD 618–906)

This rim sherd from the rounded wall of a wide mouthed jar is decorated over the cream slip with bands of brown and green, one broad green band being elaborated by a row of brown dots. The greyish buff, medium-coarse body is exposed where the transparent glaze stops on the inside below the rim.

Dimensions: 9.5 × 6.5 cm. Body: 0.5 cm.
Published: WW 1965 (9) pp. 26–56, Pl. 1:4

305
Fragment from the wall of a jar(?)
From Sichuan Qionglai (1957:7)
Tang dynasty (AD 618–906)

This wall fragment from a jar(?) has a slightly everted foot with an almost imperceptibly recessed base which is glazed. The glaze, which stops short of the foot on the outside wall, is splashed with blue-green, olive and brown. On the broad foot ring adhere the remains of a spur, on which the vessel was fired. The body material is greyish buff and medium-coarse.

Height: 8.2 cm. Width of foot: 3.5 cm. Body: 0.4 cm.
Published: WW 1965 (9) pp. 26–56, Pl. 1:6

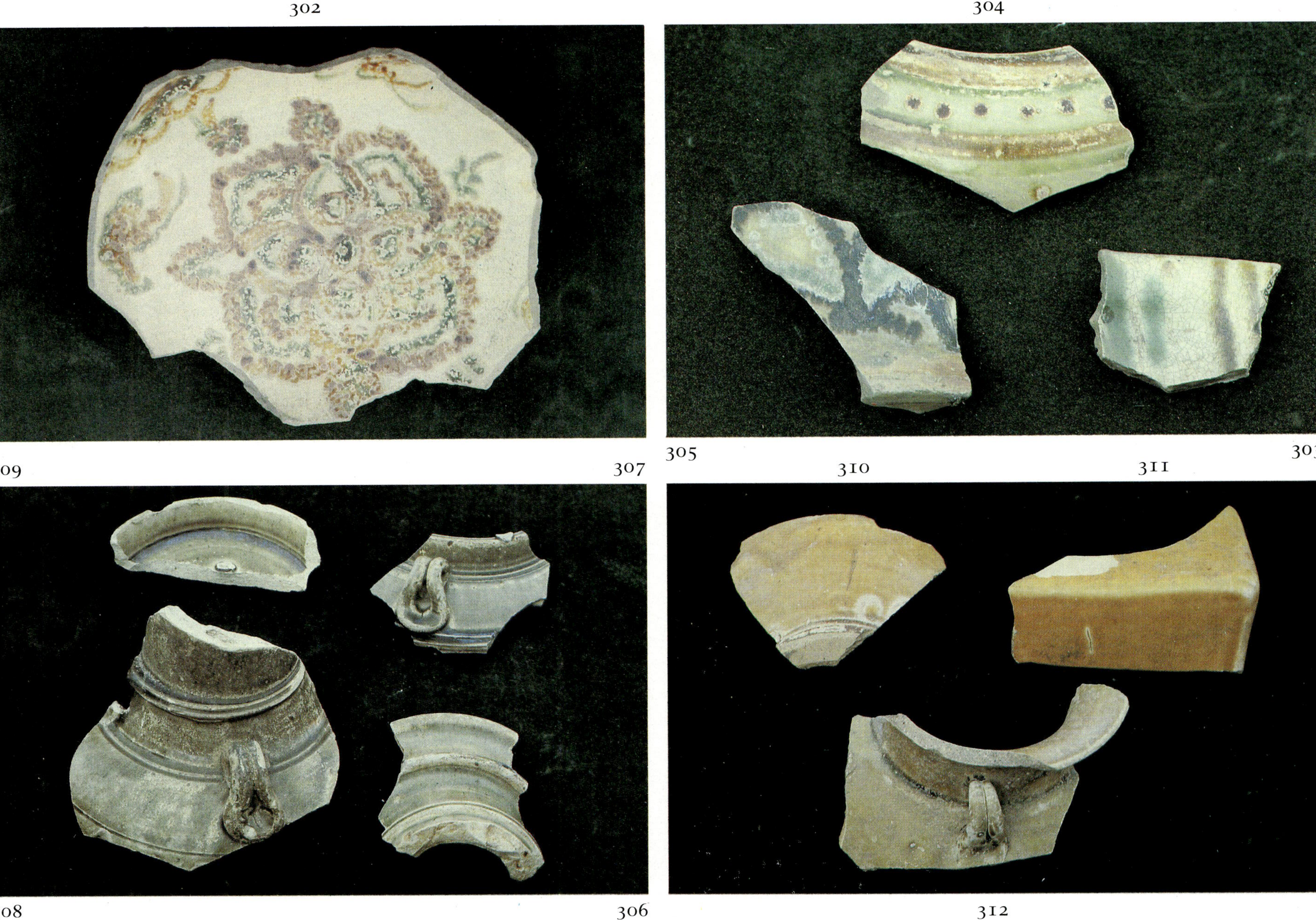
302
304
309
307
305
310
311
303
308
306
312

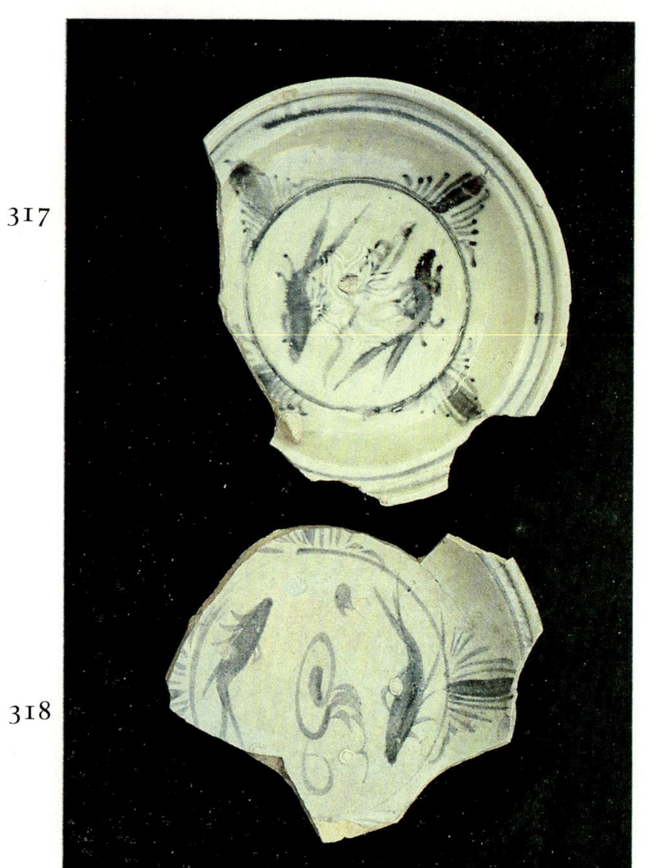

317

318

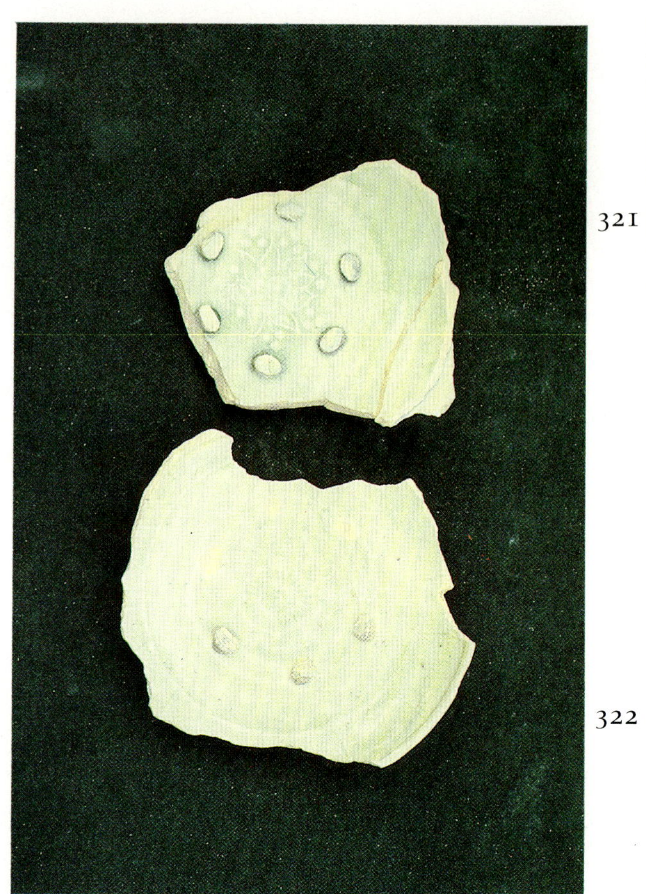

321

322

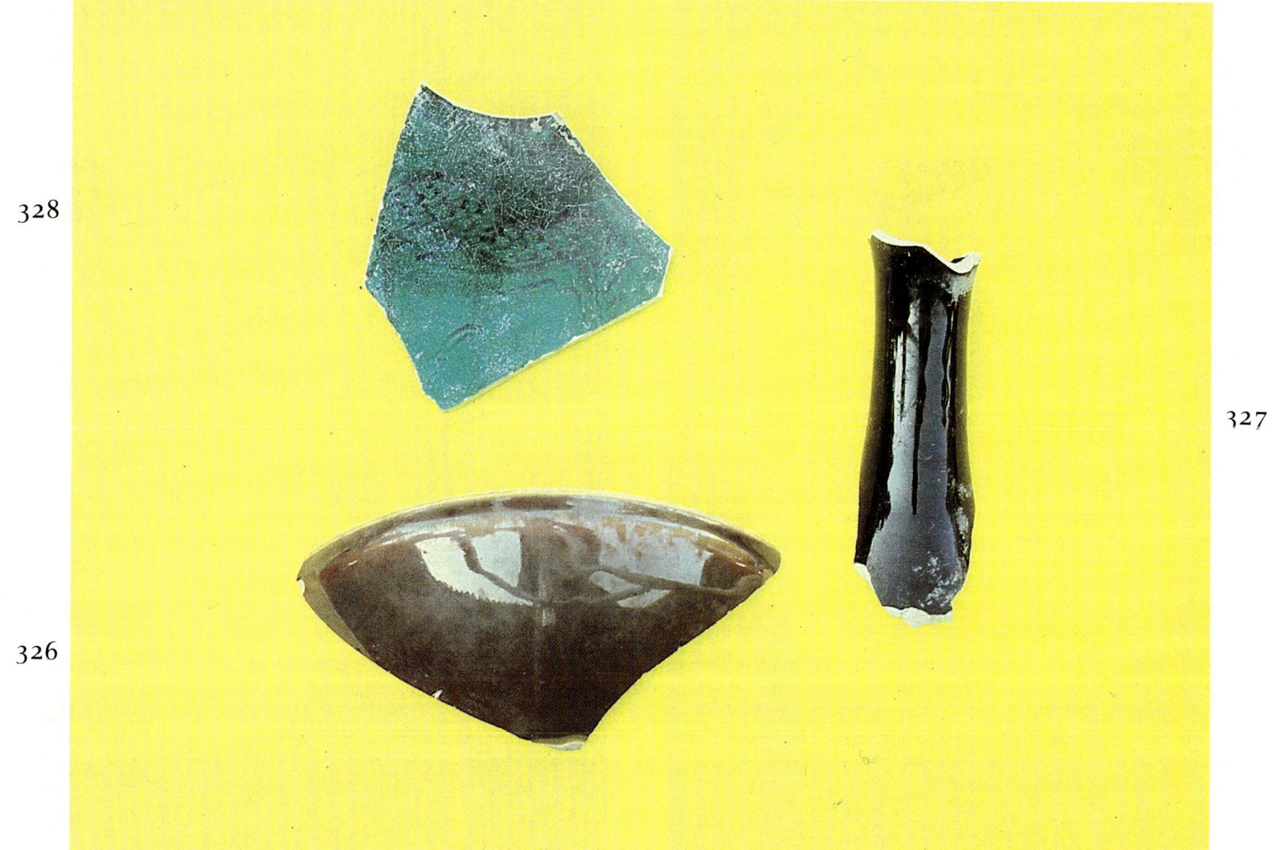

328

327

326

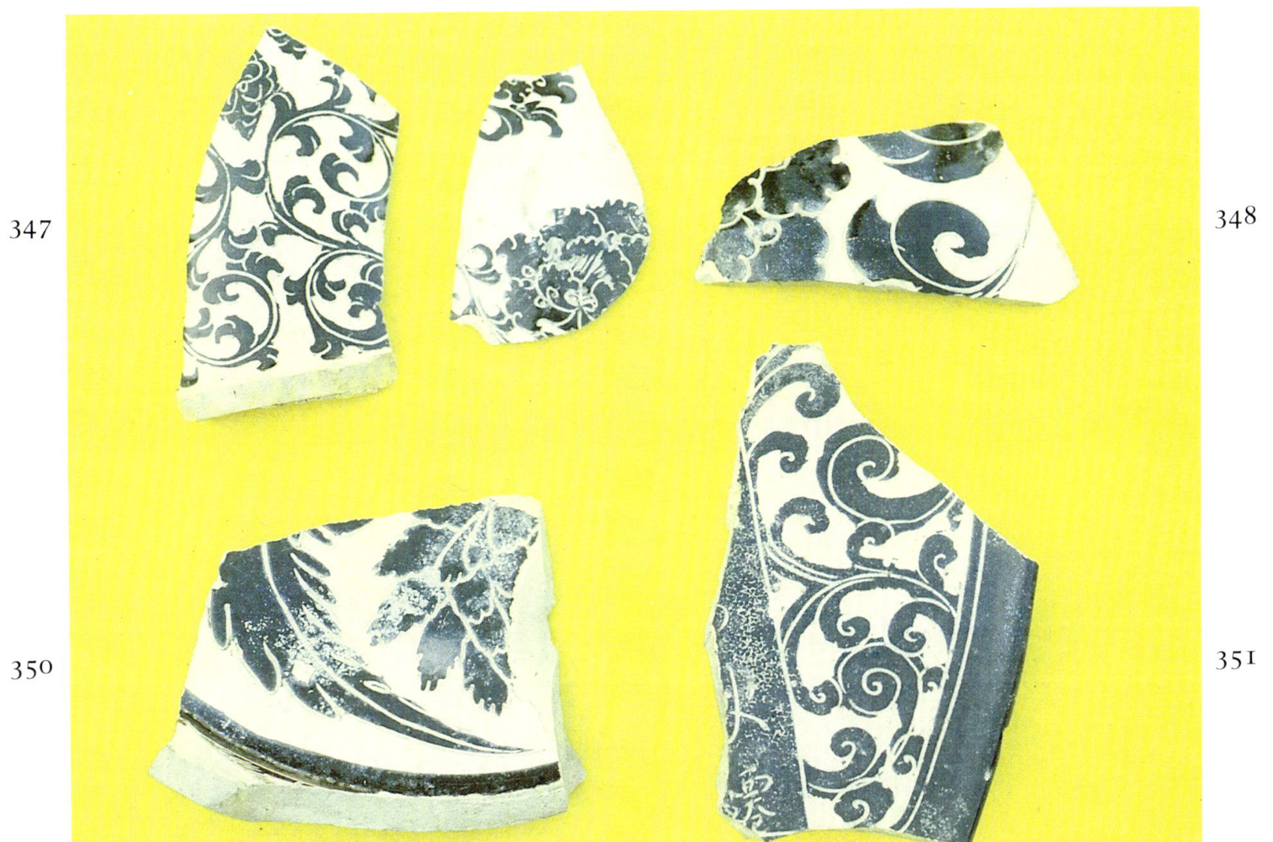

344

343

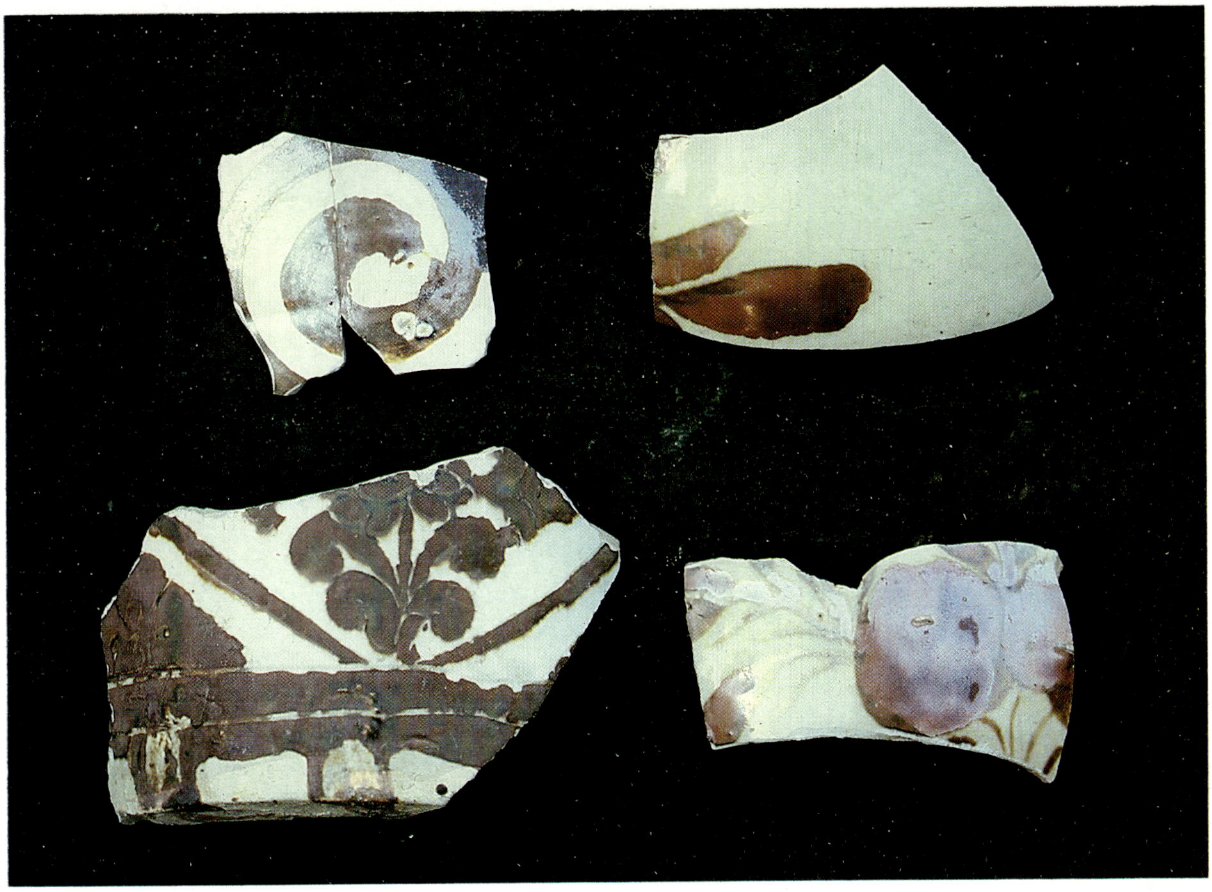

346

345

349

347

348

350

351

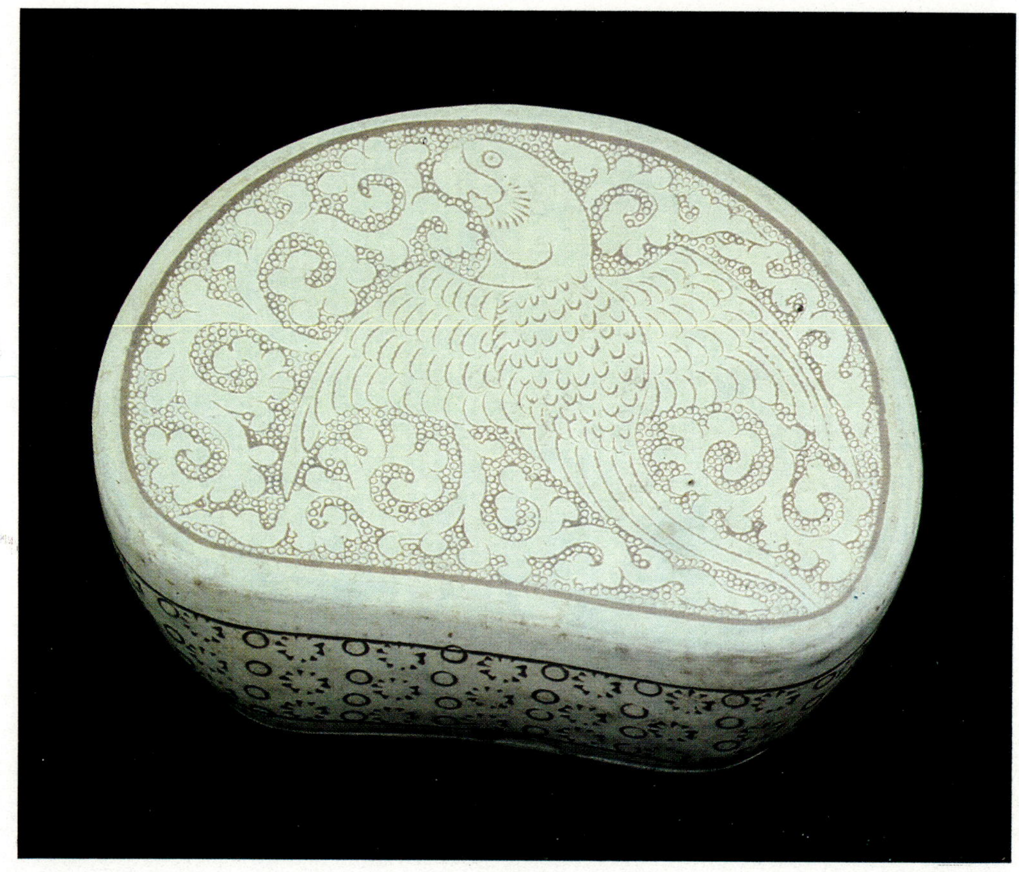

378

370

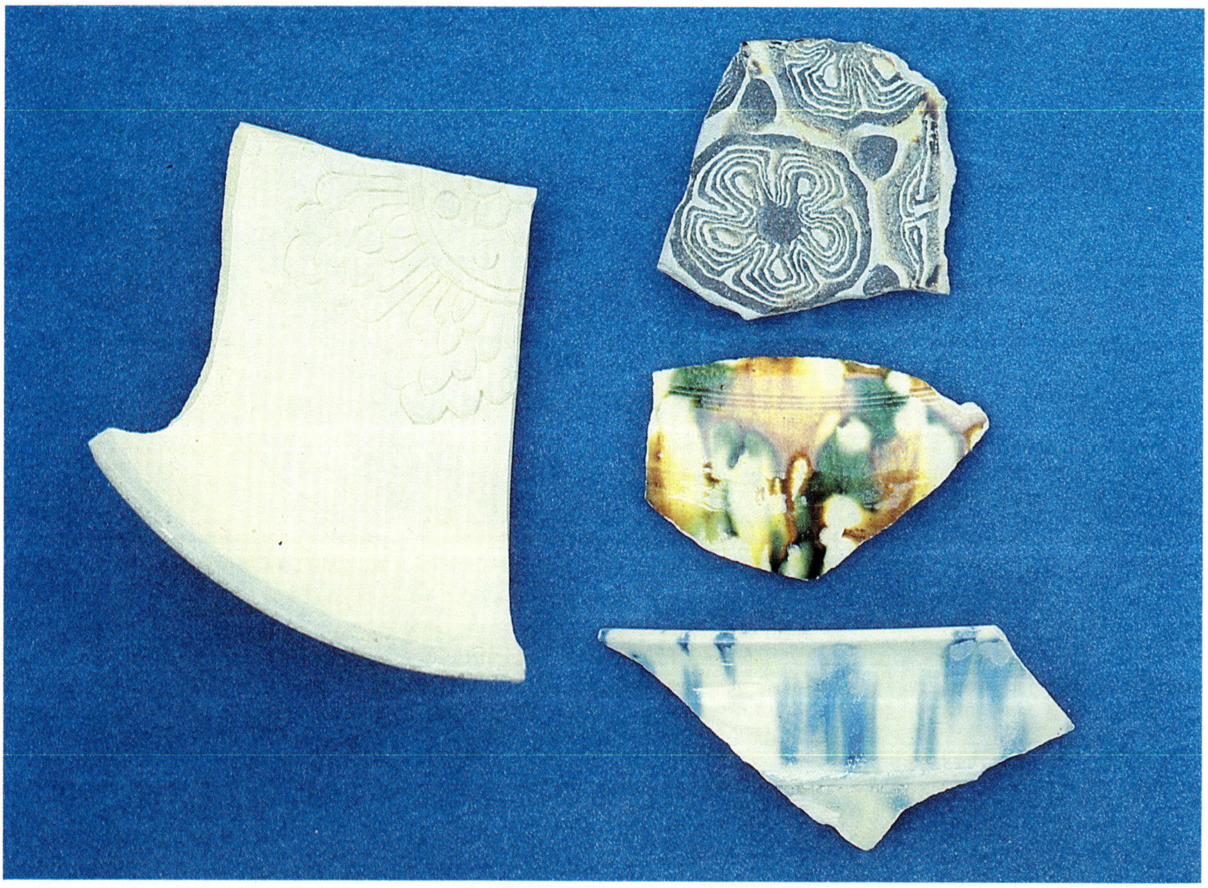

372

368

371

Just one kiln complex is shown from Anhui and is a group of the yellow wares.

Shouzhou   nos. 306–315

Shouzhou   nos. 306–315

Discovered in 1960, the six kiln sites of the complex are situated in Shou xian, 40 kilometres to the east of Gaotang Lake. When production started in the Sui at Guanjiazui green glazed wares were made, but in the Tang period pots with yellow glazes were manufactured. Among the excavated wares from Yujiagou were found remains of bowls, cups, basins, water droppers and pillows. Their yellow glaze is rich and glossy, which accords with the record in Lu Yu's 'Tea Classic' that states 'Shouzhou wares are yellow'.

306
Neck of a flask with a brownish olive glaze
From Anhui Shouzhou (1960)
Sui dynasty (AD 581–618)

This part of the neck of a flask with prominent protruding ribs, broadens in steps towards the rounded everted rim. The light grey, medium-coarse body is glazed inside and outside with an olive glaze, which appears brown and iridescent where thick, and is crazed and deteriorated in places.

Dimensions: 8 × 8 cm. Body: 0.75–1.7 cm.

307
Fragment of a jar with a brownish olive glaze
From Anhui Shouzhou (1960)
Sui dynasty (AD 581–618)

This sherd from a jar with a rounded shoulder and short upright neck is fitted with a lug handle made of a curled cylinder of clay. Bands of incised lines decorate the shoulder. The medium-coarse, grey body is covered inside and outside with a brownish olive glaze, which appears brown and iridescent blue where deep in the incisions, and which is pock-marked on the inside. A piece of kiln debris adheres to the rim.

Dimensions: 10 × 6.5 cm. Body: 0.6–0.8 cm.

308
Fragment of a jar with a brownish olive glaze
From Anhui Shouzhou (1960)
Sui dynasty (AD 581–618)

This fragment from a jar is incised with ridges around the neck, collar and shoulder. A lug handle formed of a cylinder of clay is attached to the shoulder. The brownish olive glaze which covers the dark grey coarse body on the outside runs down inside the neck. The body is burnt to a buff colour where unglazed. Under the shoulder on the inside there is a ring of glaze which is pock-marked.

Dimensions: 13 × 13 cm. Body: 0.9 cm.

309
Fragment of a tall-footed dish with a green glaze
From Anhui Shouzhou (1960)
Sui dynasty (AD 581–618)

This part of a high-footed dish has shallow walls with an everted rim. The buff, medium-coarse body is covered with a brownish olive glaze which appears brown and iridescent blue where thick round the edge. A piece of kiln debris adheres to the un-decorated inside base.

Dimensions: 11.2 × 4 cm. Body: 0.4–1.2 cm.

310
Fragment of a bowl with an amber glaze
From Anhui Shouzhou (1960)
Tang dynasty (AD 618–906)

This sherd is a fragment from a bowl with a thick, flat, unglazed foot, with rounded walls and a tapered rim. The coarse, buff body has a cream slip and a thin amber glaze which stops short of the foot on the outside, revealing the slip.

Height: 5 cm. Dimensions: 9.5 × 7 cm. Body: 0.7 cm.

311
Fragment of a pillow with an amber glaze
From Anhui Shouzhou (1960)
Tang dynasty (AD 618–906)

This corner piece from a pillow has a flat top and sides. The coarse, buff body has a cream slip and is glazed with an amber glaze.

Height: 5.5 cm. Dimensions: 10.3 × 7.8 cm.
Body: 0.4 cm.

312
Part of a ewer with a yellowish olive glaze
From Anhui Shouzhou (1960)
Tang dynasty (AD 618–906)

This piece is from a ewer with a high, rounded shoulder, a trumpet neck and a lug handle composed of twin cylinders of clay joined to the neck and body. The coarse, buff body is covered with a cream slip and glazed inside and outside with a yellowish olive glaze which is iridescent on the surface and which appears brown where it wells thick at the base of the neck.

Dimensions: 10 × 6.5 cm.
Diameter of inside neck: 8 cm. Body: 0.6–0.9 cm.

313
Fragment of a ewer with a black glaze
From Anhui Shouzhou (1960)
Tang dynasty (AD 581–618)

This fragment is part of a ewer with an eight-faceted spout. The grey-buff, coarse body is covered with a white slip before being glazed with the shiny, black glaze. The inside is unglazed except inside the spout and the neck.

Dimensions: 7 × 6 cm. Body: 0.6 cm.

314
Fragment of a ewer with a black glaze
From Anhui Shouzhou (1960)
Tang dynasty (AD 618–906)

This fragment from a ewer has a high, rounded shoulder, an upright neck, the remains of a lug handle composed of twin cylinders of clay and attached to the neck and the body, and the remains of a spout. The grey-buff coarse body has a white slip and a shiny black glaze which is speckled with brown.

Dimensions: 9 × 8.5 cm. Body: 0.6 cm.

315
Fragment of a jar with a black glaze
From Anhui Shouzhou (1960)
Tang dynasty (AD 618–906)

This piece is from the neck of a jar with a high, rounded shoulder, an upright neck which is ridged and slightly everted at the rim, and a broad lug handle joined to the neck and the shoulder. The grey coarse body which is burnt to a buff colour is covered first with a white slip and then with a shiny black glaze which is speckled with brown. Inside the jar the glaze stops short just below the mouth rim.

Dimensions: 6 × 5.5 cm. Body: 0.5 cm.

Yunnan   nos. 316–323

The discovery of a Yuan dynasty kiln in Yunnan has opened up the study of underglaze decorated wares, this appears to have been a technique practised in the western kilns and the use of cobalt seems to have been a natural part of the tradition.

Yuxi   nos. 316–323

Yuxi   nos. 316–323

In 1960 three kiln sites were discovered at Wayaocun in Yuxi xian that had made green wares with stamped decoration, and vessels decorated in underglaze blue. Among the exhibits, the *yuhuchun* bottle decorated in underglaze blue with fish and waterweeds, excavated from a Yuan dynasty burial in Lufeng xian, is typical of Yuxi ware. Although this bottle lacks the fine quality of a Jingdezhen piece, its shape and decoration are in Yuan style, and it provides fresh material for the study of Yuan blue and white ceramics.

316
Base of a bowl with moulded and underglaze blue decoration
From Yunnan Yuxi (1957)
Yuan dynasty (AD 1280–1368)

The inside of this base fragment of a dish is decorated with a rosette in stamped relief. A floral design is painted in cobalt blue on the buff body which burns to an orange buff where exposed on the inside of the high straight foot and base. The glaze is transparent with a slight greenish tinge.

Dimensions: 9.5 × 4.7 cm. Body: 0.5–0.9 cm.

317
Part of a dish decorated in underglaze blue
From Yunnan Yuxi (1957)
Yuan dynasty (AD 1280–1368)

The dish has rounded sides and a flattened rim, upturned at the edge and rounded, a straight foot and a flat base. On the inside is a stamped relief lotus motif over which is painted a decoration in cobalt blue of fish within a circle, out of which stylised waterweeds grow in four directions. A double band of blue decorates the rim. The greyish-buff body, which burns orange-buff where exposed, is similar to the green glazed pieces, nos. 321, 322. The greenish transparent glaze runs unevenly down the sides to the foot.

Diameter: 17.4 cm. Height: 4.8 cm. Body: 0.3 cm.

318
Part of a dish decorated in underglaze blue
From Yunnan Yuxi (1957)
Yuan dynasty (AD 1280–1368)

Part of a dish similar to no. 317 but without the moulded decoration in the centre, this fragment has rounded sides, a flattened rim which is upturned at the edge and rounded, a straight foot and a flat base. The decoration in cobalt blue consists of two fish among weeds inside a ring with weeds growing in four directions up the walls to the double blue ring on the rim. The outside wall is decorated with a sketchily painted scroll. The buff body burns orange where exposed on the base and inside the foot, and also shows orange through the glaze in places. There are six spurs on the inside base.

Dimensions: 16.2 × 13 cm. Height: 0.4 cm. Body: 0.4–0.5 cm.

319
Bottle decorated with fish in underglaze blue
From Yunnan Lufeng xian (1973)
Yuan dynasty (AD 1280–1368)

The bottle is decorated in underglaze blue beneath the pale greenish, transparent glaze, with three leaves around the spreading neck, four panels of fruit around the shoulder above a band of roughly painted diagonal lines, and the main band round the body of two fish among waterweeds. At the bottom, above the short, spreading foot, is a band of sketchy scroll pattern. The foot ring and flat base are unglazed revealing the buff body burnt to an orange colour.

Height: 24 cm. Diameter of base: 7.7 cm.
Diameter of mouth: 6.6 cm.
Thickness of foot: 0.5 cm.
Published: GGBWYYK 1980 (1) pp. 3–27, Fig. 13

320
Fragment from the neck of a bottle decorated in
underglaze blue
From Yunnan Yuxi (1957)
Yuan dynasty (AD 1280–1368)

The neck fragment from a bottle is decorated on the
outside with petal-like brush strokes and a band of
leaf design painted in blue on the buff body under a
clear glaze. On the inside a thick welt of clay is visible
where the neck is luted to the shoulder.

Height: 7 cm. Interior diameter of neck: 2.5 cm.
Body: 0.5 cm.

321
Part of a dish with a green glaze
From Yunnan Yuxi (1957)
Yuan dynasty (AD 1280–1368)

This fragment has a short, roughly cut, flat foot and
a recessed, flat base. The inside base is decorated
with a stamped relief design of a lotus and shows the
remains of six spurs. Part of the wall of another dish
is stuck to the inside. The greyish-buff, medium-
coarse body burns orange where exposed and dark
orange on the side where the glaze has missed. The
pale green, crazed glaze runs in a thick tear drop on
the outside, stopping short of the foot.

Dimensions: 14.5 × 13.5 cm.
Diameter of base: 8.9 cm. Body: 0.5–0.8 cm.

322
Part of a green glazed dish
From Yunnan Yuxi (1957)
Yuan dynasty (AD 1280–1368)

The dish has shallow, rounded sides with a straight
rim, and is decorated on the inside base with a
rudimentary stamped relief design of a chrysanthemum and foliage. The remains of three spurs and
three spur marks are visible on the inside base while
lumps of rough kiln support adhere to the foot. The
foot and base are roughly cut and are unglazed. The
body is similar to no. 321 and the pale green glaze
runs in tears down the outside to the foot.

Dimensions: 17.2 × 16 cm.
Diameter of base: 8.4 cm. Body: 0.6–0.8 cm. (base)

323
Part of a dish with a green glaze
From Yunnan Yuxi (1957)
Yuan dynasty (AD 1280–1368)

Part of a shallow dish with a flattened, everted rim,
small rounded foot and recessed base turned with a
pimple of clay in the centre, this fragment is glazed
with a pale green, crazed glaze. The glaze runs short
of the foot, where the greyish-buff, medium-coarse
body burns orange. Four spur marks are visible on
the base and the remains of perhaps another vessel
adhere to the inside base. Kiln grit adheres to the
glaze on the outside.

Dimensions: 9.1 × 8.3 cm.
Diameter of foot ring: 4.3 cm. Body: 0.2–0.5 cm.

The two important and influential kilns of Hebei have been freshly and more extensively investigated and reported. The full range of wares from both Ding and Cizhou are represented. Their production particularly in the Song dynasty are clearly of great significance in the general development of both technique and style in other kilns of both north and south.

Ding   nos. 324–342
Cizhou   nos. 343–363

Ding yao   nos. 324–342

The Ding kiln is one of the famous kilns of the Song dynasty. It is situated in Quyang xian, Jiancicun. Production started in the late Tang, with important developments taking place in the Northern Song. Apart from white wares, which form the bulk of the production, there were a few black wares, brown wares, and, occasionally, greenwares. The earliest wares are mostly plain, while the Northern Song wares had incised or moulded decoration, the moulded ones being the most elaborate. In order to increase production, the *fushao* firing technique was used. The rims of bowls were left unglazed. They could then be placed rim downwards in a tier within a stepped saggar (clay container), without risk of the glaze causing the bowl to adhere to the saggar. This feature was known in literature as *Mang kou* (referring to the roughness of the bowl rim), and is one of the characteristics of Ding wares. The piece of 'green Ding' in the exhibition is very unusual.

324
Fragment from the base of a dish
From Hebei Ding yao (1957:3)
Tang dynasty (AD 618–906)

The fragment from this undecorated dish has a heavy, hard, white body, a white slip, and a clear glaze which runs in tears down the outside. The wide base ring is slightly recessed in the centre and is unglazed.

Dimensions: 7.8 × 7 cm. Body: 0.4 cm.
Similar to: KG 1965 (8) p. IV, no. 5

325
Fragment of a dish
From Hebei Ding yao (1957:3)
Five Dynasties (AD 907–960)

This fragment of an undecorated dish with a rounded wall and an everted, rolled rim has a small, neatly cut foot which shows spur marks and a flat base. The greyish-white, fine body is covered with a thick, even, clear glaze which gives a very white effect. The dish is glazed inside, and outside the glaze is trimmed above the foot, leaving the foot and base unglazed.

Height: 4.5 cm. Diameter of foot: 5.2 cm.
Body: 0.2 cm.

326
Fragment of a bowl with a brown glaze
From Hebei Ding yao (1957:3)
Song dynasty (AD 960–1279)

This fragment from the rounded wall of a bowl with an inverted rim has an ivory white fine body covered with an even, glossy coffee coloured glaze.

Dimensions: 13.5 × 7 cm. Body: 0.3–0.5 cm.
Published: WW 1959 (7) p. 70, Fig. 11

327
Fragment of a bottle with a black glaze
From Hebei Ding yao (1957:3)
Song dynasty (AD 960–1279)

This part of a neck of a bottle has an ivory-coloured fine body, similar to no. 326, and an even, glossy black glaze which covers the outside and part of the way down the neck.

Length: 10 cm. Diameter: 3 cm. Body: 0.3 cm.
Published: WW 1959 (7) p. 70, Fig. 12

328
Fragment of a dish with a green glaze
From Hebei Ding yao (1957:3)
Song dynasty (AD 960–1279)

This fragment of a dish has a dragon design incised
on the inside. The body, like the brown and black
pieces, nos. 326 and 327, is ivory white and fine.
The deep bluish-green glaze which has iridised
slightly covers the inside, and the outside to the foot
ring, but the base is unglazed.

Dimensions: 9 × 9 cm. Body: 0.4 cm.
(Li Huibing: This is the larger of only two green-
glazed pieces found at Ding yao)

329
Part of the base of a dish
From Hebei Ding yao (1957:3)
Song dynasty (AD 960–1279)

This fragment is part of a dish which has carved
designs of dragons on the inside and on the outside
walls. The foot ring of the high, straight foot is
unglazed. The dish has the usual Ding yao ivory
white body and transparent glaze which gathers in
tear drops on the outside walls and base.

Dimensions: 11 × 8.3 cm. Body: 0.4 cm.

330
Part of the base of a dish
From Hebei Ding yao (1957:3)
Song dynasty (AD 960–1279)

The carved and incised decoration of a dragon on the
inside of this large dish fragment is extremely finely
detailed. The ivory white, fine body is covered with
transparent glaze on both sides.

Dimensions: 14.5 × 7.5 cm. Body: 0.5 cm.
Published: WW 1965 (9) pp. 26–56, Pl. 1:9
Also *WW 1959 (7) p. 69, fig. 5*

331
Part of the base of a dish
From Hebei Ding yao (1957:3)
Song dynasty (AD 960–1279)

A moulded design of two winged dragons among
clouds decorates the inside of this fragment of a dish.
Roughly incised through the glaze on the base are
the characters: *Shang shi ju*, translated as in no. 342,
as 'Office of imperial banqueting'. The glaze over the
characteristic ivory white fine body appears over-
fired and shows thick yellow tear marks.

Dimensions: 13 × 12 cm. Body: 0.4 cm.

332
Part of the base of a dish
From Hebei Ding yao (1957:3)
Song dynasty (AD 960–1279)

This fragment from the base of a dish with a small,
fine foot and a slightly recessed base is decorated on
the inside base with a *chi* dragon, and with a scroll of
peonies around the well. The body is ivory white and
fine, and the glaze is transparent.

Dimensions: 11 × 10 cm. Body: 0.3 cm.

333
Fragment from the base and wall of a bowl
From Hebei Ding yao (1957:3)
Song dynasty (AD 960–1279)

This sherd from a bowl with rounded walls and a
fine, slightly inverted foot has, on the inside, a
moulded decoration of waves in the centre and of
children among leaf sprays round the wall. The
ivory-white, fine body and the transparent glaze are
similar to other contemporary pieces from Ding yao.

Dimensions: 9 × 6.3 cm. Body: 0.2–0.4 cm.

334
Fragment from the base and wall of a dish
From Hebei Ding yao (1957:3)
Song dynasty (AD 960–1279)

The inside of the dish is decorated with a moulded
design of cranes on the base and of ridged panels
containing mandarin ducks in lotus ponds around
the walls. The dish, which has a fine straight foot,
has an ivory white fine body and a transparent glaze.

Dimensions: 9.5 × 7 cm. Body: 0.2–0.4 cm.

335
Fragment of a dish
From Hebei Ding yao (1957:3)
Song dynasty (AD 960–1279)

This fragment with a thin ivory-white fine body and
a thin transparent glaze has a moulded decoration
on one side of a *xiniu* gazing at the moon from an
island among waves, within a key-fret border.

Dimensions: 6.6 × 4 cm. Body: 0.15 cm.

336
Fragment of a bowl
From Hebei Ding yao (1957:3)
Song dynasty (AD 960–1279)

This fragment is the base of a bowl with a small, fine
foot and with a carved and incised decoration of fish
among waves on the inside. It has an ivory-white,
fine body and a transparent glaze, which covers the
foot and base.

Dimensions: 9 × 7.6 cm. Body: 0.2–0.4 cm.

337
Fragment of a pillow with decoration incised
through the slip
From Hebei Ding yao (1957:3)
Song dynasty (AD 960–1279)

This pillow fragment is carved with a decoration of
leaf scrolls through the white slip to the greyish-
white fine body beneath. The whole is then covered
with a transparent glaze.

Dimensions: 11.2 × 6.5 cm. Body: 0.4 cm.

338
Part of a moulded box
From Hebei Ding yao (1957:3)
Song dynasty (AD 960–1279)

This fragment of a lobed box, which has a small part
of another box fired on to the top of it, is decorated on
the flat surface with a moulded decoration of fruit
and lotus and with a moulded leaf scroll round the
lobed sides. The body is white, fine and thick and the
glaze transparent.

Height: 6.8 cm. Body: 0.5 cm.

339
Sherd from a pillow with decoration carved through
the cream slip
From Hebei Ding yao (1957:3)
Song dynasty (AD 960–1279)

This fragment of a pillow is decorated with a sketchy
design of leaf scrolls on a striated ground and within
a border of radiating lines, all carved through the
cream slip to the greyish-buff fine body and covered
with a transparent glaze.

Dimensions: 11 × 9.5 cm. Body: 0.5 cm.

340
Part of the base of a dish
From Hebei Ding yao (1957:3)
Song dynasty (AD 960–1279)

The fragment from the base of a dish is decorated
with a moulded decoration on the inside of scrolling
lotus with a surrounding band of key-fret pattern,
and with a peony scroll round the wall. The dish,
which has an ivory white, fine body, has a fine,
straight, glazed foot ring. The transparent glaze
appears slightly over-fired and has crawled on the
outside, becoming thin and dry.

Dimensions: 12 × 12 cm. Body: 0.4 cm.

341
Part of the base of a dish inscribed with the character
Guan, 'Official'
From Hebei Ding yao (AD 960–1279)
Song dynasty (AD 960–1279)

Inscribed through the glaze on the flat base of the
dish fragment is the character *Guan*, 'official'. The
foot ring is narrow and bevelled. The greyish-white,
fine body is covered inside and outside with a
transparent glaze, to which kiln dirt adheres on both
sides.

Diameter of base: 8.6 cm. Body: 0.3 cm.

342
Part of the base of a dish inscribed with two of the
characters for the 'Office of imperial banqueting'
From Hebei Ding yao (1957:3)
Song dynasty (AD 960–1279)

Incised through the glaze on the base of this dish
fragment are the final two characters of title of the
palace kitchen *Shang shi ju*, previously translated as
the 'Office of imperial banqueting'. The inside has a
moulded decoration of a phoenix among peonies,
which is surrounded by a band of daisies around the
well. The transparent glaze, which covers the
greyish-white, fine body, runs in tears down the
outside to the foot, which has been sliced off.

Dimensions: 10 × 5.3 cm. Body: 0.3–0.4 cm.

Cizhou nos. 343–363

Cizhou wares are one of the famous popular northern wares of the Song
dynasty. The kilns are situated in Ci xian at Guantaizhen, Dong'aikoucun,
Yezicun and Pengchenzhen. The excavation of a large group of kilns has
produced rich remains, with many types of pot decorated in various ways, the
most characteristic and effective being a black design on a white ground. The
subjects of the decoration reflect a popular taste.

343

Fragment of a jar (see no. 345)
From Hebei Cizhou (1964:4)
Song dynasty (AD 960–1279)

This fragment of the rounded wall of a jar is decorated with two leaves painted in rust brown on a cream slip over the grey medium-fine body. On the outside the glaze makes the slip appear grey while the inside is covered with a brown glaze.

Dimensions: 9 × 6 cm. Body: 0.3 cm.
Illustrated: GGBWYYK 1980 (1) pp. 3–27, Pl. 5:10
Also *WW 1964 (8) pp. 37–48, fig. 11 (still one piece with no. 345)*

344

Fragment of a jar
From Hebei Cizhou (1964:4)
Song dynasty (AD 960–1279)

The body of this curved wall fragment is a similar hard grey fine body to that of the previous sherd. The cream slip, however, this time shows through the transparent glaze quite clearly, contrasting with the rust-brown painted spiral decoration. A black glaze covers the inside and there is a spot of it on the outside.

Dimensions: 5.6 × 5.2 cm. Body: 0.4 cm.
Published: GGBWYYK 1980 (1) pp. 3–27, Pl. 5:12
Also *WW 1964 (8) pp. 37–48, fig. 11*

345

Part of the same jar as no. 343
From Hebei Cizhou (1964:4)
Song dynasty (AD 960–1279)

This fragment was originally joined to sherd no. 343. The body, slip and glaze are therefore identical and this part of the decoration shows a fruiting spray.

Dimensions: 9.5 × 4.8 cm. Body: 0.3 cm.
Published: GGBWYYK 1980 (1) pp. 3–27, Pl. 5:11
Also *WW 1964 (8) pp. 37–48, fig. 11 (still joined to no. 343)*

346

Part of a jar with brown painted decoration
From Hebei Cizhou (1964:4)
Song dynasty (AD 960–1279)

This fragment from the base and wall of a jar is decorated with painting in brown over a cream slip of a floral motif inside a panel which tapers to a point at the double brown lines around the foot. The jar has a broad foot ring and a slightly recessed base to which brown slip and kiln grit adhere. There is another accidental splash of the brown slip on the inside which has a cream slip under the transparent glaze that also covers the outside. The body material is grey and medium-coarse.

Height: 6.2 cm. Width: 11.5 cm. Body: 0.7 cm.
Published: GGBWYYK 1980 (1) pp. 3–27, Pl. 5:13

347

Fragment of a bottle with black painted designs with incised details
From Hebei Cizhou (1964:4)
Song dynasty (AD 960–1279)

This fragment from the rounded wall of a bottle has a design of a peony scroll painted in black over a white slip. Details, such as the stems and veins of the foliage and the petals of the peony, are incised through the black to the white. The body is creamy-buff coloured and medium-fine, and the outside is covered with a transparent glaze, while the inside remains unglazed.

Dimensions: 10.2 × 5.3 cm. Body: 0.8 cm.
Published: GGBWYYK 1980 (1) pp. 3–27, Pl. 5:4
Also *WW 1964 (8) pp. 37–48, Pl. 1:1*

348

Fragment of a jar with black painted decoration and incised details
From Hebei Cizhou (1964:4)
Song dynasty (AD 960–1279)

The fragment is decorated with a large, bold decoration of a peony scroll painted in black with the details of the leaves and petals incised through the black to the white slip beneath. The creamy-buff medium-fine body and the transparent glaze on the outside are similar to no. 347. This fragment is also unglazed on the inside.

Dimensions: 10.3 × 5.1 cm. Body: 0.6 cm.
Published: GGBWYYK 1980 (1) pp. 3–27, Pl. 5:2
Also *WW 1964 (8) pp. 37–48, Pl. 1:1*

349

Fragment of a jar with black painted decoration with incised detail
From Hebei Cizhou (1964:4)
Song dynasty (AD 960–1279)

This fragment, similar in body, slip, glaze and technique to the previous two sherds shows yet another variant on the peony scroll design, with more detail incised on the more specific and less stylised flower.

Dimensions: 8 × 5 cm. Body: 0.6 cm.
Published: GGBWYYK 1980 (1) pp. 3–27, Pl. 5:1
Also *WW 1964 (8) pp. 37–48, Pl. 1:1*

350
Part of the base of a large dish
From Hebei Cizhou (1964:4)
Song dynasty (AD 960–1279)

This sherd comes from the flat base of a large dish
which has an inclined foot, straight on the inside.
The decoration on the inside of a spiky peony and its
leaf within a black band is painted in black, with the
central vein of the large leaf and the divisions of the
petals within the silhouette of the flower incised
through to the white slip ground beneath. The
transparent glaze covers the inside of the dish, while
traces of the white slip and the glaze on the outside
are trimmed short of the foot. Body: As for no. 347.

Dimensions: 5.3 × 10.5 cm. Body: 0.8 cm.
Published: GGBWYYK 1980 (1) pp. 3–27, Pl. 5:3
Also *WW 1964 (8) pp. 37–48, Pl. 1:1*

351
Fragment of a pillow with painted and incised
decoration
From Hebei Cizhou (1964:4)
Song dynasty (AD 960–1279)

This fragment from the edge of the top of a pillow is
decorated with a panel of leaf scroll design painted in
black with the central leaf veins and the overlap of
the leaves picked out in incised line. Round the edge
is a broad black band incised through to the white
slip beneath towards the inside. A black band across
the scroll decoration is incised with the characters
huo qian. Creamy-buff, medium-coarse body,
transparent glaze.

Dimensions: 12.8 × 8 cm. Body: 0.4 cm.
Published: GGBWYYK 1980 (1) pp. 3–27, Pl. 5:5
Also *WW 1964 (8) pp. 37–48, Pl. 1:1*

352
Fragment of the base of a bowl with incised
decoration
From Hebei Cizhou (1964:4)
Song dynasty (AD 960–1279)

This part of the base of a bowl is decorated on the
inside base with a design of a fish among water
weeds incised through the cream slip to the buff,
medium-fine body beneath. The inside is covered
with a transparent glaze which runs thickly in
places. The outside walls and the high, straight foot
are glazed with a brown-black glaze while the foot
ring and the deeply recessed base are left unglazed.

Dimensions: 14.4 × 11.5 cm.
Diameter of foot: 6.4 cm. Body: 0.2–0.6 cm.
Published: GGBWYYK 1980 (1) pp. 3–27, Pl. 5:7

353
Fragment of a large bowl with decoration incised
through the slip
From Hebei Cizhou (1964:4)
Song dynasty (AD 960–1279)

This sherd is part of the side of a large bowl decorated
with a peony leaf scroll on a striated background.
The design is incised through the white slip to the
buff medium-fine body beneath and coated with a
transparent glaze. On the outside walls, the V-shaped
foot, and the base (but not the foot ring) is a black
glaze which has iridised in places.

Dimensions: 13.5 × 11.5 cm. Body: 0.1–0.7 cm.
Published: GGBWYYK 1980 (1) pp. 3–27, Pl. 5:6

354
Fragment of a pillow
From Hebei Cizhou (1964:4)
Song dynasty (AD 960–1279)

This fragment from the corner of a pillow is
decorated with a moulded leaf design within an
incised border and with yellow and green glazes. An
incised design is visible on the side. The body is buff,
medium-fine.

Dimensions: 6.5 × 6.2 cm. Body: 0.5 cm.
Published: WW 1964 (8) pp. 37–48, Fig. 9

355
Fragment of a pillow with a black painted decoration
under a green glaze
From Hebei Cizhou (1964:4)
Song dynasty (AD 960–1279)

This fragment is part of the side of a pillow with
remains of the projecting rim of the top, and of the
unglazed base. Over the buff, medium-fine body and
the white slip is a decoration of leaf scroll painted in
black under a green glaze.

Height: 10.5 cm. Width: 9.5 cm. Body: 0.4–0.6 cm.
Published: WW 1964 (8) pp. 37–48, Fig. 9

356
Part of a moulded miniature figure holding a dog
From Hebei Cizhou (1964:4)
Song dynasty (AD 960–1279)

This fragment of the body of a figure holding a dog is
decorated over the white slip with underglaze brown
painting for the dog and with green, orange and
yellow enamels over the transparent glaze for the
robes. The figure is unglazed on the inside where the
potter's finger marks remain after pressing the clay
of the buff, medium-fine body into the mould. The
green enamel is slightly iridescent.

Dimensions: 7.3 × 3.7 cm. Body: 0.1–0.4 cm.
Published: WW 1964 (8) pp. 37–48, Fig. 9

357

Part of a pillow with decoration in black
From Hebei Cizhou (1964:4)
Song dynasty (AD 960–1279)

This fragment from the top of a pillow is decorated with a design painted in black of a crane among reeds, edged with one narrow and one broad painted band. On the underside a sausage of clay is visible where the top is luted to the side. This join is undercut so that the top projects over the sides. The body is buff, medium-fine and the glaze transparent. The inside of the pillow is unglazed.

Dimensions: 17.6 × 13.5 cm. Body: 0.4 cm.
*Published: GGBWYYK 1980 (1) pp. 3–27, Pl. 5:8
Also WW 1964 (8) pp. 37–48, Pl. 1:4*

358

Fragment from a pillow with incised decoration on a ground of small circles
From Hebei Cizhou (1964:4)
Song dynasty (AD 960–1279)

This fragment comes from the top of a pillow with a projecting rim. The main decoration of a leaf scroll on a ground of small circles is edged with two plain bands separated by a thin band of ring-matting. The lines incised through the white slip appear to contain brown pigment. The transparent glaze is crazed. Body: buff, medium-fine.

Dimensions: 15.1 × 13.6 cm. Body: 0.8 cm.
*Published: GGBWYYK 1980 (1) pp. 3–27, Pl. 5:9
Also WW 1964 (8) pp. 37–48, Pl. 1:2*

359–363

Unglazed fragments of pillows stamped with marks of the Zhang family
From Hebei Cizhou (1964:4)
Song dynasty (AD 960–1279)

These fragments from the unglazed bases of pillows have varying stamped marks indicating that they were made by the Zhang family. The body material in each case is buff and medium-fine.

359. The remains of the stamp reads (from right to left): . . . *jia zao* '. . . family made'

Dimensions: 9 × 4.4 cm. Body: 0.4 cm.
Published: WW 1964 (8) pp. 37–48, Fig. 24

360. This fragment appears to have kiln-grit burnt on to it. It is stamped, rather hard, with the characters reading horizontally: *Zhang jia zao*, 'Made by the Zhang family'.

Dimensions: 8.5 × 6 cm. Body: 0.4 cm.
Published: WW 1964 (8) pp. 37–48, Fig. 24

361. This fragment has the inscription stamped to read vertically: *Zhang jia*, 'Zhang family', and has the remains of a stamped scroll design above the characters.

Dimensions: 10.2 × 4.3 cm. Body: 0.4 cm.
Published: WW 1964 (8) pp. 37–48, Fig. 24

362. This stamp reads vertically: *Zhang jia zhen*, 'Zhang family pillow'. At each end of the stamp is an impressed lotus motif.

Dimensions: 11.5 × 6.8 cm. Body: 0.4 cm.

363. This fragment shows the bottom part of a stamp reading vertically: . . . *jia zao*, '. . . family made'. The stamp is decorated at the end with a floral motif.

Dimensions: 7.4 × 6.3 cm. Body: 0.2 cm.
Published: WW 1964 (8) pp. 37–48, Fig. 24

Henan   nos. 364–428

A range of the many kilns of Henan are represented, notably the group which is related to the Cizhou kilns just across the border in Hebei. The identification of Gong xian kilns is illustrated and the point is made, as at Ding, that major kilns made a great variety of wares in styles popular at the time.

Gong xian	nos. 364–372
Mi xian	nos. 373–381
Dengfeng	nos. 382–393
Yu xian	nos. 394–402
Lushan	nos. 403–416
Baofeng	nos. 417–428

Gong xian   nos. 364–372

In 1959 three kiln sites were discovered, the largest in scale being that at Tiejianglucun. The manufacture of pots in Gong xian began in the Sui, with important developments taking place in the Tang. The white wares, which formed the bulk of the production, were made as tribute wares for the palace in the *Kaiyuan* reign period (AD 713–756). In the Tang dynasty, at Gong xian, *san cai*, or 'three colour', wares were also being produced. It is the only kiln producing *san cai* wares of the Tang period to have been discovered. The unglazed vessels were given a preliminary firing, and the successful pieces were then glazed and fired a second time. Fragments of marbled pillows have also been found at the kiln site, and it seems likely, therefore, that Tang dynasty pillows of marbled clay, with the inscriptions 'Pillow decorated by the Du family' or 'Pillow decorated by the Pei family', were products of Gong xian.

364

Fragment of a bowl with cream slip and transparent glaze
From Henan Gong xian (1957:7)
Tang dynasty (AD 618–906)

This part of a bowl has a rounded wall with a straight rim tapering from the outside and a wide foot with a shallow recessed base tooled to leave a nipple of clay in the centre. The body material is greyish white and medium-coarse. It has a cream slip and the transparent glaze runs in tears on the outside to the foot.

Dimensions: 10.8 × 8.8 cm. Diameter of base: 7 cm.
Body: 0.7 cm.

365

Part of a foliated bowl with a cream slip and a clear glaze
From Henan Gong xian (1957:7)
Tang dynasty (AD 618–906)

This fragment is part of a bowl with spreading sides and a foliated rim. Ribs on the cavetto correspond with the foliations. The wide foot ring surrounds the shallow recessed base which is glazed. Spur marks are visible inside the bowl and have been trimmed off round the foot ring. The greyish white, fine body has a cream slip and a transparent glaze which runs thickly outside to the foot.

Height: 4 cm. Diameter: 14 cm. (approx.)
Body: 0.3–0.6 cm.

366

Part of a bowl with cream slip and transparent glaze
From Henan Gong xian (1957:7)
Tang dynasty (AD 618–906)

This fragment is part of the side of a rounded bowl with an everted rim, a wide foot ring which is straight on the outside and inclined on the inside. The bowl was fired on the foot ring. Kiln grit adheres to the outside of the foot. The flat base is glazed. The creamy white, fine body is slipped and glazed with a clear glaze which is minutely crazed.

Dimensions: 10 × 10 cm. Body: 0.5 cm.

367

Part of a bottle with a blue glaze
From Henan Gong xian (1957:7)
Tang dynasty (AD 618–906)

This piece is part of a bottle with a globular body, a high, spreading foot everted at the base. There is a thin ring of glaze on the base inside the foot ring which has been sliced off. The bottle is unglazed on the inside and glazed on the outside with a dark blue lead glaze. The body material is off-white earthenware.

Height: 14 cm. Diameter of body: 11.7 cm.
Diameter of foot: 7.2 cm. Body: 0.7 cm.
Published: WWCKZL 1959 (3) p. 57, Fig. 7

368
Fragment of a jar with green and brown splashed
glaze (*san cai*)
From Henan Gong xian (1957:7)
Tang dynasty (AD 618–906)

This section from the rounded shoulder of a jar is
incised with a band of four lines. The outside is
decorated with a green and brown splashed lead
glaze. The body is a chalky pinkish-white
earthenware.

Dimensions: 8.5 × 5.5 cm. Body: 0.4 cm.
Published: GGBWYYK 1980 (1) pp. 3–27, Fig. 18
Also *WWCKZL 1959 (3) pp. 56–58, Fig. 6*

369
Part of a ewer with a black glaze
From Henan Gong xian (1957:7)
Tang dynasty (AD 618–906)

This piece is part of a ewer with a rounded shoulder,
a high flaring neck and a short, straight spout. The
black iron oxide glaze with iridescent streaks covers
the pale buff, coarse body on the outside of the ewer
and partially inside.

Dimensions: 13 × 10.5 cm. Body: 0.6 cm.

370
Fragment of a pillow with a design in marbled clay
From Henan Gong xian (1957:7)
Tang dynasty (AD 618–906)

This fragment of a pillow shows, on the unglazed
underside, a smooth buff body. On the top surface the
body is overlaid with a floral design in marbling of
black and grey clay. Traces of a clear glaze are visible
over the marbling. There are fabric impressions on
the body on the underside.

Dimensions: 8.5 × 8.3 cm. Body: 0.6 cm.
Published: GGBWYYK 1980 (1) pp. 3–27, Fig. 18

371
Sherd of a bowl with a blue-splashed glaze
From Henan Gong xian (1957:7)
Tang dynasty (AD 618–906)

This sherd of a bowl with an everted rim and a ridge
around the outside is decorated with blue splashes in
the glaze over a thin, cream slip. The glaze is
iridescent in places. The body is chalky-white
earthenware.

Dimensions: 12.2 × 6 cm. Body: 0.6 cm.
Published: GGBWYYK 1980 (1) pp. 3–27, Fig. 18

372
Part of an unglazed dish with stamped decoration
From Henan Gong xian (1957:7)
Tang dynasty (AD 618–906)

This fragment is part of a dish with a flat base, a
rounded wall and a square cut rim, slightly
constricted on the outside. In the centre of the inside
base is a single formalised flower impressed into the
buff body. There is a cream slip on the inside but the
dish is unglazed except for an accidental splash of
green glaze on the outside wall.

Height: 6 cm. Radius: 9.6 cm. Body: 0.6–0.8 cm.
Published: GGBWYYK 1980 (1) pp. 3–27, Fig. 18

Mi xian nos. 373–381

Two kiln sites were discovered in Mi xian. Remains of the Tang and Song
periods at Xiguan demonstrate that, in addition to pots with incised decoration
against a ring-punched background, white wares, yellow glazed, blue glazed
and black glazed wares were also made at the kiln. Xiguan seems to have been
the earliest source of vessels with decoration against a ring-punched ground, a
technique derived from metalwork of the Tang dynasty. The other kiln at
Yaogou has produced Jin and Yuan remains. White wares were the main
product, but pots with simple designs in black on a white ground were also
made.

373
Part of a bowl with a cream slip and clear glaze
From Henan Mi xian (1962:5)
Tang dynasty (AD 618–906)

This fragment is part of a bowl with a rounded wall,
a flattened and constricted rim, and a wide, shallow
foot which is recessed in the centre. The light grey,
smooth body is visible where the cream slip and clear
glaze stop short of the foot. There are three spur
marks on the inside base and three on the foot ring.

Height: 3.6 cm. Width: 9.6 cm.
Diameter of base: 5.2 cm. Body: 0.4 cm.

374
Section of the neck of a ewer with a yellow glaze
From Henan Mi xian (1962:5)
Tang dynasty (AD 618–906)

This section of the neck of a ewer has a band of
incised grooves around the outside, and two lug
handles composed of double cylinders of clay, one on
the neck and one joined to the shoulder. The neck is
glazed inside and out with the remains of a yellow
glaze. The grey medium-coarse body, which contains
black specks, is covered with a cream slip before
glazing.

Height: 4.3 cm. Diameter of neck: 6.5 cm.
Body: 0.4 cm.

375
Fragment from the side of a pillow with incised
decoration on a background of small circles
From Henan Mi xian (1962)
Tang dynasty (AD 618–906)

This section from the side of a pillow has a band of
floral decoration against a background of small
circles incised through the cream slip. The incisions
appear to be filled with ferruginous slip under the
clear glaze. The body is of a grey-buff, medium-
coarse material. The pillow is unglazed on the inside.

Dimensions: 10.7 × 7.5 cm. Body: 0.5 cm.
Published: WW 1964 (3) pp. 47–55, 45, Fig. 8:4

376
Fragment of a pillow with designs stamped through
the cream slip
From Henan Mi xian (1962)
Tang dynasty (AD 618–906)

The sherd from the side of a pillow has a band of
decoration consisting of alternate vertical rows of
circles and daisy-like motifs stamped through the
cream slip and filled with a rust brown ferruginous
slip under the clear glaze. The grey-buff, medium-
coarse body is unglazed on the inside.

Dimensions: 7 × 5.1 cm. Body: 0.7 cm.
Published: WW 1964 (3) pp. 47–55, 45, Fig. 8:2

377
Part of the top of a pillow with incised decoration
against a background of small circles
From Henan Mi xian (1962)
Tang dynasty (AD 618–906)

This piece from the top of a kidney-shaped pillow is
decorated with a quail among foliage against a
background of small circles incised through the
cream slip. The incisions appear filled with brown,
ferruginous slip under the clear glaze. The fragment
has a grey-buff, medium-coarse body and is unglazed
on the inside. The remains of another item adheres
to the top.

Dimensions: 11.7 × 10 cm. Body: 0.5 cm.
Published: WW 1964 (3) pp. 47–55, 45, Fig. 7

378
Pillow with an incised decoration of a parrot among
foliage on a background of circles
Henan Mi xian type (From the Gugong, Peking)
Tang dynasty (AD 618–906)

This kidney-shaped pillow is decorated on the top
with a design (incised through the cream slip and
filled with ferruginous slip) of a parrot among
scrolling foliage against a background of small
circles. Round the sides is a band of alternate vertical
rows of three daisy-like rosettes and four rings
between two lines. There is a hole in the back of the
pillow. The buff body is covered with a cream slip on
all sides, including the base, but the glaze runs short
of the base on which the pillow was fired.

Height: 7 cm (back), 6 cm. (front)
Dimensions: 17 × 12 cm.
*Published: Chūgoku Nisen nen no Bi (Beauty of Two
Thousand Years in China), Tokyo, 1965, Pl. 73*

379
Fragment of a bowl with decoration incised through
the slip
From Henan Mi xian (1962:5)
Song dynasty (AD 960–1279)

This sherd from the base of a bowl is decorated on the
inside with a floral design incised through the cream
slip to the grey-buff, medium-coarse body. The wide
foot ring, which is rounded and slightly inverted, is
slipped. Both the foot ring and base are unglazed.

Dimensions: 4.6 × 4.2 cm. Body: 0.8 cm.

380
Fragment of a brush washer with decoration incised
through the slip
From Henan Mi xian (1962:5)
Song dynasty (AD 960–1279)

This sherd is a fragment of a brush washer with a flat
unglazed base. The rounded walls and inside base
are decorated with a floral design incised through
the cream slip to the grey-buff, medium-coarse body,
and covered with a clear glaze.

Height: 5.3 cm. Width of base: 3 cm.
Body: 0.4–0.6 cm. (base)
Published: WW 1964 (3) pp. 47–55, 45, Fig. 9:4

381
Sherd from the wall of a jar with incised decoration
on a ground of small circles
From Henan Mi xian (1962:5)
Song dynasty (AD 960–1279)

This sherd from the foliated wall and everted rim of a
jar has an incised decoration of a scroll band beneath
the rim on the inside and outside, and beneath that
on the outside a floral design on a ground of tiny
circles. The decoration is incised through the cream
slip to the grey-buff, medium-coarse body. The piece
is glazed with a transparent glaze.

Dimensions: 6 × 6 cm. Body: 0.4 cm.
Published: WW 1964 (3) pp. 47–55, 45, Fig. 8:3

Dengfeng   nos. 382–393

This kiln at Quhezhen was active from the Tang to the Yuan dynasty, reaching
its peak in the Song dynasty. Pots decorated with incised designs against ring-
punched backgrounds were made in abundance. A large number of examples of
different types of bottles, some of more than 40 centimetres in height, have also
survived, fragments of pillows with incised and ring-punched decoration have
been found in large quantities at the 10 kilns in the provinces of Henan, Hebei
and Shanxi, and many have been excavated from Song tombs in the north.

382
Part of a jar with a black glaze
From Henan Dengfeng (1962:5)
Song dynasty (AD 960–1279)

This fragment of a jar with lobed sides and an
everted rim has a black glaze on the outside and a
white slip with a transparent glaze inside. The coarse
body appears buff.

Dimensions: 7.7 × 4.7 cm. Body: 0.3 cm.

383
Part of a bowl with a cream slip and a clear glaze
From Henan Dengfeng (1962:5)
Song dynasty (AD 960–1279)

This fragment is part of a bowl with rounded sides
and a small, neat foot. The piece was fired on small
supports on the foot. The grey, fine body is covered
all over with the cream slip, but the clear glaze stops
short of the foot.

Height: 4.2 cm. Diameter: 10.8 cm.
Diameter of foot: 4.4 cm. Body: 0.4 cm.

384
Part of the neck and shoulder of a *meiping* vase with
incised designs on a background of small circles
From Henan Dengfeng (1962:5)
Song dynasty (AD 960–1279)

This fragment from a *meiping* vase has a short neck
with an inverted rim, stepped on the inside to
accommodate a lid. The rounded shoulder is
decorated with a band of peony scroll on a ground of
small circles incised through the cream slip. The
incisions appear to be filled with dark brown
ferruginous slip. The body material is medium-coarse
and is glazed inside and out with a clear glaze.

Dimensions: 12 × 5.5 cm. Body: 0.5 cm.
The body is as thick as 1.0 cm. in places.

385
Section of the top of a pillow with a peony decoration
on a background of small circles
From Henan Dengfeng (1962:5)
Song dynasty (AD 960–1279)

This sherd from the top of a pillow has a design of a
peony scroll on a ground of small circles incised
through the cream slip and filled with brown
ferruginous slip. The medium-coarse body appears
orange-buff where it is exposed on the underside.
The outside is glazed with a transparent glaze.

Dimensions: 8.7 × 6.5 cm. Body: 0.7 cm.

386
Part of the base and wall of a *meiping* vase with
incised decoration
From Henan Dengfeng (1962:5)
Song dynasty (AD 960–1279)

This fragment from the lower part of a *meiping* vase
has an incised decoration of a band of lotus petals
above which is a part of the background of small
circles for the main band of design. The dark grey,
coarse body appears black beneath the slip. The
inside is unglazed. The recessed base and inside of
the inclined, roughly cut foot ring are merely slipped.
The outside is glazed with a clear glaze.

Height: 12.5 cm. Body: 0.5–1.0 cm.

387
Part of a cup with carved grooves under a cream slip
and a clear glaze
From Henan Dengfeng (1962:5)
Song dynasty (AD 960–1279)

This is part of a globular cup with deeply carved
grooves up the sides. The inverted rim has two
horizontal ridges on the outside. The cream slip and
clear glaze stop short of the flat foot and the recessed
base, where the buff, medium-coarse body has burnt
reddish brown. Kiln grit adheres to the outside of
the cup.

Height: 4.8 cm. Diameter of base: 3.6 cm.
Body: 0.3 cm.

388
Part of a cup with grooves carved through the slip
into the body
From Henan Dengfeng (1962:5)
Song dynasty (AD 960–1279)

This fragment is from the base of a cup with rounded
sides, a minimal foot ring and a recessed base. The
inside of the cup is slipped and glazed, while the
outside walls are carved with grooves through the
cream slip into the dark brownish-buff body under a
clear glaze. The slip and glaze are trimmed above the
foot. Three spur marks are visible inside the cup.

Dimensions: 11 × 10.5 cm. Body: 0.4–0.9 cm.
Published: WW 1964 (3) pp. 47–55, 45, Fig. 13

389
Fragment of a flask with decoration carved and
incised through the cream slip
From Henan Dengfeng (1962:5)
Song dynasty (AD 960–1279)

This sherd from the wall of a flask has a lotus design
deeply carved, and with details incised, through the
cream slip to the dark grey coarse body. The cream
slip and clear glaze are on the outside only.

Dimensions: 6.4 × 6.4 cm. Body: 0.4–0.7 cm.

390
Part of a jar with a yellow glaze
From Henan Dengfeng (1962:5)
Song dynasty (AD 960–1279)

This fragment is part of a jar with a globular body, a
straight neck and a flat constricted rim. The body is
light buff and medium-coarse, and is covered with a
cream slip and a yellow-olive glaze, except on the rim
which is unglazed.

Height: 7 cm. Width: 8.3 cm. Body: 0.4–0.5 cm.

391
Fragment from the corner of a pillow
From Henan Dengfeng (1962:5)
Song dynasty (AD 960–1279)

This sherd from the corner of a pillow has a flat top
and, on the side, the remains of a moulded monster
face. The outside is decorated with green and amber
splashed glazes. On the unglazed underside fabric
impressions are visible where the top and side are
slabbed together. The top protrudes over the join.
The body is a chalky buff colour.

Dimensions: 8 × 3 cm. Body: 0.5 cm.

392
Fragment of a pillow with a green glaze
From Henan Dengfeng (1962:5)
Song dynasty (AD 960–1279)

This sherd from the edge of the top of a pillow has an
incised feather-like spray within two incised lines
around the rim under a green lead glaze. The chalky,
pinkish-white coarse earthenware body has a splash
of green glaze on the inside which is otherwise
unglazed.

Dimensions: 8.5 × 7.7 cm. Body: 1.0 cm.

393
Fragment of a dish with incised decoration under
green and amber glaze painting
From Henan Dengfeng (1962:5)
Song dynasty (AD 960–1279)

Fragment from the base of a dish with a thick, flat
base, incised on the inside base with a peony. On top
of the chalky-buff body is a layer of slip and a
transparent glaze with green and amber lead glaze
painting.

Dimensions: 10 × 7.4 cm. Body: 1.5 cm.

Yu xian   nos. 394–402

Almost a hundred kilns, active from the Tang to the Yuan dynasties, have been discovered in Yu xian. The excavation of the kiln at Baguadong, which can be taken as representative, provided evidence of the source of the large quantity of Jun ware boxes, vases, and brush washers with numbers inscribed on the base, that have survived. The excavated specimens show that these pieces were made for the court in the latter part of the Northern Song. Apart from Jun ware, greenwares with moulded decoration were also produced at Baguadong, as well as other types of ware for popular use, such as those with black designs painted on a white ground. The later limit of the kilns' activity lay in the Jin or Yuan period.

394
Fragment of a basin with a pale blue glaze
From Henan Yu xian Jun ware kiln (1973)
Song dynasty (AD 960–1279)

This sherd is part of a basin constructed in a mould with a straight, square cut rim below which are two raised lines containing a row of studs on the rounded wall above the foot ring, to which is attached a small bracket foot. The body is fine and buff coloured, darkening to grey towards the glazed exterior. The glaze is predominantly pale blue and is brown on the base and foot ring. The size number 8 is stamped into the base.

Height: 6 cm. Dimensions: 10.2 × 11 cm. Body: 0.6 cm.

395
Part of a basin with a pale blue glaze
From Henan Yu xian Jun ware kiln (1973)
Song dynasty (AD 960–1279)

This sherd is part of a basin constructed in a mould with a rounded wall, and a row of 'drum nail' studs above the short, stout foot ring, to which a small bracket foot is attached. It is stamped number 7 on the base under the glaze. The glaze is predominantly pale bluish lavender in colour, powder blue on the foot, and khaki on the base, foot ring and studs. The glaze is pitted and runs in rivers on the inside. The body is fine and buff coloured.

Dimensions: 9 × 8.3 cm. Body: 0.4–0.7 cm.

396
Fragment of a 'drum nail' basin with a purple glaze
From Henan Yu xian Jun ware kiln (1973)
Song dynasty (AD 960–1279)

This fragment of a 'drum nail' basin has a flat base and the remains of two bracket feet. The glaze is purple outside, and pale blue on the inside base spreading to purple on the walls. The base is glazed brown and stamped with the number 9. The body is grey, appearing reduced to white between body and glaze.

Dimensions: 11 × 7.2 cm. Body: 0.5–0.6 cm.

397
Fragment of a basin with a sky blue glaze
From Henan Yu xian Jun ware kiln (1973)
Song dynasty (AD 960–1279)

This part of a basin has a rounded wall and a row of 'drum nail' studs beneath the square cut rim and between two raised ridges, and another row above the foot ring, to which would probably have been attached small feet, such as on nos. 394 and 395. The glaze is predominantly sky blue, streaked with a whitish blue, and is khaki and brown on the base. The body is fine and buff, turning to grey towards the exterior.

Dimensions: 17.5 × 7.5 cm. Body: 0.5–1.0 cm.

398
Fragment of a flower pot with blue and purple glaze
From Henan Yu xian Jun ware kiln (1973)
Song dynasty (AD 960–1279)

This fragment is part of a flower pot with straight,
spreading sides and a small foot at the corner where
two sides join. The flat base is pierced with five holes
and inscribed with the number 10. The glaze is a
pale blue opalescent colour with purple tinges. The
glaze on the base is khaki. The body is fine and buff
coloured.

Height: 9 cm. Body: 0.8–1.0 cm.

399
Part of a foliated flower pot with coloured glazes
From Henan Yu xian Jun ware kiln (1973)
Song dynasty (AD 960–1279)

This part of a flower bowl has a foliated shape, small
cabriole legs and a flat base inscribed with the
number 7. The glaze on the inside base is an
opalescent blue merging to a purple towards the
well. The base is glazed brown and khaki. The
greyish-buff body appears paler towards the exterior.

Dimensions: 11 × 9.6 cm. Body: 0.7 cm.

400
Fragment of a flower pot with coloured glazes
From Henan Yu xian Jun ware kiln (1973)
Song dynasty (AD 960–1279)

This fragment has a rounded wall, a thick, spreading
foot and a flat recessed base pierced with four (out of
five) holes, and stamped with the number 6. The
piece is glazed purple on the outside, pale blue inside,
and green and brown on the base. The fine, buff body
appears grey where exposed on the base.

Dimensions: 13.5 × 12 cm. Body: 0.7–0.9 cm.

401
Fragment of a vessel (*zun*) with coloured glazes
From Henan Yu xian Jun ware kiln (1973)
Song dynasty (AD 960–1279)

This fragment has a rounded wall, a thick spreading
foot and a flat base which is pierced with a hole and
inscribed with the number 1. Inside the glaze is a
streaky pale blue, and outside a pinkish purple
merging to blue on the foot. On the base the glaze is a
khaki colour. The body appears grey, whitening
towards the edges.

Dimensions: 14 × 9 cm. Body: 0.5–0.8 cm.
(Thickness of foot: 1.0 cm.)

402
Base of a flower pot with a sky blue glaze
From Henan Yu xian Jun ware kiln (1973)
Song dynasty (AD 960–1279)

This fragment of a flower pot with rounded,
spreading sides and a thick, spreading, rounded foot
is pierced through the base with a hole. The glaze is a
bright sky blue on the inside base and the outside of
the foot, and brown on the base and foot ring. The
fine buff body appears dark grey towards the edge on
the underside.

Diameter of base: 15 cm.
Body: 1.2 cm. (base)–1.4 cm. (foot ring)

Lushan   nos. 403–416

The Duandian kiln site at Lushan has been re-examined, and it is now known
that vessels with a black glaze decorated with paler mottling were being made
there as early as the Tang dynasty. Ten pieces of the 'decorated ceramic drums
from Lushan', mentioned in the Tang dynasty work, *Jie Qu Lu*, were found in
the kiln, thus providing evidence of the location of the kiln where the surviving
ceramic drums were made. In the Song dynasty the quantity and range of
wares produced greatly increased. Examples in the exhibition, such as the white
wares with combed decoration, have rarely been found at other kilns, and the
san cai, or 'three colour', pottery pillow in the form of a lion and the lamp carved
with a lotus petal decoration, have distinctive features, characteristic of Lushan.

426
427
413
424
391
425
393
382
404
390
392
403

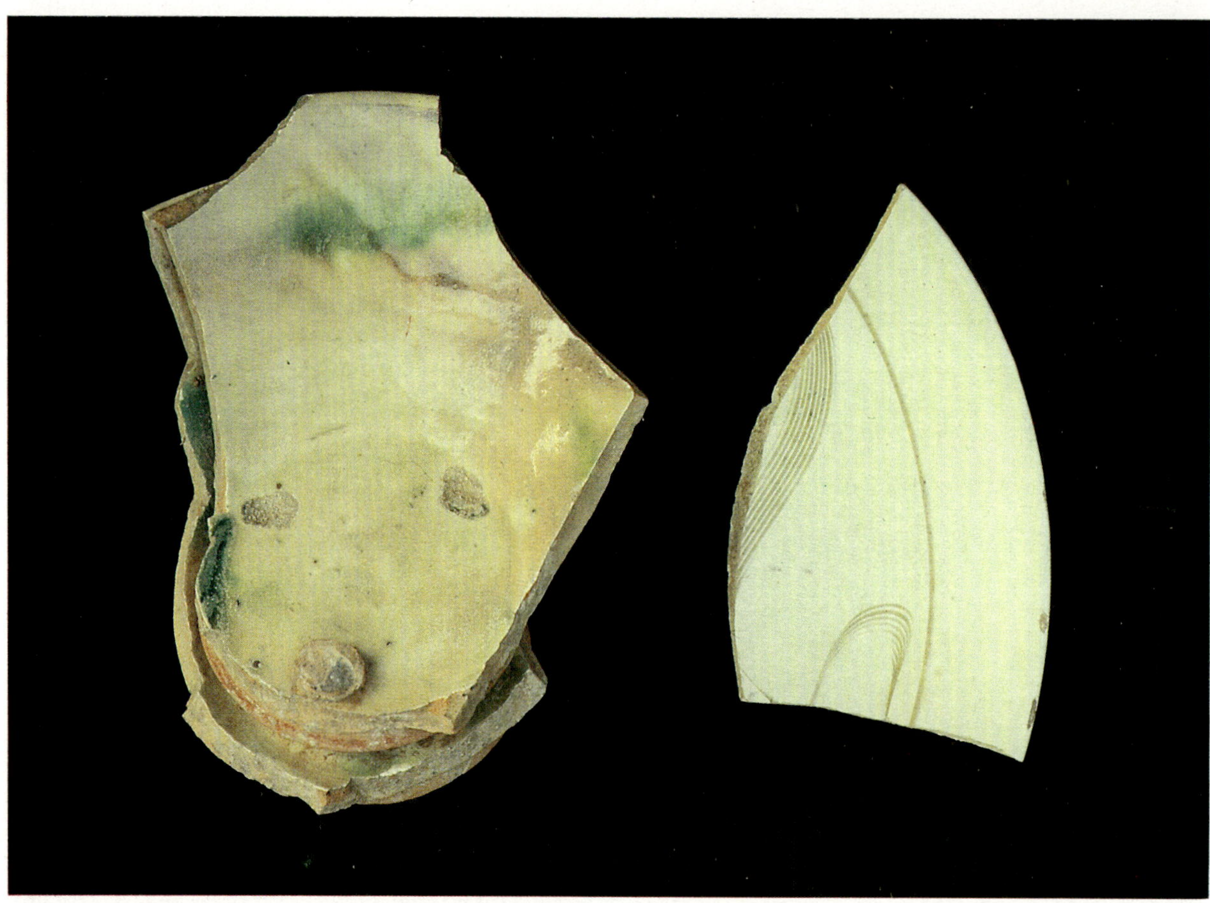

431 432

433 434

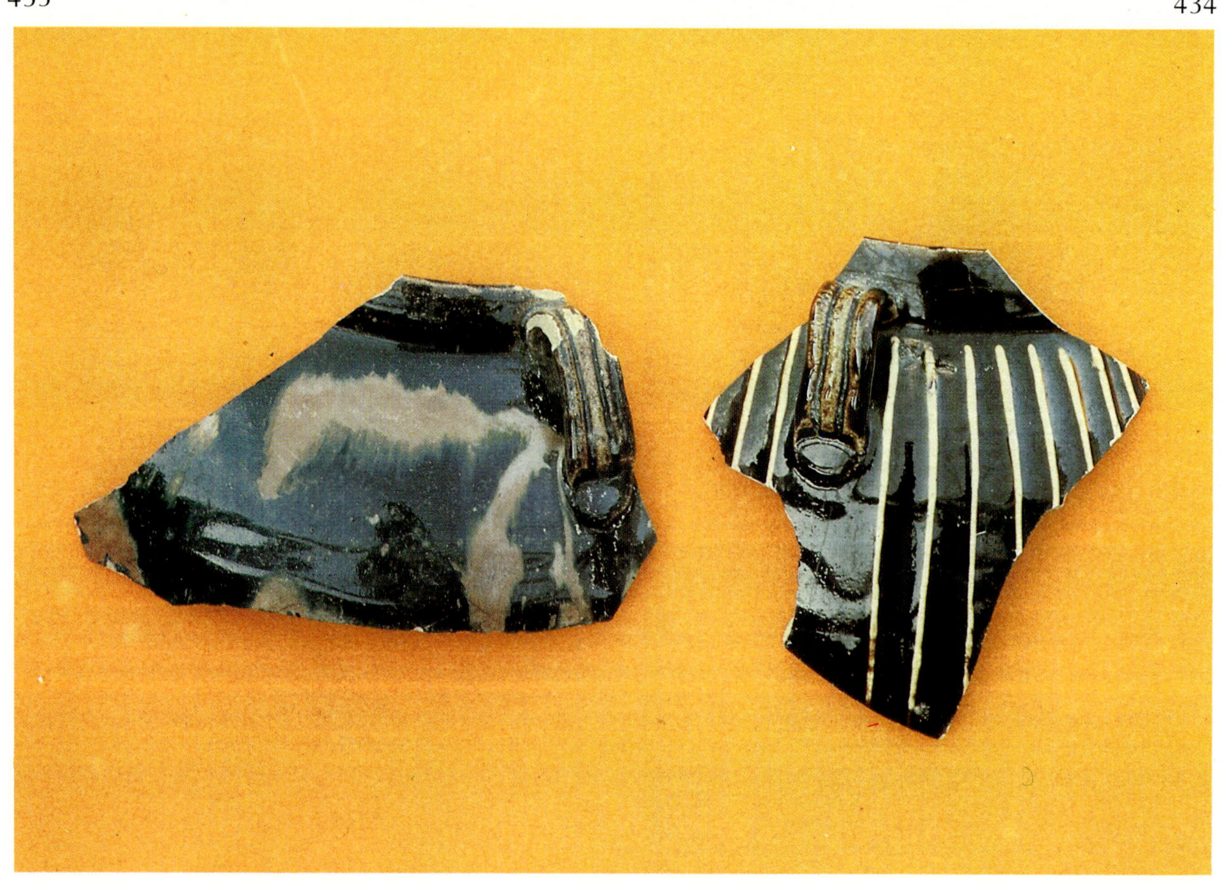

403
Fragment of a drum with a black glaze with bluish
mottling
From Henan Lushan (1977:4)
Tang dynasty (AD 618–906)

This sherd is a fragment of a drum which tapers at
the waist where it is decorated with ribs. The outside
is glazed with a black ash glaze with bluish splashes.
The light grey body is coarse and hard.

Dimensions: 15.6 × 10 cm. Body: 1.1 cm.
Published: GGBWYYK 1980 (1) pp. 3–27, Fig. 19
Also WW 1980 (5) pp. 52–60, Fig. 2

404
Fragment of a drum with a brown glaze with bluish
patches
From Henan Lushan (1977:4)
Tang dynasty (AD 618–906)

This part of the ribbed waist of a drum is glazed on
the outside with an ash glaze with a brown tea dust
effect with bluish-white splashes. The body is grey,
coarse and hard.

Dimensions: 16.4 × 10.1 cm. Body: 0.4–0.8 cm.
Published: GGBWYYK 1980 (1) pp. 3–27, Fig. 19

405
Fragment of a vase with decoration incised through
the slip and a ring-punched ground
From Henan Lushan (1977:4)
Song dynasty (AD 960–1279)

This sherd from the wall of a vase is decorated with a
horizontal petal band on a ringed background and
vertical bands enclosing repeated circles filled with
smaller circles. The decoration is incised through the
cream slip, appears filled with black ferruginous slip
and covered with a clear glaze. The inside of the vase
is unglazed. The light greyish-buff body is coarse and
dry.

Dimensions: 7.2 × 7 cm. Body: 0.5 cm.
Published: WW 1980 (5) pp. 52–60, Fig. 11

406
Fragment of a vase with decoration incised through
the slip and a ring-punched ground
From Henan Lushan (1977:4)
Song dynasty (AD 960–1279)

This sherd from the wall of a vase is decorated with a
horizontal band of leaf scroll, on a ground of
relatively loosely punched rings, incised through the
cream slip to reveal the greyish-buff, coarse, dry body
which has a slight iron tinge. The outside is glazed
with a clear glaze and the inside of the vase is
unglazed.

Dimensions: 7.8 × 6.6 cm. Body: 0.6 cm.
Published: WW 1980 (5) pp. 52–60, Fig. 11

407
Fragment of a vase with decoration incised through
the slip and a ring-punched ground
From Henan Lushan (1977:4)
Song dynasty (AD 960–1279)

This sherd from the wall of a vase is decorated with a
camellia on a tightly packed ring-punched ground.
The decoration is incised through the cream slip and
the incisions appear filled with dark brown
ferruginous slip. The outside is coated with a clear
glaze. The inside is unglazed. The light grey-buff
body is coarse and dry.

Dimensions: 8.8 × 6.5 cm. Body: 0.4 cm.
Published: WW 1980 (5) pp. 52–60, Fig. 11

408
Fragment of a pillow with incised decoration under a
green glaze
From Henan Lushan (1977:4)
Song dynasty (AD 960–1279)

This sherd from the top of a pillow has an incised
floral decoration within a band of double line around
the edge. The green lead glaze covers the chalky
white, medium-coarse body on the outside of the
pillow.

Dimensions: 8.7 × 6.3 cm. Body: 0.6 cm.
Published: WW 1980 (5) pp. 52–60, Fig. 10

409
Part of a lamp with incised decoration and green and
amber glaze
From Henan Lushan (1977:4)
Song dynasty (AD 960–1279)

This fragment of a lamp has a round neck with a
broad, flattened rim which curves downwards on the
outside edge and which is slightly ridged where
joined to the neck. The rim is decorated with an
incised petal design under a runny green glaze. On
the underside it is glazed with an amber glaze. The
medium-coarse body is a chalky white material.

Width of rim: 3.8 cm. Overall length: 10.5 cm.
Body: 0.5 cm.

410
Sherd from the wall of a vase with decoration incised
through the slip
From Henan Lushan (1977:4)
Song dynasty (AD 960–1279)

This sherd from the wall of a vase is decorated with
sketchy panels incised in the cream slip, the incisions
being filled with a dark brown ferruginous slip. The
outside is glazed with a clear glaze and the inside is
unglazed. The body is dry and coarse, and greyish
buff with a slight iron tinge.

Dimensions: 6.7 × 5 cm. Body: 0.5 cm.

411

Fragment of a pillow with a wave design incised and combed through the cream slip
From Henan Lushan (1977:4)
Song dynasty (AD 960–1279)

This sherd from the rim of a pillow is decorated with an incised and combed design of waves within a foliated panel bordered by two lines. The lines incised through the cream slip reveal a light grey body, but the section and unglazed interior show a second, darker and more coarse layer of body material.

Dimensions: 10.8 × 6.7 cm. Body: 0.6 cm.
Published: WW 1980 (5) pp. 52–60, Fig. 11

412

Fragment of a pillow with decoration painted in dark brown over a cream slip
From Henan Lushan (1977:4)
Song dynasty (AD 960–1279)

This fragment from the curved edge of a pillow is decorated on top with bands of varying widths enclosing a petal band painted in dark brown over the cream slip, and on the side with a band of meandering key-fret pattern reversed in white on a dark brown ground. The buff body is coarse and thick, and the outside is glazed with a clear glaze.

Height: 3.2 cm. Dimensions: 8.8 × 6.3 cm.
Body: 1.4 cm.

413

Part of a lid with a black glaze and white ribs
From Henan Lushan (1977:4)
Song dynasty (AD 960–1279)

This large sherd is a fragment of a lid in the shape of a lotus leaf with a foliated upturned rim and a high domed top, down which radiate ribs in groups of three made of white slip. The whole of the top of the lid is glazed with a black iron oxide glaze, while the inside and the underside of the rim are unglazed. The light grey body is coarse and dry.

Inside diameter: 14.5 cm.
Maximum diameter: 19.5 cm. Body: 0.5 cm.

414

Fragment of a pillow with green and yellow lead glazes
From Henan Lushan (1977:4)
Song dynasty (AD 960–1279)

This fragment from the corner of a pillow with a flat top which protrudes over the sides and a flat, unglazed base is decorated with a monster face moulded in relief and covered with green and yellow lead glazes. The finger prints of the potter who pressed the clay into the mould are still clearly visible on the inside. The body is a chalky white material.

Height: 9 cm. Width: 9.2 cm. Body: 0.4 cm.
Published: WW 1980 (5) pp. 52–60, Fig. 10

415

Meiping vase with designs combed through the cream slip
Henan Lushan type (From the Gugong, Peking)
Song dynasty (AD 960–1279)

This vase has a high rounded shoulder tapering towards the flat broad foot ring and the flat recessed base. The short neck is surmounted by a sloping lip. Combed through the cream slip are five double bands of wavy lines separated by five bands of straight lines. The base is slipped but unglazed and the outside of the vase is covered with a clear glaze. The piece has been extensively repaired.

Height: 21 cm. Diameter of base: 8.2 cm.

416

Fragment of a vase with decoration combed through the cream slip
From Henan Lushan (1977:4)
Song dynasty (AD 960–1279)

This sherd from the rounded shoulder of a vase is decorated with vertical bands of combed lines, one band of straight lines for every two of waves. The decoration is combed through the cream slip and appears to be filled with brown ferruginous slip. The vase has a grey body and is covered with a clear glaze.

Dimensions: 10.5 × 7 cm. Body: 0.4 cm.
Published: WW 1980 (5) pp. 52–60, Fig. 11

Baofeng   nos. 417–428

The kiln, at the Qindong Temple, was discovered in 1950 and re-examined in 1977. Among the rich variety of products were found green wares with moulded and carved decoration, white wares with incised designs or decoration in green, *san cai*, or 'three colour', pottery as well as black glazed and brown glazed wares. Most of the black glazed wares were decorated in fine, raised lines; those with grain-like incisions in the glaze being the most unusual. The Baofeng kiln was active in the Song and Jin dynasties, and the wares show a certain influence from Yaozhou and Cizhou wares.

417
Part of a lid with a design cut through the glaze
From Henan Baofeng (1977:4)
Song dynasty (AD 960–1279)

This sherd is a fragment of a lid with a domed top and a horizontal rim with a vertical flange beneath. On the dome and as a border for the rim is a pattern of 'rice grain' nicks through the brownish-black glaze to the putty-coloured fine body. The inside of the dome is glazed but the underside of the rim is unglazed.

Dimensions: 7 × 3.7 cm. Body: 0.3 cm.
Published: GGBWYYK 1980 (1) pp. 3–27, Pl. 5:16

418
Fragment of a jar with a floral motif carved through the black glaze
From Henan Baofeng (1977:4)
Song dynasty (AD 960–1279)

This sherd has a thin wash of black glaze on the inside, and on the outside a layer of thick black glaze through which is carved a flower-like motif, consisting of two concentric circles of radiating 'melon pip' nicks, within a square panel. The body beneath the glaze is fine and putty-coloured.

Dimensions: 9.2 × 4.7 cm. Body: 0.3 cm.
Published: GGBWYYK 1980 (1) pp. 3–27, Pl. 5:14

419
Part of a black jar with white ribs
From Henan Baofeng (1977:4)
Song dynasty (AD 960–1279)

This sherd is part of a jar with an upright neck and a rolled rim, and with a small lug handle high on the rounded shoulder which is decorated with ribs of white slip. The black iron oxide glaze, which is thin enough on the ribs to allow the contrasting white through, has iridised with brown streaks on the inside of the jar. The body is fine and putty-coloured.

Height: 6.2 cm. Width: 11 cm. Body: 0.4 cm.
Published: GGBWYYK 1980 (1) pp. 3–27, Pl. 5:15

420
Fragment of a vase with an olive glaze
From Henan Baofeng (1977:4)
Song dynasty (AD 960–1279)

This sherd from the wall of a vase has the remains of a thick out-turned lip and is decorated on the outside with deeply carved vertical grooves, every second one carved more deeply and with a serrated edge forming a stylised petal design. The shiny, crackled olive glaze covers the outside and part of the inside below the neck. The grey body is thick and medium-coarse.

Dimensions: 13.5 × 8 cm. Body: 0.2–1.2 cm.
Published: GGBWYYK 1980 (1) pp. 3–27, Fig. 20

421
Fragment of a bowl with carved and combed
decoration under an olive glaze
From Henan Baofeng (1977:4)
Song dynasty (AD 960–1279)

This sherd from the spreading wall of a bowl with a
straight rim is decorated on the inside with a carved
and combed design of peony leaves. The piece is
glazed inside and out with the shiny and crazed
green glaze. The body is light grey and medium-
coarse.

Dimensions: 10.5 × 6.8 cm. Body: 0.3–0.5 cm.
Published: GGBWYYK 1980 (1) pp. 3–27, Fig. 20

422
Fragment of a dish with lotus decoration carved
through the cream slip
From Henan Baofeng (1977:4)
Song dynasty (AD 960–1279)

This sherd is a fragment from the base of a bowl with
a broad square cut foot. Spur marks are visible on
the foot ring as well as on the inside base which is
decorated with a design of lotus carved and incised
through the cream slip to the buff, medium-coarse
body. The clear glaze and the slip stop short of the
foot on the outside.

Dimensions: 10.6 × 7.5 cm. Body: 0.5 cm.

423
Part of a ewer with green splashing in the glaze
From Henan Baofeng (1977:4)
Song dynasty (AD 960–1279)

This sherd is part of a ewer with a foliated body.
There are the remains of a handle attached to the
shoulder which is grooved where it begins to taper
towards the neck. The grey coarse body which tends
to buff on the unglazed inside is slipped on the
outside with a cream slip and decorated with green
splashing in the transparent glaze.

Dimensions: 9 × 9 cm. Body: 0.5 cm.

424
Fragment from the corner of a pillow with a monster
face under an amber glaze
From Henan Baofeng (1977:4)
Song dynasty (AD 960–1279)

This sherd from the corner of a pillow with a flat
projecting top is decorated on the side with a
moulded monster face, similar to those from
Dengfeng (no. 391), and Lushan (no. 414). On the
top inside a double lined border is a pattern of lightly
incised marks which resemble animal fur. The
outside is glazed with a shiny amber glaze and as
with the other pillows the potter's finger prints are
clearly visible in the chalky white body on the inside.

Length: 11.5 cm. Body: 0.5 cm.

425
Part of a lamp with a green glaze
From Henan Baofeng (1977:4)
Song dynasty (AD 960–1279)

This sherd from the neck of a lamp has a wide
horizontal rim decorated with lightly incised lines.
Where it is joined to the neck there is an everted
ridge. The wall of the neck is carved with vertical
grooves. The whole piece is glazed with a shiny,
crazed green glaze over the chalky white body.

Height: 5.5 cm. Length: 10.5 cm. Body: 0.5 cm.

426
Sherd from a pillow with yellow and green glazes
over incised decoration
From Henan Baofeng (1977:4)
Song dynasty (AD 960–1279)

This sherd from a pillow is decorated with an incised
leaf design under a cream slip and with glazes of
yellow and green. The chalky white earthenware
body is unglazed on the inside.

Dimensions: 8 × 3.5 cm. Body: 0.7 cm.

427
Fragment of a pillow with amber and green glazes
over incised decoration
From Henan Baofeng (1977:4)
Song dynasty (AD 960–1279)

This sherd from the edge of the top of a pillow is
decorated with a repeated incised design of simple
quatrefoliate motifs with small circles in the
diamond-shaped spaces between them. The border
and leaves are glazed with green, and the spaces
with amber. The coarse grey body has a cream slip
under the glaze.

Dimensions: 6.5 × 5.6 cm. Body: 0.9 cm.

428
Fragment of a vase with incised and punched
decoration
From Henan Baofeng (1977:4)
Song dynasty (AD 960–1279)

This sherd from the wall of a vase has a band of
petals separated by two lines from another band of
decoration with a ring punched ground. The
decoration is incised through the cream slip and
filled with ferruginous slip. The outside is glazed with
a clear glaze, and the body appears grey, thick and
coarse on the unglazed inside.

Dimensions: 6.5 × 5.8 cm. Body: 0.9 cm.

Shandong   nos. 429–437

Ceramics from Shandong have not yet been fully studied but the investigation of
the kiln area near to Zibo show a kiln in a strong tradition close to Cizhou active
over several centuries.

Zibo   nos. 429–437

Zibo   nos. 429–437

In 1976 an intensive excavation was carried out at Cicun, 10 kilometres to the south-west of Zibo city. The excavated objects show that the kiln was active for six hundred years, from the Tang to the Yuan dynasties. In the Tang period the kiln mainly produced black glazed wares but in the Song changed to making white wares decorated with cut or incised decoration. In the Jin and Yuan periods the black glazed ware had a standing equal to that of the white. Decoration included the use of marbled clay, black painting on a white ground, and decoration in red and green on a white slip, all these types showing the influence of Cizhou wares.

429
Part of a bowl with a black glaze
From Shandong Zibo (1976)
Tang dynasty (AD 618–906)

This fragment is part of a bowl with rounded sides everted at the rim, a broad foot ring and a slightly recessed base with a nipple of clay in the centre. The side is sharply undercut where it meets the foot. The body is buff coloured and coarse and the very shiny iron black glaze is trimmed well short of the foot on the outside, to which kiln grit adheres.

Height: 9.4 cm. Width: 15 cm. Body: 0.6 cm.

430
Part of a dish with a black glaze
From Shandong Zibo (1976)
Tang dynasty (AD 618–906)

This fragment is part of a dish with a thick, flat base, spreading sides and an everted rim. Three spur marks are visible on the outside and inside base. The light grey coarse body burns light brown where exposed. The glossy black glaze covers the inside of the dish and is trimmed well short of the base on the outside.

Dimensions: 10.5 × 9.5 cm. Body: 0.4 cm.

431
The remains of two bowls stuck together during firing
From Shandong Zibo (1976)
Tang dynasty (AD 618–906)

This piece consists of two bowls with spreading sides, straight rims, broad foot rings and slightly recessed bases, which have stuck together during the firing. The bases of the bowls are separated by three spurs while the remains of one spur and two spur marks are visible on the inside base of the top dish and on the base of the lower one. The light grey, coarse body has oxidised to a reddish colour where exposed. The cream slip, green splash and transparent glaze cover the inside of the bowls and a short way down the outside.

Diameter of base: 7.6 cm. Length of side: 8.6 cm. Body: 0.5–0.7 cm.

432
Fragment of a bowl
From Shandong Zibo (1976)
Jin dynasty (AD 1115–1234)

This rim fragment of a bowl with curved, spreading sides is decorated with a swirling combed design within an incised line border which cuts through the cream slip to reveal the creamy-buff medium-coarse body beneath. The cream slip and transparent glaze cover the inside of the bowl and just over the rim on the outside.

Dimensions: 14.2 × 7 cm. Body: 0.3 cm.

433

Fragment of a two-handled jar
From Shandong Zibo (1976)
Jin dynasty (AD 1115–1234)

This fragment consists of part of the neck and
shoulder of a jar with a rounded body, upright
curved neck and a lug handle composed of three
cylinders of clay attached to the neck and shoulder.
The coarse, grey body has a black iron oxide glaze
with brown and bluish 'tortoise shell' markings.

Height: 8.4 cm. Width: 14.5 cm. Body: 0.8 cm.

434

Fragment of a two-handled jar with white ribs
From Shandong Zibo (1976)
Jin dynasty (AD 1115–1234)

This piece is from the neck and shoulder of a jar with
rounded sides and an upright curved neck. The lug
handle, composed of three cylinders of clay, is
pinched onto the neck and shoulder. The medium-
coarse grey body and white ribs made of cylinders of
slip are covered with a black iron oxide glaze which,
where thin on the ribs, reveals their contrasting
white colour.

Dimensions: 12 × 11 cm. Body: 0.4–0.5 cm.

435

Fragment from the rim of a dish
From Shandong Zibo (1976)
Yuan dynasty (AD 1280–1368)

This rim sherd of a dish with a rounded cavetto and
broad flaring rim with constricted outside edge is
decorated on the cavetto with a design, painted in
brown on the white slip, of loops, and on the rim a
bracket-like decoration in a broad and a narrow
band, bordered on the inside with a band of three
thin lines. The fragment has a chalky white body
and is unglazed on the underside where it is stained
dark with smoke and to which kiln grit adheres.

Dimensions: 15.5 × 8 cm. Body: 0.3–1.0 cm.

436

Fragment from the base of a dish decorated in brown
on a white slip
From Shandong Zibo (1976)
Yuan dynasty (AD 1280–1368)

This sherd is part of a very thick base of a dish with a
broad base ring, slightly recessed in the centre. The
decoration of a fish among weeds is executed in
brown painted over the white slip and under a
transparent glaze. The coarse, chalky-white body is
unglazed on the base and outside wall.

Dimensions: 10 × 6 cm. Body: 1.5 cm.

437

Fragment of a large dish with decoration painted in
brown on a white slip
From Shandong Zibo (1976)
Yuan dynasty (AD 1280–1368)

This fragment from the flat base of a dish, unglazed
on the outside base and on the outside of the walls, is
decorated with a design painted in brown on the
white slip of a band of leaf scroll, a broad plain band
and a thin band of dots between two narrow lines.
The body consists of a greyish-white, coarse, hard
material.

Dimensions: 10 × 5.5 cm. Body: 1.0 cm.

Shaanxi   nos. 438−454

The very important kilns of this province are dominated by the Yaozhou group
which produced green glazed wares of the 11th and 12th centuries. This
influential kiln, producing tribute wares and fine quality greenware continued
in production into the Jin and Yuan dynasties as examples in the exhibition
show.

Yaozhou	nos. 438−447
Xunyi	nos. 448−454

Yaozhou   nos. 438–447

The site of Yaozhou is situated in Tongchuan city. It was first discovered in
1954 and later surveyed and extensively excavated. Four kilns were discovered,
concentrated at Huangbaozhen. Yaozhou started production in the Tang and
stopped again in the Yuan period, reaching its peak during the Northern Song
dynasty. The principal wares made were greenwares with carved and moulded
decoration, the carving being sharp and powerful and the moulding rich and
varied. The influence on kilns of the surrounding area was so great that they
form what is known as the 'Yaozhou kiln complex'.

438
Cover of a box with painted decoration
From Shaanxi Yaozhou (1959)
Tang dynasty (AD 618–906)

This box cover is decorated on the top with a stylised
floral motif painted in black glaze over a white slip.
Further splashes of the black decorate the outside
walls. The inside of the top is glazed while the insides
of the walls are unslipped and unglazed, revealing
the light grey, fine body.

Height: 1.5 cm. Diameter: 7.3 cm. Body: 0.4 cm.
Published: Shaanxi Tongchuan Yaozhou yao, Pl. VII:14

439
Fragment from the base of a bowl with a green glaze
From Shaanxi Yaozhou (1959)
Song dynasty (AD 960–1279)

This fragment forms the base of a bowl with rounded
spreading sides and a short, straight foot. The inside
is decorated with a carved design of a duck among
waves under an olive green glaze. The glaze shades
to brown near the foot, and the inside foot, to which
kiln grit adheres, and the base have a brown glaze.
The body is fine and pale grey.

Dimensions: 10.5 × 6.7 cm. Body: 0.4 cm.
Drawing: Shaanxi Tongchuan Yaozhou yao, p. 39, Fig. 4
Published: Shaanxi Tongchuan Yaozhou yao,
Plate XXIII:2

440
Fragment from the base of a bowl with a green glaze
From Shaanxi Yaozhou (1959)
Song dynasty (AD 960–1279)

This sherd forms part of the base of a bowl with
rounded spreading sides and a short, straight foot. The
inside base is decorated with a carved decoration of a
lotus petal under a green olive glaze which is broadly
crazed. Kiln grit adheres to the glaze on the inside
and outside of the foot, and the foot ring is unglazed.
The fine pale grey body burns reddish where exposed
and pieces of debris adhere to the inside of the bowl.

Dimensions: 8.4 × 7.8 cm. Body: 0.3 cm.
Drawing: Shaanxi Tongchuan Yaozhou yao, p. 27, Fig. 2

441
Fragment of a bowl with a green glaze
From Shaanxi Yaozhou (1959)
Song dynasty (AD 960–1279)

This sherd from the wall of a bowl with straight sides
and an inverted rim has a carved and combed
decoration of waves under a *terre verte* glaze. The fine
body is pale grey in colour.

Dimensions: 10.9 × 7.7 cm. Body: 0.3 cm.

442
Fragment of a dish
From Shaanxi Yaozhou (1959)
Song dynasty (AD 960–1279)

This sherd forms part of a dish with short, spreading
sides, a flat base ring which is unglazed and within
which is a small recessed circle. The inside base is
decorated with a carved and combed design of
waves. The pale grey fine body burns rust coloured
where exposed on the base and the olive green glaze
appears yellowish where thin on the walls.

Dimensions: 10.5 × 6 cm. Body: 0.4–0.5 cm.

443
Fragment of a bowl with carved decoration under a
green glaze
From Shaanxi Yaozhou (1959)
Song dynasty (AD 960–1279)

This rim sherd from the rounded wall of a bowl is
decorated with a carved decoration of chrysanthemum scroll. This very thin fragment has a fine,
pale grey body and a thin, pale grey-olive glaze.

Dimensions: 6.4 × 4.6 cm. Body: 0.25 cm.
Drawing: Shaanxi Tongchuan Yaozhou yao, p. 27, Fig. 6

444
Fragment from the base of a dish with a green glaze
From Shaanxi Yaozhou (1959)
Song dynasty (AD 960–1279)

The inside of this fragment of a dish is decorated with
a moulded dragon design. The green glaze covers the
inside of the dish and is trimmed half way down the
square cut foot. Under the glaze on the deeply
recessed base is an incised two-character inscription.
Iron spots are visible in the glaze on the outside and
the grey, medium-coarse body is burnt iron brown
where exposed on the foot.

Dimensions: 17.5 × 17 cm. Diameter of foot: 8.7 cm.
Body: 0.5 cm.
Published: Shaanxi Tongchuan Yaozhou yao, Pl. XV:4

445
Fragment from the neck of a ewer with a green glaze
From Shaanxi Yaozhou (1959)
Song dynasty (AD 960–1279)

This sherd from a ewer has a trumpet shaped neck
carved with vertical petals, and a stiff leaf ornament
applied like a lug handle to the neck and shoulder.
The fine, pale grey body is covered with a grey-olive
glaze.

Height: 4.8 cm. Inside diameter: 2.8 cm.
Body: 0.5 cm.

446
Bowl with carved decoration under a green glaze
Shaanxi Yaozhou type (from the Gugong, Peking)
Jin dynasty (AD 1115–1234)

This bowl with rounded spreading sides, a thick,
constricted rim and short, slightly everted foot, is
decorated on the inside with a carved design of a
xiniu gazing at the moon within a four-petalled panel
which is surrounded by a leaf scroll. The grey body is
burnt a brownish buff where exposed on the foot
ring. The convex base and the inside of the foot are
covered with the grey-green glaze which is severely
crazed.

Height: 7.8 cm. Diameter: 21 cm.
Drawing: Shaanxi Tongchuan Yaozhou yao, p. 40, Fig. 3

447
Fragment of a bowl with carved decoration under a
green glaze
From Shaanxi Yaozhou (1959)
Jin dynasty (AD 1115–1234)

This fragment from the base of a bowl has on the
inside a carved decoration of a *xiniu* gazing at the
moon on a background of leaf scrolls. The bowl has
rounded spreading sides, with a spreading foot and
slightly convex base. The pale grey, fairly fine body is
glazed with a grey-olive glaze which covers the foot
and base but leaves the foot ring exposed. Kiln grit
adheres to the inside of the foot.

Dimensions: 9 × 8 cm. Body: 0.4–0.7 cm.

Xunyi   nos. 448–454

Xunyi is 70 kilometres to the south-west of Yaozhou. The glaze of the
greenwares, which formed the main product, is often a yellowish colour. Many
bowls have unglazed ring on the inside, and, in this respect, are similar in style
to wares of the Jin dynasty from Yaozhou. Decoration was carved or moulded;
incised or combed designs of wares or lotus leaves are arranged in a manner
similar to that on vessels from Yaozhou. Indeed Xunyi falls within the sphere of
the 'Yaozhou kiln complex'.

448

Bowl with a carved and combed decoration under a yellowish-green glaze
Shaanxi Xunyi type (from the Gugong, Peking)
Jin dynasty (AD 1115–1234)

This bowl with rounded, spreading sides, slightly everted rim and short, spreading foot is decorated with a carved and combed design of six waves rising around an unglazed ring in the centre. This ring shows the grey body burnt to a greyish buff with rust-coloured spots from the kiln support of another bowl fired inside this one. Outside the exposed body appears brownish buff with iron spots. On the outside the yellowish-olive glaze runs from a thick welt under the rim to half way down the side.

Diameter: 19.4 cm. Height: 7.6 cm.

449

Fragment of a bowl with a wave design under an olive glaze
From Shaanxi Xunyi (1959)
Jin dynasty (AD 1115–1234)

This fragment is part of a bowl, similar to no. 448, with spreading sides, a rounded mouth rim and an everted foot which is straight on the inside. The bowl is decorated on the inside with a carved and combed design of waves rising around an unglazed ring. The ring shows the grey fine body burnt to an orange-brown in firing and has kiln material adhering. The olive glaze is crazed and has iron spots on the outside where it stops short of the foot.

Dimensions: 10.5 × 7.5 cm. Body: 0.3–0.5 cm.
Published: GGBWYYK 1980 (1) pp. 3–27, Fig. 15

450

Part of a bowl decorated with a carved design under a yellowish-olive glaze
From Shaanxi Xunyi (1959)
Jin dynasty (AD 1115–1234)

This item is part of a bowl with rounded sides, a spreading foot and a slightly convex base. The inside of the bowl is decorated with a formalised quatre-foliate lotus design surrounded by leaf scrolls. An unglazed ring on the inside base shows the remains of a kiln support. The grey, fine body is burnt greyish buff where exposed, and the yellowish olive glaze runs short of the foot on the outside where the potter's fingernail marks are visible in the body and in the glaze.

Available diameter: 16.5 cm. Diameter of foot: 6 cm.
Body: 0.3–0.6 cm.
Published: GGBWYYK 1980 (1) pp. 3–27, Fig. 15

451

Part of a bowl with carved decoration under a yellowish-olive glaze
From Shaanxi Xunyi (1959)
Jin dynasty (AD 1115–1234)

This fragment of the base of a bowl with rounded spreading sides, which are undercut where they meet the slightly everted foot, and a slightly recessed base is decorated on the inside with a carved design of a lotus leaf scroll. An unglazed ring on the inside base shows the grey fine body fired to a greyish-buff colour. The body burns to a rust brown. The yellowish-olive glaze is trimmed short of the foot on the outside.

Dimensions: 13.5 × 9 cm. Body: 0.6 cm.
Published: GGBWYYK 1980 (1) pp. 3–27, Fig. 15

452

Fragment of a bowl with carved decoration under a yellowish-olive glaze
From Shaanxi Xunyi (1959)
Jin dynasty (AD 1115–1234)

This fragment from a bowl with rounded spreading sides and an everted foot chamfered on the outside is decorated with a carved decoration of a peony scroll. The grey body is fired to a greyish-buff where exposed on the foot and on the unglazed ring on the inside base to which kiln material adheres. The yellowish-olive glaze is trimmed short of the foot on the outside where iron spots are visible.

Dimensions: 11 × 7.5 cm. Body: 0.2–0.9 cm.

453

Fragment from a bowl with carved decoration under a yellowish-green glaze
From Shaanxi Xunyi (1959)
Jin dynasty (AD 1115–1234)

This fragment from a bowl with rounded sides is decorated on the inside wall with a carved decoration of lotus leaf scroll. In the centre is an unglazed ring where the grey body is fired to a greyish-buff colour. The yellowish-olive glaze is trimmed short of the foot on the outside.

Dimensions: 7 × 6 cm. Body: 0.3–0.8 cm.
Published: GGBWYYK 1980 (1) pp. 3–27, Fig. 15

454

Fragment of a bowl with a carved decoration under a yellowish-olive glaze
From Shaanxi Xunyi (1959)
Jin dynasty (AD 1115–1234)

This fragment from a bowl with rounded spreading sides and an everted foot is decorated on the inside with a carved decoration of radial panels, one of which contains a deer, and another a peony leaf scroll. The grey body appears greyish buff on the unglazed ring in the centre to which kiln material adheres. The yellowish-olive glaze is trimmed short of the foot on the outside.

Dimensions: 7.5 × 5.3 cm. Body: 0.4–0.9 cm.
Published: GGBWYYK 1980 (1) pp. 3–27, Fig. 15

Shanxi   nos. 455–500

A group of five kilns in this province underline the relationship of this area with kilns to the east.

Jiexiu	nos. 455–464
Huozhou	nos. 465–474
Datong	nos. 475–480
Hunyuan	nos. 481–495
Huairen	nos. 496–500

Jiexiu   nos. 455–464

In 1959 a kiln site was discovered at Hongshanzhen. Production continued for eight or nine hundred years from the Northern Song, throughout the Jin, Yuan, Ming, and Qing dynasties to the Republic. In the Song period the kiln produced white wares and dishes and bowls with a black glaze and moulded decoration, all of which show the influence of Ding ware from Hebei. The wares with decoration painted in black on a white slip are likewise related to those from Cizhou. The wares with brown decoration on a white glaze are, on the other hand, characteristic of Jiexiu. One with red designs belongs to an extremely rare group. In the Jin dynasty many brown glazed bowls, with moulded decoration of children floating boats on lotus ponds, were made. These are rarely seen at other kilns.

455
Parts of two bowls stuck together during firing
From Shanxi Jiexiu (1977:5)
Song dynasty (AD 960–1279)

Of these two fragments of bowls with a chalky-grey coarse body which have become stuck together during the firing, the smaller, outside fragment is covered with a black glaze. The larger fragment with rounded wall, a straight rim and a broad, heavy foot ring with a round recessed base, is decorated with a design of leaf sprays painted in brown over a cream slip. The slip and the transparent glaze stop short of the base on the outside.

Dimensions: (Inner) 11.5 × 8.2 cm.
Body: (Inner) 0.5 cm. (Outer) 0.4 cm.

456
Part of a lid decorated with painted designs in brown on a cream slip
From Shanxi Jiexiu (1977:5)
Song dynasty (AD 960–1279)

This part of a lid with a flat top, with a V-shaped profile, and rounded sides has a black glaze on the inside. The top is decorated with a sketchy flower motif with four leaves, and the sides with feather-like leaf sprays. This design is painted in brown over a cream slip and beneath a transparent glaze.

Dimensions: 14 × 10 cm. Diameter of top: 10.2 cm.
Body: 0.7–1.1 cm.

457
Fragment of a jar decorated with brown painting over a cream slip
From Shanxi Jiexiu (1977:5)
Song dynasty (AD 960–1279)

This sherd from the rounded wall of a jar is decorated with a design painted in brown of a bird among leaf scrolls. The body is grey, hard, medium-coarse, covered with cream slip, brown painting and a transparent glaze on the outside. The inside is unglazed.

Dimensions: 12.6 × 7.4 cm. Body: 0.6 cm.

458
Part of the base of a dish with a design painted in brown with incised details
From Shanxi Jiexiu (1960:5)
Song dynasty (AD 960–1279)

This fragment from the base of a large dish is decorated on the inside base with half palmettes, the details incised through the brown slip to reveal the cream slip and body. A transparent glaze covers the inside base and outside wall leaving the flat base and broad, shallow foot ring unglazed, where the grey, hard medium-coarse body has oxidised to a yellowish-brown.

Dimensions: 18.7 × 10.7 cm. Body: 0.9 cm.
*Published: GGBWYYK 1980 (1) pp. 3–27, p. 23,
Fig. 16*
Also WW 1965 (9) pp. 26–56, Pl. 2:1

459
Fragment of a mould
From Shanxi Jiexiu (1977:5)
Song dynasty (AD 960−1279)

Fragment of a mould with an unglazed, hard, grey, partially reduced body. The decoration intended for a bowl consists of a peony pattern bordered by a palmette scroll with flowers around the well.

Dimensions: 7 × 4.3 cm. Body: 0.5 cm.

460
Sherd from a pillow with decoration incised through the slip
From Shanxi Jiexiu (1977:5)
Song dynasty (AD 960−1279)

This sherd from a pillow is decorated with leaf sprays incised through the greyish white slip to the brown dressing which covers the grey, coarse body. The sketchily dotted ground appears to have been done with half a ring-stamping tool. The under side of the fragment is undecorated and unglazed.

Dimensions: 5 × 5 cm. Body: 0.5 cm.

461
Fragment from a pillow
From Shanxi Jiexiu (1977:5)
Song dynasty (AD 960−1279)

This sherd from the foliated rim of a pillow is decorated with a flower design within a lobed border incised through the slip, with the background cut away revealing the grey, coarse body and glazed with a transparent glaze.

Dimensions: 9.2 × 7.2 cm. Body: 0.4 cm.

462
Large pillow fragment with decoration incised through the slip
From Shanxi Jiexiu (1962:5)
Song dynasty (AD 960−1279)

This fragment from the top of a pillow, which has the remains of a side luted to it, is decorated with a sketchy lotus scroll incised through the cream slip to the buff, medium-coarse body beneath and is glazed with a transparent glaze. The underside is unglazed.

Dimensions: 16.8 × 12 cm. Body: 0.5 cm.
Published: WW 1965 (9) pp. 26−56, Pl. 2:3

463
Fragment of a moulded bowl with brown glaze
From Shanxi Jiexiu (1977:5)
Jin dynasty (AD 1115−1234)

This fragment from the rounded wall of a bowl is decorated with a moulded design of lotus and leaves inside and is glazed with a brown glaze which is slightly iridescent on the moulded relief surfaces. The thin body is buff and medium-coarse.

Dimensions: 8 × 7.8 cm. Body: 0.3−0.5 cm.

464
Large fragment of a dish with a yellow glaze
From Shanxi Jiexiu (1977:5)
Jin dynasty (AD 1115−1234)

This part of a dish with spreading sides, straight rim, wide sloping foot and deeply recessed base has a yellow glaze which covers the foot on the outside but leaves the foot ring and base unglazed with only accidental splashes, and an unglazed ring on the inside base where pieces were stacked in the kiln. The decoration on the inside is a moulded design of children in a boat and fish in a lotus pond. The thick body is chalky-buff and coarse. Kiln grit adheres to both sides of the bowl.

Diameter: 23 cm. Diameter of foot: 9.5 cm.
Body: 0.5−1.4 cm.
Published: GGBWYYK 1980 (1) pp. 3−27, Fig. 16
Similar one: WW 1958 (10) pp. 36−37, Fig. 2

Huo zhou   nos. 465–474

The kiln site is in the area of Chencun. White wares were the main product; among these were many unglazed examples, some with a moulded decoration of children. The wares were fired on five spurs, the marks of which remain on the inside and base. Cao Zhao mentions in the *Ge Gu Yao Lun* that 'Peng Junbao copied ancient Ding wares making "waisted" vessels (contracting sharply towards the foot) which were very neat. The white ones are similar to Ding wares'. Remains of these 'waisted' dishes, found at the site, demonstrate that this was the location of the kiln making 'Peng' ware. Manufacture at Huo xian started in the Jin dynasty and flourished into the Yuan. Cao Zhao called the vessels the new Ding.

465

Stem cup
Shanxi Huozhou type (from the Gugong, Peking)
Yuan dynasty (AD 1280–1368)

This stem cup, with its spreading foot with three bamboo-joint-like ribs, rounded sides and everted rim is made of a fine, creamy white clay, and has a cream slip and transparent glaze. It is unglazed on the inside of the foot and on the small base. Four spur marks are visible on the inside base, and four faintly visible on the foot ring.

Height: 5.5 cm. Diameter: 10.9 cm.
Diameter of foot: 3.4 cm.

466

Dish with moulded peony design
Shanxi Huozhou type (from the Gugong, Peking)
Yuan dynasty (AD 1280–1368)

This dish, with a flattened rim, shallow sides cut in towards the base on the outside while on the mould, a short, slightly splayed foot and a flat recessed base, has short incisions on the outside walls which come through to the inside as ribs. The fine creamy-white body is slipped white and glazed with a transparent glaze which stops short of the foot, leaving the foot and base unglazed. On the inside is a moulded design of two peonies and five tiny spur marks.

Height: 3.3 cm. Diameter: 13.1 cm.
Diameter of foot: 4 cm.

467

Part of a dish with a moulded peony decoration
From Shanxi Huozhou (1977:5)
Yuan dynasty (AD 1280–1368)

This sherd is part of a dish with a flattened rim and is decorated on the inside base with a moulded peony. The short foot is inclined on the inside towards the small base, which has a pimple of clay in the centre. The fine, creamy-white body has a white slip and a transparent glaze which runs short of the foot where kiln grit adheres. Kiln grit and two spur marks are also visible on the inside base.

Height: 3 cm. Diameter of base: 3.9 cm.
Body: 0.2–0.3 cm.

468

Part of a dish
From Shanxi Huozhou (1977:5)
Yuan dynasty (AD 1280–1368)

This fragment is part of a dish with rounded sides and straight rim. The short spreading foot is chamfered on the outside, has a roughly trimmed foot ring and inside slopes in towards the recessed base which has a pimple of clay in the centre. The body material is fine and creamy white and covered with a white slip. There is an unglazed ring on the inside base and the transparent glaze partially covers the outside, with a tear running down to the foot.

Height: 4.2 cm. Diameter of foot: 3.7 cm.
Body: 0.15 cm.

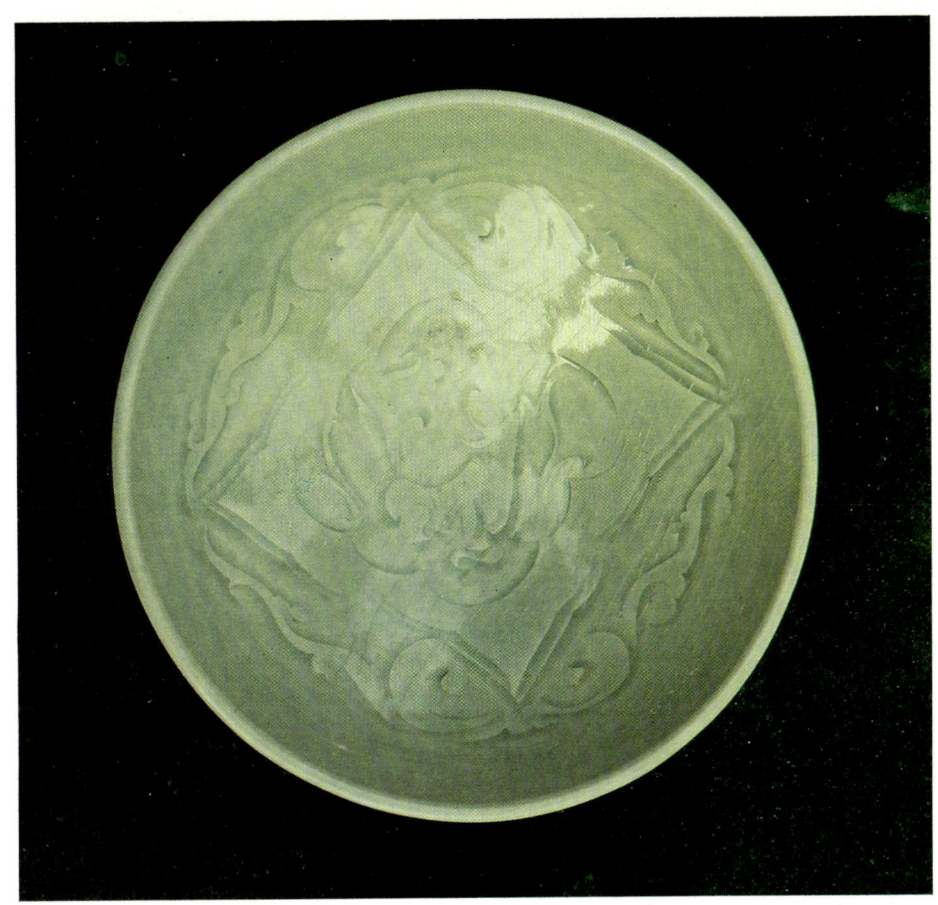

446

448

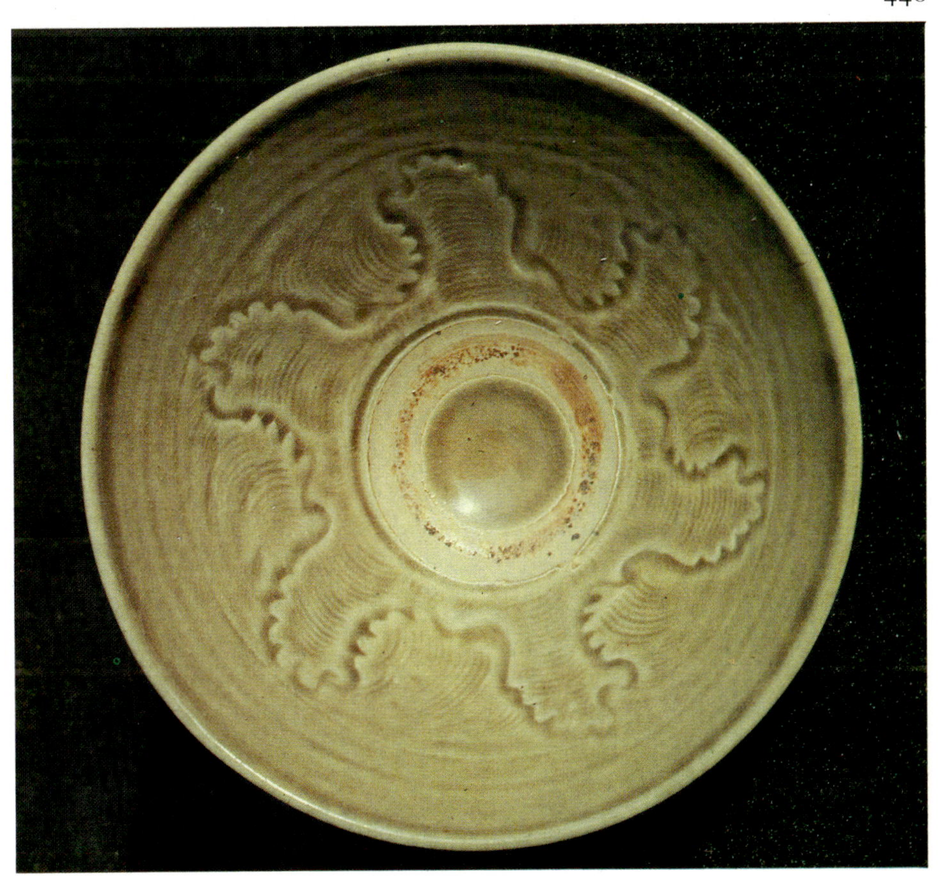

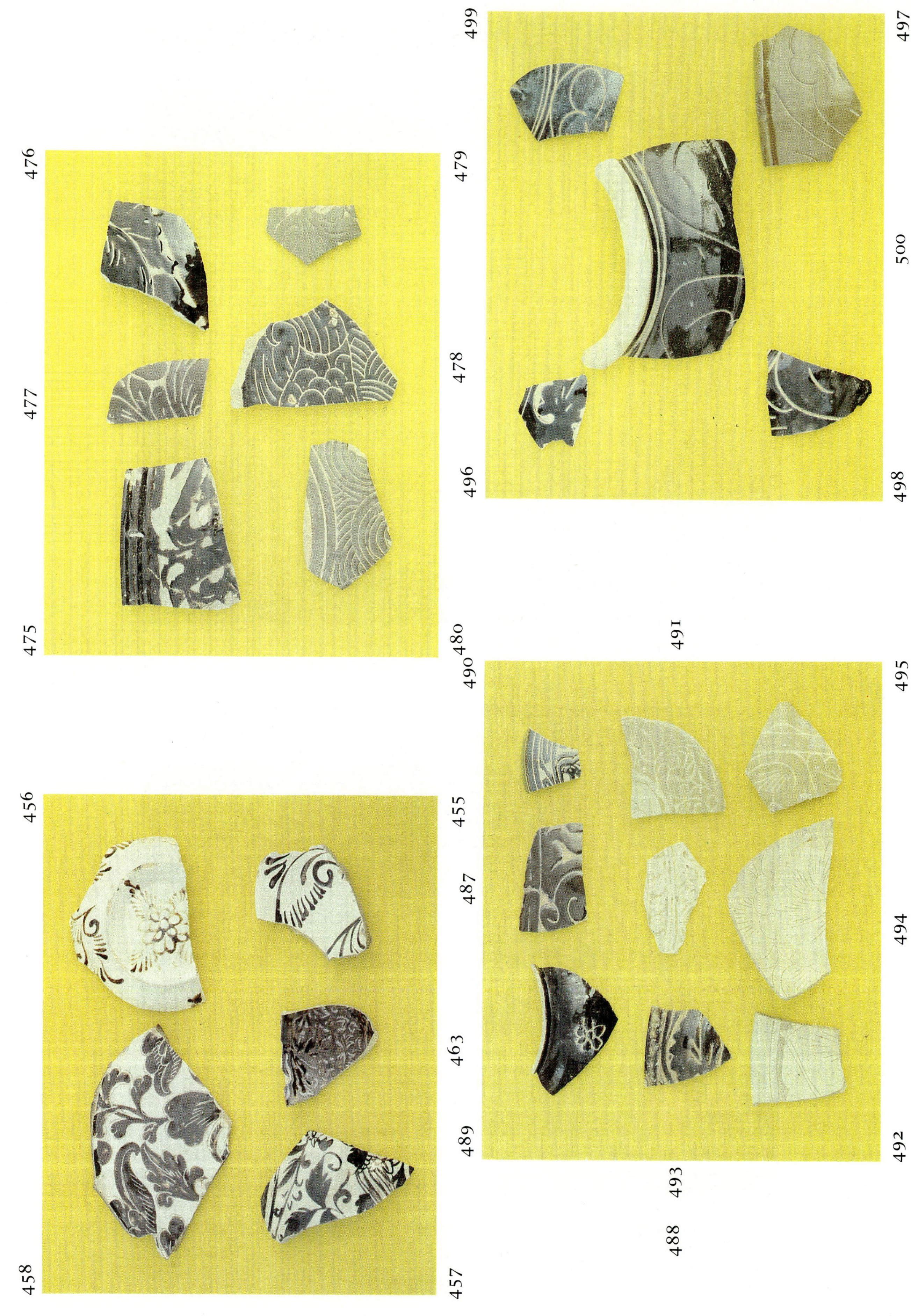

469

Foot of a cup
From Shanxi Huozhou (1977:5)
Yuan dynasty (AD 1280–1368)

This part of the underside of a cup has a spreading
foot with a flat foot ring on which five tiny, neat
conical spurs remain. The cup has the typical
Huozhou fine, creamy-white body, white slip and the
transparent glaze which covers the inside and part of
the outside. The inside of the cup is undecorated but
four (out of five) spur marks are visible on the inside
base.

Dimensions: 6.5 × 5.5 cm. Body: 0.2 –0.3 cm. (foot)
Diameter of foot: 3.7 cm.

470

Part of a dish
From Shanxi Huozhou (1977:5)
Yuan dynasty (AD 1280–1368)

This fragment is part of a dish with a carinated
external profile, an everted rim and a short, neat,
straight foot. The body is fine and creamy white, the
slip white, and the crazed glaze transparent, running
in tears down the outside. Two spur marks are
visible on the inside base.

Dimensions: 7.8 × 7 cm. Height: 2.6 cm.
Diameter of foot: 4 cm. Body: 0.3 cm.

471

Foot of a stem cup
From Shanxi Huozhou (1977:5)
Yuan dynasty (AD 1280–1368)

This fragment from the base of a stem cup has a
spreading foot, with two bamboo-joint-like ribs,
chamfered at the bottom where the foot ring is flat
and neat. The fine, creamy-white body has a white
slip and a transparent glaze which only partially
covers the foot on the outside and leaves the inside of
the foot and the base unglazed. Two spur marks are
visible on the inside base.

Height: 4.3 cm. Height of foot: 2.8 cm.
Diameter of foot: 3.5 cm. Body: 0.2 –0.3 cm.

472

Fragment of a bowl with moulded peony design
From Shanxi Huozhou (1977:5)
Yuan dynasty (AD 1280–1368)

This sherd was part of a bowl with a rounded wall
and a short foot with a flat, narrow foot ring on
which one small conical spur remains. The inside
base is decorated with a lightly moulded design of a
peony and shows the marks of five spurs. The fine
body and white slip with transparent glaze give a
more cream-coloured appearance than the other
pieces from the same kiln. The glaze runs short of the
foot, leaving the inside of the foot and the small,
recessed base unglazed.

Height: 2.7 cm. Diameter of foot: 3.9 cm.
Body: 0.2 –0.3 cm.

473

Fragment of a bowl with moulded chrysanthemum
design
From Shanxi Huozhou (1977:5)
Yuan dynasty (AD 1280–1368)

This fragment from the base of a bowl has a high,
straight foot and a flat base. The foot ring shows the
remains of three spurs and three (out of five?) spur
marks are visible on the inside base which is
decorated with a moulded floral roundel (chrysanthemum) within a band of florets with dots between
their four petals. This band is repeated at the base of
the walls. The off-white fine body has a slip of a more
brilliant white than other pieces from Huozhou.

Dimensions: 7.3 × 6.5 cm. Diameter of base: 4.5 cm.
Body: 0.3 –0.5 cm.

474

Fragment of a bowl with a moulded peony design
From Shanxi Huozhou (1977:5)
Yuan dynasty (AD 1280–1368)

This part of the base of a bowl has a small, rather
roughly cut foot which slopes inwards on the inside
towards the base. On the inside base is a moulded
decoration of a peony. The creamy-white, fine body
has a cream slip and a transparent glaze which stops
short of the foot on the outside.

Dimensions: 8.6 × 6.7 cm. Diameter of foot: 4.4 cm.
Body: 0.2 –0.4 cm. (base)

Datong   nos. 475–480

The kiln site is at Wayaogou, and is the greenware kiln mentioned in the *Datong Fu Zhi*. The kiln area is not very large and the remains consist predominantly of black glazed wares, among which are a few with a 'tealeaf' glaze. The forms include bottles, jars, and basins, that are decorated with cut-glaze or incised designs. The cut-glaze wares are somewhat rough in quality while the incised wares are comparatively fine. Quite a few have wave patterns, but those with fish among the waves are less common. The kilns were active in the Jin and Yuan dynasties.

475
Fragment of a jar with a cut-glaze decoration
From Shanxi Datong (1977:5)
Jin dynasty (AD 1115–1234)

This sherd from the rim of an open-mouthed jar has a rounded wall which has a crude floral design on the outside cut through the black glaze to the light grey, thick coarse body beneath. The piece is glazed also on the inside but the black glaze is trimmed off along the thick square cut rim below which, on the outside, are glazed ridges forming a border to the cut-glaze design.

Dimensions: 12.2 × 9.8 cm.
Body: 0.7–1.7 cm. (at rim)
Published: GGBWYYK 1980 (1) pp. 3–27, Pl. 4:1

476
Fragment of a jar with a black cut-glaze decoration
From Shanxi Datong (1977:5)
Jin dynasty (AD 1115–1234)

This fragment from the wall of a jar is covered on the inside and outside with a black glaze which is cut through to the light grey, coarse body with the design of a leaf.

Dimensions: 13 × 8.2 cm. Body: 0.7 cm.

477
Fragment of a bottle with a brown cut-glaze design
From Shanxi Datong (1977:5)
Jin dynasty (AD 1115–1234)

This sherd from the rounded wall of a bottle has a brown glaze inside and outside. The glaze is cut through on the outside to the grey, medium-coarse body with a floral design.

Dimensions: 10.2 × 4.4 cm. Body: 0.6 cm.
Published: GGBWYYK 1980 (1) pp. 3–27, Pl. 4:2

478
Fragment of a basin with a cut-glaze fish design
From Shanxi Datong (1977:5)
JIn dynasty (AD 1115–1234)

This sherd from the base of a basin is decorated on the inside base with a design of a fish among waves cut through the brownish glaze to the grey, medium-coarse body beneath. The unglazed base is flat with a small, slightly recessed circle in the middle, like a jade *bi*.

Dimensions: 13.2 × 8.4 cm.
Body: 0.8 cm. (centre); 1.5 cm. (base)
Published: GGBWYYK 1980 (1) pp. 3–27, Pl. 4:3

479
Fragment of a jar with a cut-glaze design
From Shanxi Datong (1977:5)
Jin dynasty (AD 1115–1234)

This sherd from the wall of a jar has a brown glaze inside, and on the outside a greenish-brown 'tea dust' glaze which is carved through to the grey, medium-coarse body in a leaf design.

Dimensions: 8 × 4.8 cm. Body: 0.4 cm.
Published: GGBWYYK 1980 (1) pp. 3 27, Pl. 4:5

480
Fragment of a jar with a cut-glaze pattern of waves
From Shanxi Datong (1977:5)
Jin dynasty (AD 1115–1234)

This sherd from a jar has a greenish-brown, 'tea dust' glaze inside and outside. On the outside the glaze is cut with a stylised pattern of waves consisting of overlapping circles of concentric lines. The design is bordered by two lines incised through the glaze to the grey, medium-coarse body.

Dimensions: 11.8 × 6.8 cm. Body: 0.8 cm.
Published: GGBWYYK 1980 (1) pp. 3–27, Pl. 4:4

Hunyuan   nos. 481–495

At Hunyuan is one of the earliest kiln sites discovered in the area of Shanxi. Three kilns have been found in all. Of these, the first, Guci yao, started up in the Tang dynasty, and from that time survive many examples of bowls and jars with white and black glaze. Although the basketware designs used are similar to those of the Henan style, bowls decorated with white on the inside and black on the outside represent a local taste. In the Jin and Yuan dynasties many designs cut into the black glaze typical of this part of north China, were used. In addition to these varieties white wares with incised, cut, and moulded decoration were also made. Such a wide range of different types is rare in this northern region.

481
Part of a bowl
From Shanxi Hunyuan (1977:5)
Tang dynasty (AD 618–906)

This fragment of a bowl with spreading sides, a straight rim, broad flat foot and small recessed base on which there is a pimple of clay, has a grey, fairly fine body with a cream slip and a transparent glaze, which are both trimmed short of the foot. Two spur marks are visible on the inside base, which is undecorated.

Height: 4 cm. Diameter of base: 6.9 cm.
Body: 0.5 cm.
Published: GGBWYYK 1980 (1) pp. 3–27, Fig. 17

482
Part of a bowl
From Shanxi Hunyuan (1977:5)
Tang dynasty (AD 618–906)

The fragment forms part of a bowl with rounded, spreading sides and an everted rim. The body is undercut where it meets the flat, slightly concave base. Two spur marks and kiln grit are visible on the inside which is undecorated. The grey, fairly fine body is covered with a cream slip and a transparent glaze which are trimmed short of the foot.

Height: 4.2 cm. Diameter of base: 6.7 cm.
Available diameter: 12.2 cm. Body: 0.5 cm.
Published: GGBWYYK 1980 (1) pp. 3–27, Fig. 17

483
Fragment of a bowl with a brown glaze
From Shanxi Hunyuan (1977:5)
Tang dynasty (AD 618–906)

This fragment is part of a bowl with rounded sides and an everted rim, a short, straight foot and a flat base. The inside of the bowl and the rim are covered with a cream slip and a transparent glaze, and the outside from below the rim to the base, which is unglazed, with a brown glaze. Kiln grit and an accidental incision are visible on the outside; one spur mark is visible on the inside. Body: grey, medium-coarse.

Height: 7 cm. Diameter of base: 10.8 cm.
Body: 0.6 cm.
Published: GGBWYYK 1980 (1) pp. 3–27, Pl. 4:21

484
Part of a bowl
From Shanxi Hunyuan (1977:5)
Tang dynasty (AD 618–906)

This sherd is part of a bowl with spreading sides which are undercut where they meet the short spreading foot. The outside walls are glazed with a brown glaze down to the base which is unglazed except for a small recessed convex circle in the centre. Cream slip and transparent glaze cover the grey, medium-coarse body of the bowl on the inside where one spur mark is visible.

Height: 5.2 cm. Diameter of base: 6.3 cm.
Body: 0.4–1.2 cm.
Published: GGBWYYK 1980 (1) pp. 3–27, Pl. 4:20

485
Fragment of a small jar with matting patterns under the glaze
From Shanxi Hunyuan (1977:5)
Tang dynasty (AD 618–906)

This sherd is part of a small jar with a flattened rim, undercut on the outside. The rounded wall is glazed inside and outside with an olive brown glaze which runs into a thick welt down the outside and into the depressions of the matting pattern impressed on to the grey, medium-coarse body under the glaze. The flat surface of the rim is half glazed and half unglazed.

Dimensions: 9 × 7.5 cm. Body: 0.5–0.9 cm.
Published: GGBWYYK 1980 (1) pp. 3–27, Pl. 4:19

486
Part of a mortar bowl
From Shanxi Hunyuan (1977:5)
Tang dynasty (AD 618–906)

This fragment of a mortar bowl has rounded spreading sides with an inverted rim. The bowl has a grey, medium-coarse body. The brown glaze on the outside and over the rim is trimmed short of the flat base, everted on the outside. The base is unglazed, as is the inside of the bowl which is incised with radial and concentric lines to form sharp edges for grating.

Height: 4.4 cm. Diameter available: 16 cm.
Body: 0.5–0.7 cm.
Published: GGBWYYK 1980 (1) pp. 3–27, Pl. 4:17

487
Sherd from a jar with a cut-glaze decoration
From Shanxi Hunyuan (1977:5)
Jin dynasty (AD 1115–1234)

This sherd from the wall of a jar has a dark brown glaze inside and out. On the outside a scrolling pattern is cut through the glaze to the coarse grey chalky body beneath, and is bordered by a band of double incised line.

Dimensions: 8.5 × 5.8 cm. Body: 0.5 cm.
Published: GGBWYYK 1980 (1) pp. 3–27, Pl. 4:16

488
Rim of a jar with a cut-glaze decoration
From Shanxi Hunyuan (1977:5)
Jin dynasty (AD 1115–1234)

This sherd comes from the everted rim of a jar which has a black glaze on the inside, and a brownish-black glaze on the outside where a leaf design is carved through the glaze to the coarse grey, chalky body.

Dimensions: 7.2 × 6.5 cm. Body: 0.4 cm.
Published: GGBWYYK 1980 (1), pp. 3–27, Pl. 4:14

489
Rim sherd from a jar with cut-glaze decoration
From Shanxi Hunyuan (1977:5)
Jin dynasty (AD 1115–1234)

This fragment is part of a jar with everted rim and rounded shoulder. It is glazed on both sides with a black glaze which is slightly iridescent in places. The mouth rim is unglazed. The outside is decorated with a floret (plum blossom) incised through the glaze to the coarse, grey, chalky body.

Dimensions: 10.8 × 6.3 cm. Body: 0.3 cm.
Published: GGBWYYK 1980 (1) pp. 3–27, Pl. 4:15

490
Fragment from the lid of a box with cut-glaze decoration
From Shanxi Hunyuan (1977:5)
Jin dynasty (AD 1115–1234)

This fragment from the lid of a box has a floral design bordered by a crude key-fret pattern carved through the dark brown glaze to reveal the greyish-white medium-coarse body. Round the sides are incised bands and sparse sketchy designs. The inside of the lid has a transparent glaze.

Dimensions: 5.4 × 5 cm. Body: 0.3 cm.
Published: GGBWYYK 1980 (1) pp. 3–27, Pl. 4:13

491
Fragment from a pillow
From Shanxi Hunyuan (1977:5)
Jin dynasty (AD 1115–1234)

This sherd from the top of a pillow is decorated with a band of scrolling leaf designs incised through a pale olive slip to a cream slip beneath. This band surrounds a central roundel which has an incised design incised through the cream slip to the pale olive. The body is buff and medium-coarse, unglazed on the underside. The slip decoration is covered with a transparent glaze.

Dimensions: 11.8 × 8.1 cm. Body: 0.6 cm.
Published: GGBWYYK 1980 (1) pp. 3–27, Fig. 17

492
Fragment of a bowl with decoration carved through the slip
From Shanxi Hunyuan (1977:5)
Jin dynasty (AD 1115–1234)

This fragment is part of a bowl with an everted rim. A petal decoration is incised through the cream slip, and the background is carved away to reveal the buff, medium-coarse body. The whole is glazed with a transparent glaze.

Dimensions: 7.5 × 7 cm. Body: 0.5 cm.
Published: GGBWYYK 1980 (1) pp. 3–27, Fig. 17

493
Fragment from a pillow with moulded decoration
From Shanxi Hunyuan (1977:5)
Jin dynasty (AD 1115–1234)

This fragment of a pillow is decorated with a deeply moulded band of florets, separated by a double ridge from a band of formalised leaf scroll. The grey, medium-coarse body is unglazed on the inside and has, on the outside, a cream slip and a transparent glaze which has a greenish tinge where thick in the depressions in the decoration.

Dimensions: 9 × 5.1 cm. Body: 0.6 cm.
Published: GGBWYYK 1980 (1) pp. 3–27, Fig. 17

494
Fragment from the base of a bowl
From Shanxi Hunyuan (1977:5)
Jin dynasty (AD 1115–1234)

This sherd is from the base of a bowl with a low broad foot ring and a flat, slightly convex base. The inside of the bowl is decorated with a simple lotus flower incised through the cream slip to reveal the grey, medium-coarse body. The slip and the transparent glaze stop short of the foot on the outside.

Dimensions: 15 × 8 cm. Body: 0.4 cm.
Published: GGBWYYK 1980 (1) pp. 3–27, Fig. 17

495
Fragment of a jar
From Shanxi Hunyuan (1977:5)
Jin dynasty (AD 1115–1234)

This sherd from the rounded wall of a jar is decorated with a band of leaf design, bordered by two straight lines and one wavy line, incised through the pale olive slip to reveal the cream slip beneath. A transparent glaze covers the outside but the inside is unglazed. Body: buff, chalky, medium-coarse.

Dimensions: 8.2 × 8 cm. Body: 1.1 cm.
Published: GGBWYYK 1980 (1) pp. 3–27, Fig. 17

Huairen   nos. 496–500

Altogether three kiln sites have been discovered, the earliest being that at Xiaoyu. Black wares were the main products, and were made as bottles and jars with decoration of raised lines known as 'bow strings'; many had simple designs cut through the pitch black, glossy glaze. The wide-mouthed jars have a coarse, thick rim unlike the flattened mouth rim of the pots from Datong. A few 'oil spot' glazed wares were discovered, and also a few vessels with their bases painted black.

496
Fragment of a jar with a black cut-glaze decoration
From Shanxi Huairen (1977:5)
Jin dynasty (AD 1115–1234)

This fragment is part of the rounded wall of a jar which is glazed on both sides with a black glaze. On the outside it is decorated with a crude leaf scroll pattern cut through the glaze to the buff, chalky, medium-coarse body.

Dimensions: 7.5 × 5.7 cm. Body: 0.4 cm.
Published: GGBWYYK 1980 (1) pp. 3–27, Pl. 4:8

497
Fragment of a jar with a design incised through the glaze
From Shanxi Huairen (1977:5)
Jin dynasty (AD 1115–1234)

This sherd from the rim of a jar is decorated on the outside with a floral design incised through the olive 'tea dust' glaze to the buff, chalky, medium-coarse body. The inside below the rim is glazed brown.

Dimensions: 11 × 8.5 cm. Body: 0.7 cm.
Published: GGBWYYK 1980 (1) pp. 3–27, Pl. 4:7

498
Fragment of a jar with decoration incised through the glaze
From Shanxi Huairen (1977:5)
Jin dynasty (AD 1115–1234)

This sherd from the rounded wall of a jar is decorated on the outside with a rudimentary pattern incised through the brownish black glaze to the buff, chalky, medium-coarse body. The inside is partially glazed.

Dimensions: 8.7 × 7 cm. Body: 0.6 cm.
Published: GGBWYYK 1980 (1) pp. 3–27, Pl. 4:10

499
Fragment from a wide mouthed jar with decoration incised through the glaze
From Shanxi Huairen (1977:5)
Jin dynasty (AD 1115–1234)

This fragment from the wall of a jar has a scrolling design with a border of incised lines cut through the brown-black glaze to the grey-brown, chalky, medium-coarse body. The glaze is slightly iridescent in places.

Dimensions: 9.5 × 6.7 cm. Body: 0.5 cm.
Published: GGBWYYK 1980 (1) pp. 3–27, Pl. 4:9

500
Fragment from a wide mouthed jar with decoration incised through the glaze
From Shanxi Huairen (1977:5)
Jin dynasty (AD 1115–1234)

This sherd from a wide mouthed jar with a thick, rolled rim, flattened on top, is glazed on the outside and inside walls with a brown-black glaze. The outside wall is decorated with a scroll design incised through the glaze to the grey, chalky, medium-coarse body. The rim is coated with cream slip.

Dimensions: 17 × 10 cm. Body: 0.7–1.2 cm.
Thickness of rim: 2.5 cm.
Published: GGBWYYK 1980 (1) pp. 3–27, Pl. 4:11

Chronological table

Neolithic period	about 7000–1600 BC
Shang dynasty	about 1600–1027 BC
Western Zhou dynasty	1027–771 BC
Eastern Zhou dynasty	770 – 221 BC
Spring and Autumn period	770–475 BC
Warring States period	475–221 BC
Qin dynasty	221–207 BC
Western Han dynasty	206 BC –AD 8
Xin dynasty (Wang Mang)	AD 9–23
Eastern Han	AD 24–220
Six dynasties period	AD 220–580
Northern and Southern dynasties	AD 420–580
Sui dynasty	AD 581–618
Tang dynasty	AD 618–906
Liao dynasty	AD 907–1125
Five dynasties	AD 907–960
Song dynasty	AD 960–1279
Northern Song dynasty	AD 960–1127
Southern Song dynasty	AD 1128–1279
Jin dynasty	AD 1115–1234
Yuan dynasty	AD 1280–1368
Ming dynasty	AD 1368–1644
Qing dynasty	AD 1644–1912
Republic	AD 1912–1949
People's Republic	AD 1949–

Appendix

Excavation Reports in Chinese Periodicals

Abbreviations:

KGXB	Kaogu xuebao, 1936–1964, 1973–
KGTX	Kaogu tongxun, 1955–1958
KG	Kaogu, 1959–
WWCKZL	Wenwu cankao ziliao, 1955–1961
WW	Wenwu, 1962–

Zhejiang	Shangyu	*WW* 1963 (1) pp. 43–49
	Ningbo	*KG* 1980 (4) pp. 343–346
	Deqing	*WWCKZL* 1957 (10) pp. 60–62
		WWCKZL 1959 (12) pp. 51–52
		KG 1961 (7) pp. 359–360
	Xiaoshan	*WWCKZL* 1955 (3) pp. 66–73
		WWCKZL 1955 (8) pp. 111–113
		WWCKZL 1957 (4) pp. 84–85
	Shanglinhu	Chen Wanli: *Zhongguo qingci shi lue* Shanghai, 1956
		WWCKZL 1958 (8) pp. 42–46
	Yin xian	*KG* 1964 (4) pp. 182–187
		WW 1973 (5) pp. 30–40
	Wenzhou	*WWCKZL* 1955 (8) pp. 111–113
		WWCKZL 1956 (11) pp. 1–7
		KG 1962 (10) pp. 531–534
		WW 1965 (11) pp. 21–43
	Huangyan	*KG* 1958 (9) p. 44
	Longquan	*KG* 1962 (10) pp. 535–538
		WW 1963 (1) pp. 27–49
Fujian	Dehua	*WWCKZL* 1955 (4) pp. 55–66
		WWCKZL 1957 (9) pp. 56–58
		WW 1979 (5) pp. 51–61, 62–65, 66–70
	Anxi	*WW* 1977 (7) pp. 58–67
	Tong'an	*WWCKZL* 1957 (9) pp. 56–59
		WWCKZL 1958 (2) pp. 32–33
		WWCKZL 1959 (6) pp. 62–64
		WW 1974 (11) pp. 80–84
	Nan'an	*WWCKZL* 1957 (12) pp. 53–55
	Quanzhou	*WWCKZL* 1957 (9) pp. 56–59
		WW 1973 (1) p. 63
	Putian	*WW* 1979 (12) pp. 37–42
	Lianjiang	*WWCKZL* 1958 (2) pp. 27–31
Guangdong	Chaozhou	*WWCKZL* 1957 (3) pp. 36–39
		KG 1964 (4) pp. 194–195
		KG 1979 (5) pp. 440–444
	Xicun	*Guangzhou Xicun gu yao yizhi* Peking, Wenwu Press, 1958
Jiangxi	Nanfeng	*KG* 1963 (12) pp. 686–689
	Jingdezhen	Chen Wanli: *Jingdezhen ji ge gudai yaozhi de diaocha*
		WWCKZL 1953 (9) p. 82 ff.
	Yangmeiting	*WWCKZL* 1953 (9) p. 82 ff.
	and Hutian	*WWCKZL* 1955 (8) pp. 111–113
	Ganzhou	*WWCKZL* 1956 (8) p. 77
	Jizhou	*WWCKZL* 1953 (9) p. 88 ff.
		Jiang Xuanyi: *Jizhou yao*, Peking, 1958

Yunnan	Yuxi	*KG* 1962 (2) p. 85
Hunan	Xiangyin	*WWCKZL* 1953 (9) p. 77 ff.
		KGTX 1957 (3) pp. 37–43
		WW 1978 (1) pp. 69–81
	Changsha	*WWCKZL* 1960 (3) pp. 67–70, 71–74
		KGXB 1980 (1) pp. 67–96
Sichuan	Qionglai	*WWCKZL* 1958 (2) pp. 38–42
Anhui	Shouzhou	*WW* 1961 (12) pp. 60–66
Henan	Gong xian	*WWCKZL* 1959 (3) pp. 56–58
	Mi xian	*WW* 1964 (2) pp. 54–62
	and Dengfeng	*WW* 1964 (3) pp. 47–55
	Yu xian	*WW* 1964 (8) pp. 27–36
	Lushan	*KG* 1951 (2) pp. 53–56
	and Baofeng	
	Lushan	*WW* 1980 (5) pp. 52–60
Shandong	Zibo	*WW* 1978 (6) pp. 46–58
Hebei	Ding yao	*KG* 1965 (8) pp. 394–412
		WWCKZL 1953 (9) p. 91 ff.
		WWCKZL 1959 (7) pp. 67–71
	Cizhou	*WWCKZL* 1959 (6) pp. 59–61
		WWCKZL 1952 (1) p. 56 ff.
		KG 1959 (10) pp. 546–548
		WW 1964 (8) pp. 37–48
		Gugong bowuyuan yuankan (2) pp. 104–108
		WW 1965 (9) p. 35
Shanxi	Jiexiu	*WWCKZL* 1958 (10) pp. 36–37
Shaanxi	Yaozhou	*WWCKZL* 1955 (4) pp. 72–74, 75–78
		WWCKZL 1959 (8) pp. 72–75
		KG 1959 (12) pp. 671–673
		KG 1962 (6) pp. 312–317
		Gugong bowuyuan yuankan (1) pp. 56–60
		Shaanxi Tongchuan Yaozhou yao Peking, 1965

For the most recent summary of kiln sites excavated in China see:

Gugong Bowuyuan Yuankan 1980 (1) pp. 3–27

Translations of Chinese articles published by the Victoria and Albert Museum, in association with the Oriental Ceramic Society

1. 'Important Finds of Ancient Chinese Ceramics since 1949'
   by Feng Hsien-ming
   (*WW* 1965 (9) pp. 26–56)

2. 'Report on the Excavation of Lung-Ch'üan Celadon Kiln-sites in Chekiang'
   by Chu Po-chien
   (*WW* 1963 (1) pp. 27–35)

3. 'Report on the Investigation of Kiln-sites of Ju type and Chün ware in Lin-ju Hsien, Honan'
   by Feng Hsien-ming
   (*WW* 1964 (8) pp. 15–26)

4. 'Investigation of the Ting ware Kiln-site at Chien-tz'u ts'un, Hopei'
   by Chih Pi-che and Lin Hung
   (*KG* 1965 (8) pp. 394–412)

5. 'Kiln-site Investigations'
   (1) 'Tz'u-chou ware kiln-sites'
       by Li Hui-ping
       (*WW* 1964 (8) pp. 37–48, p. 56)
   (2) 'Kiln-site at Hao-pi-chi, Honan'
       by the Staff of the Honan Culture Bureau
       (*WW* 1964 (8) pp. 1–14)
   (3) 'Tang and Sung Kiln-sites in Mi-hsien and Teng-feng hsien, Honan'
       by Feng Hsien-ming
       (*WW* 1964 (3) pp. 47–55, p. 45)

6. 'Yüeh ware kiln-sites in Chekiang'
   (1) 'Yü-yao hsien'
       by Chin Tsu-ming
       (*KGXB* 1959 (3) pp. 107–109)
   (2) 'Huang-yen hsien'
       by the Staff of the Chekiang Bureau of Antiquities
       (*KGTX* 1958 (8) pp. 44–47)
   (3) 'Wenchou'
       by the Staff of the Chekiang Bureau of Antiquities
       (*WW* 1965 (11) pp. 21–34)

7. 'Technical studies in Long-ch'üan celadons of successive dynasties'
   by Chou Jen, Chang Fu-k'ang and Cheng Yung-fu
   (*KGXB* 1973 (1) pp. 131–156)

8. (1) 'Problems concerning the development of Chinese porcelain'
       by Feng Hsien-ming
       (*WW* 1973 (7) pp. 20–29)
   (2) 'A study of *mang-k'ou* wares and the *fu-shao* technique of Sung and Yüan at Ching-te-chen'
       by Lin Hsin-kuo
       (*KG* 1974 (6) pp. 386–393, p. 405)

9. 'Report on the excavation of fifty-six ancient tombs at the Hsiu-ling reservoir in Huang-yen, Chekiang'
   by Chin Tsu-ming
   (*KGXB* 1958 (1) pp. 111–133)

Kiln Sites represented in the Exhibition

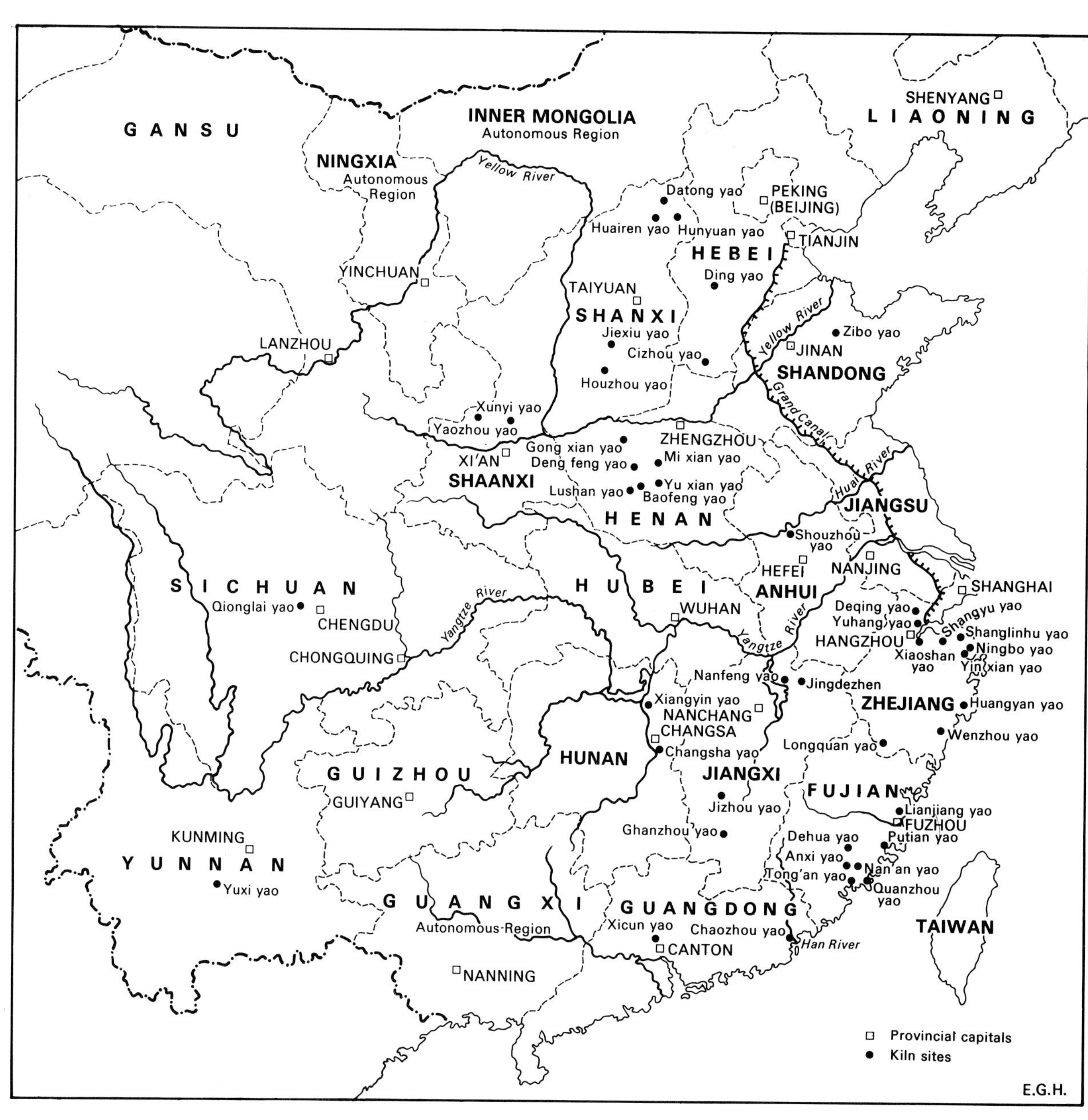

Illustrations

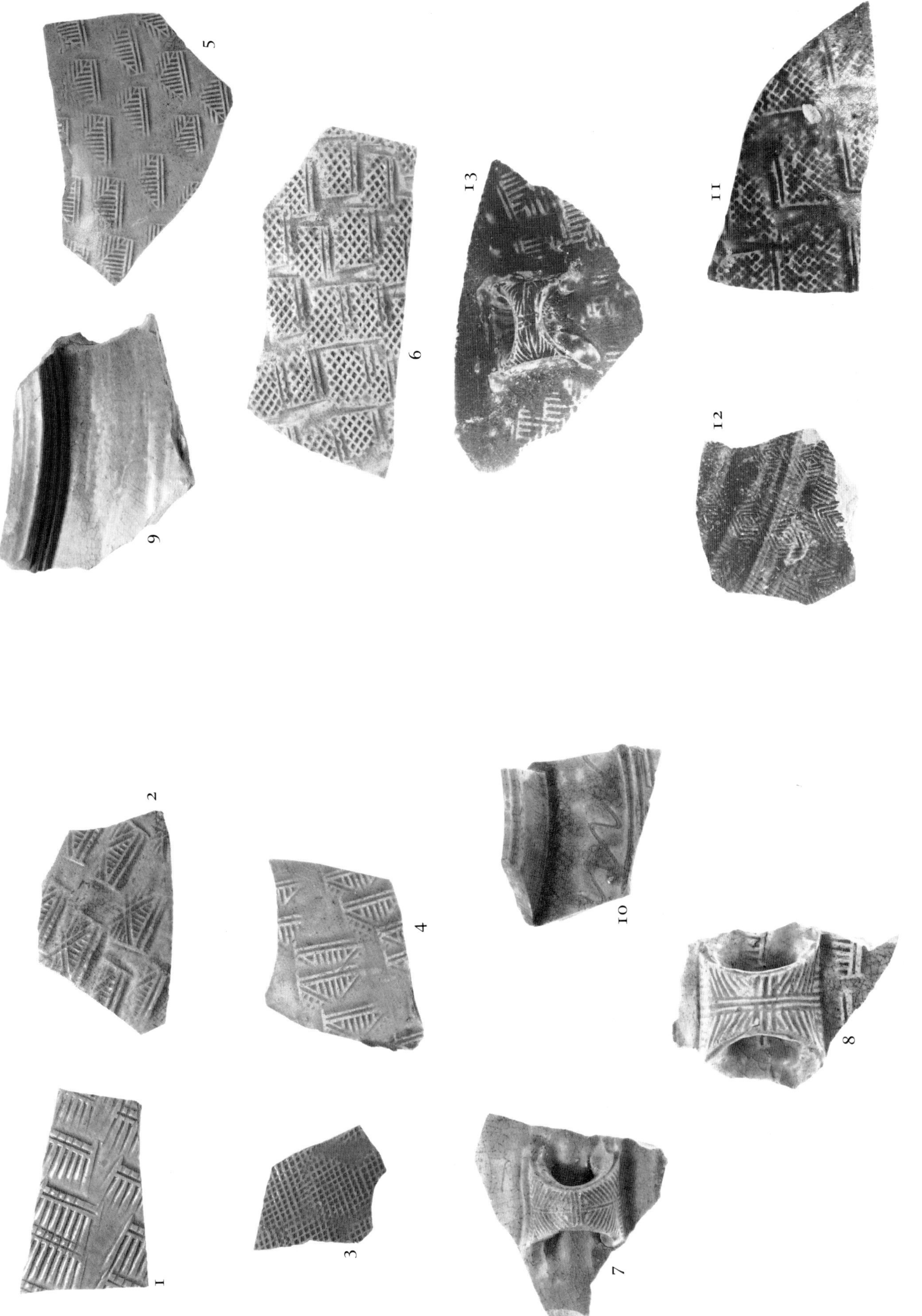

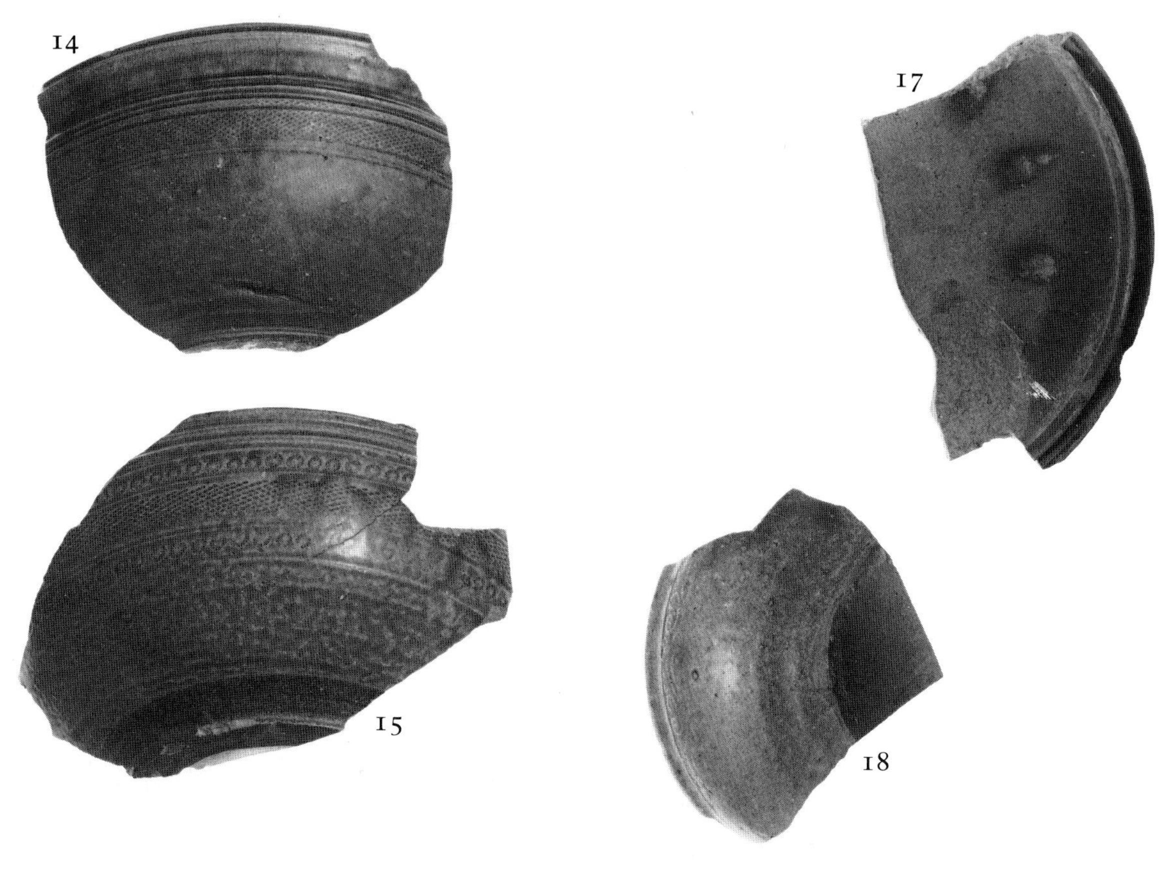

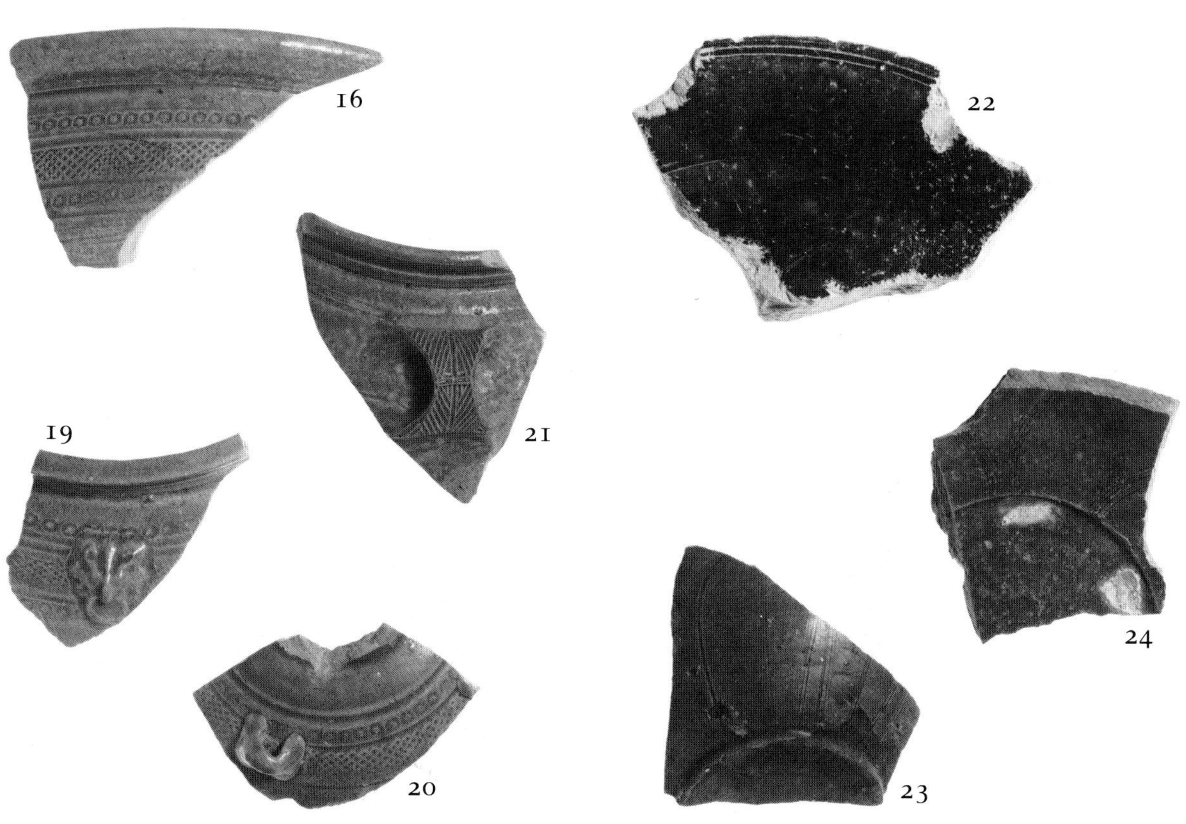

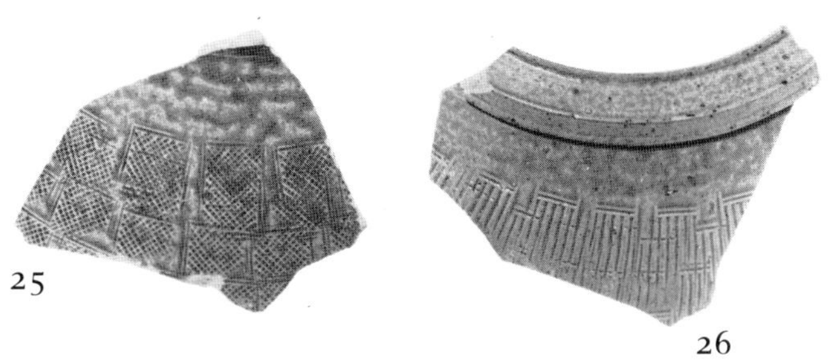

25

26

27

28

29

40

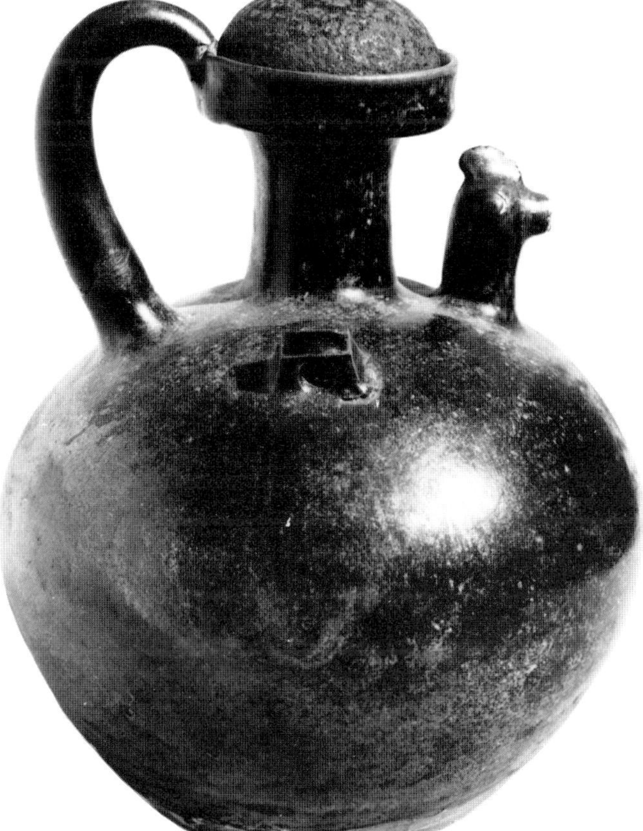

41

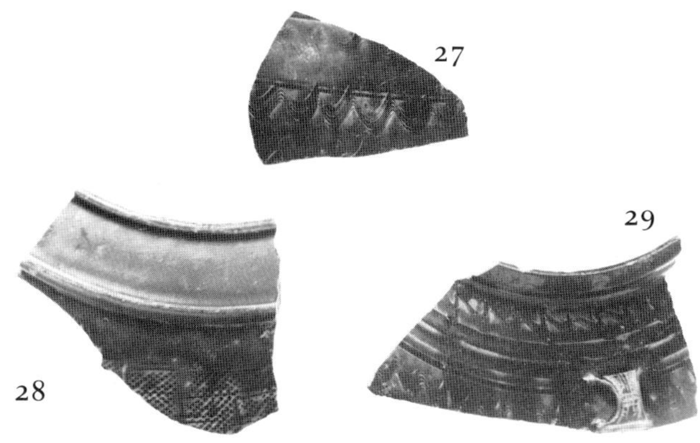

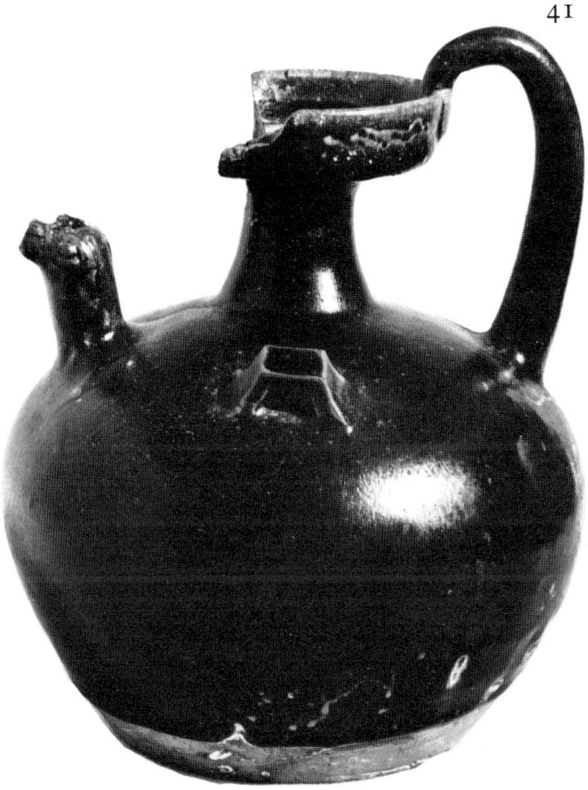

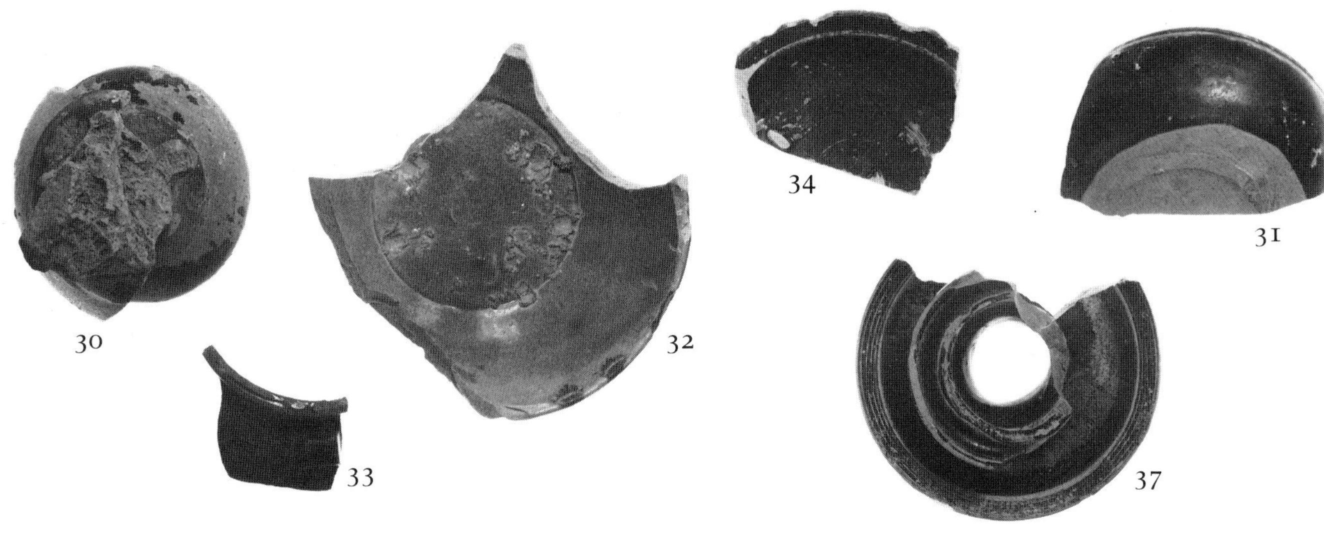
30
33
32
34
31
37

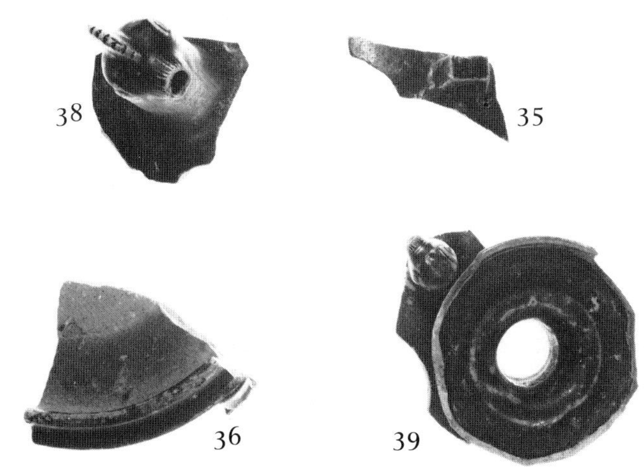
38
35
36
39

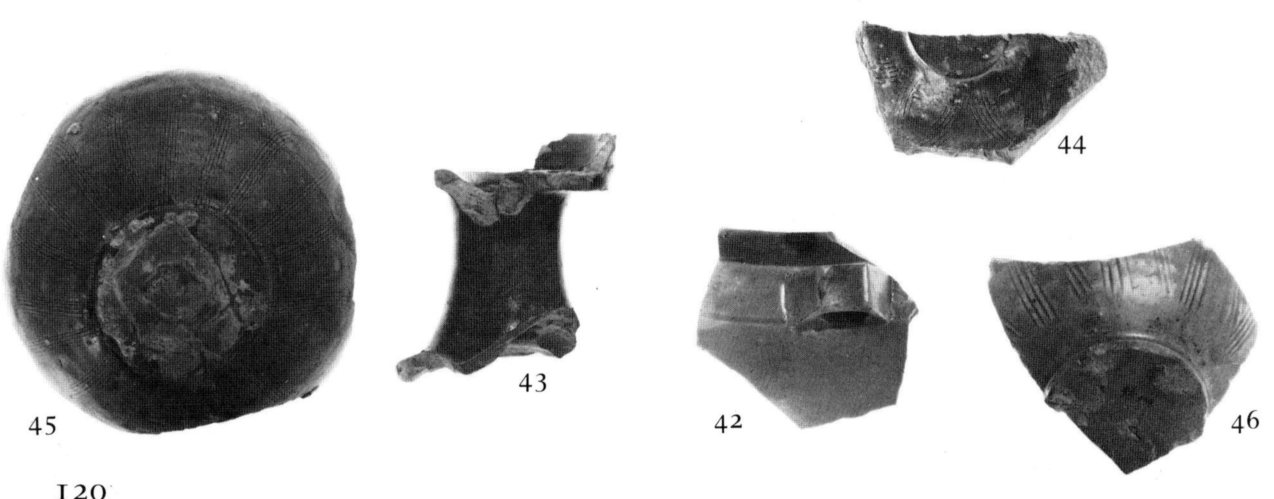
44
45
43
42
46

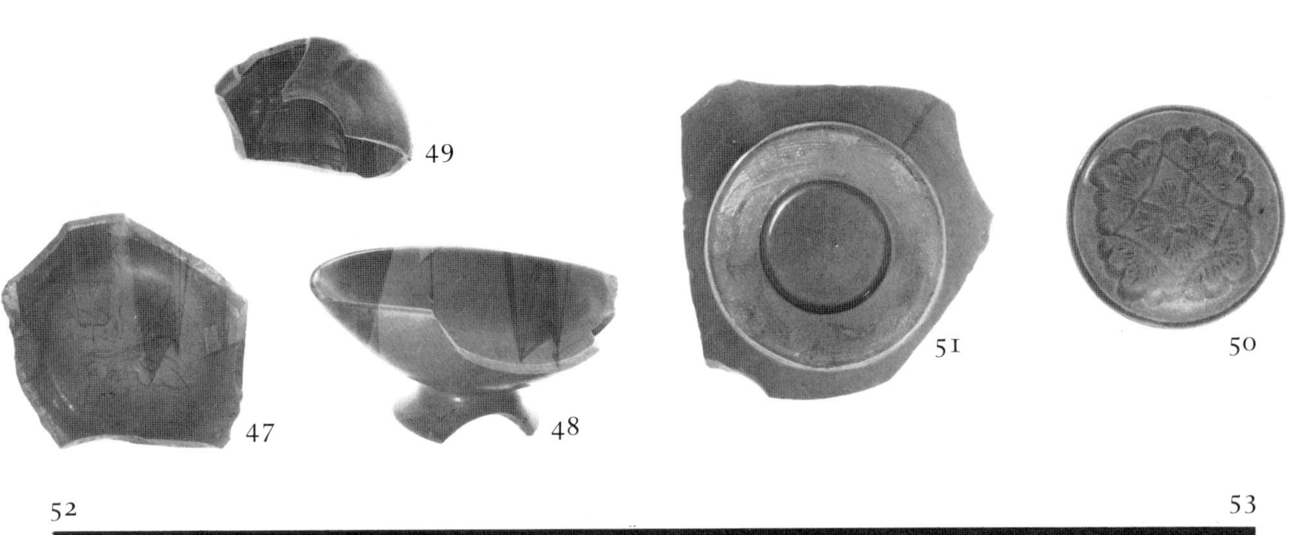

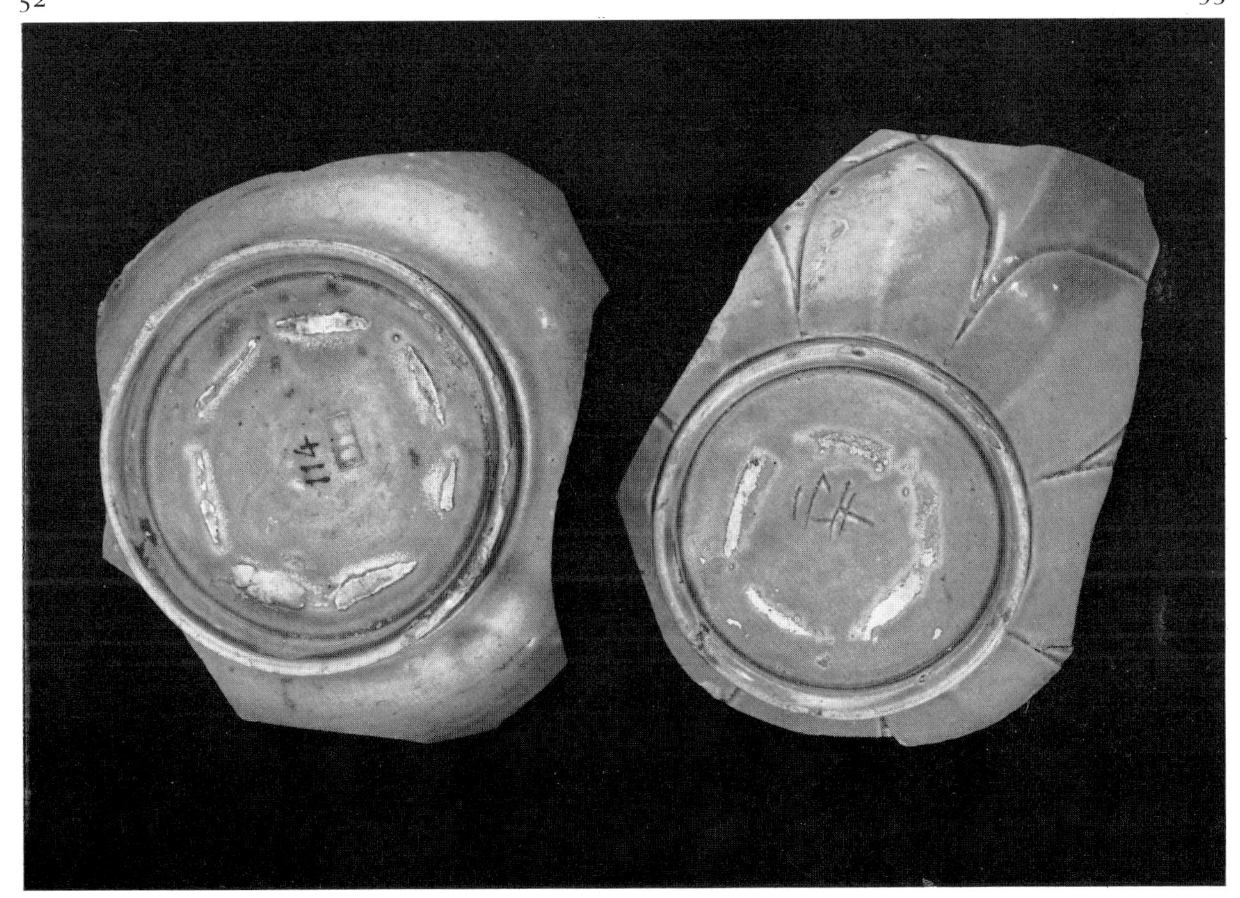

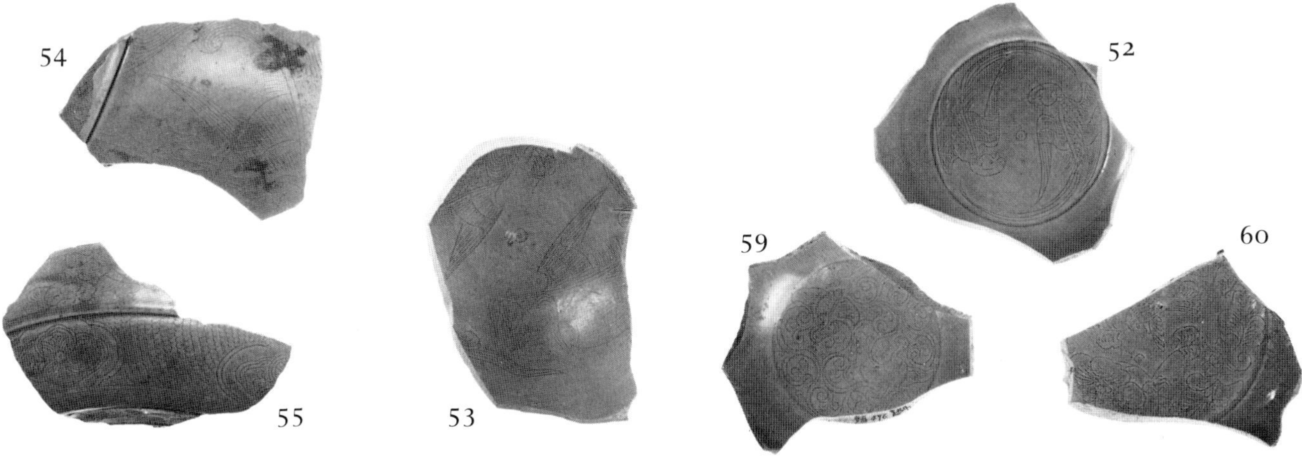

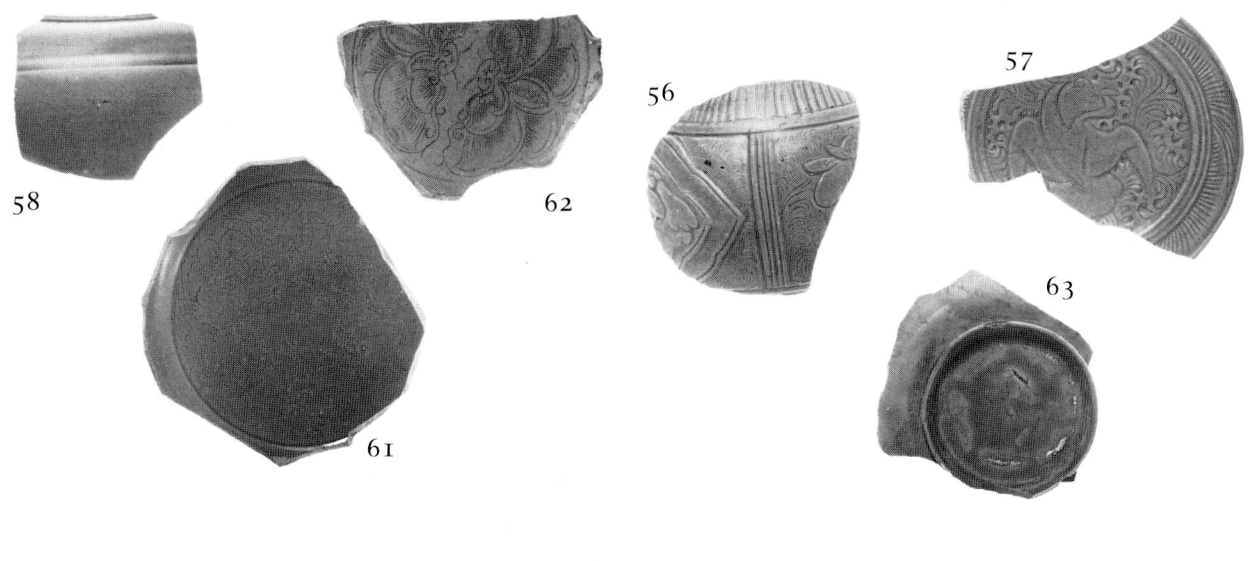

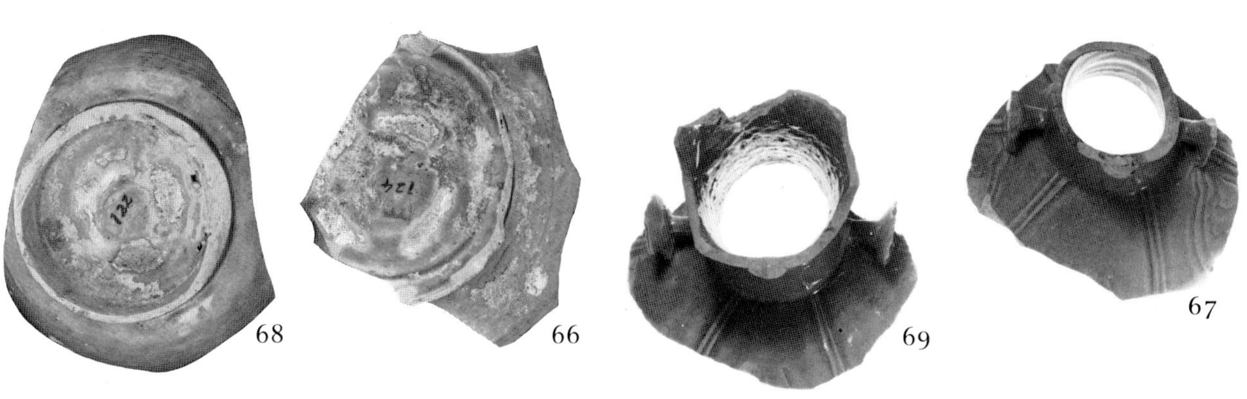

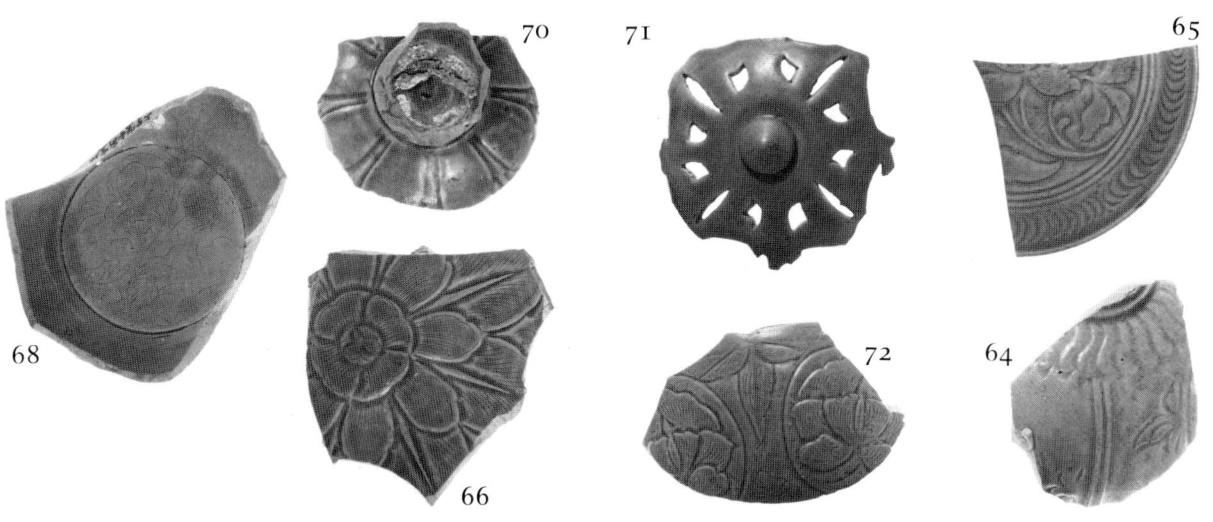

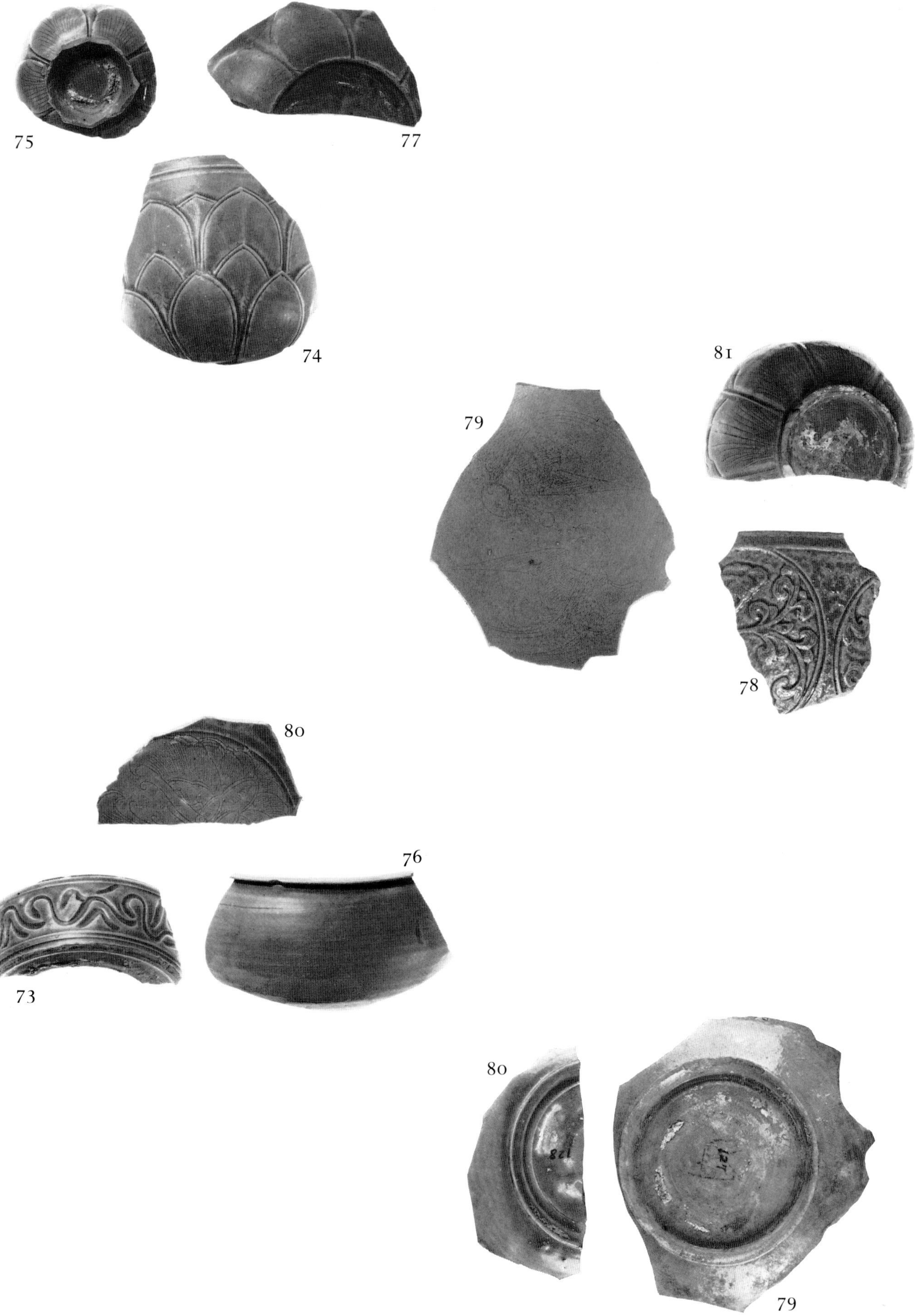

75
77
74
79
81
78
80
76
73
80
79

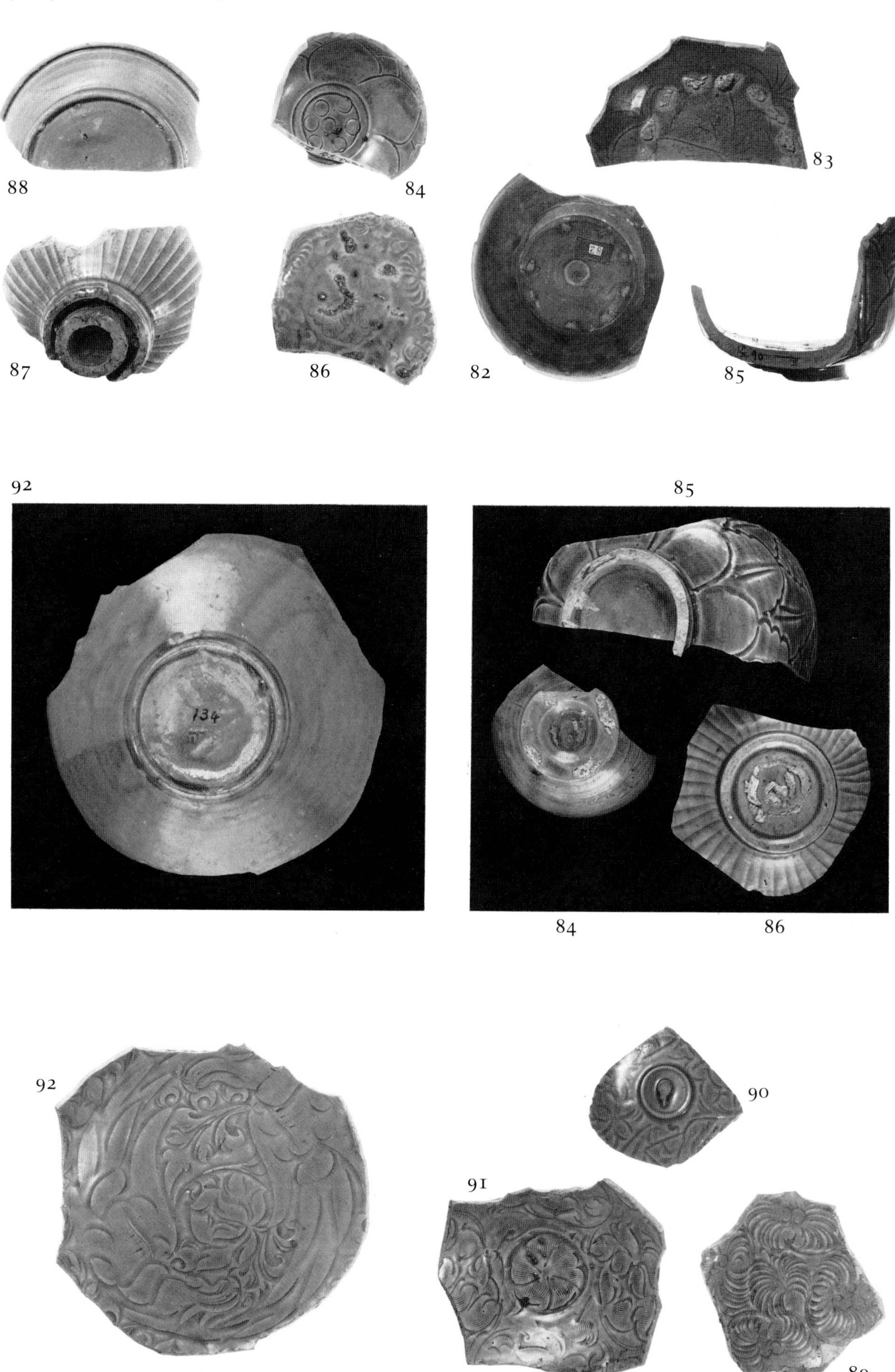

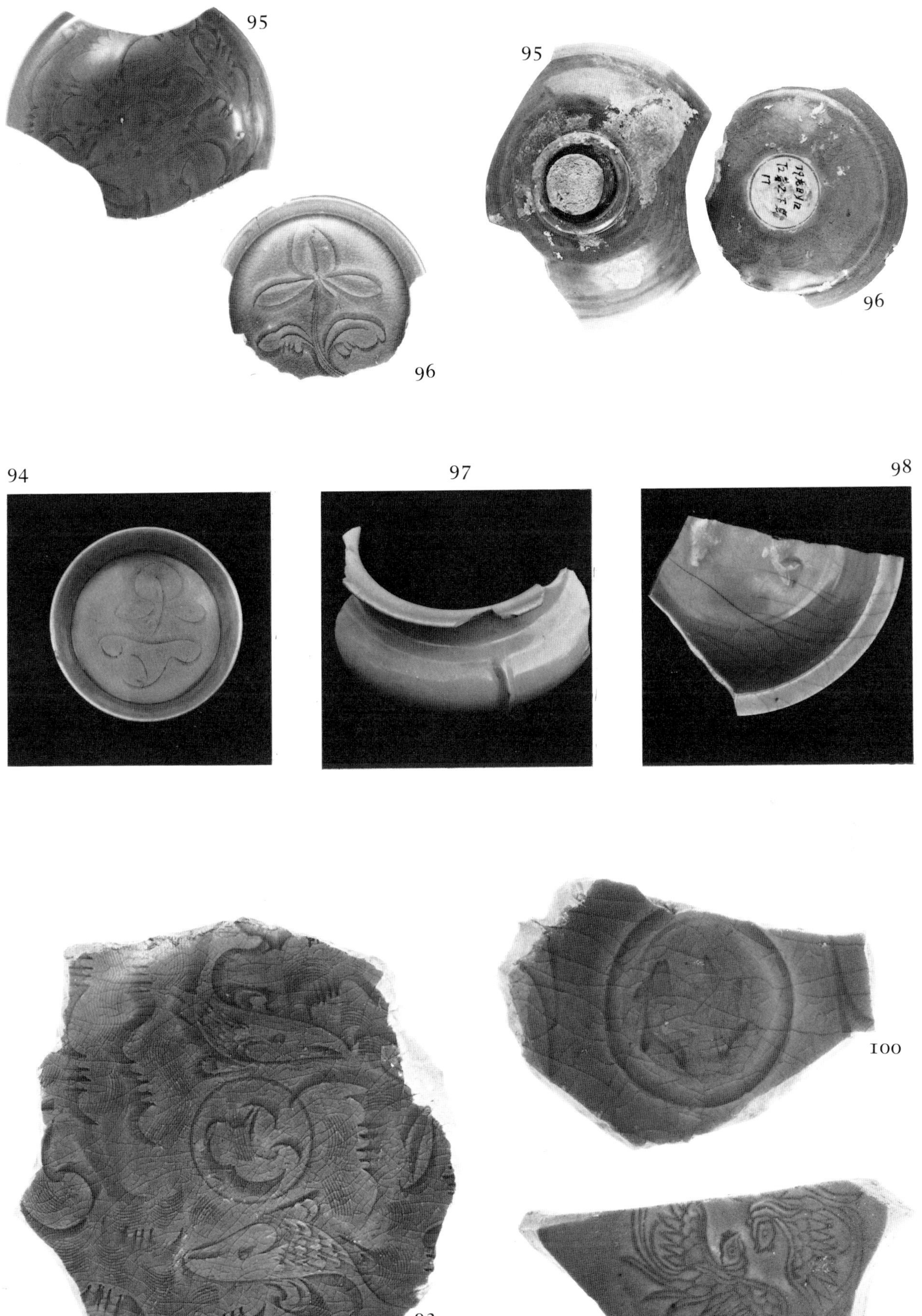

95
95
96
96
94
97
98
93
100
99

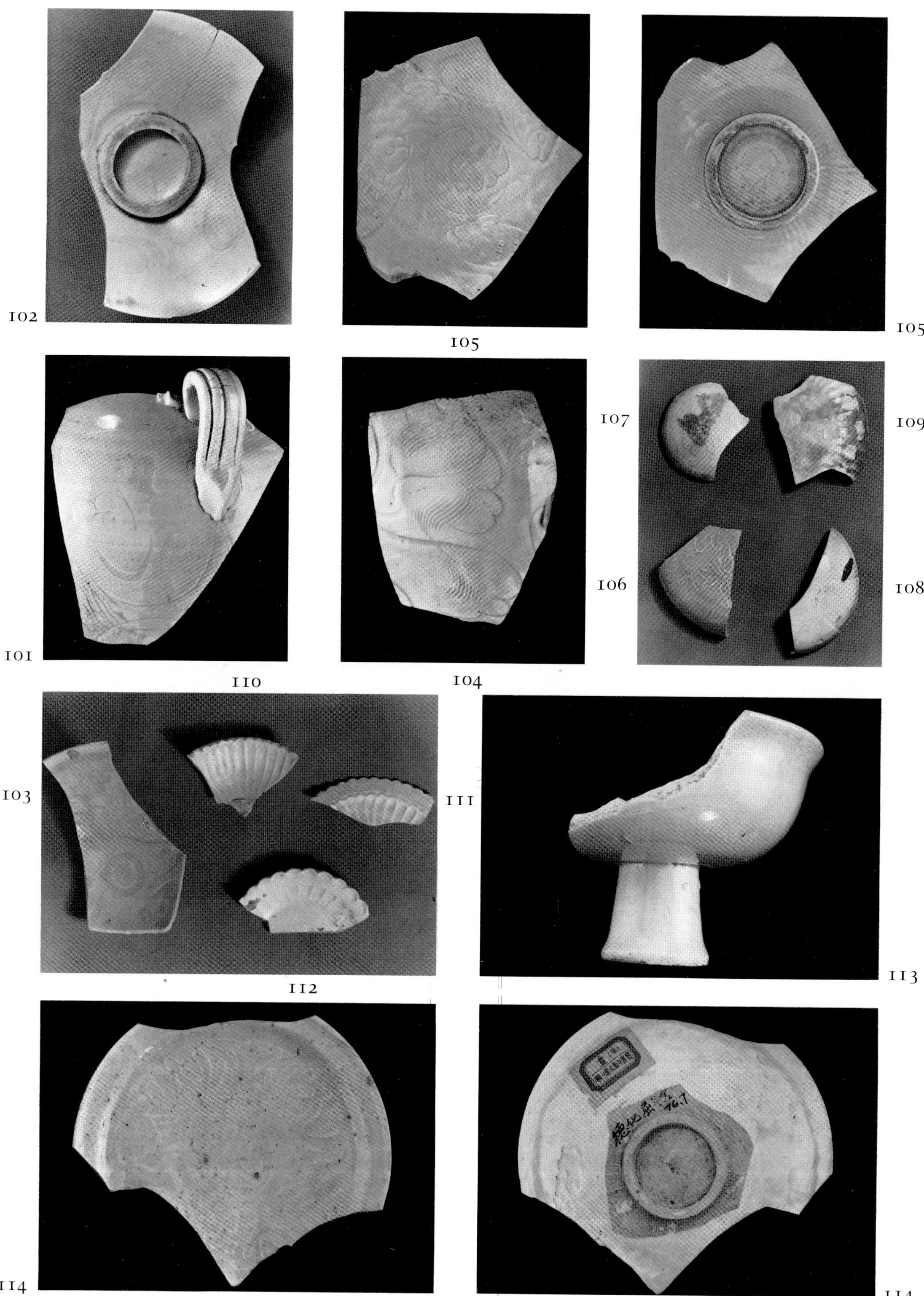

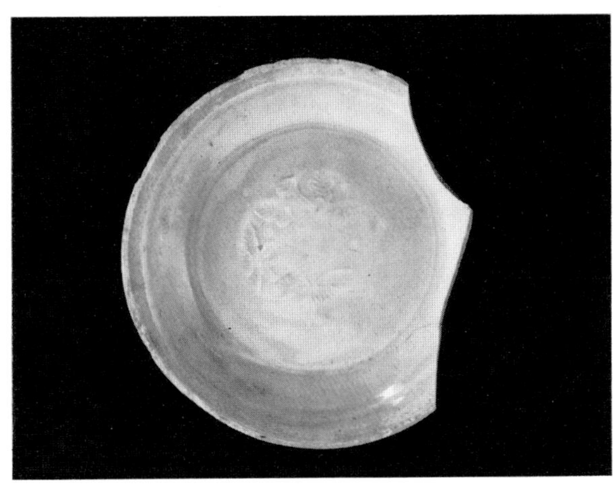

120

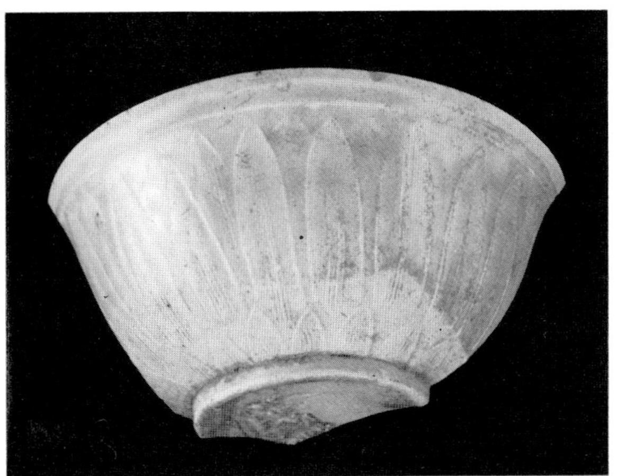

115

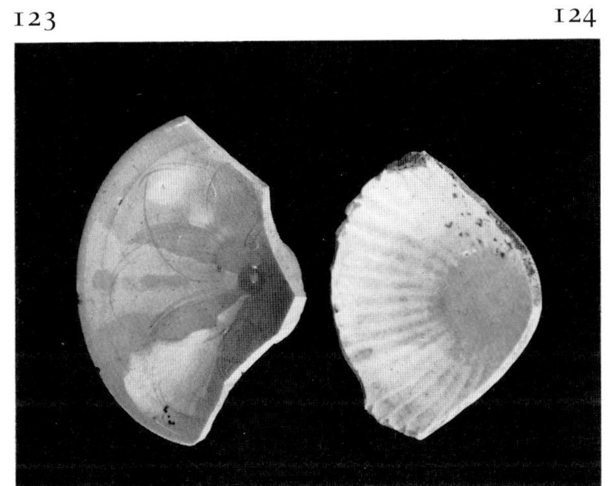

123   124

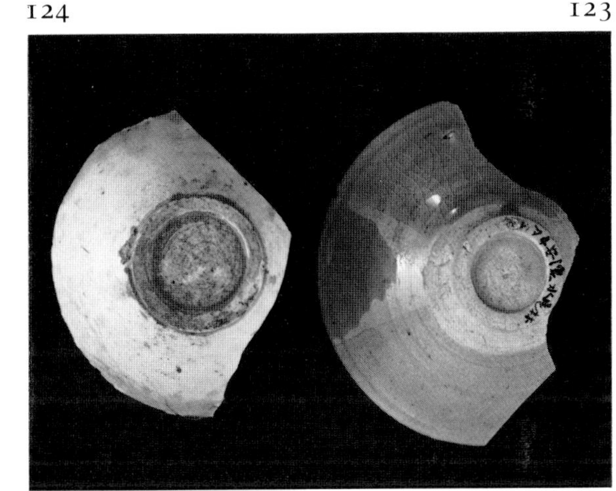

124   123

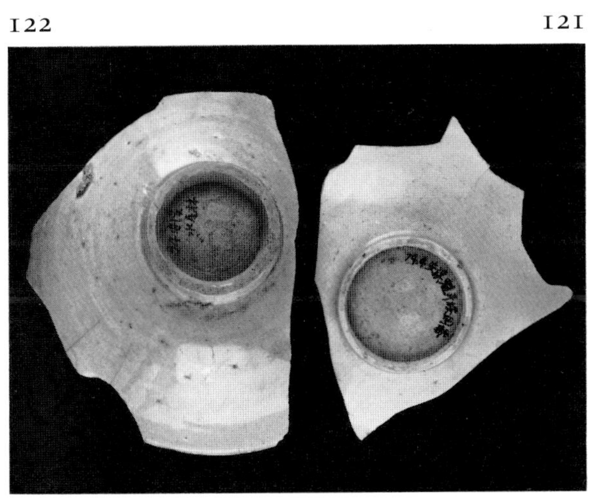

122   121

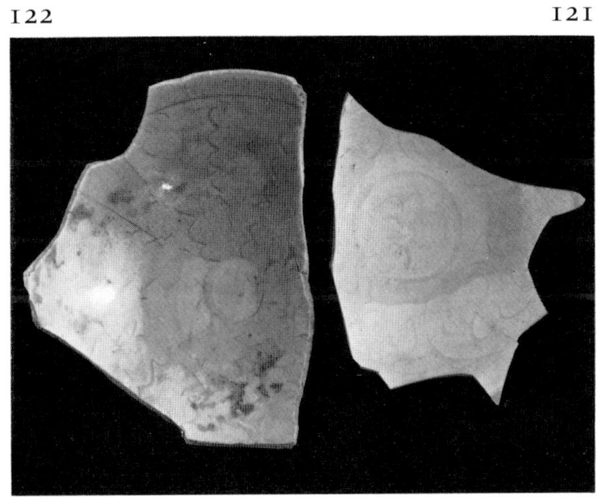

122   121

127

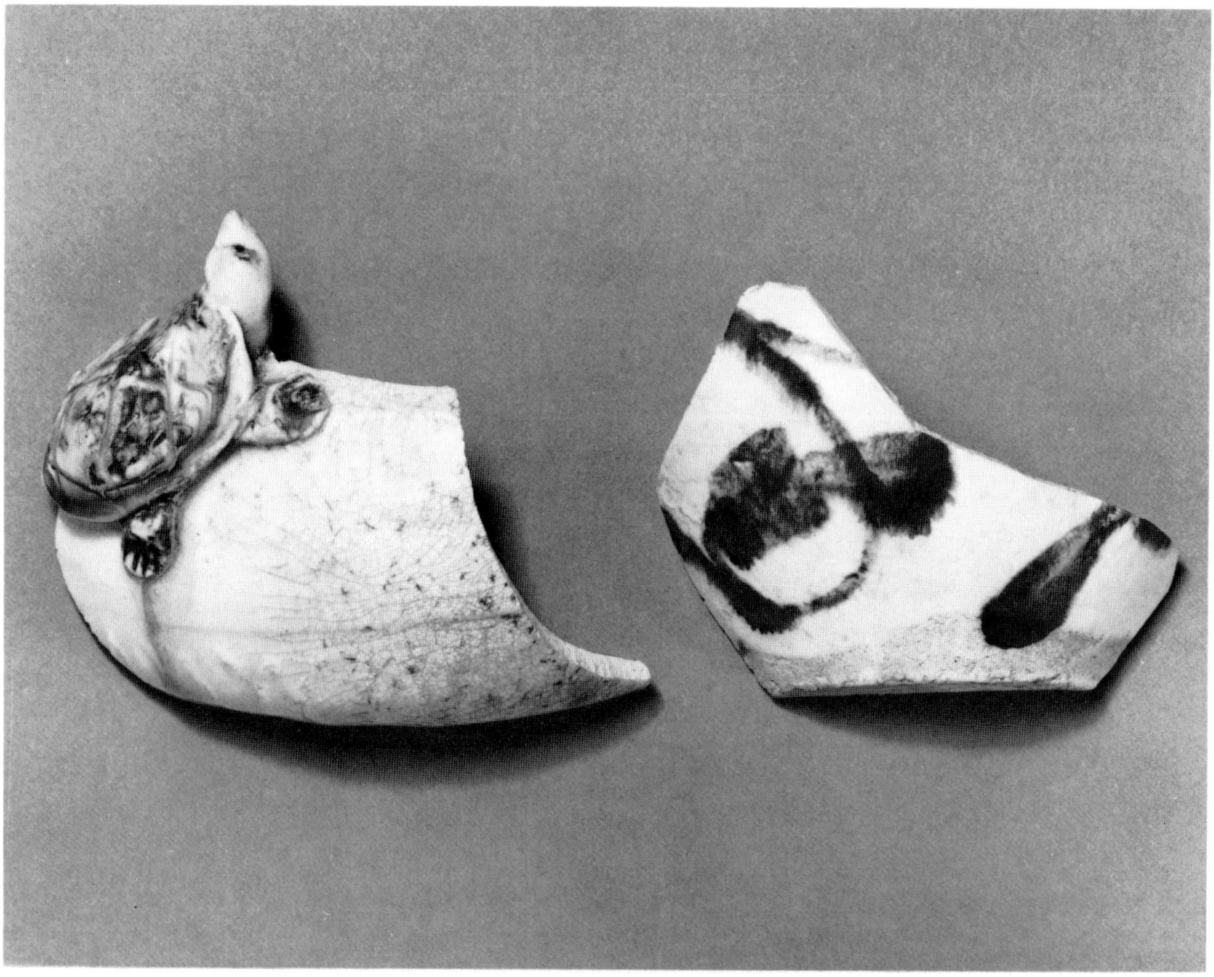

118

119

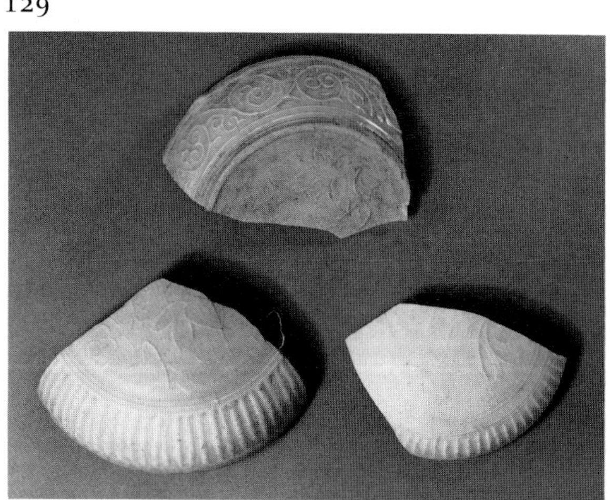

129

116

117

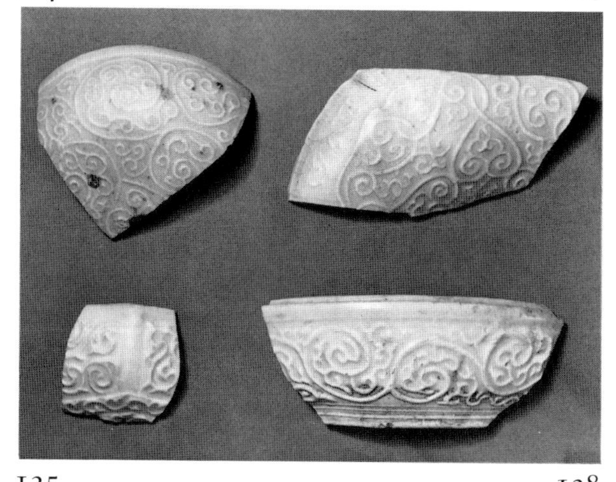

127

126

125

128

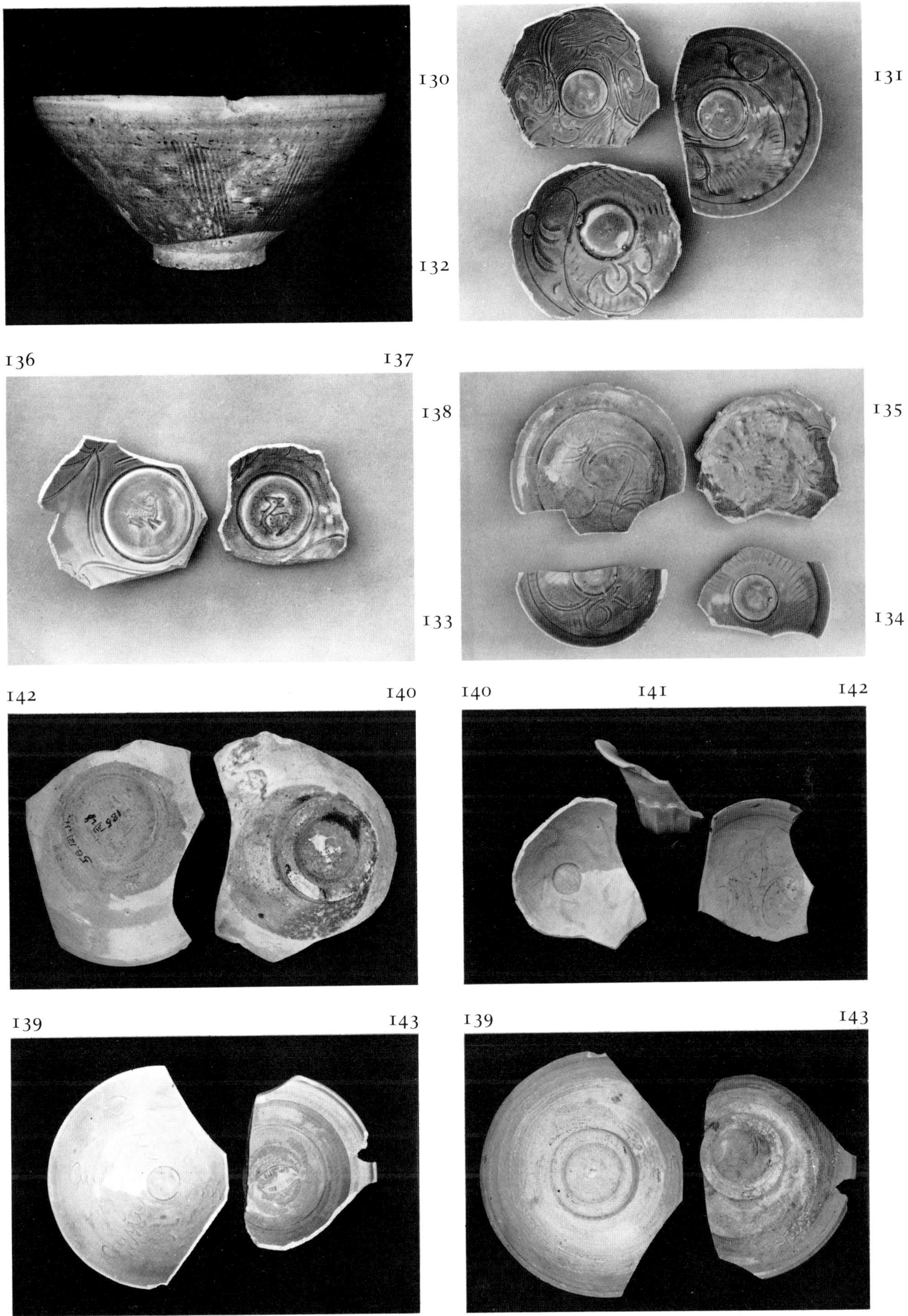

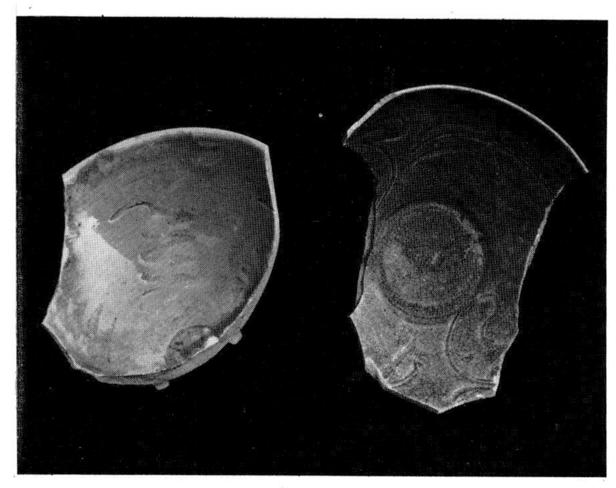

144   145

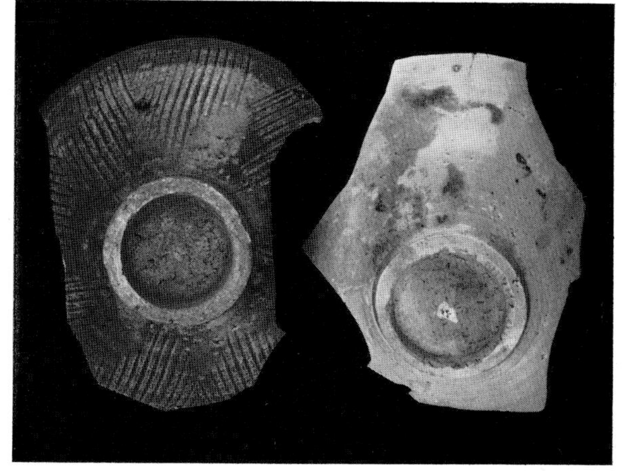

145   150

147   152

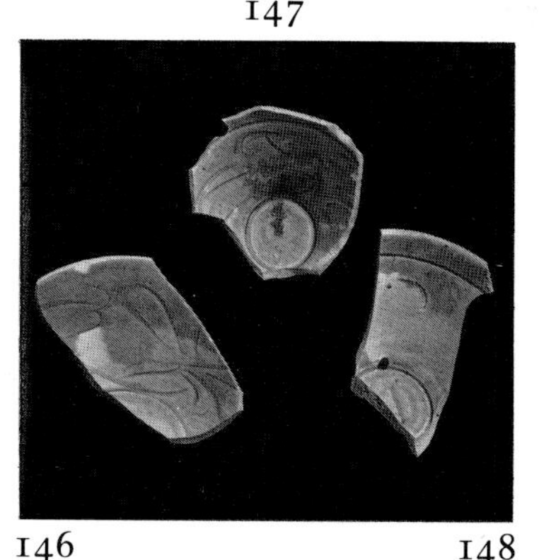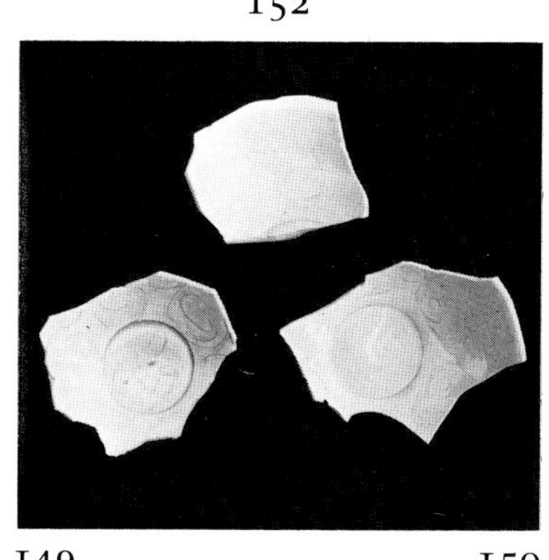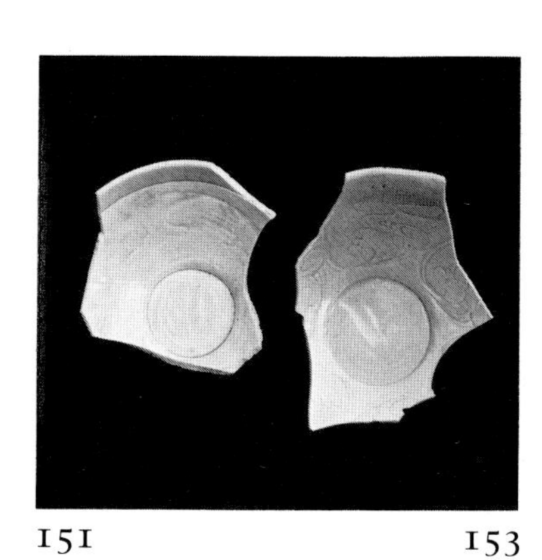

146   148   149   150   151   153

154   154

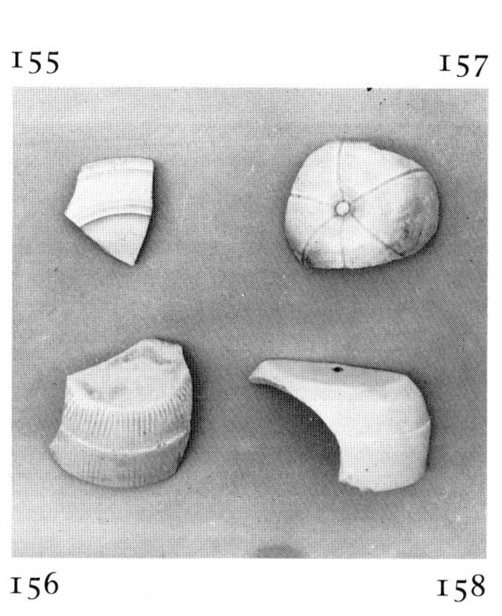

155   157

156   158

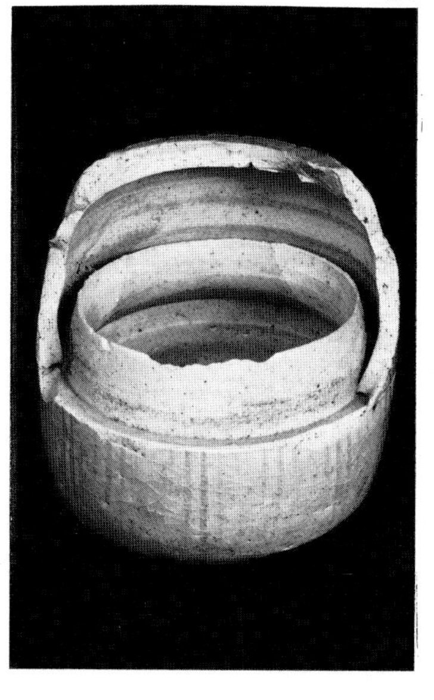

164

163

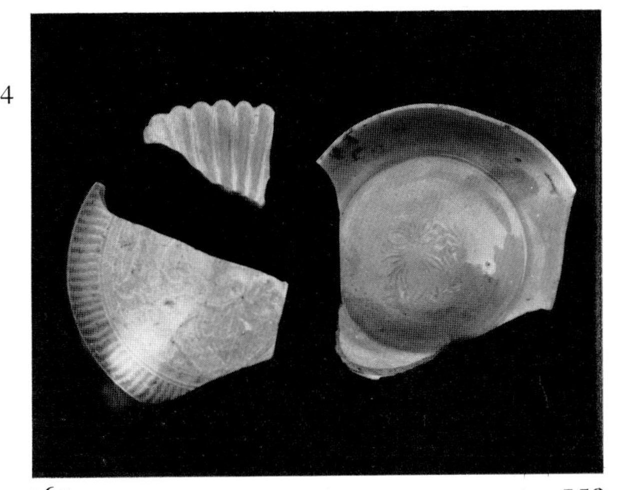

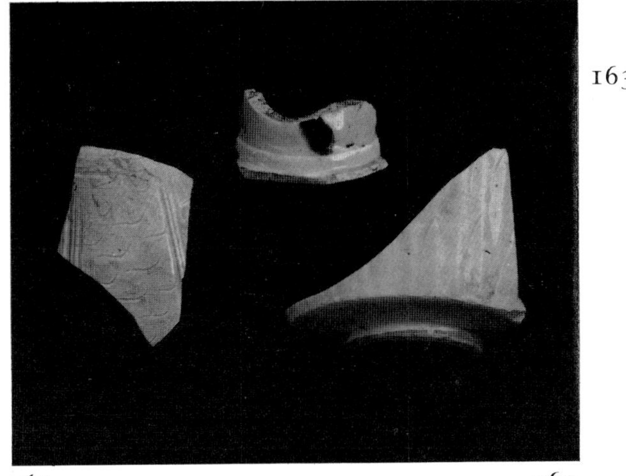

162 159 161 160

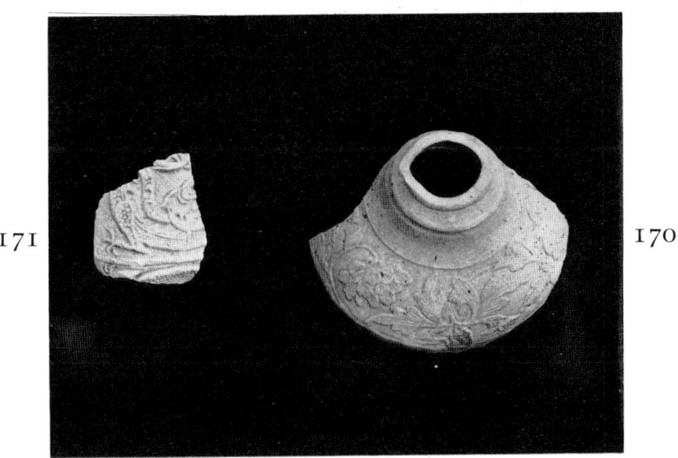

171 170

166 165

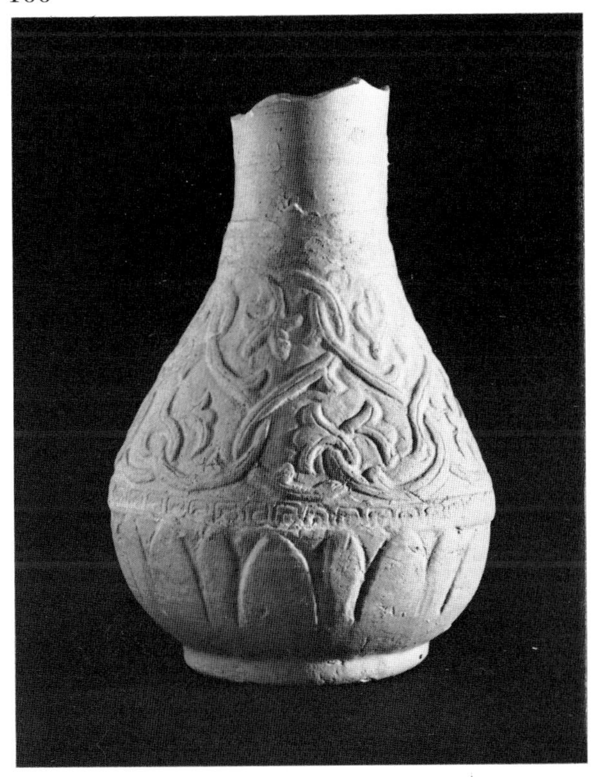

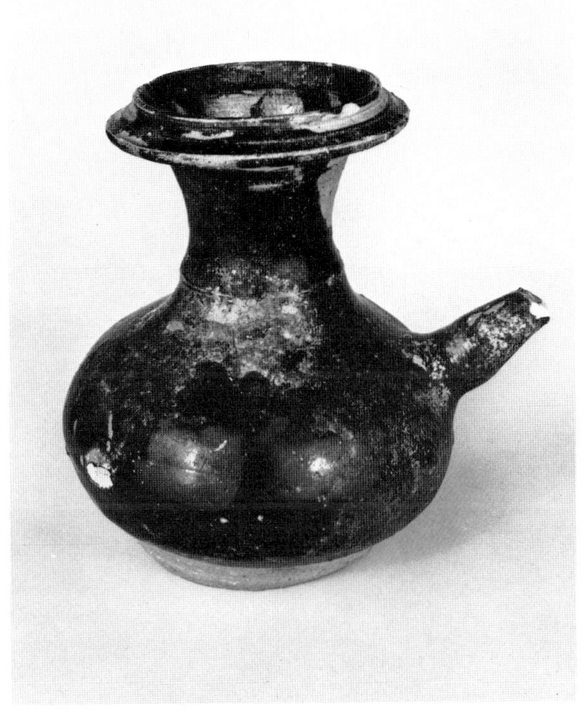

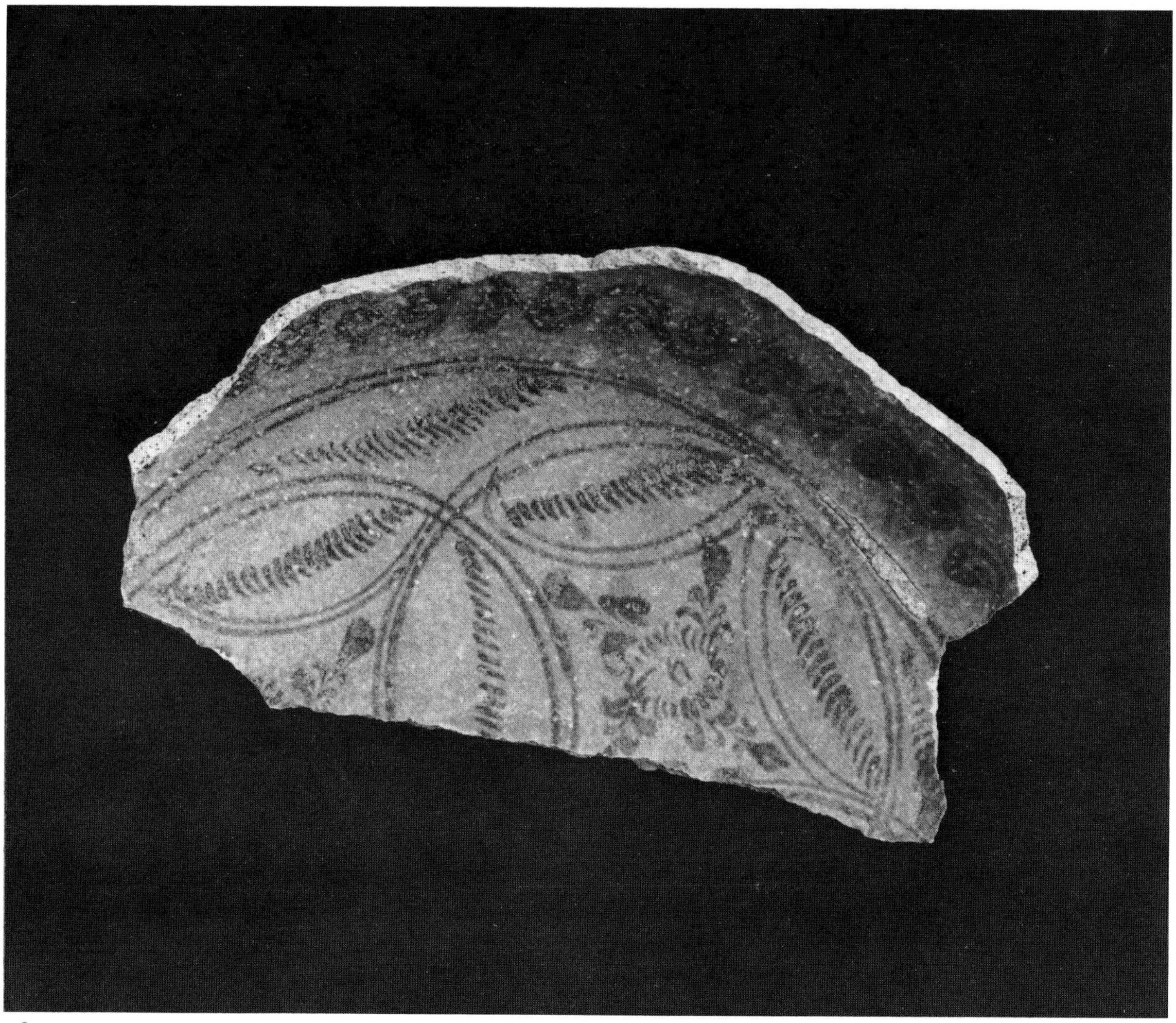

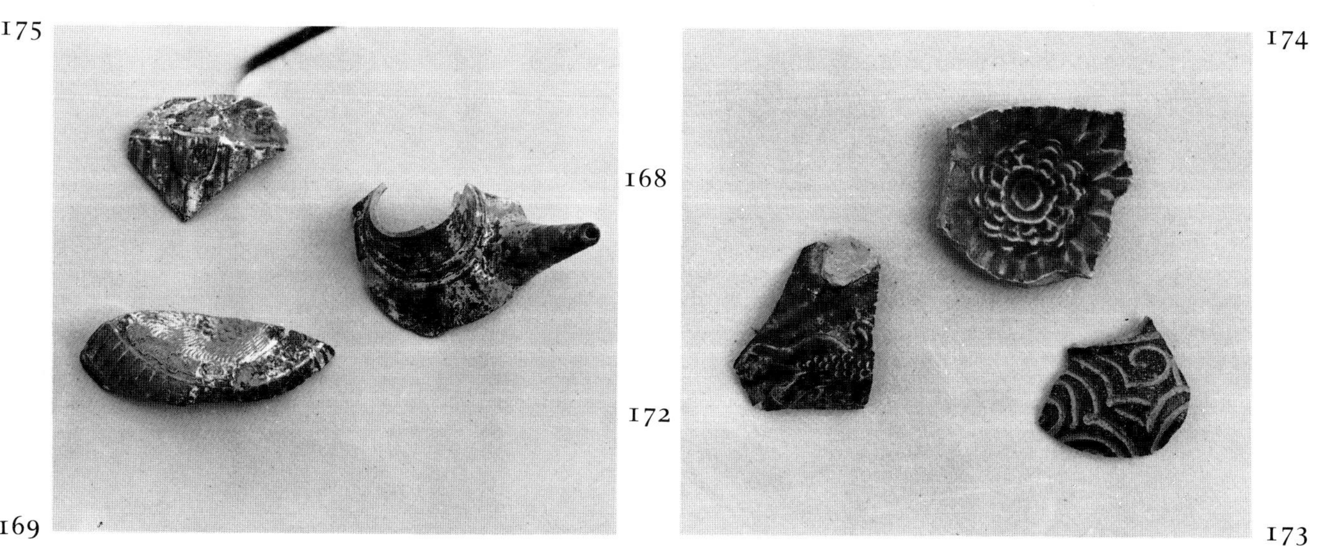

167

175   174

168

172

169   173

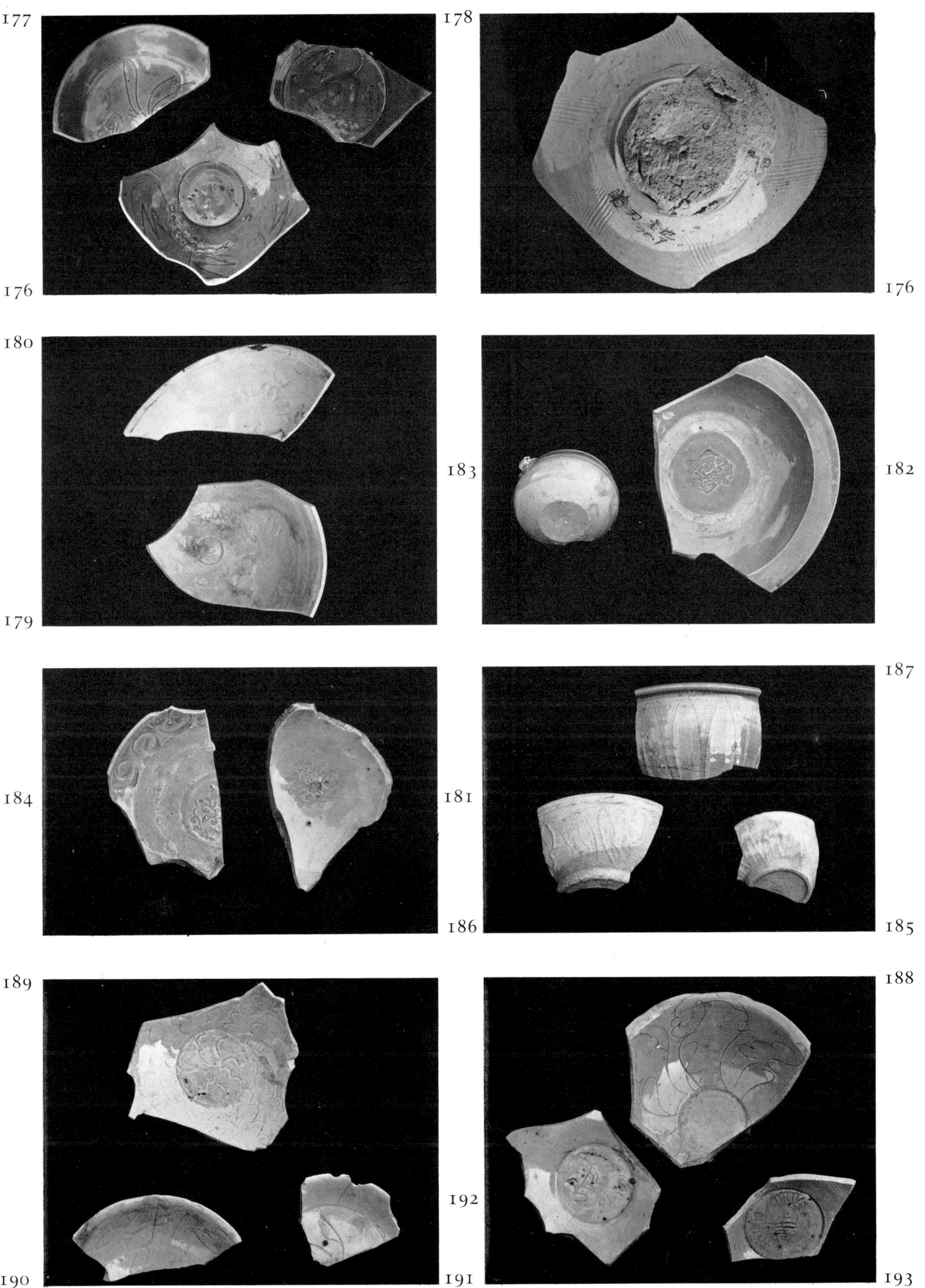

177

178

176

176

180

183

182

179

187

184

181

186

185

189

188

192

190

191

193

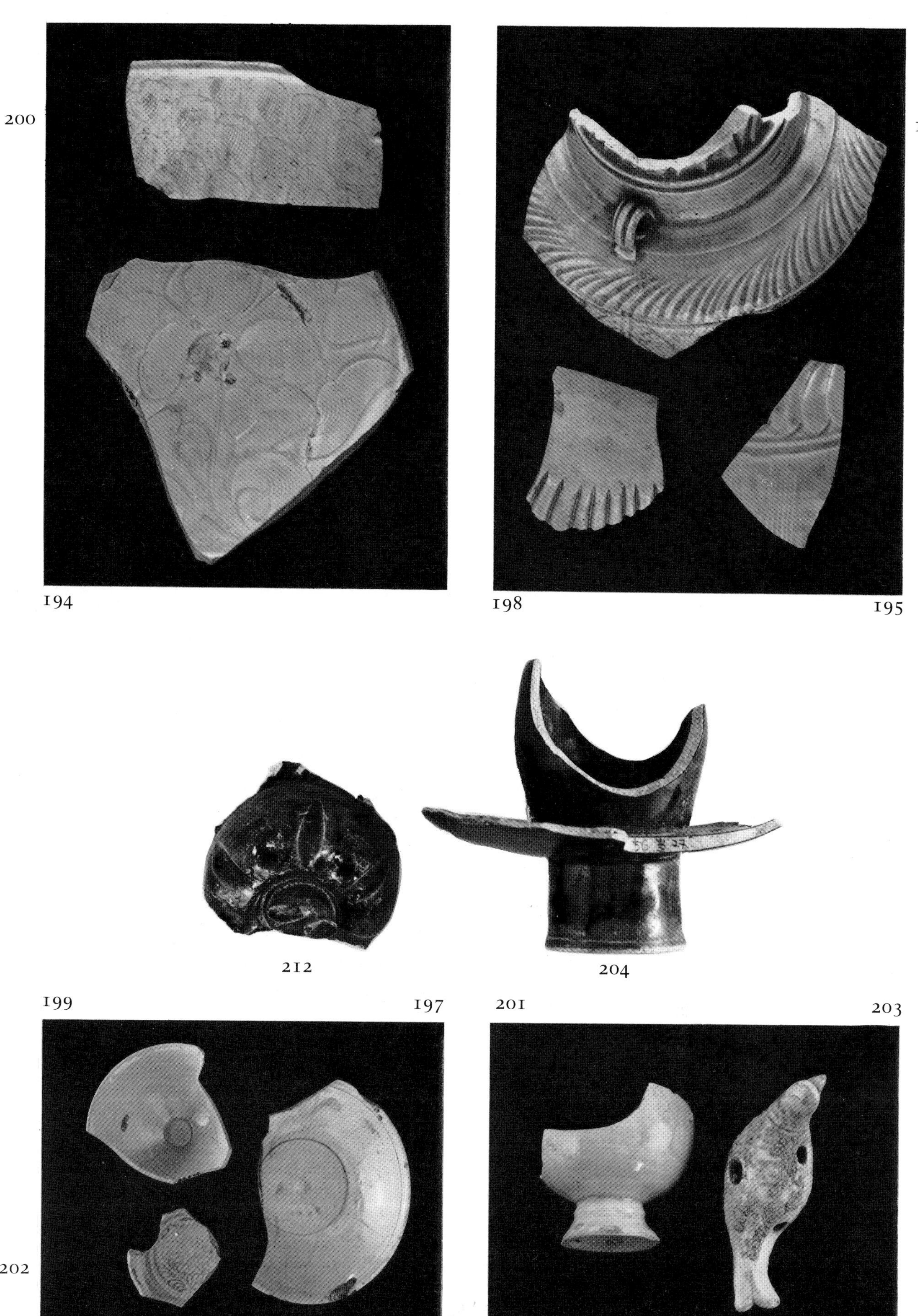

200

196

194

198

195

212

204

199 197 201 203

202

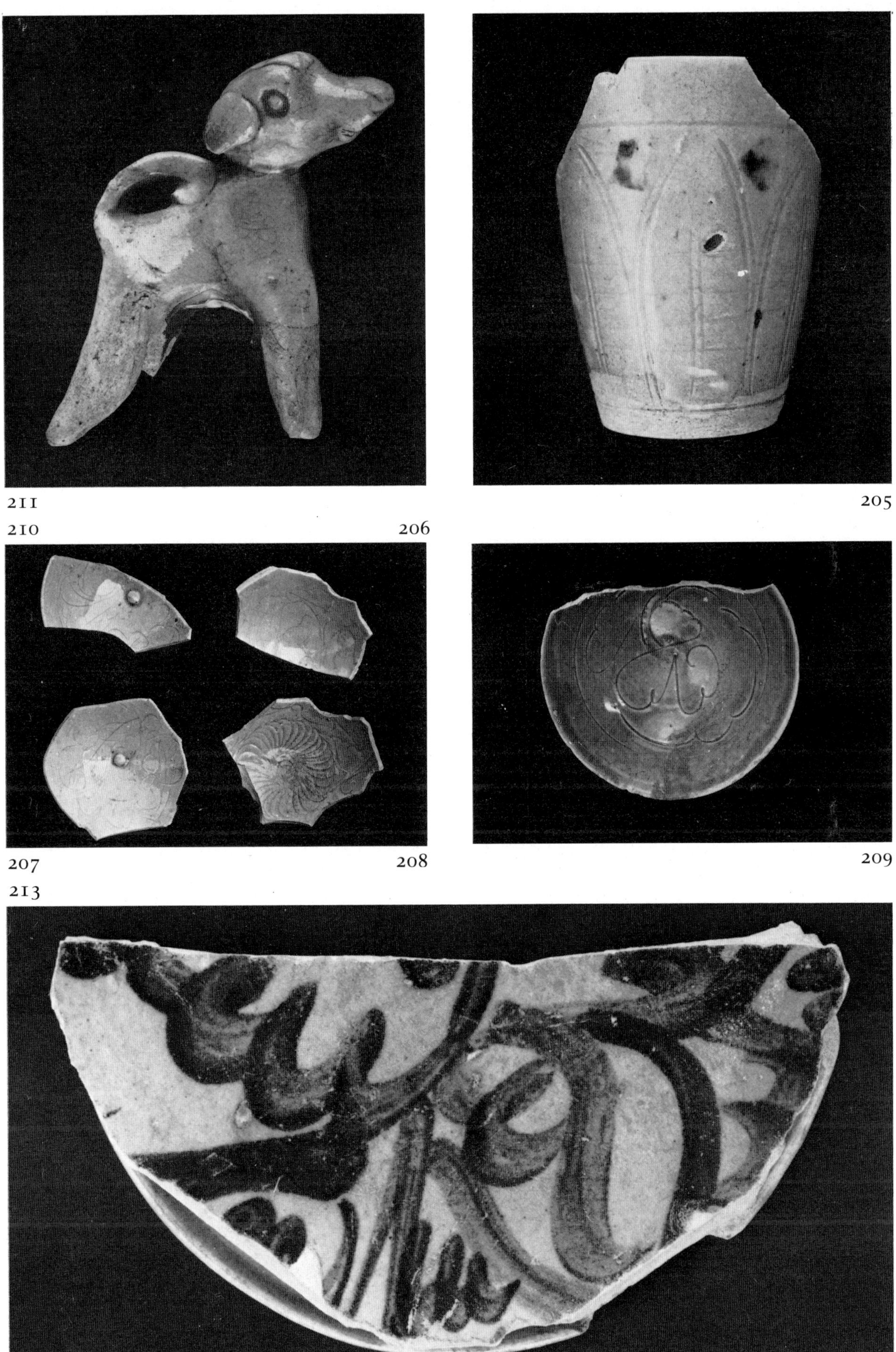

211

205

210
206

207
208

209

213

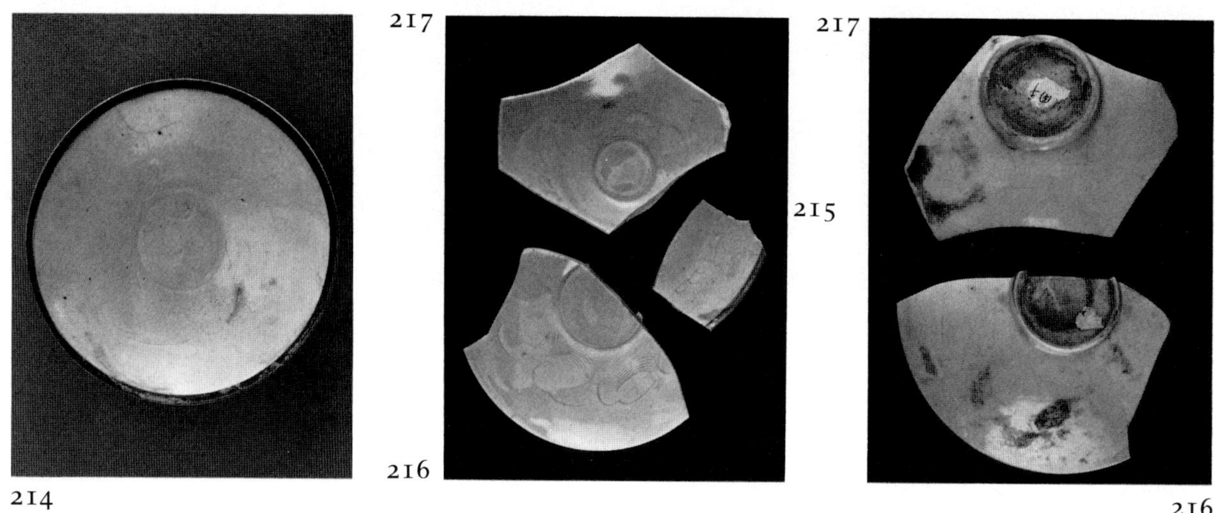

214

217

216

217

215

216

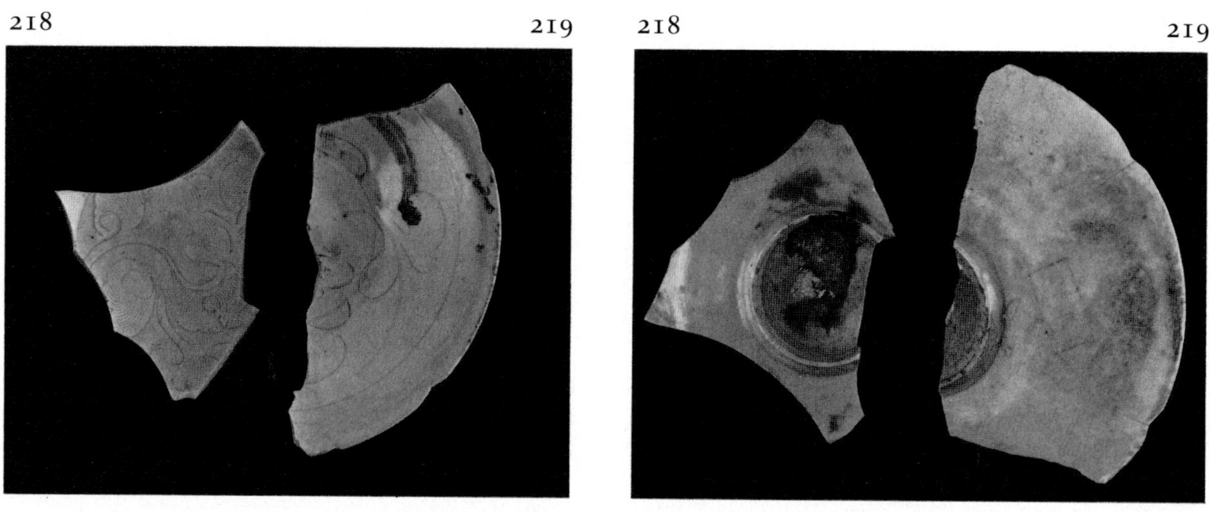

218

219

218

219

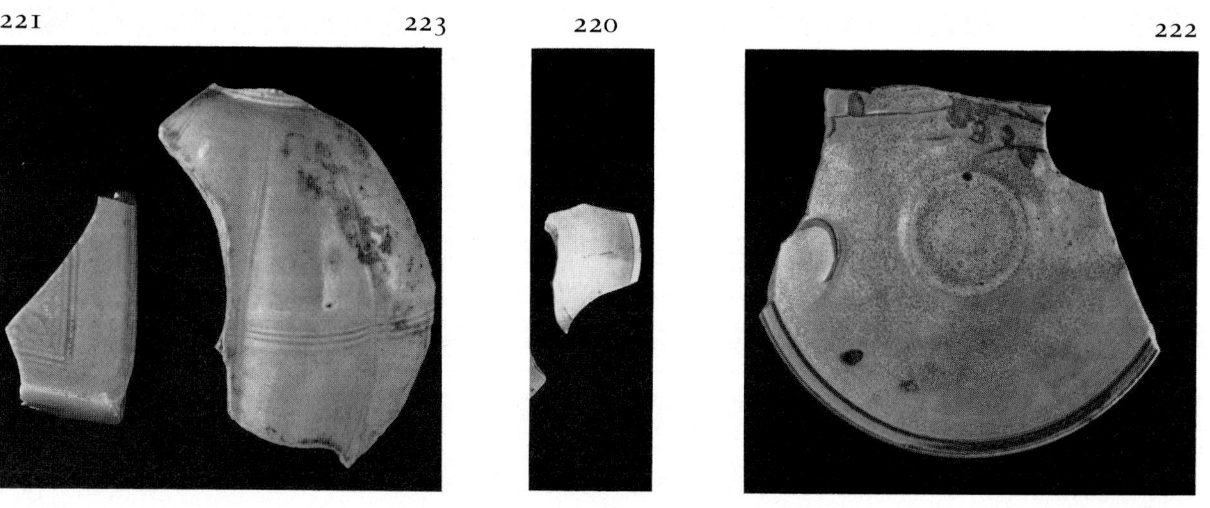

221

223

220

222

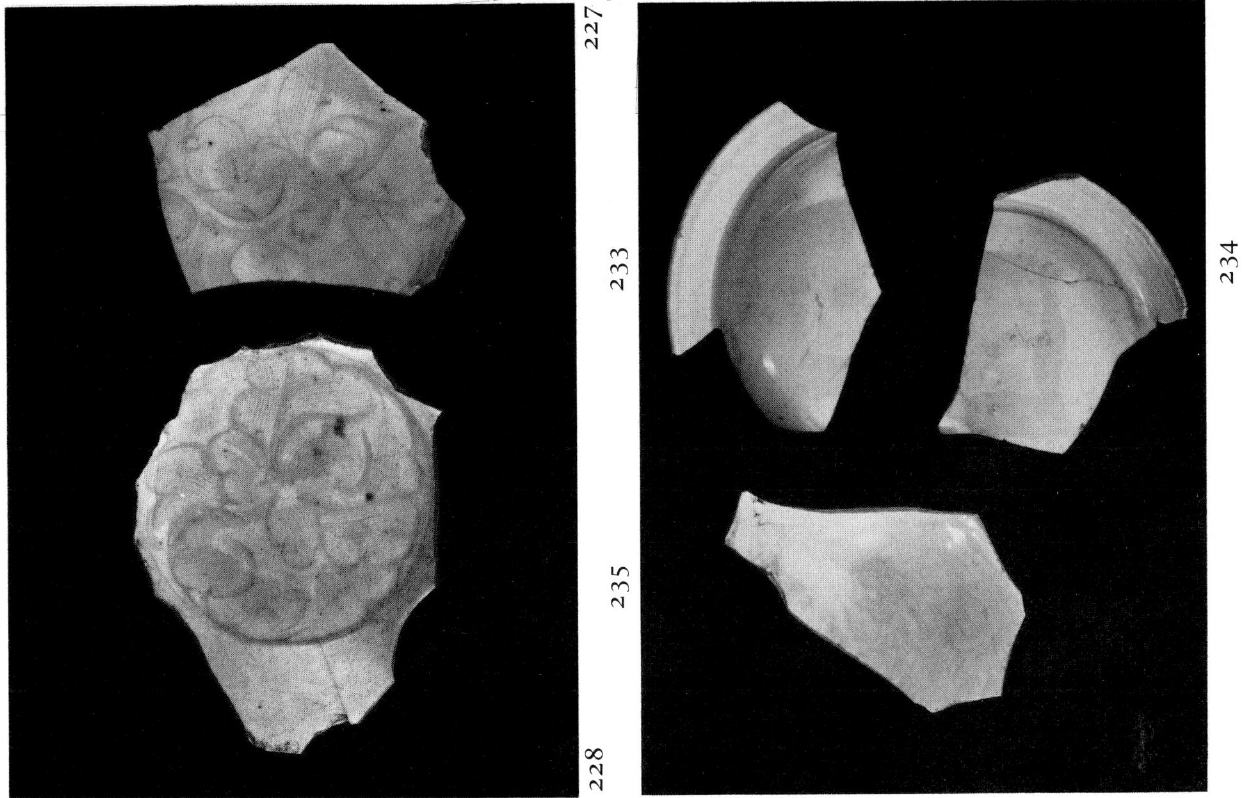

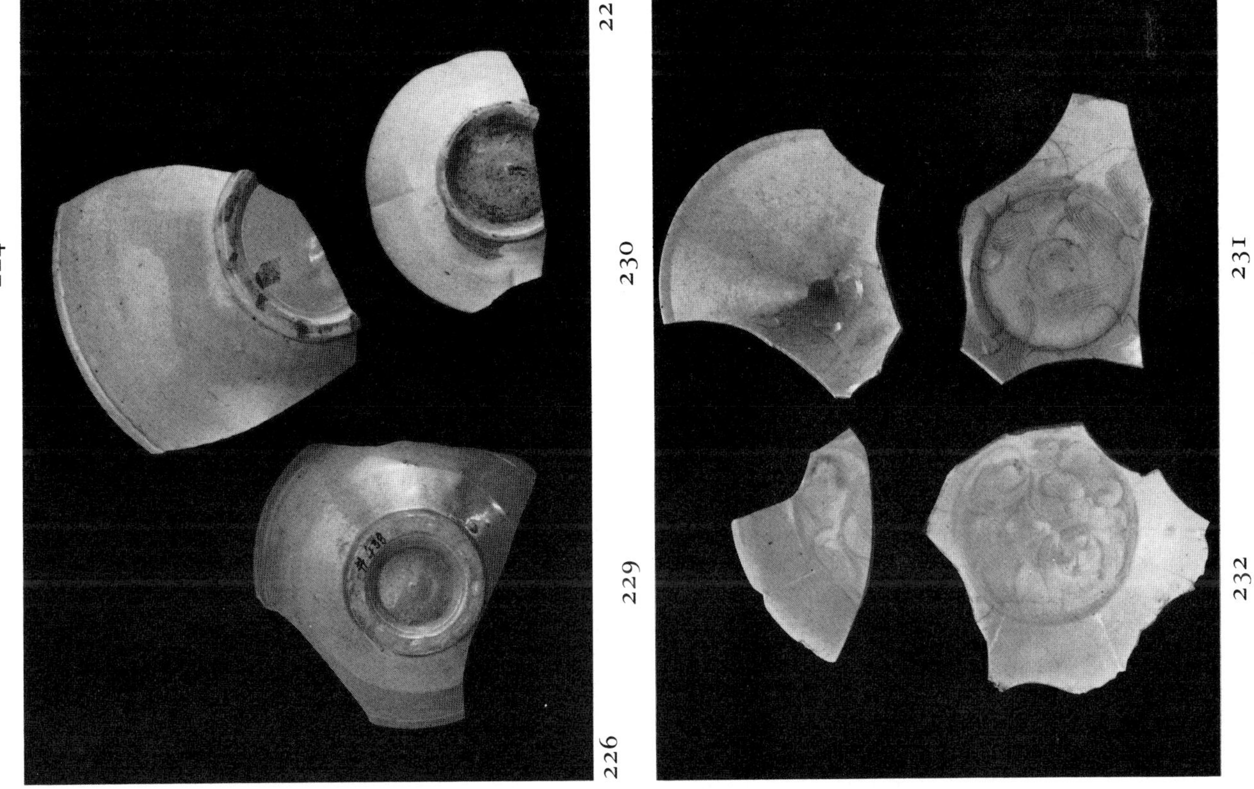

236

237

237

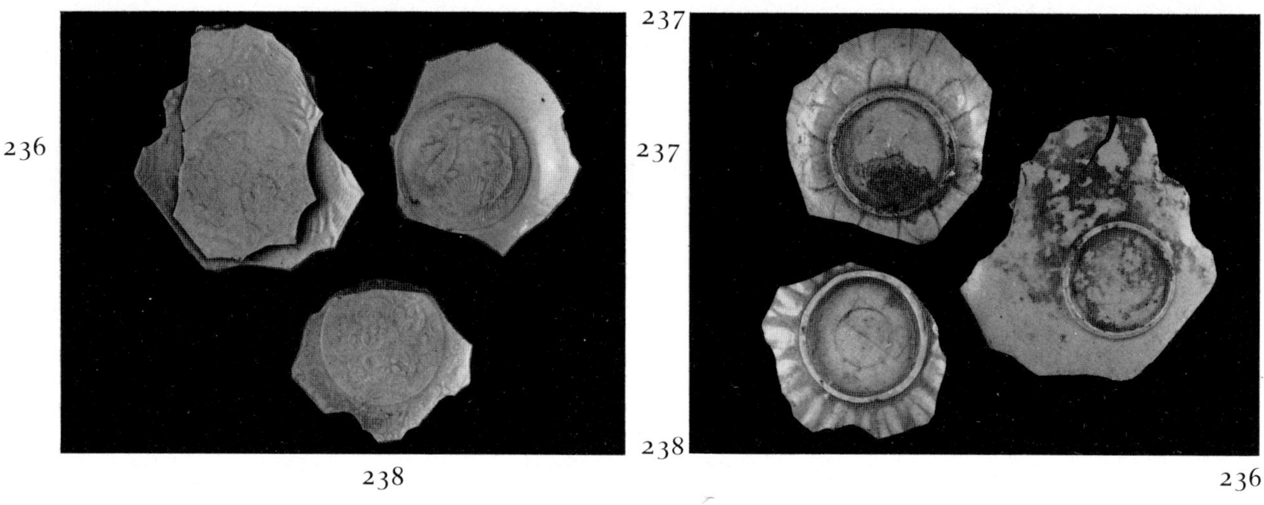

238

238

236

241

239

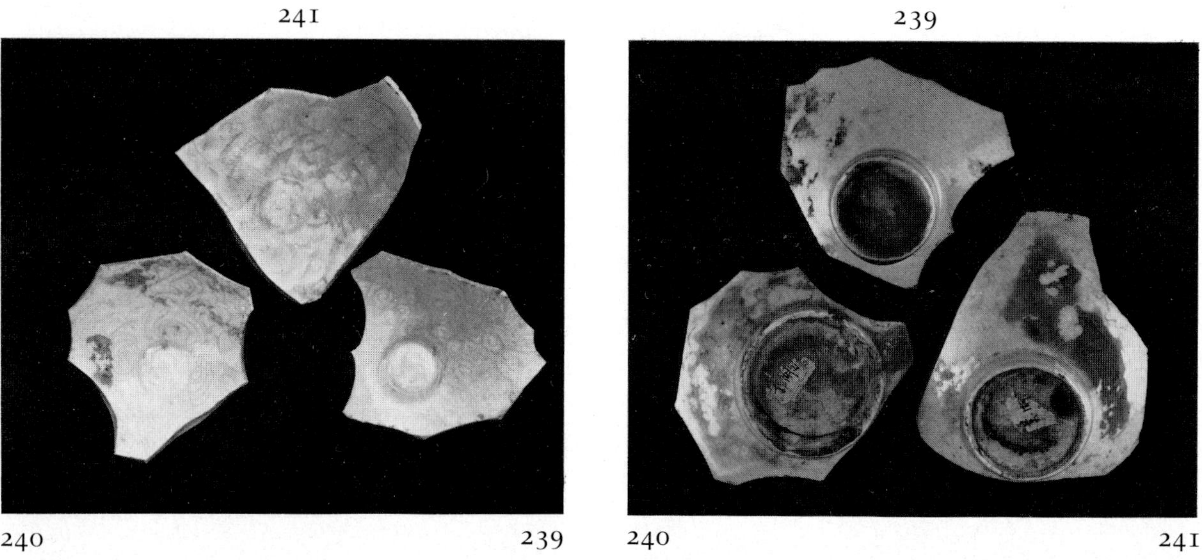

240

239

240

241

249

250

244

245

242

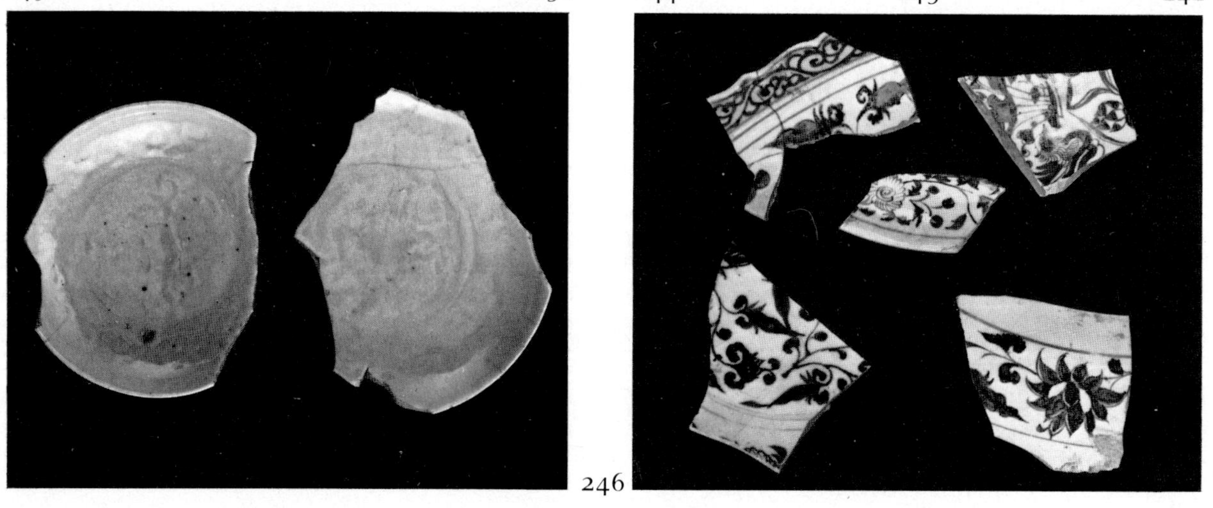

240

246

247

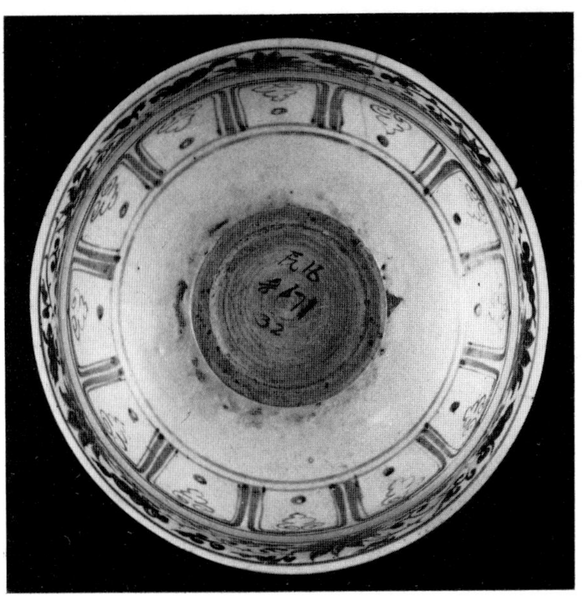

243

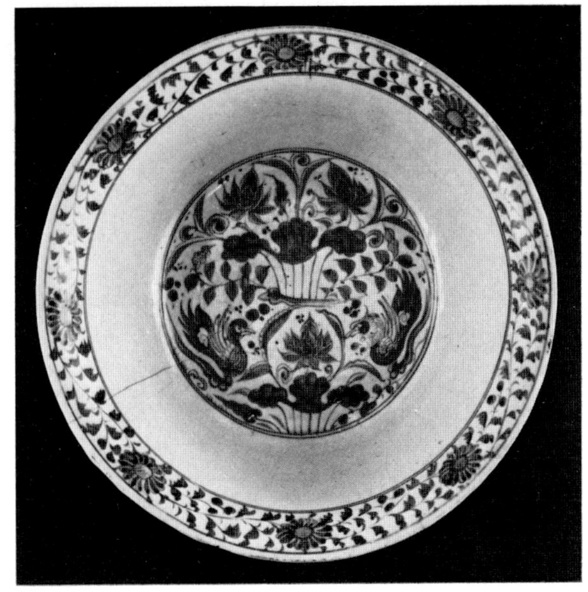

243

243

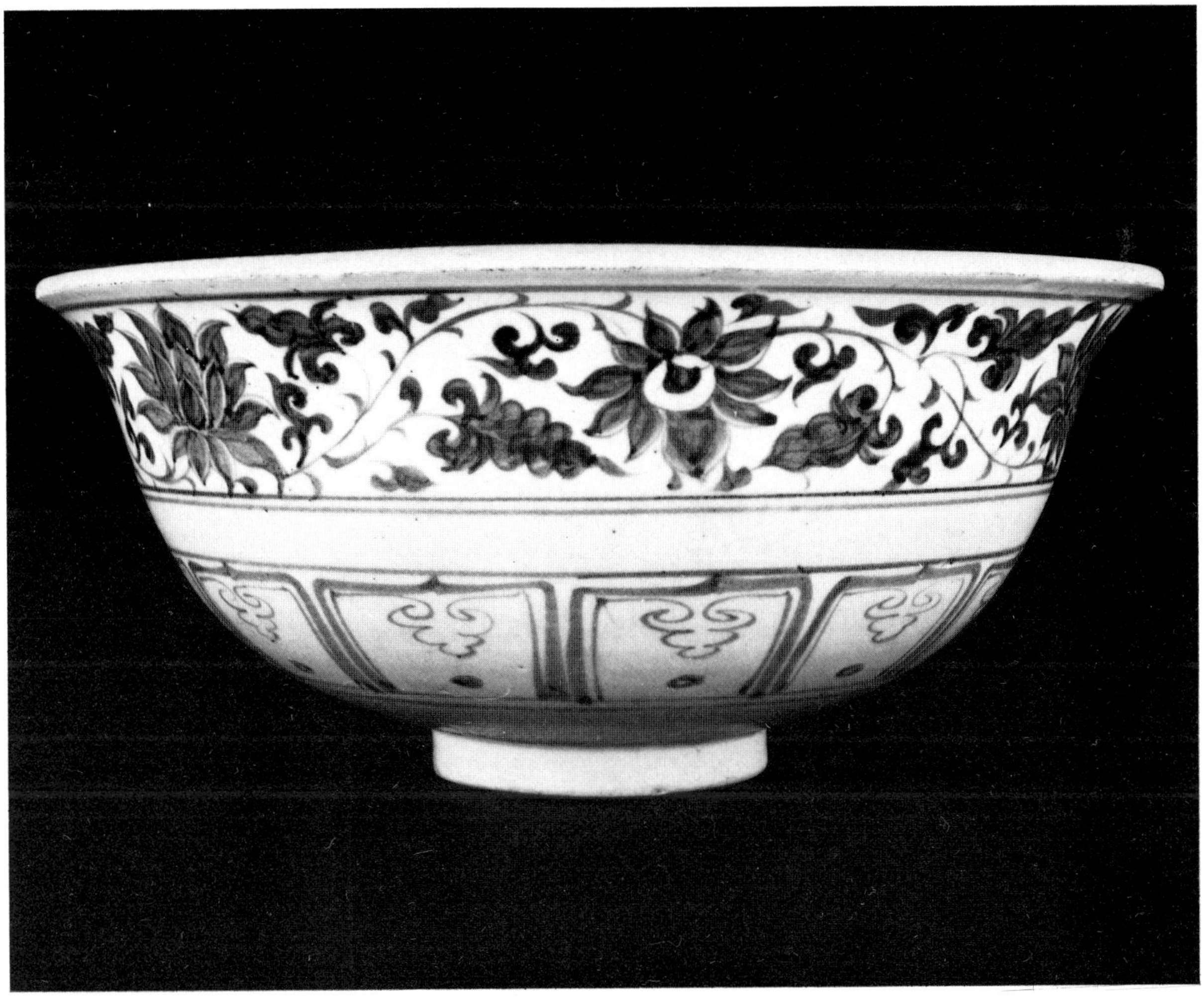

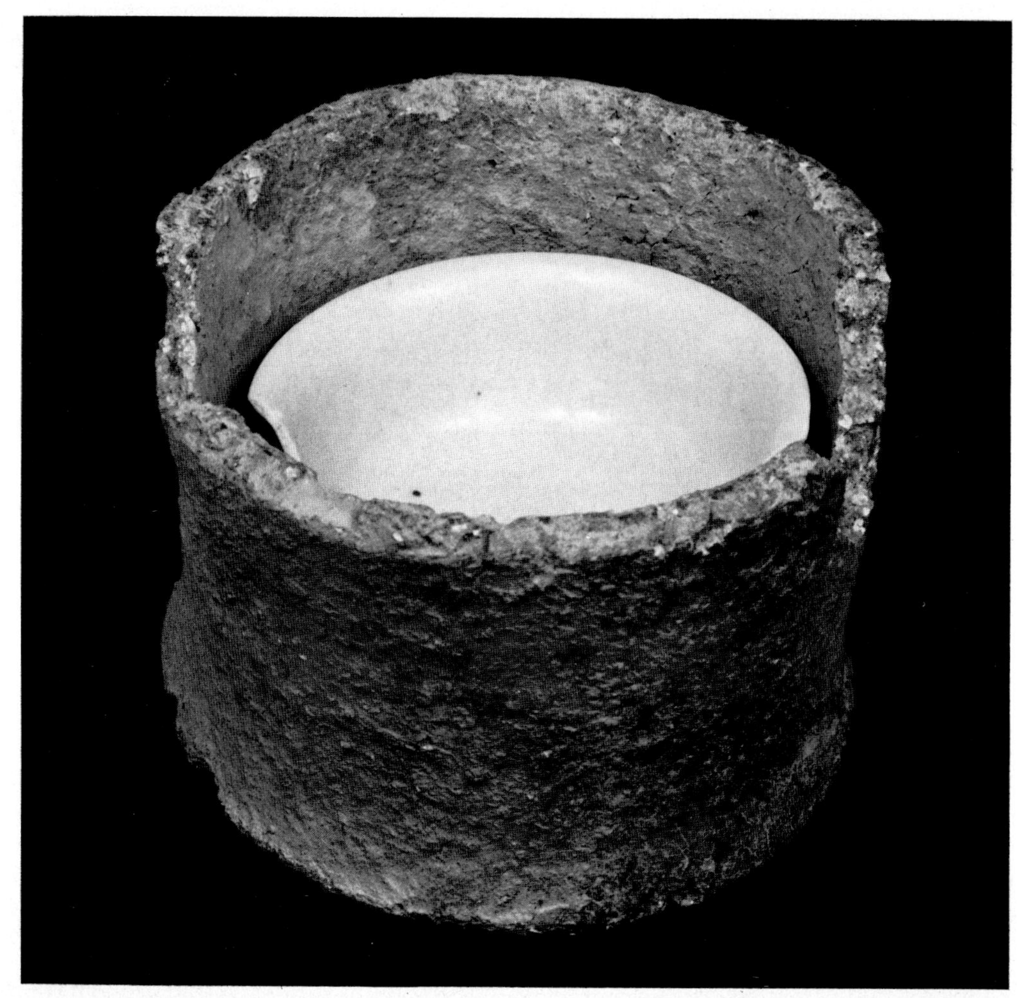

248

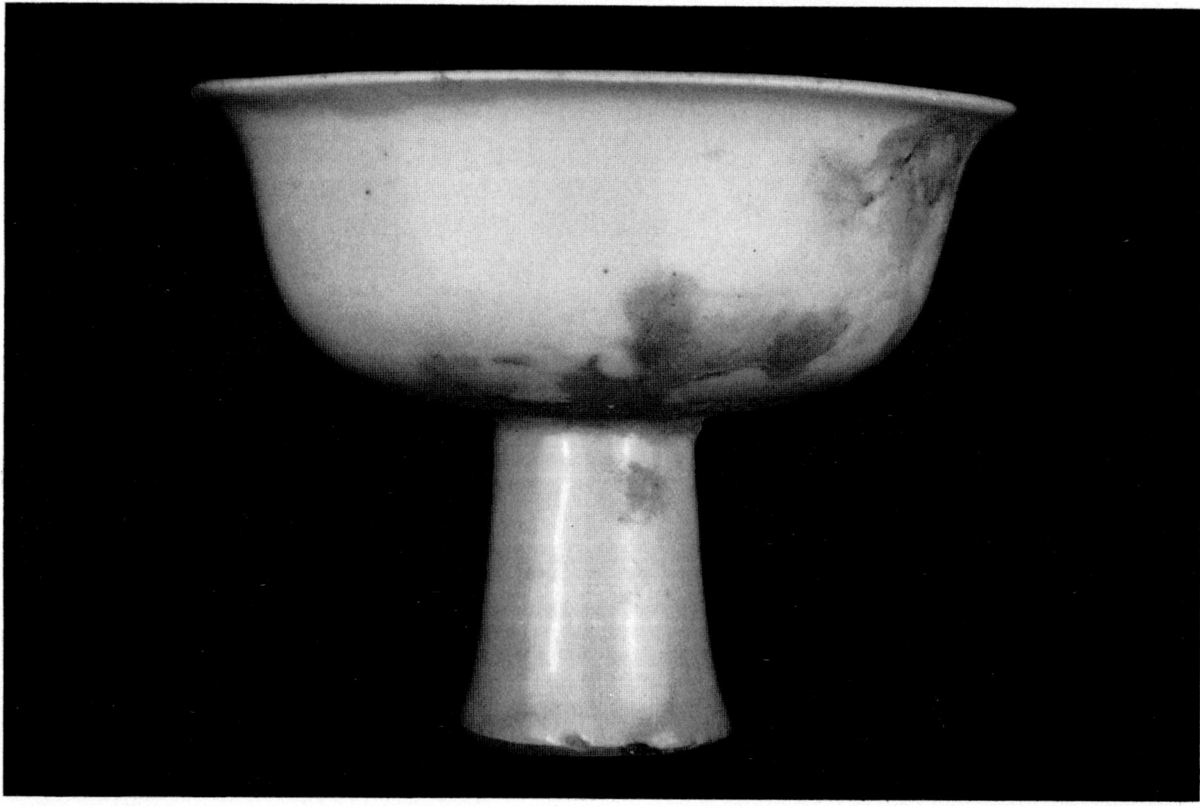

248

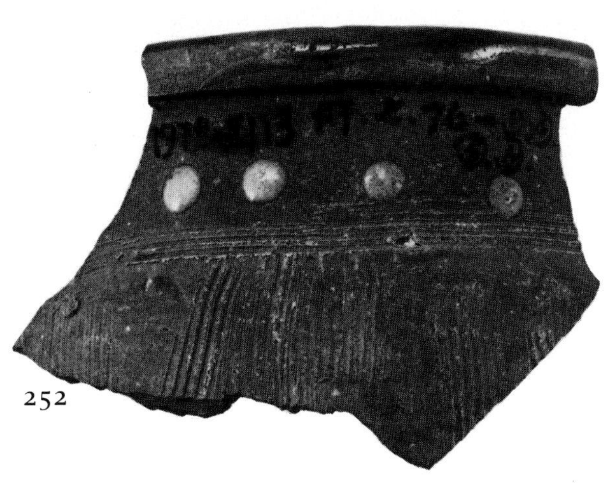

252

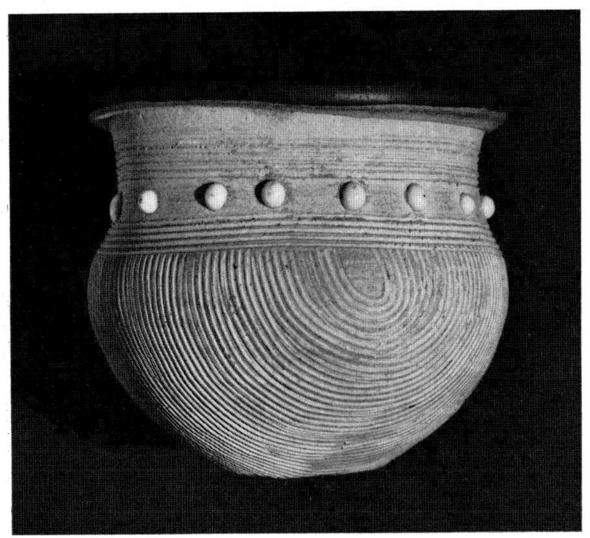

251
264

263

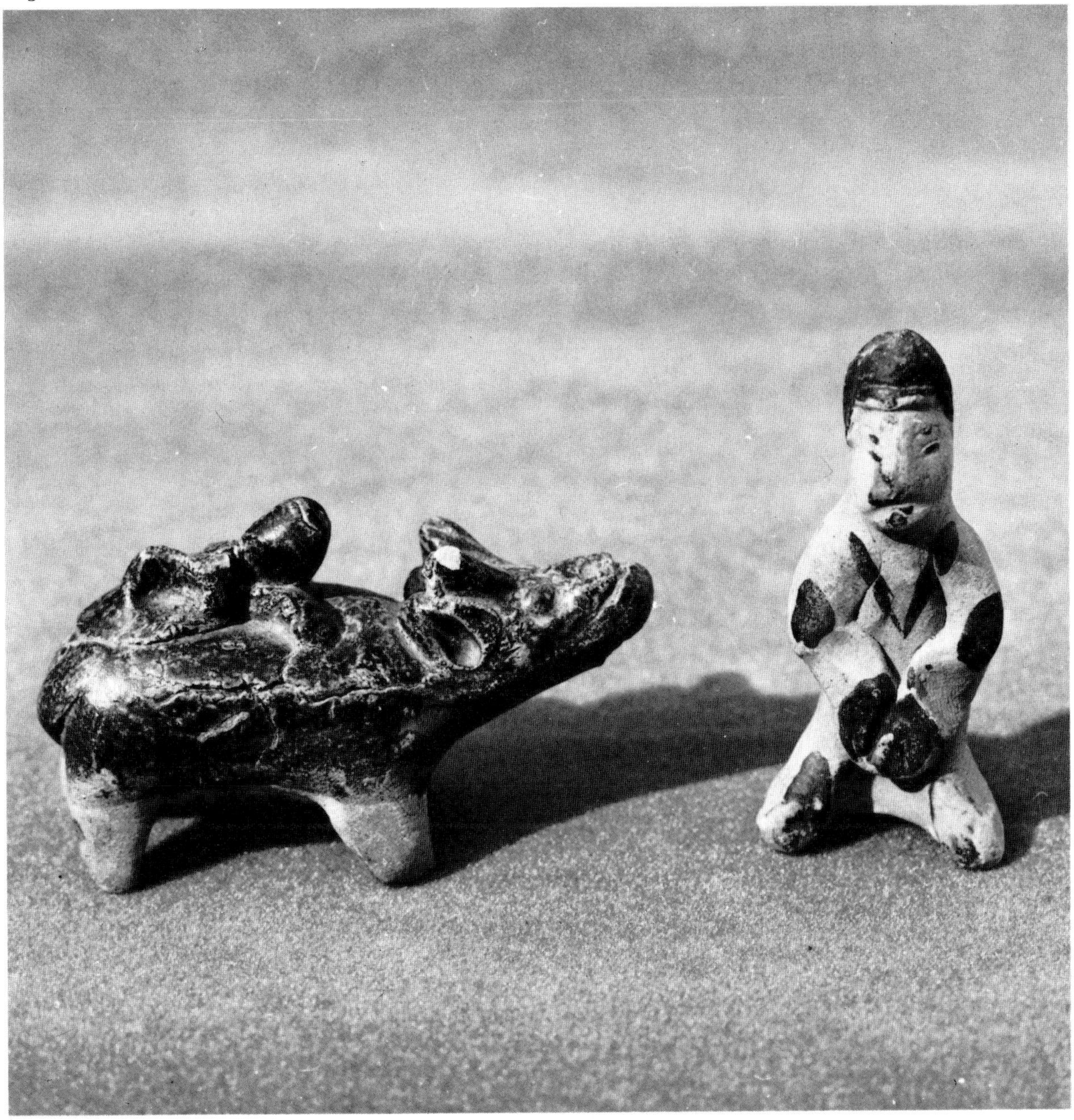

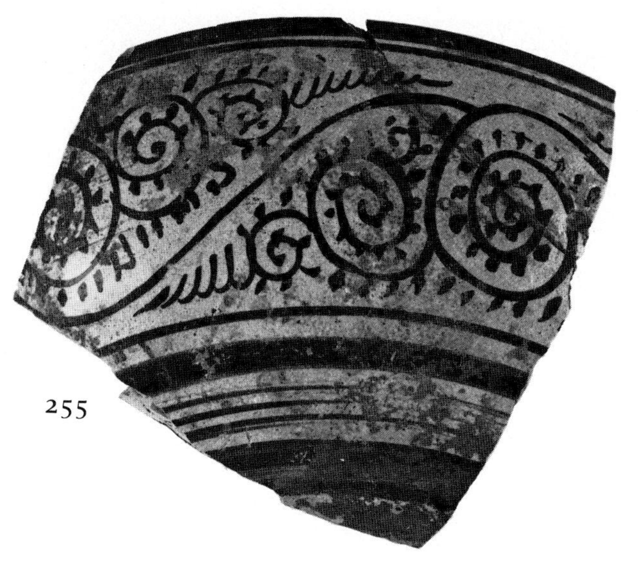

255

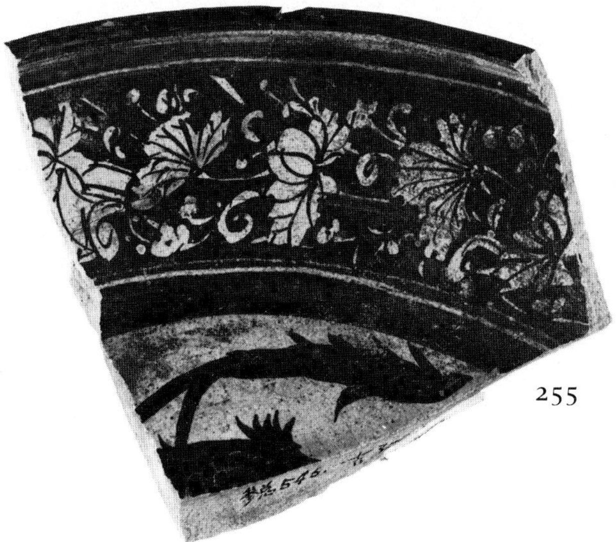

255

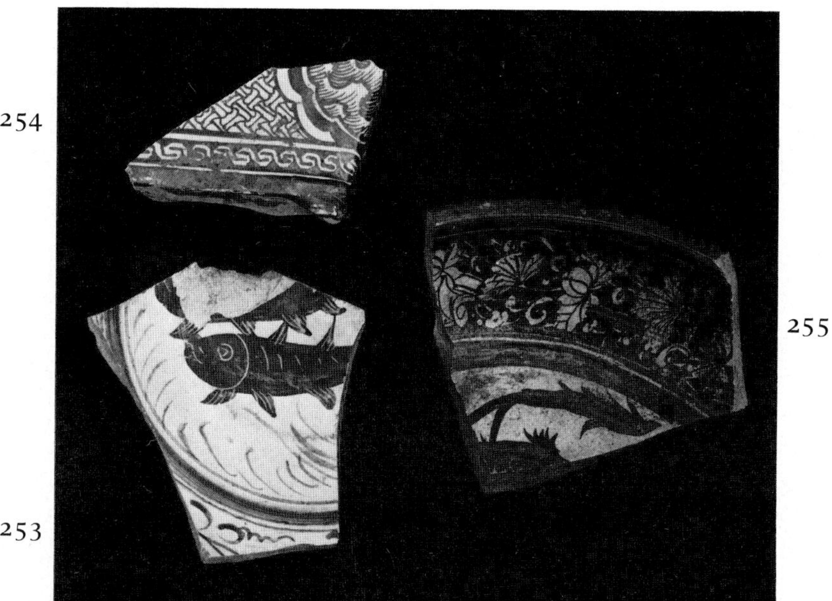

254

255

253

256

260

262

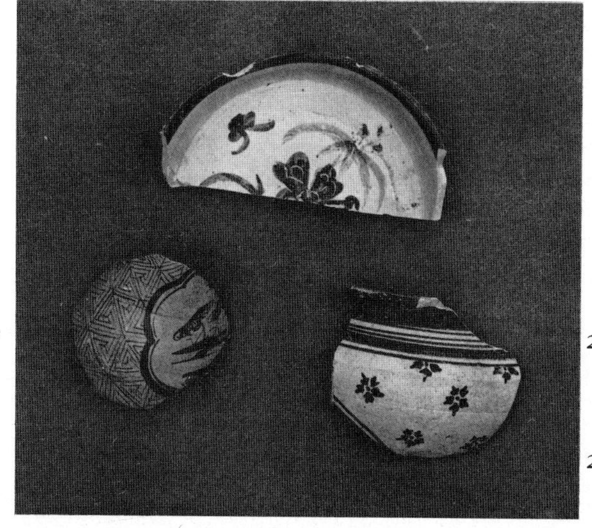

257

258

259

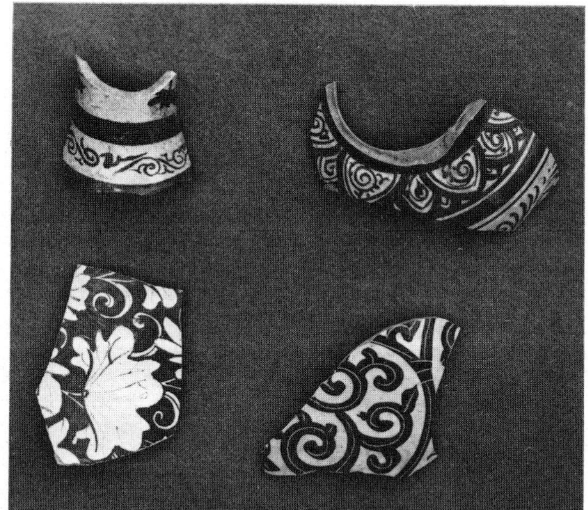

261

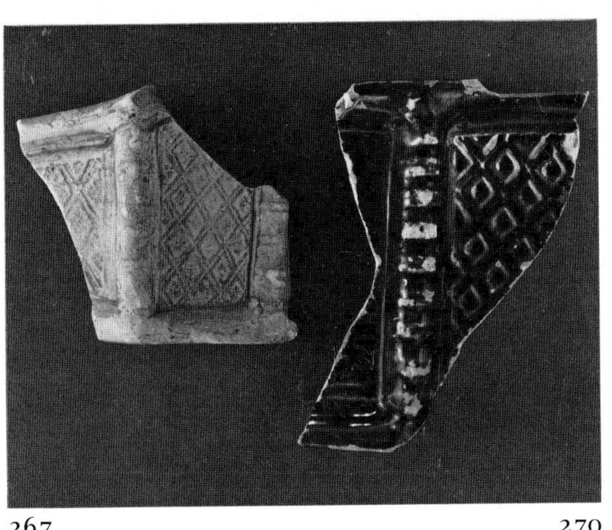

267

270

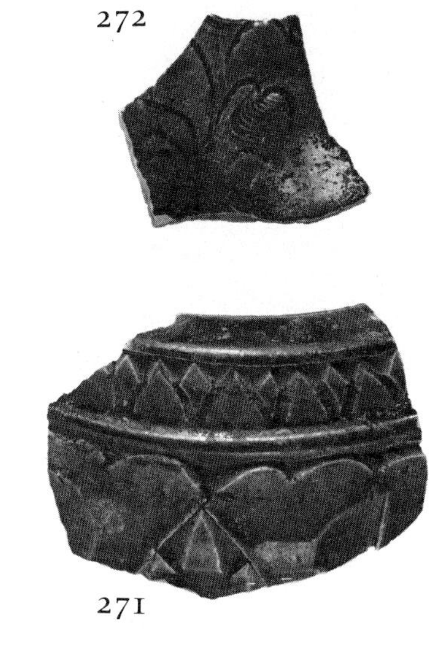

272

271

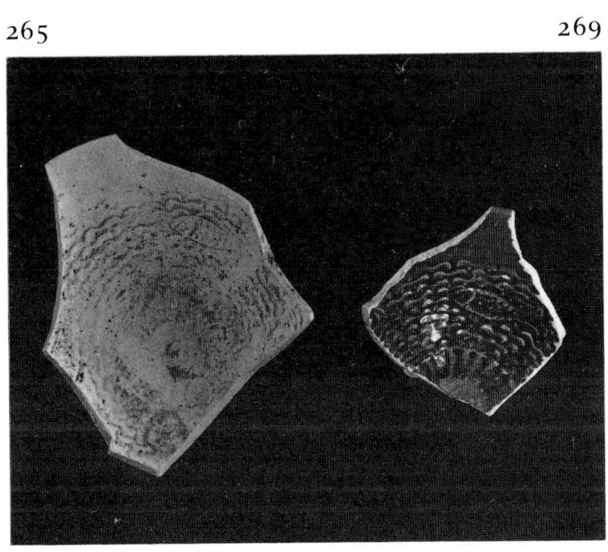

265

269

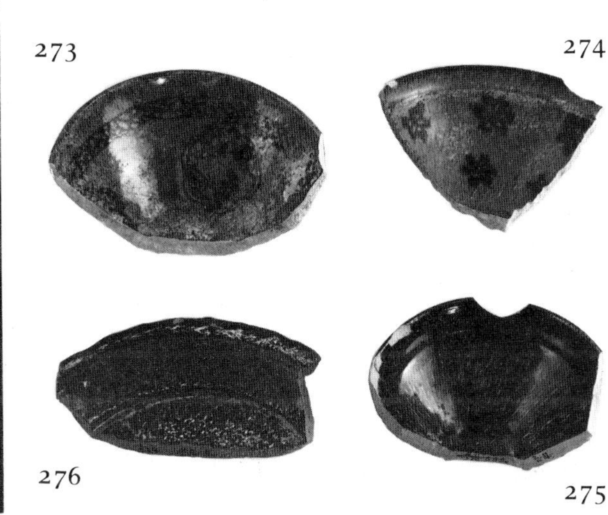

273

274

276

275

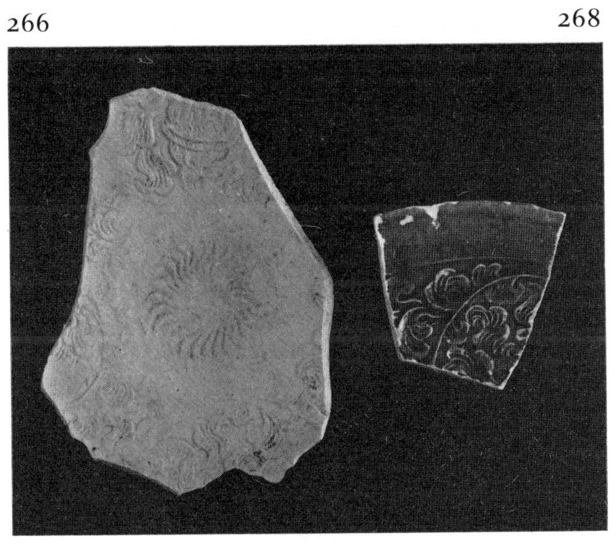

266

268

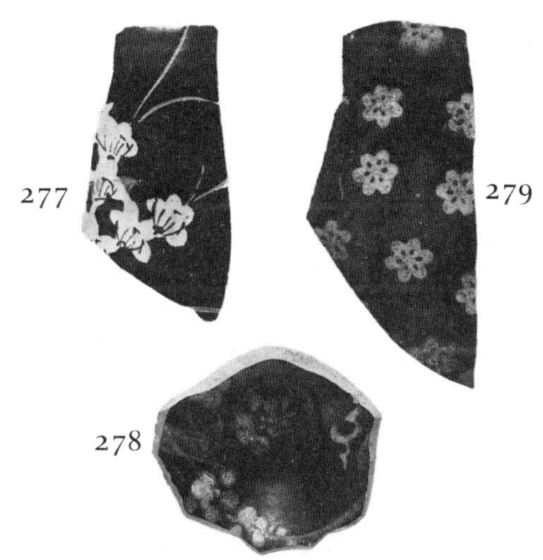

277

279

278

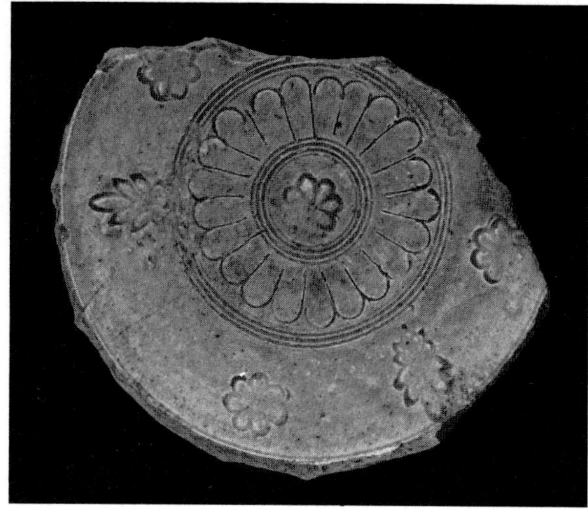

282

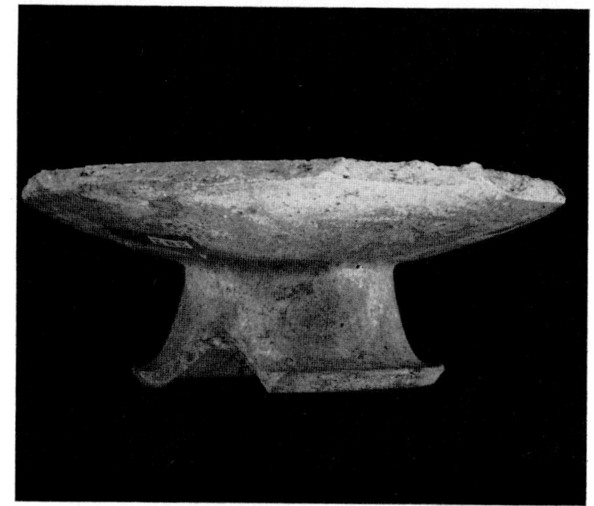

282

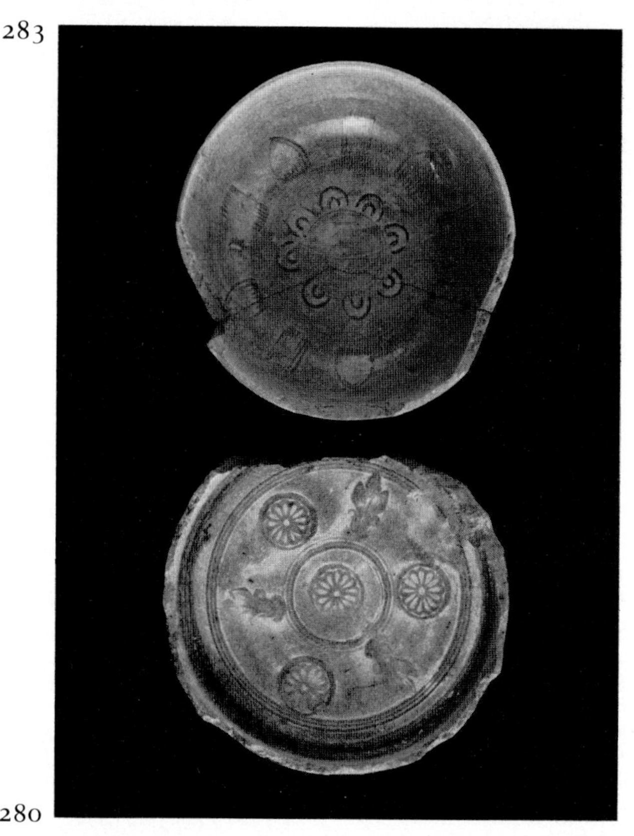

283

280

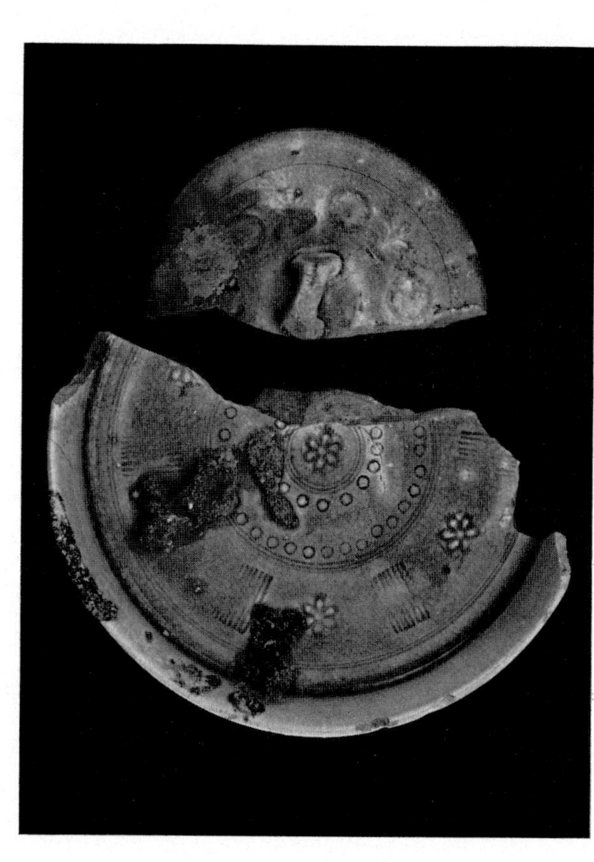

284

281

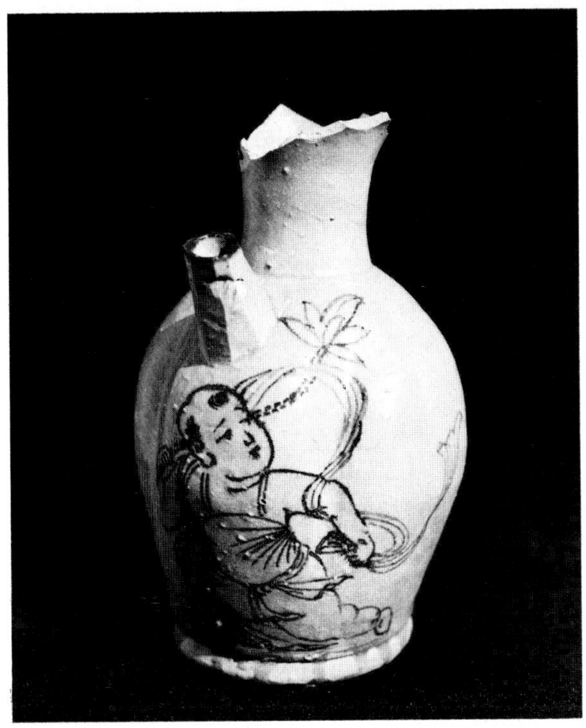

285

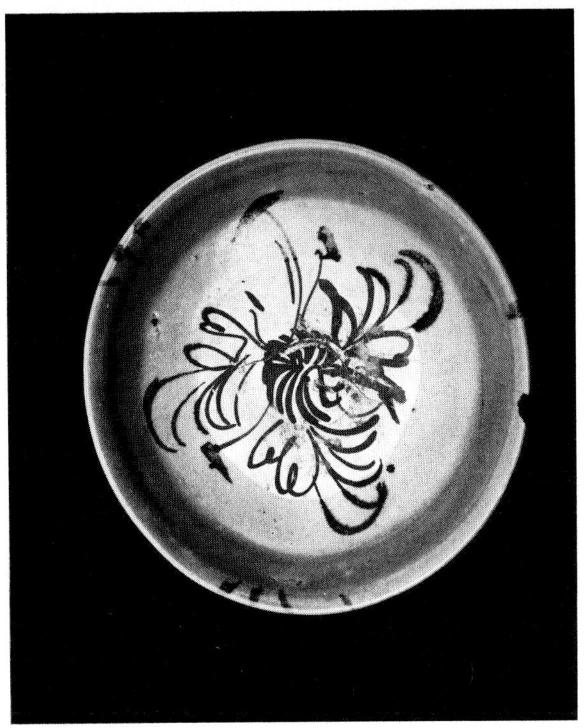

286

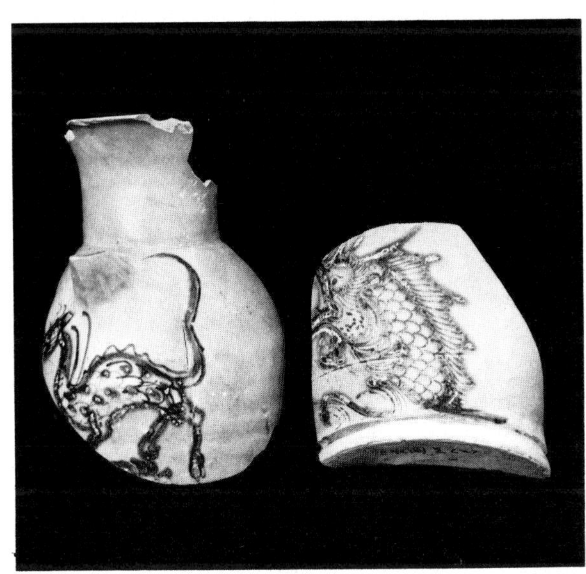

287 290

291 289

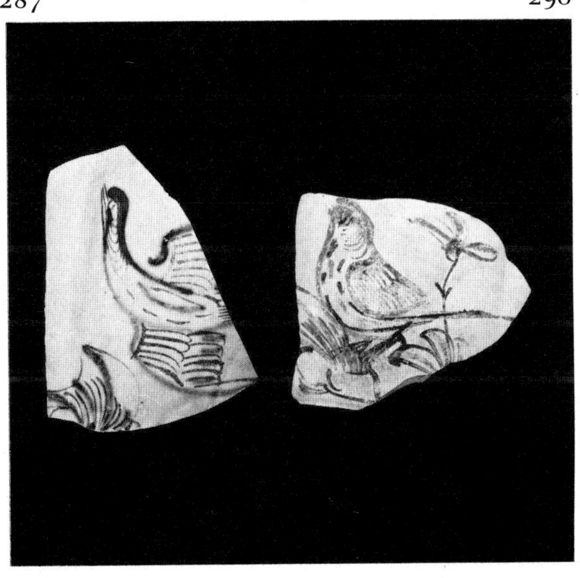

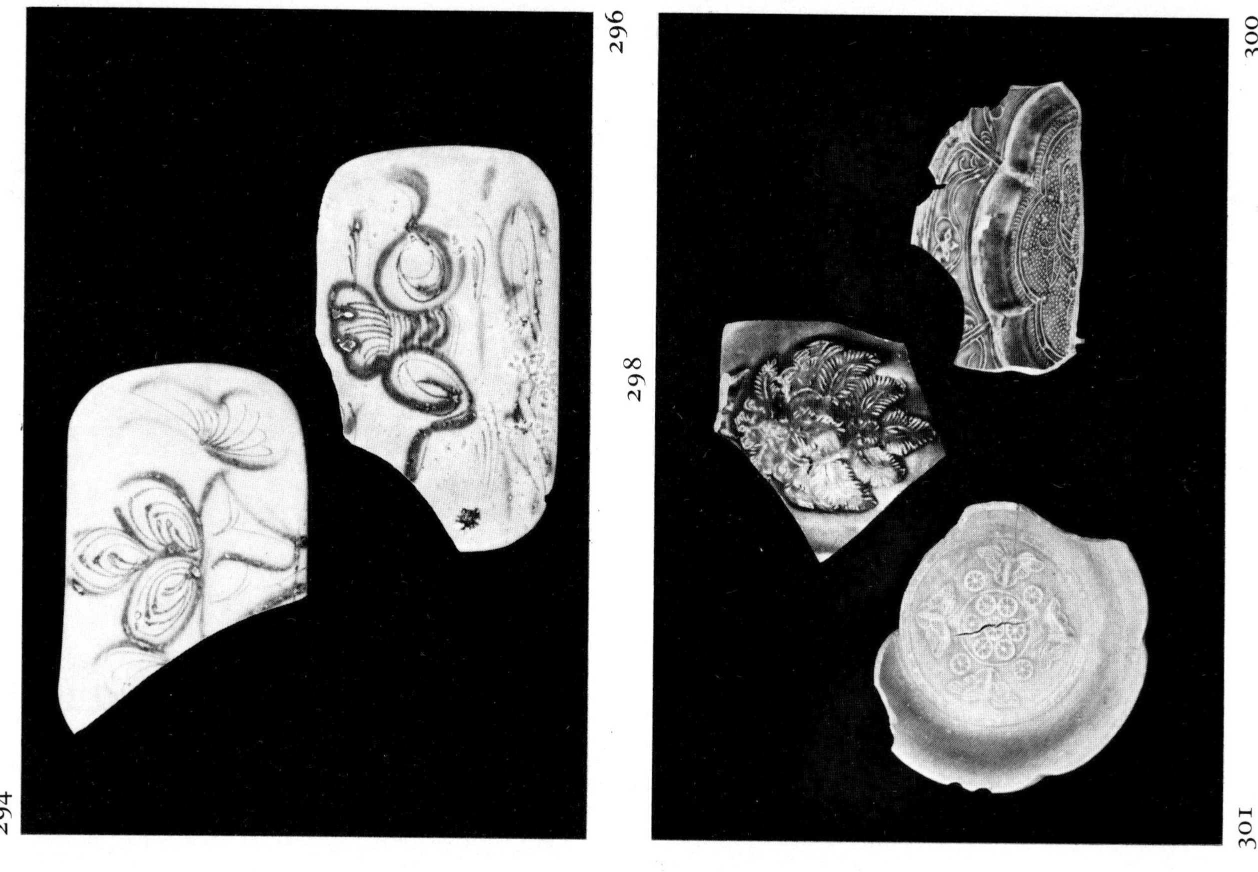

294
296
298
300
301

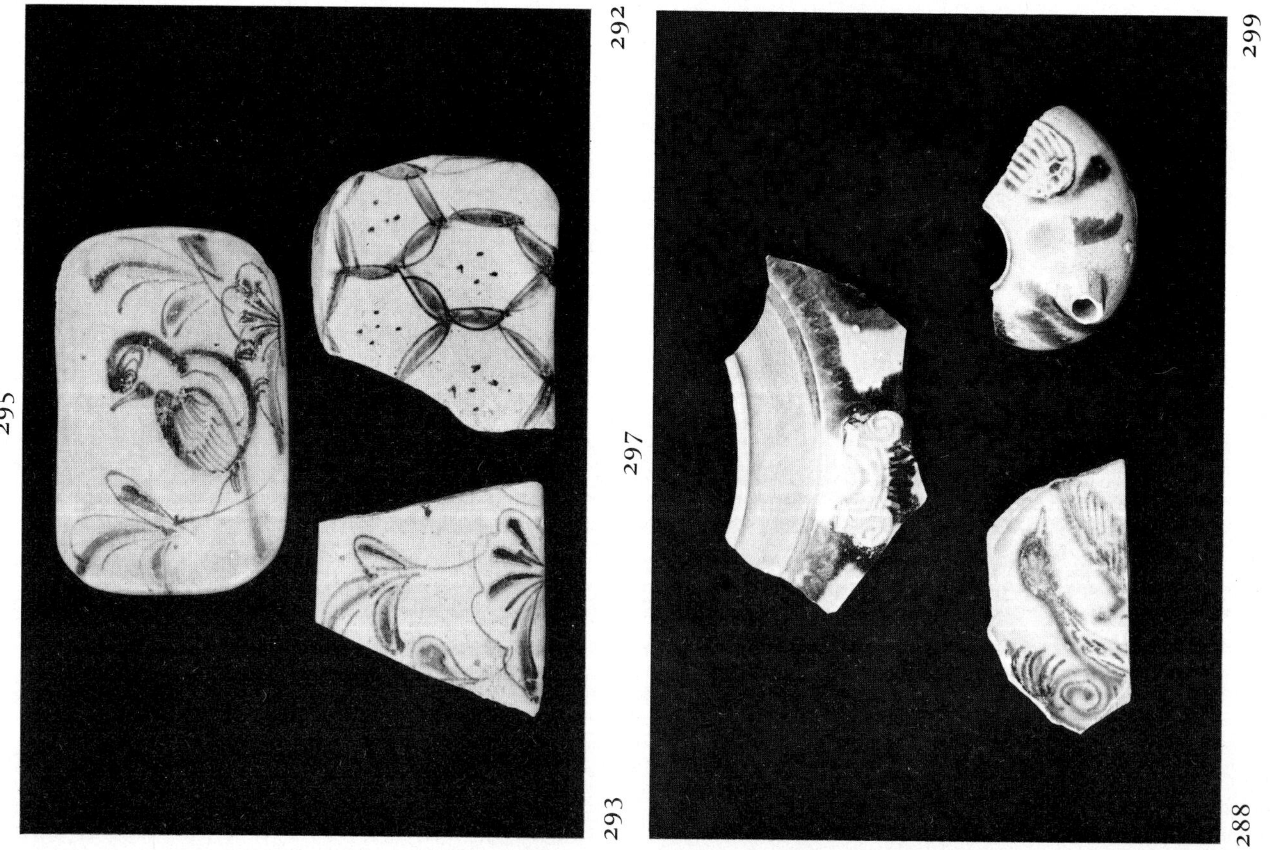

295
292
297
299
293
288

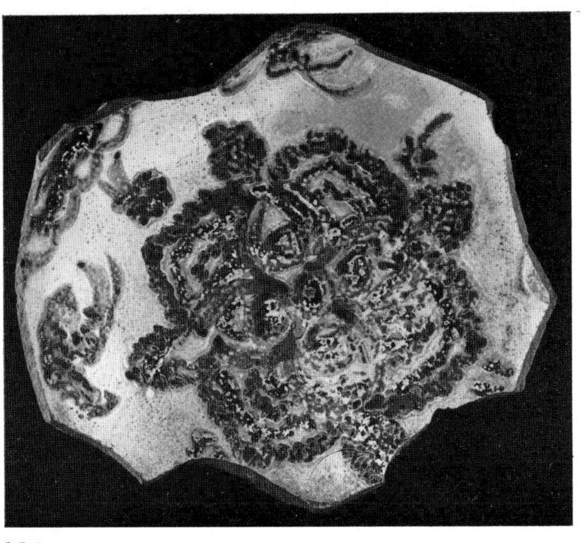

302

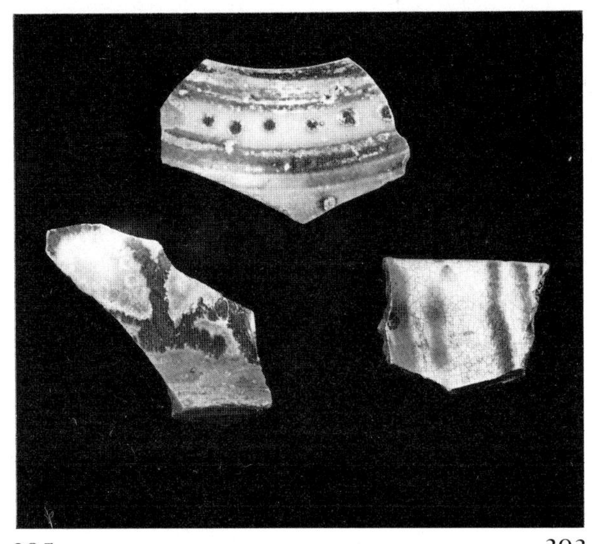

304

305 303

315 313

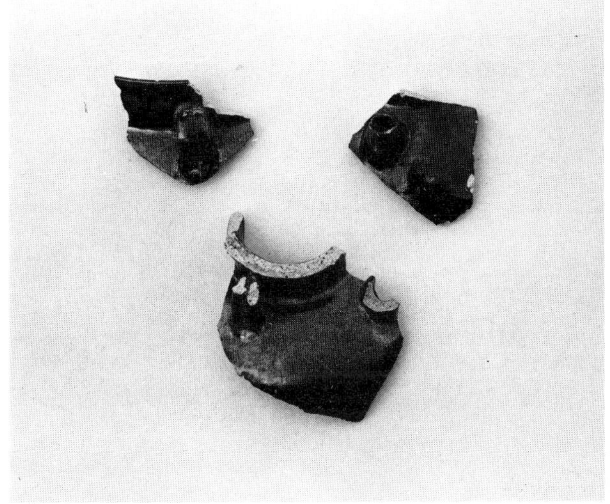

314

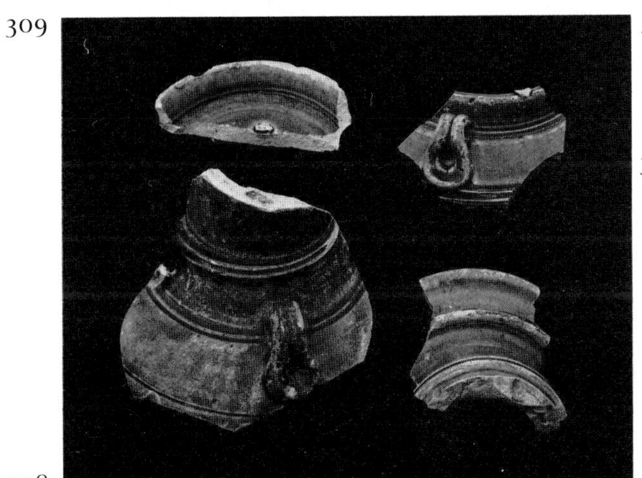

309 307

310

308 306

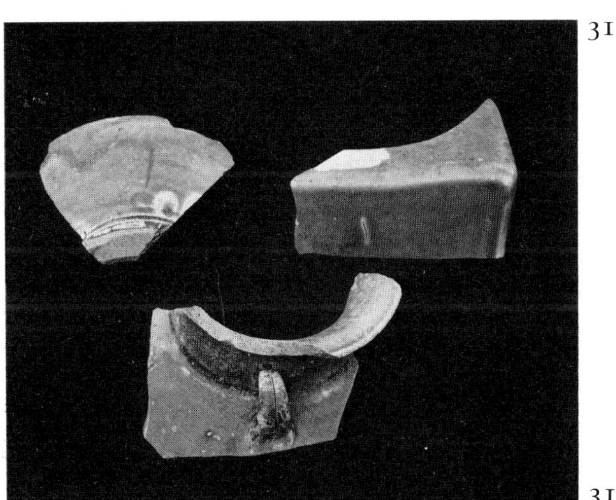

311

312

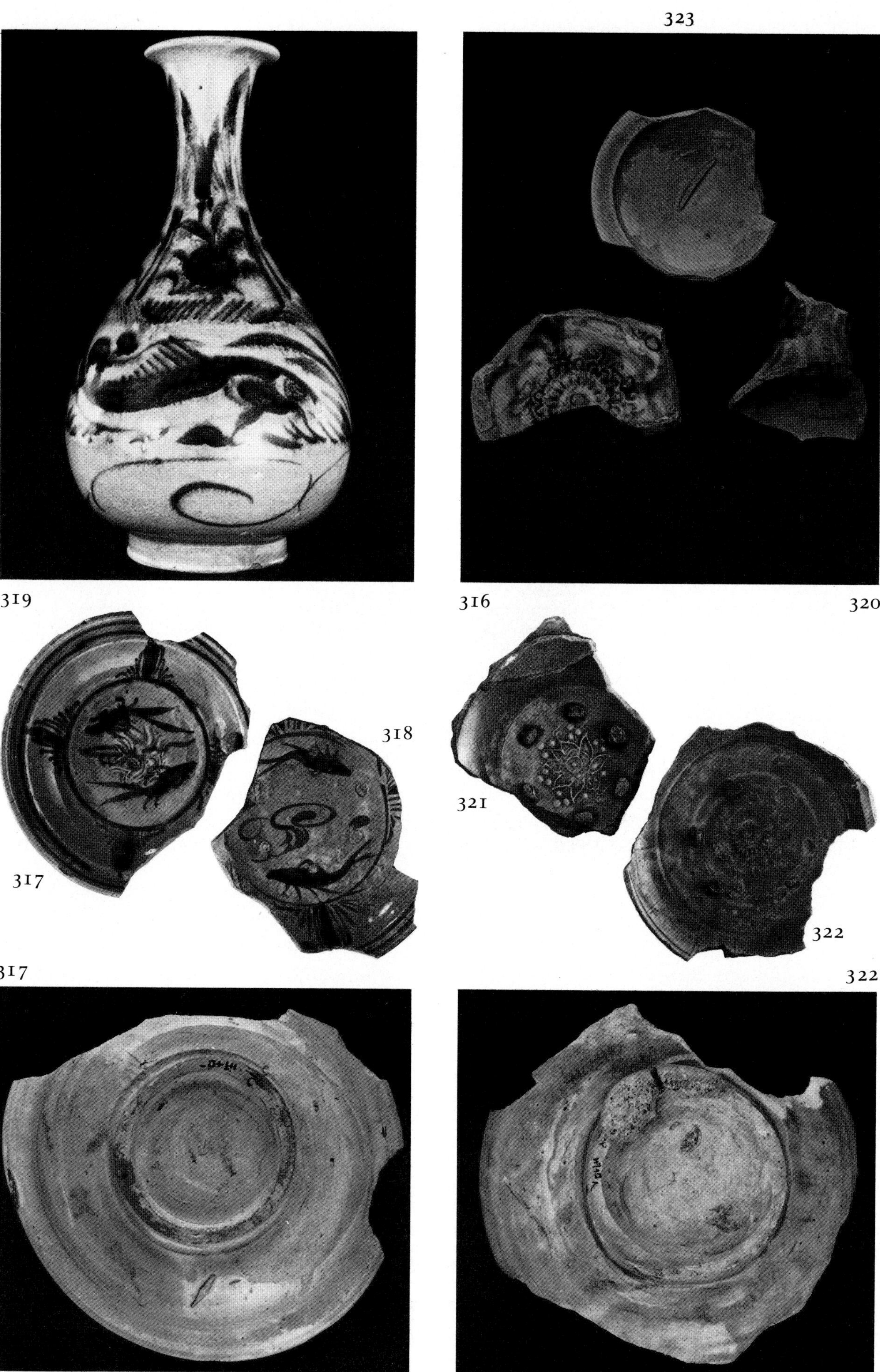

323
319
316
320
318
321
317
322
317
322

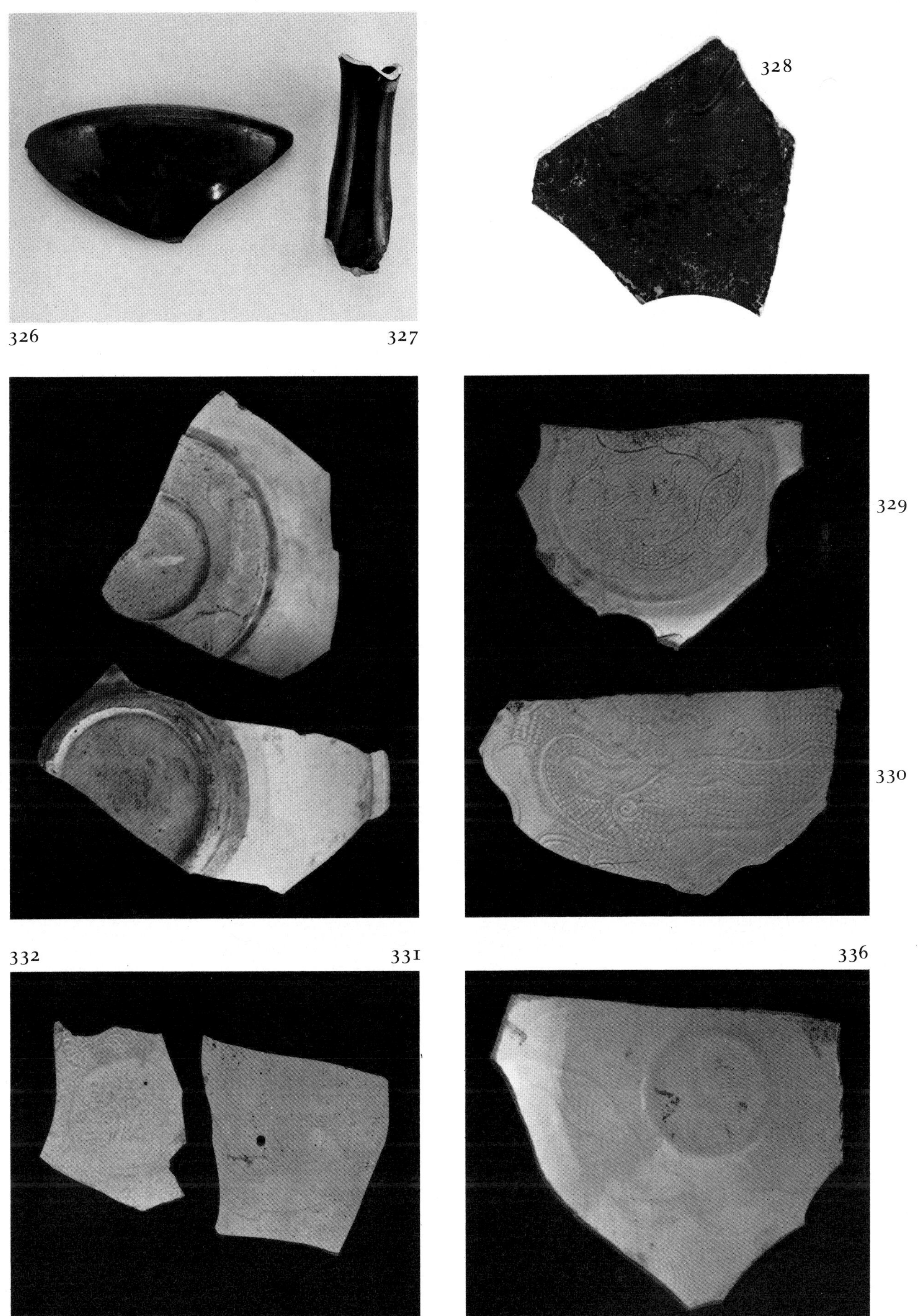

328
326
327
324
329
325
330
332
331
336

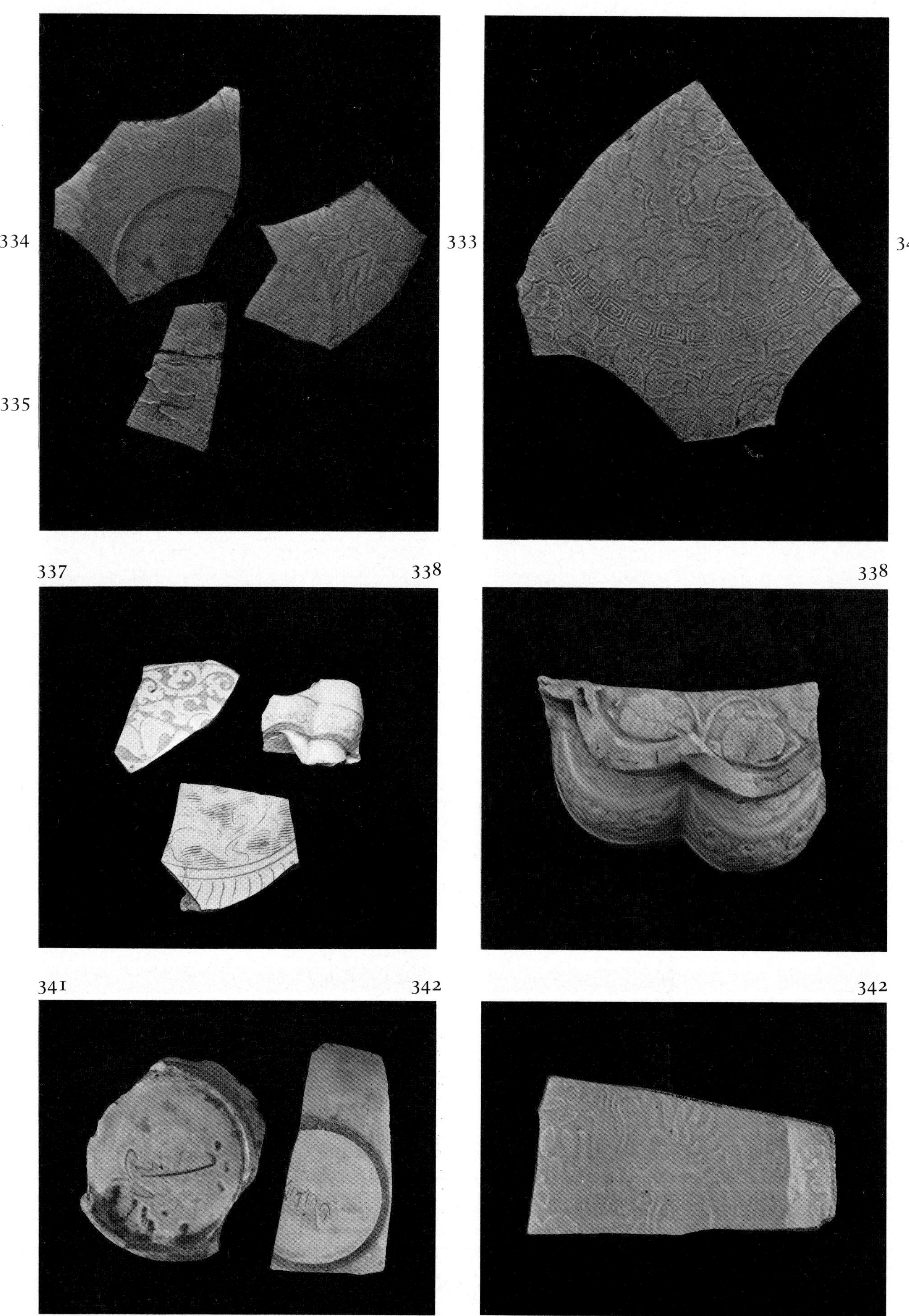

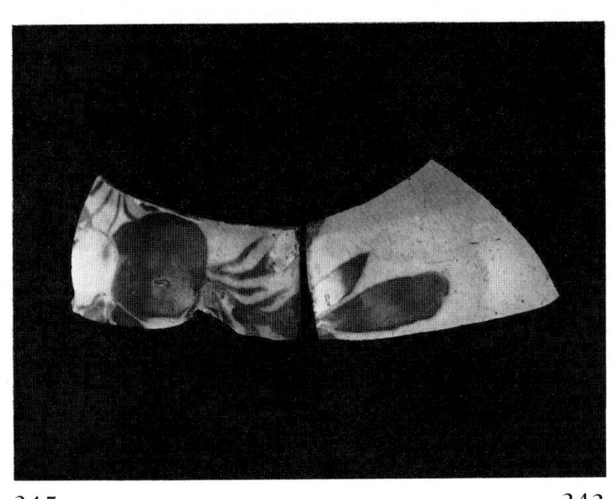

345   343

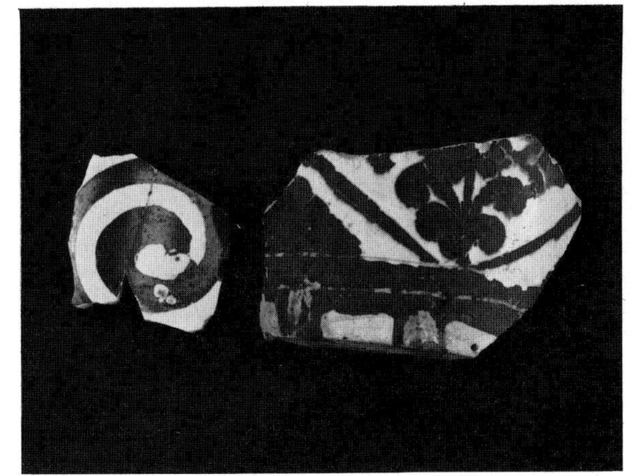

344   346

347   349   348

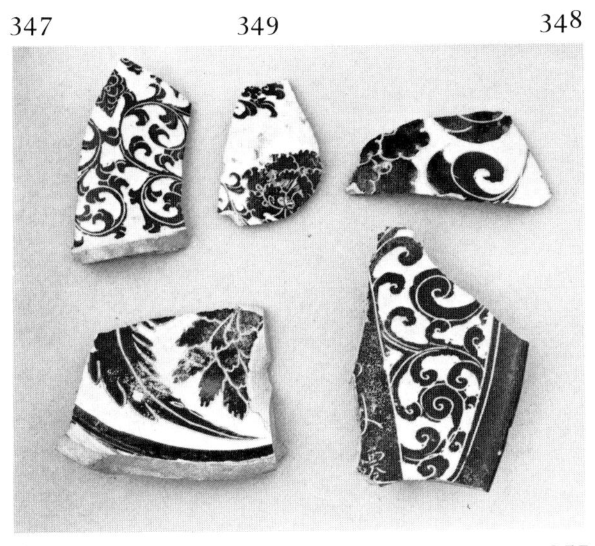

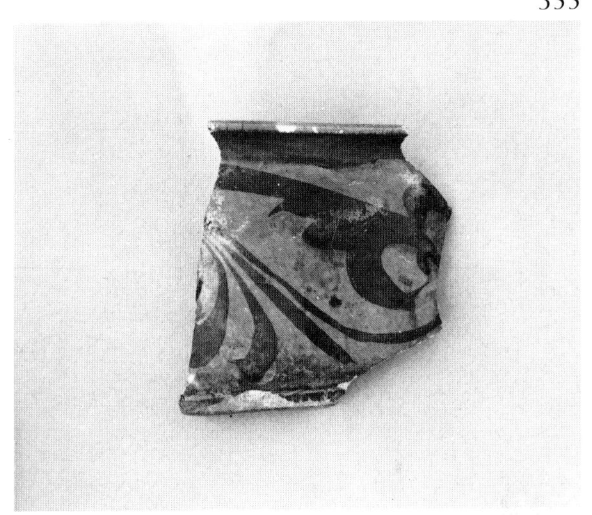

355

350   351

353   352

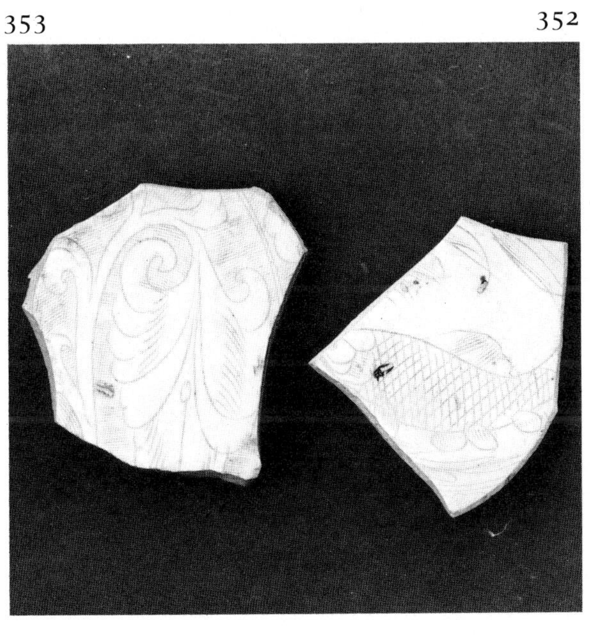

356

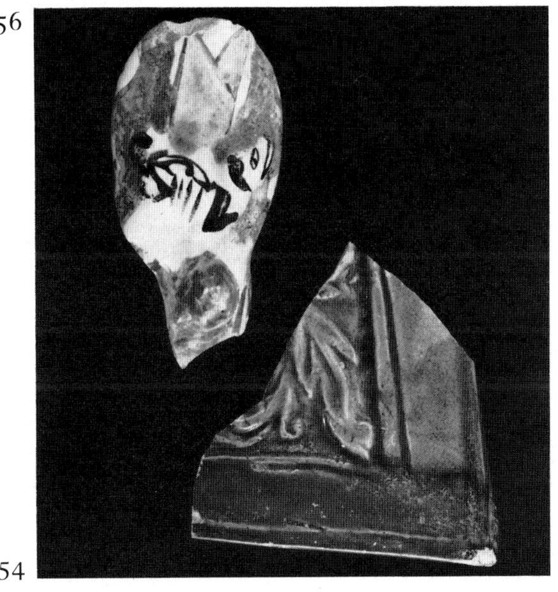

354

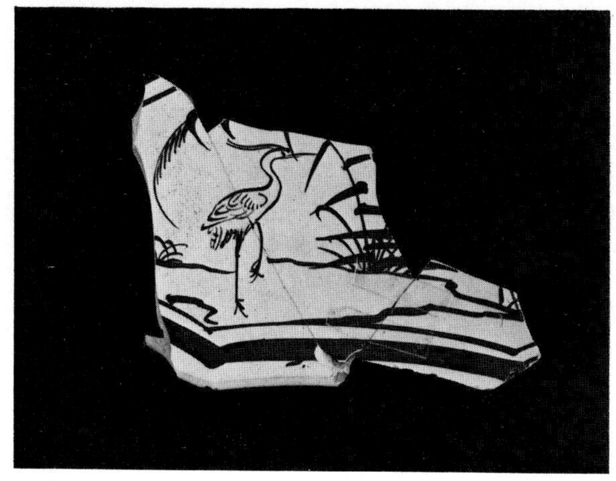

357

358

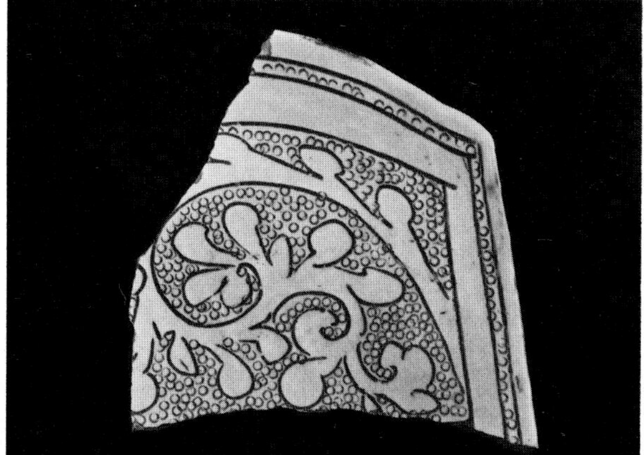

359

362

360

361

363

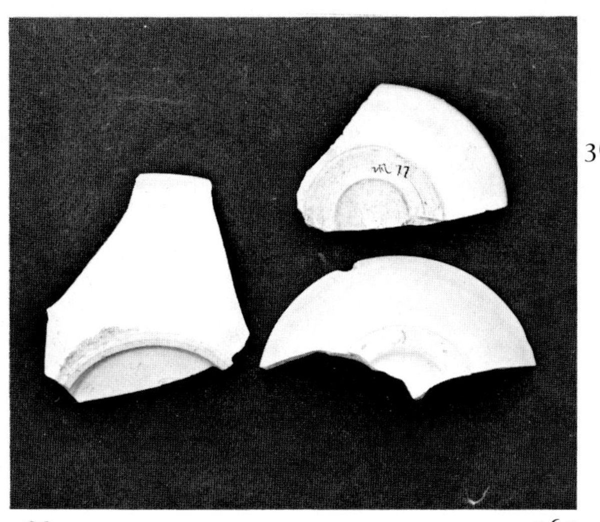

364

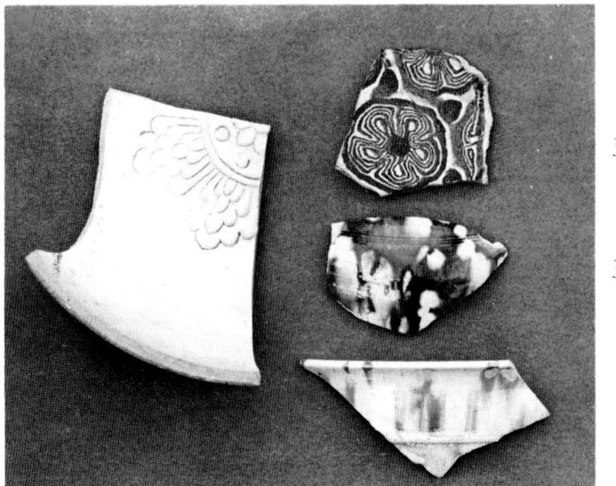

370

368

366 365

372 371

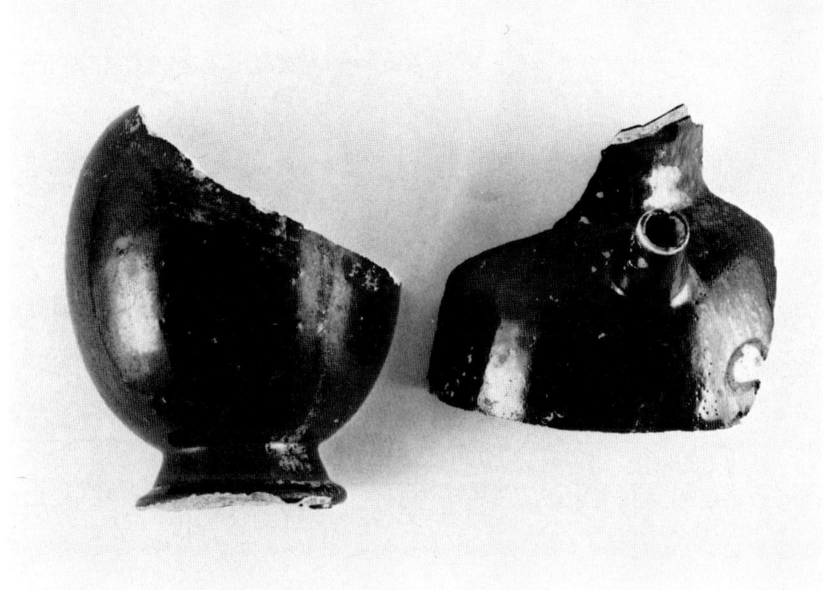

367 369

373 374

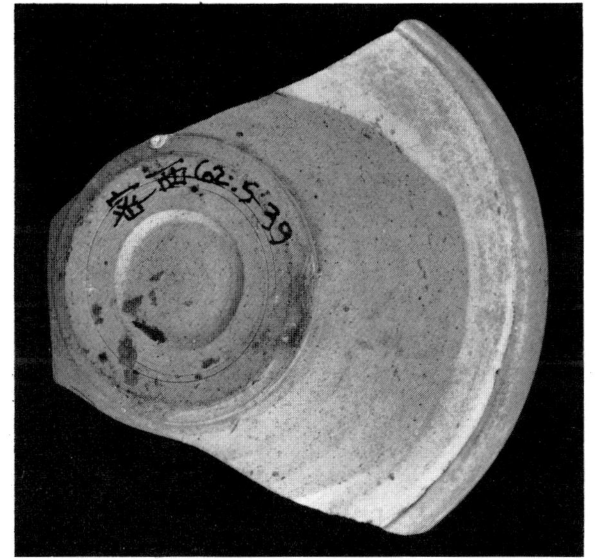

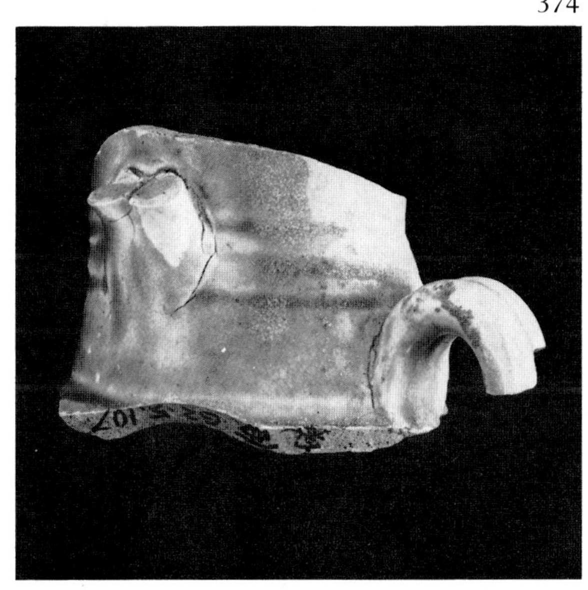

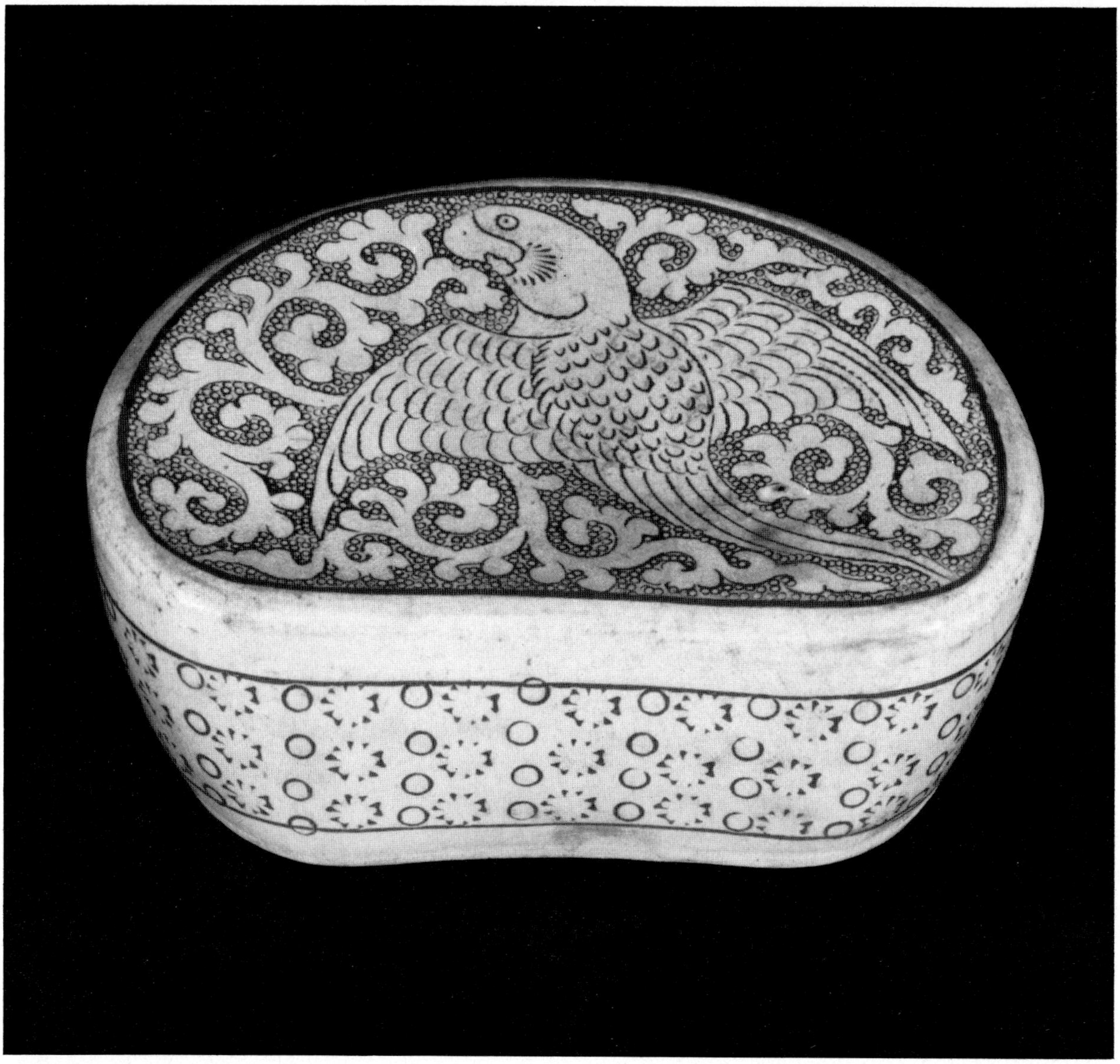

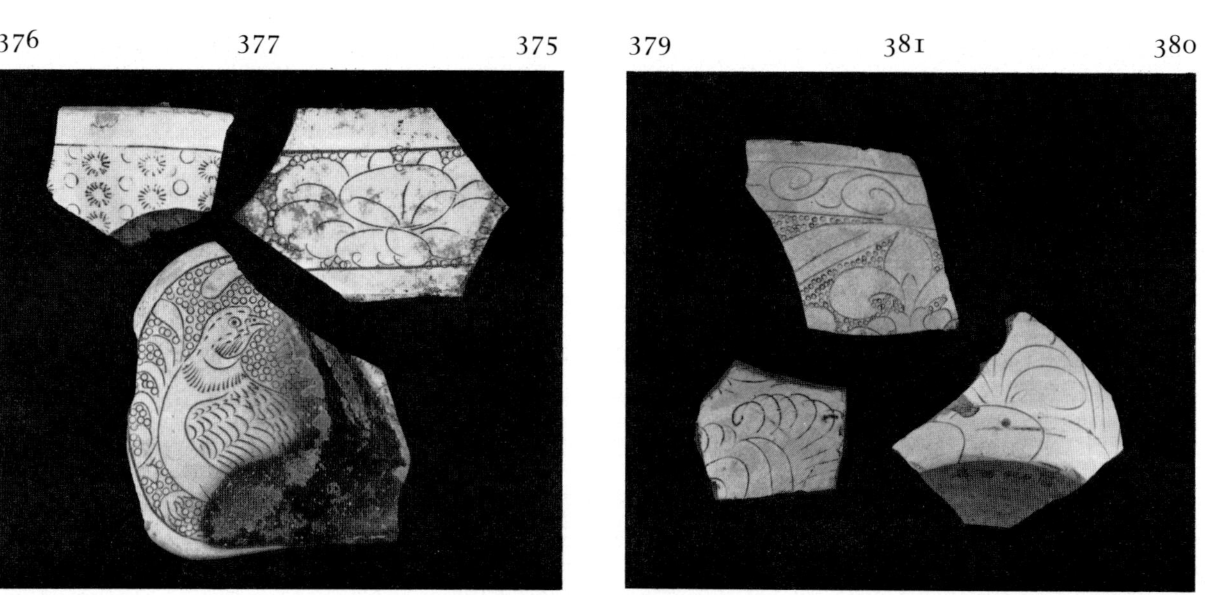

378

376   377   375   379   381   380

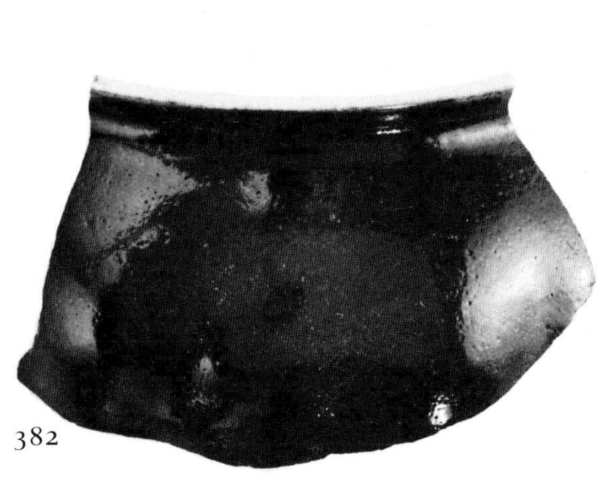

382

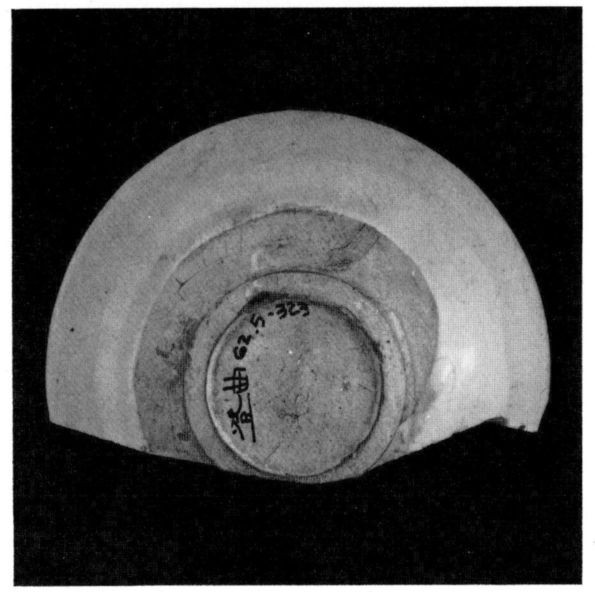

383

384

391

389

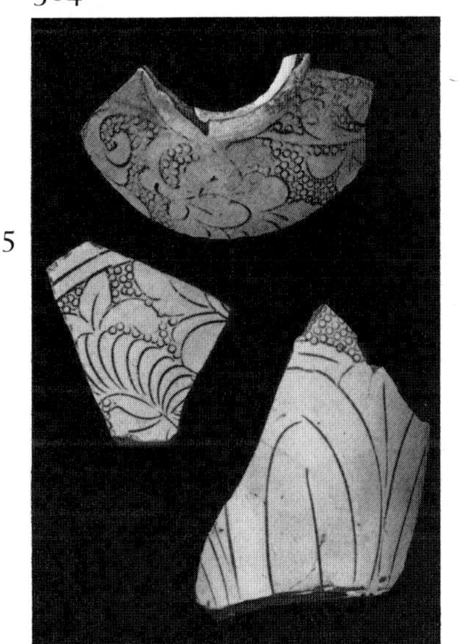

385

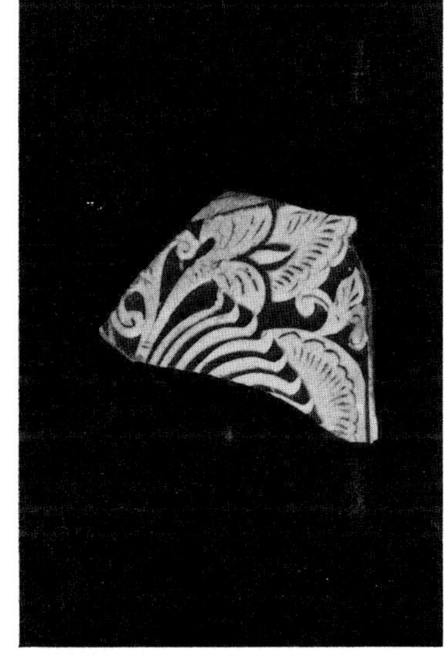

386

392

393

387

388

390

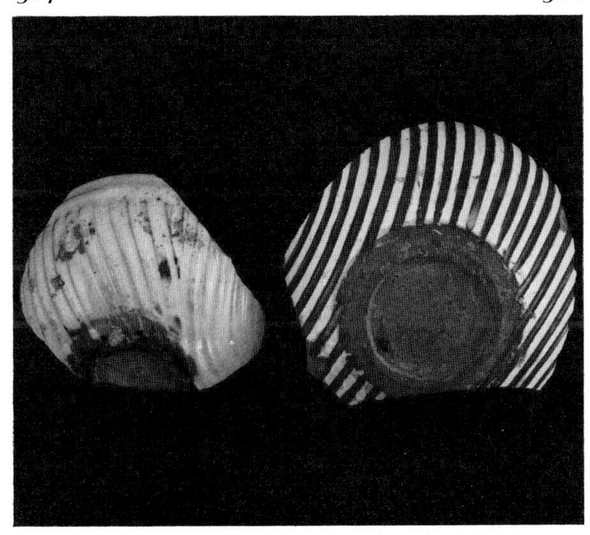

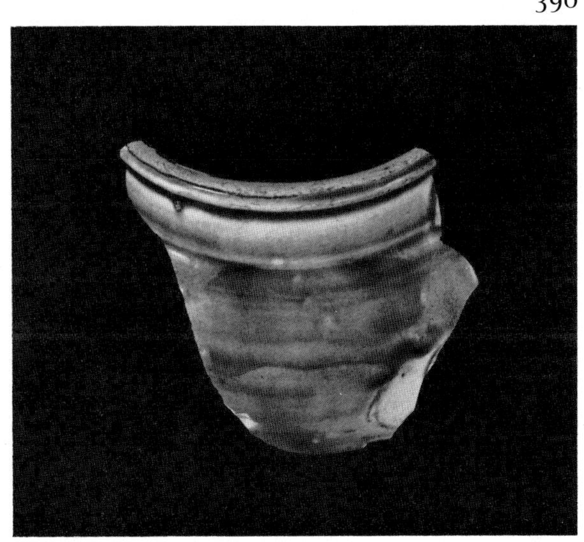

394

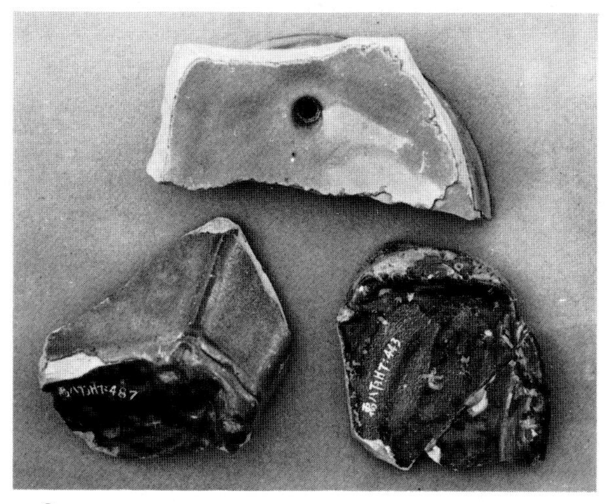

395

402

397

398

399

396

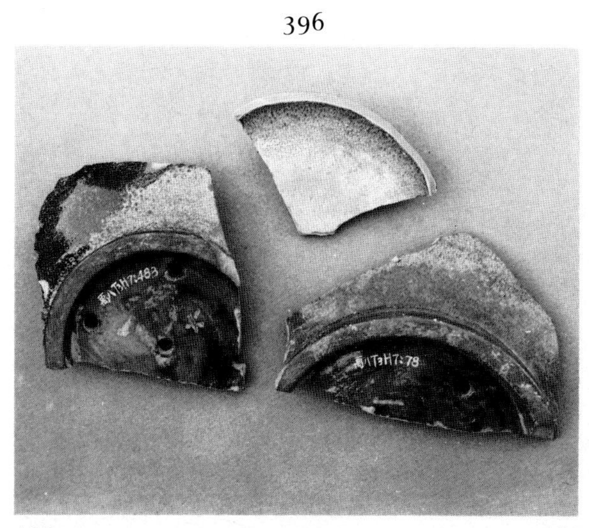

403

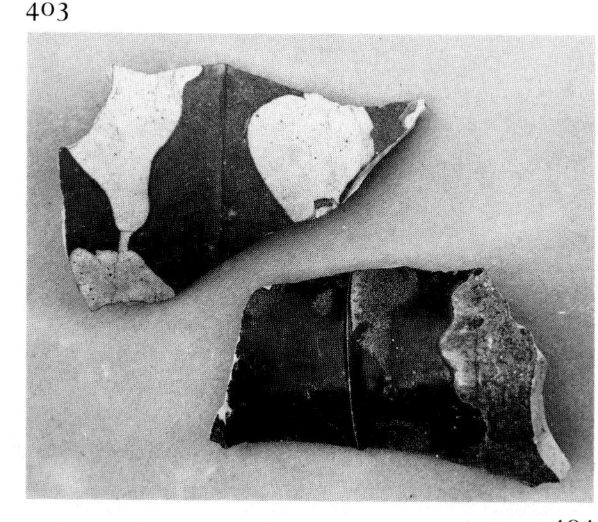

400

401

404

409

414

413

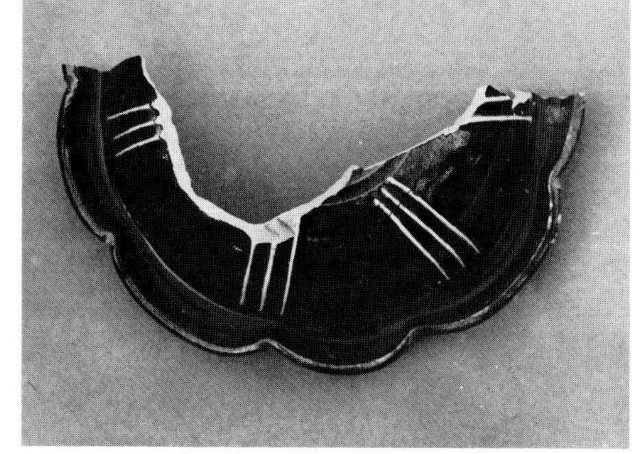

408

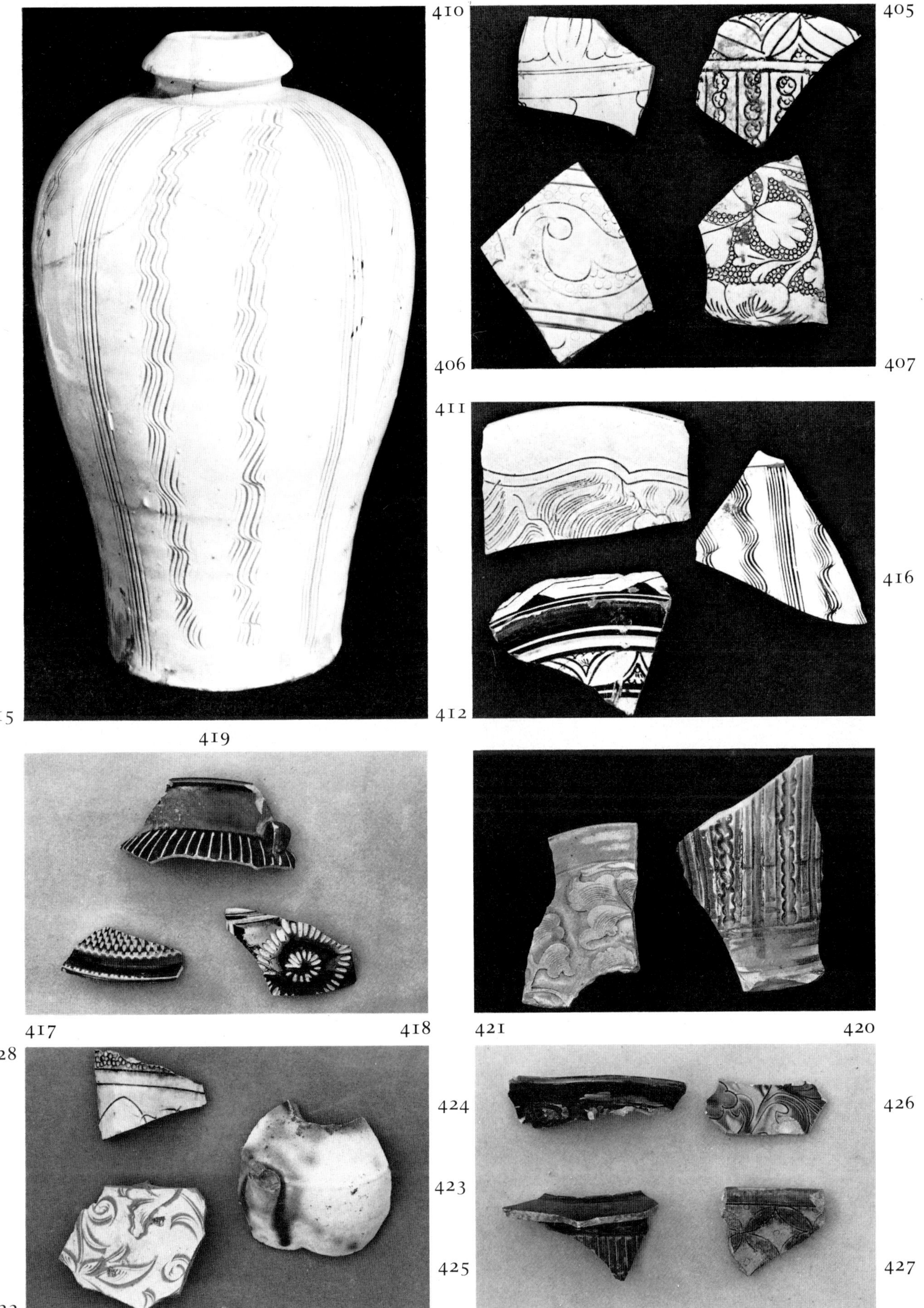

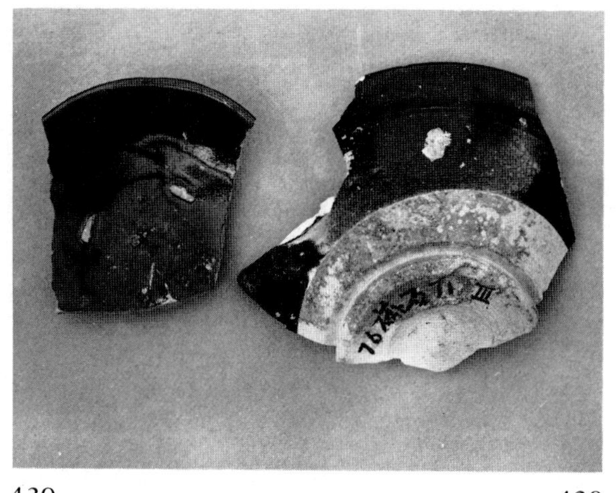

430

429

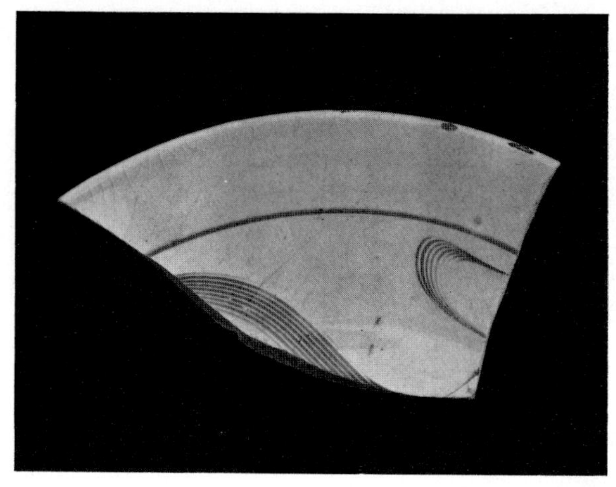

432

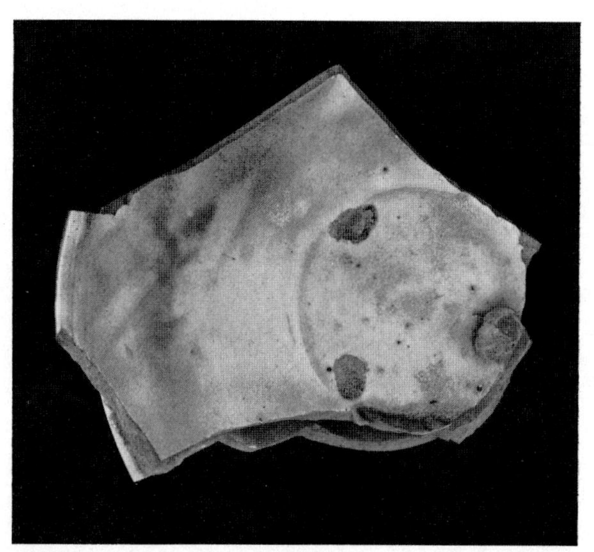

431

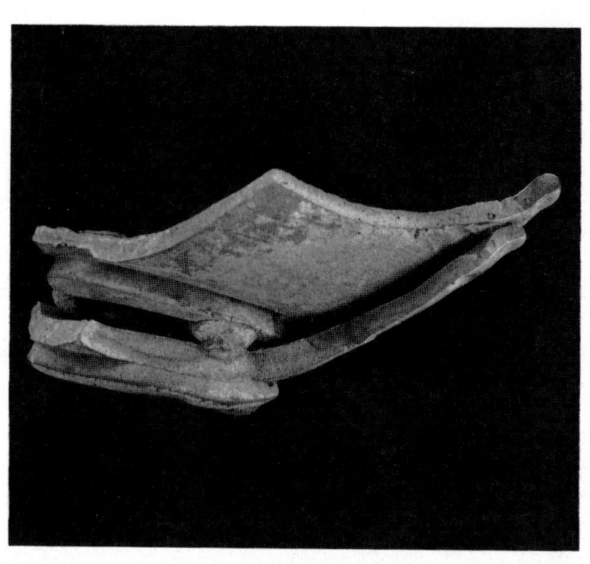

431

433

434

435

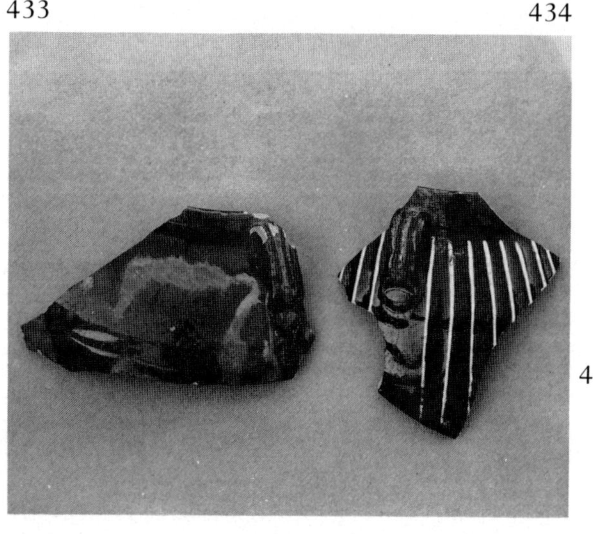

436

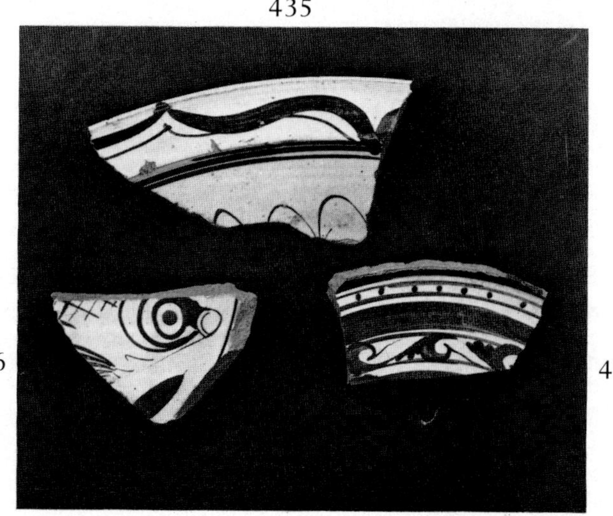

437

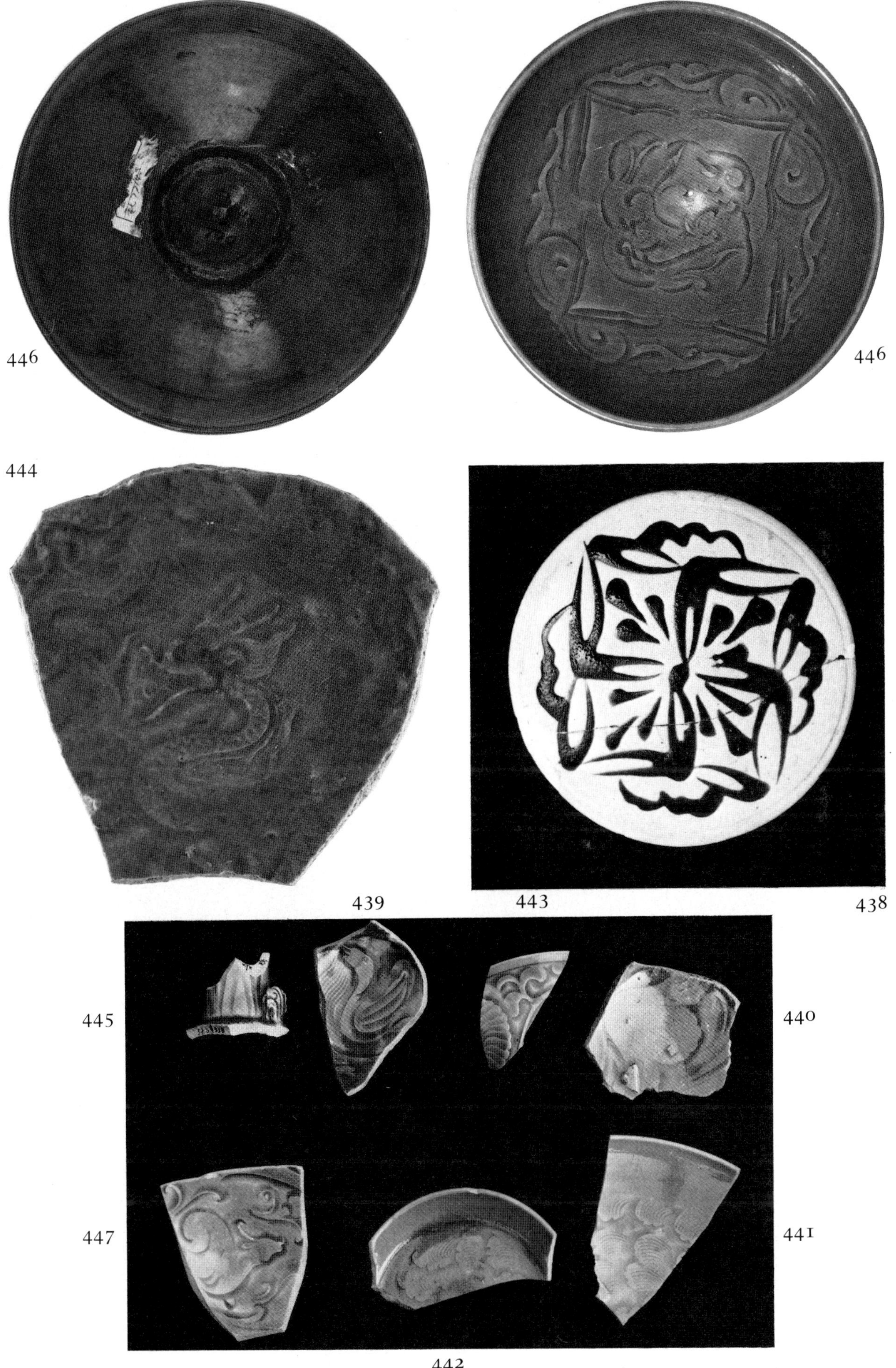

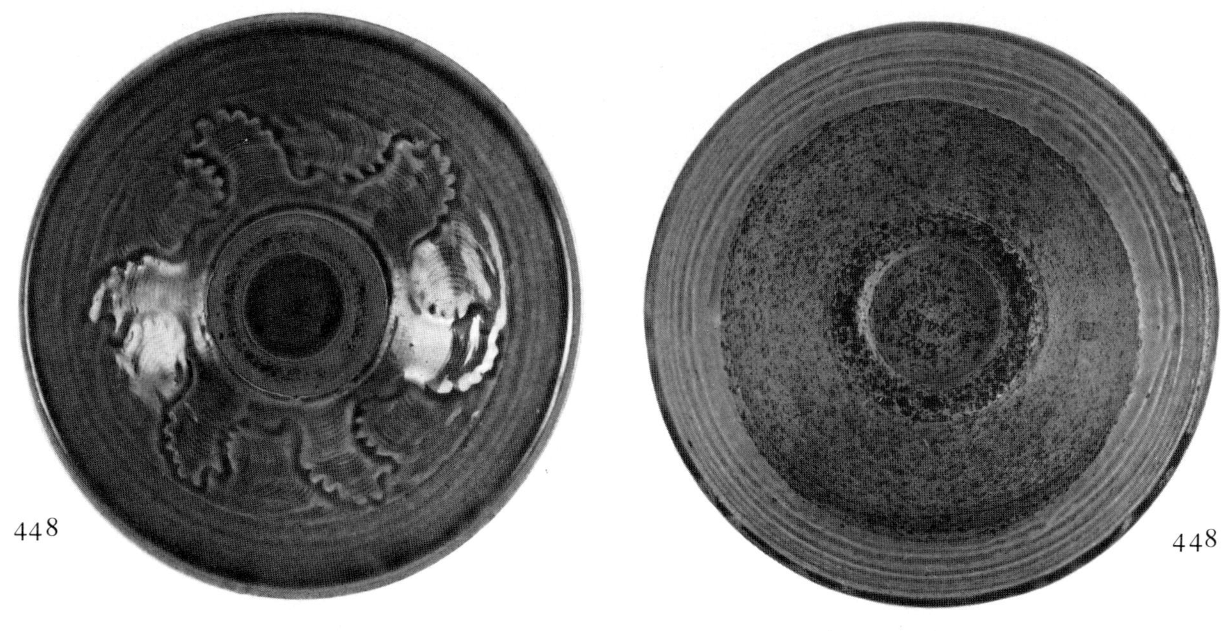

448   448

448

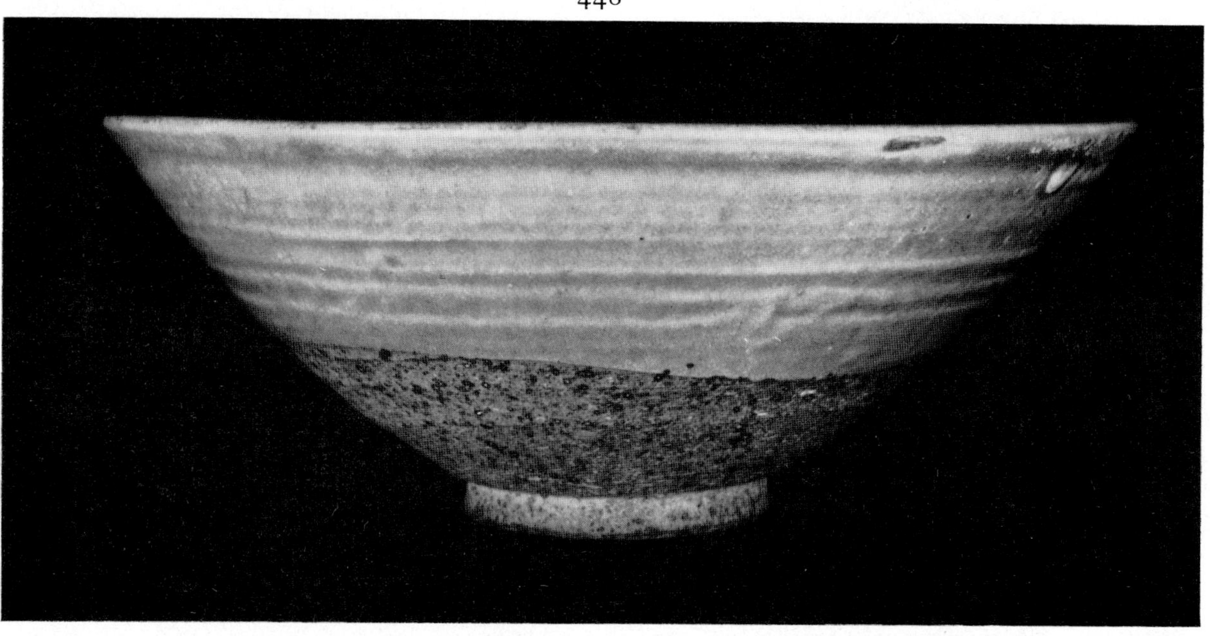

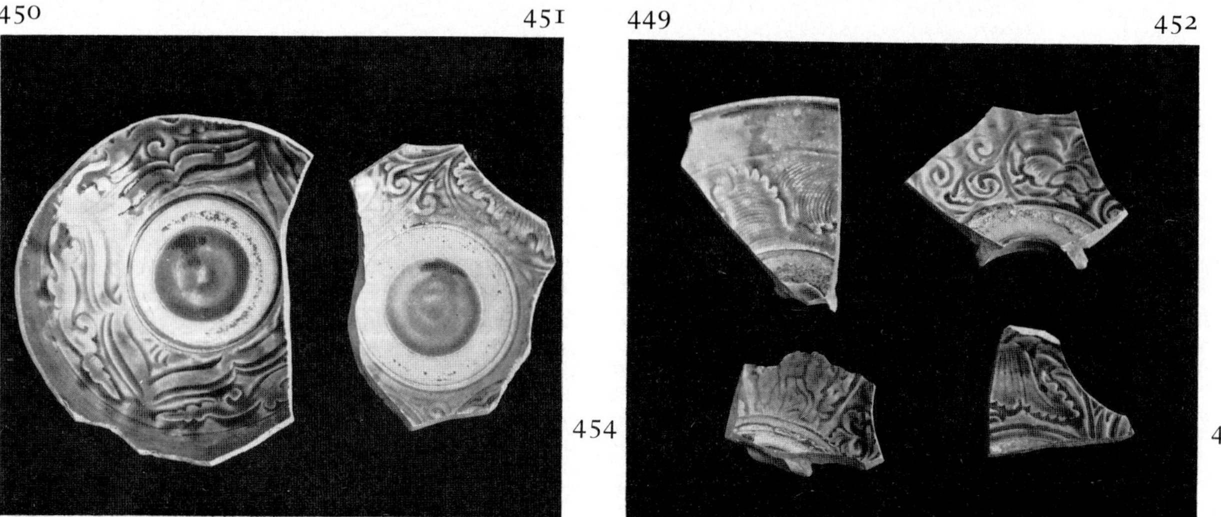

450   451   449   452

454   453

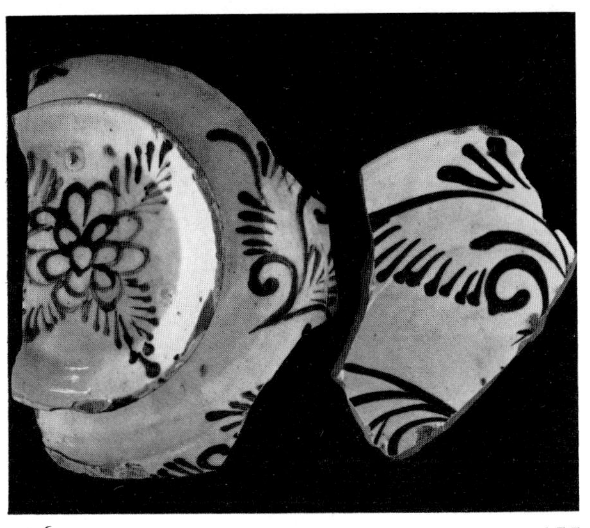

456

455

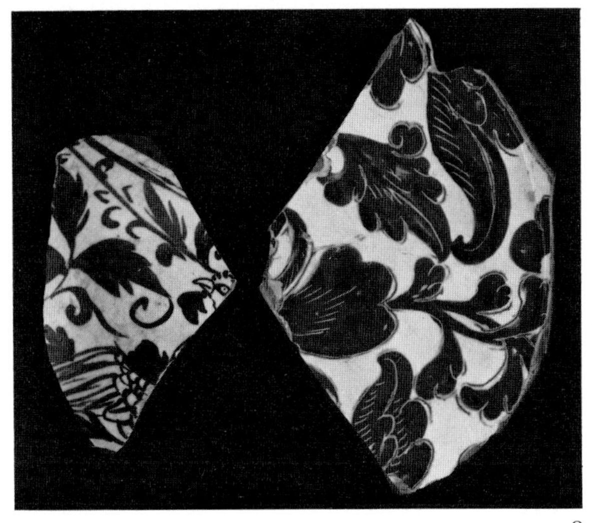

457

458

461

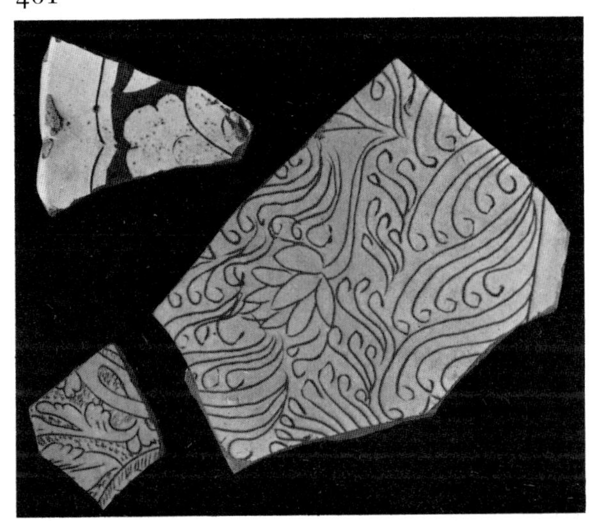

460

462

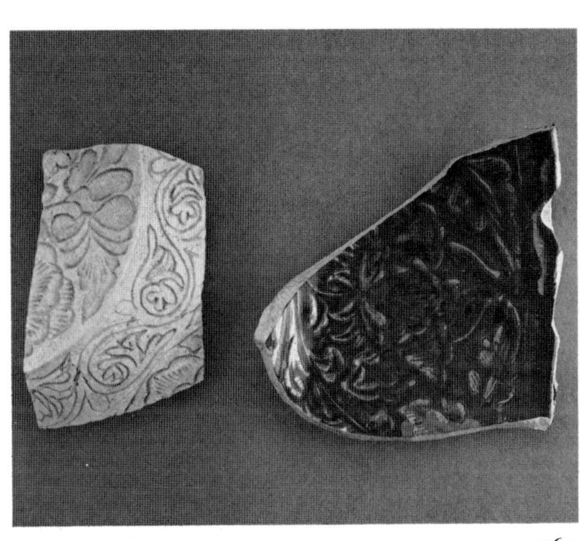

459

463

464

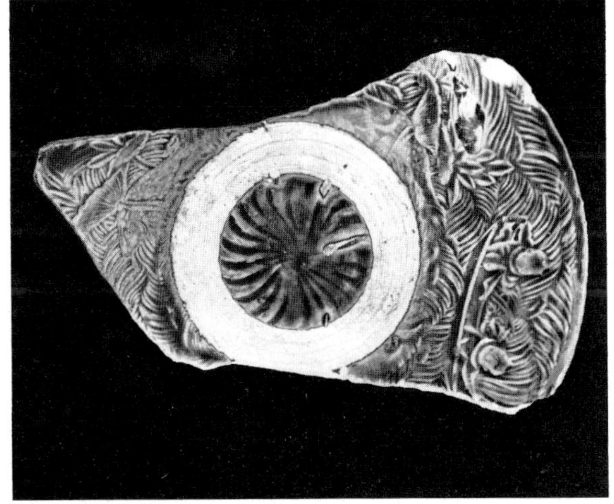

464

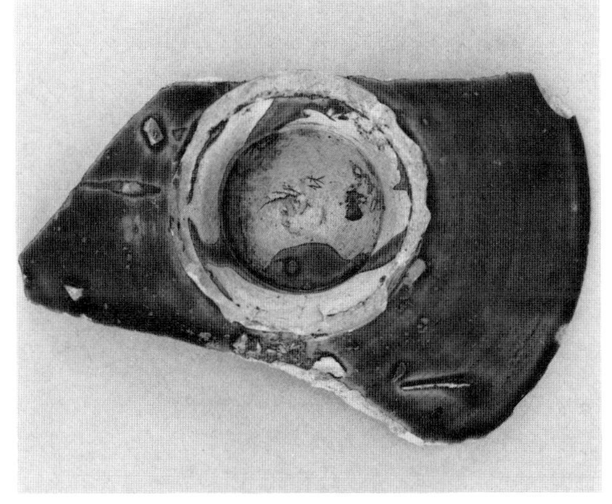

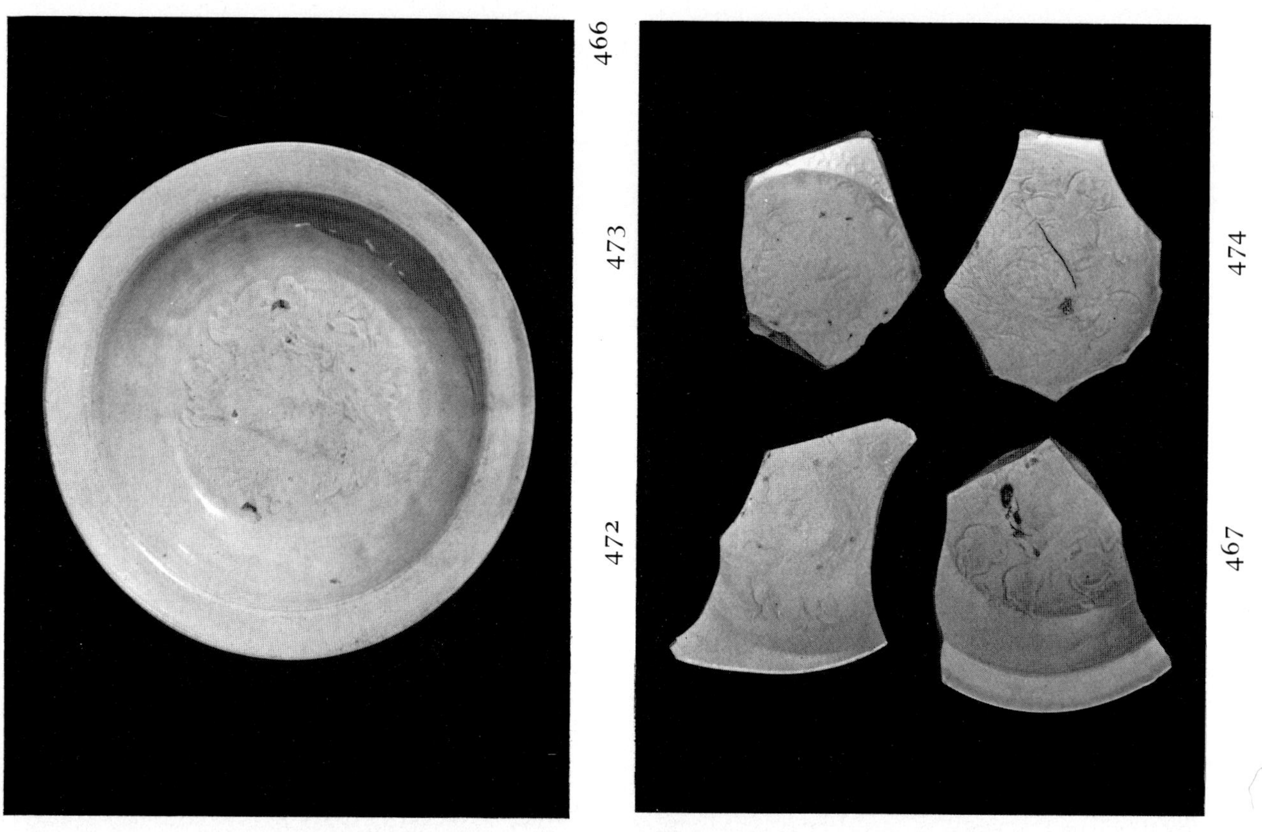

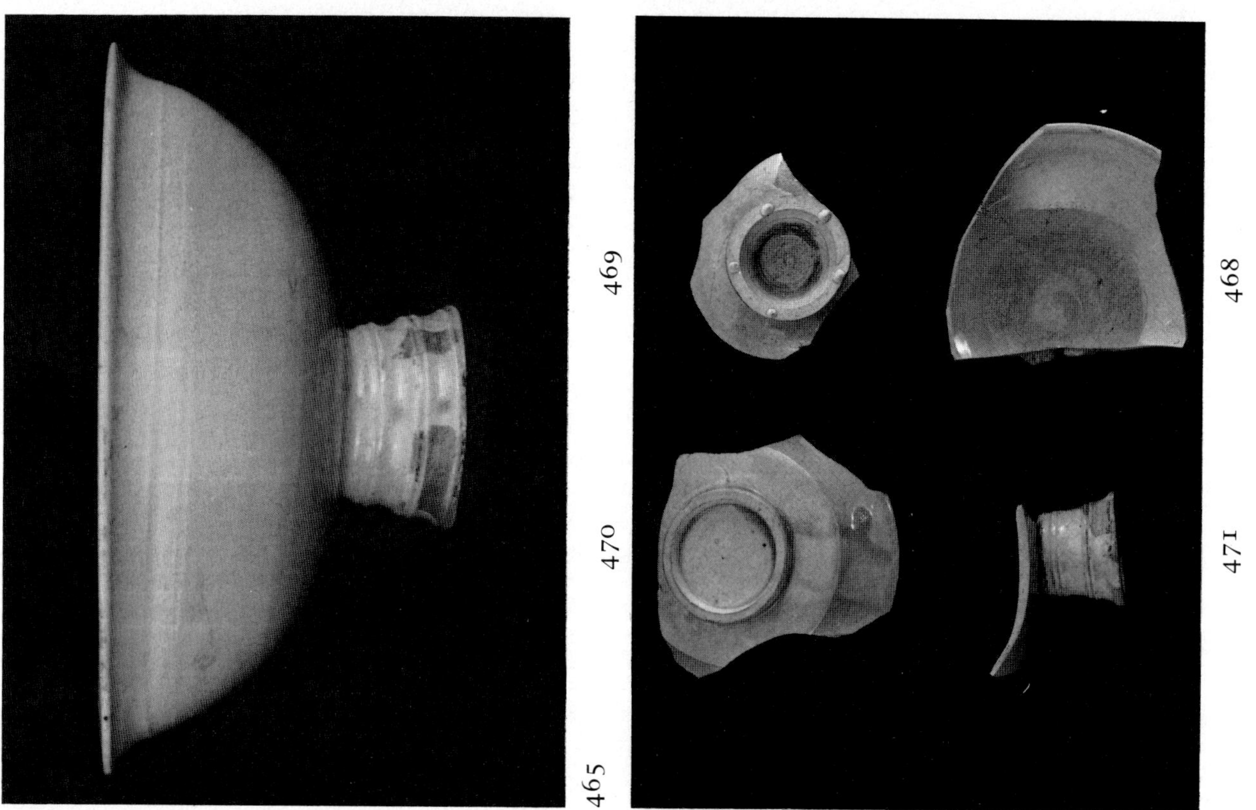

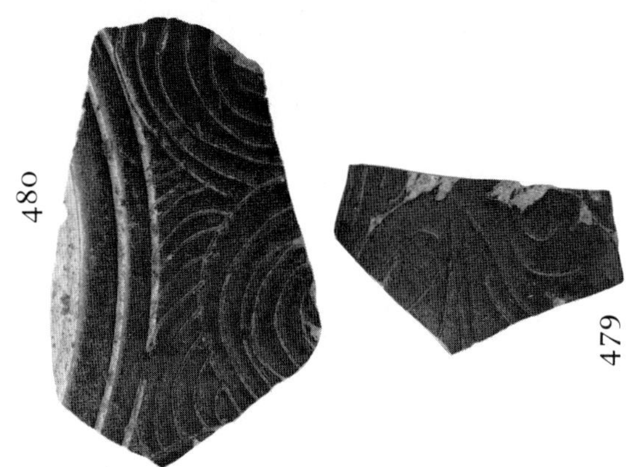

480

479

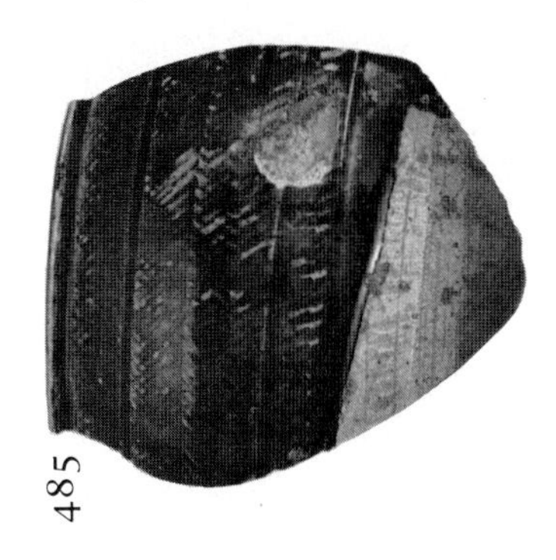

485

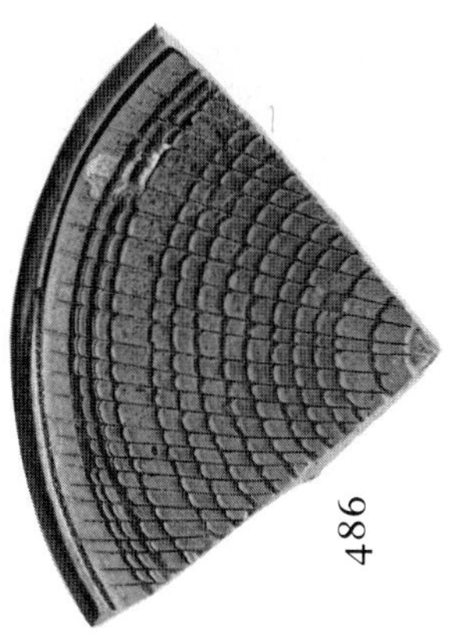

486

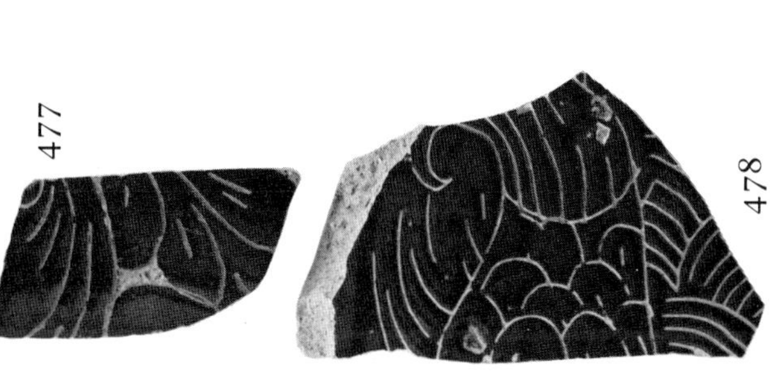

477

478

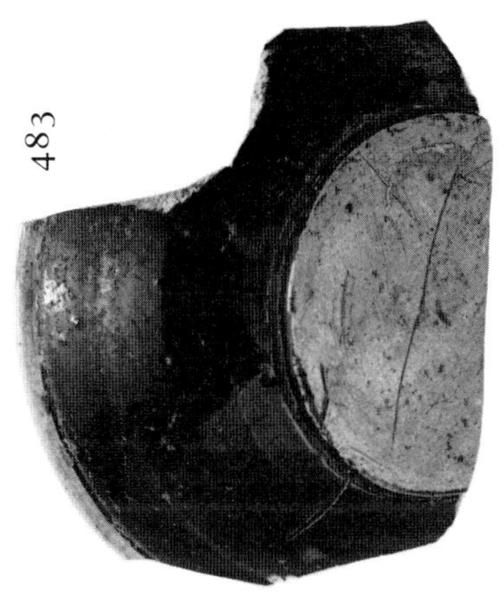

483

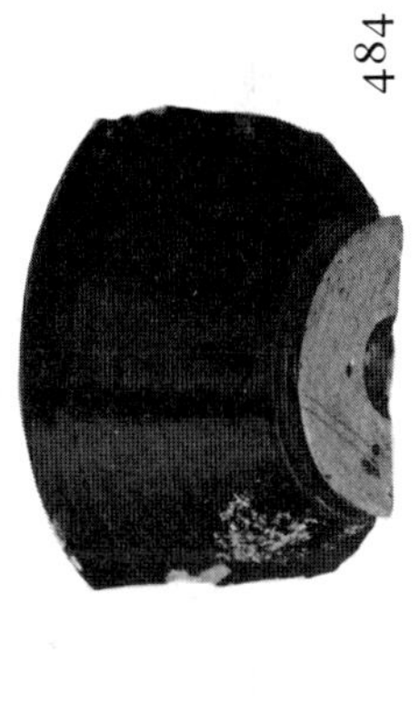

484

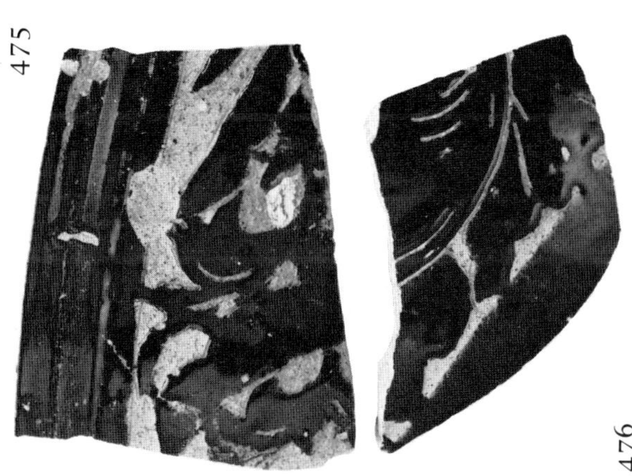

475

476

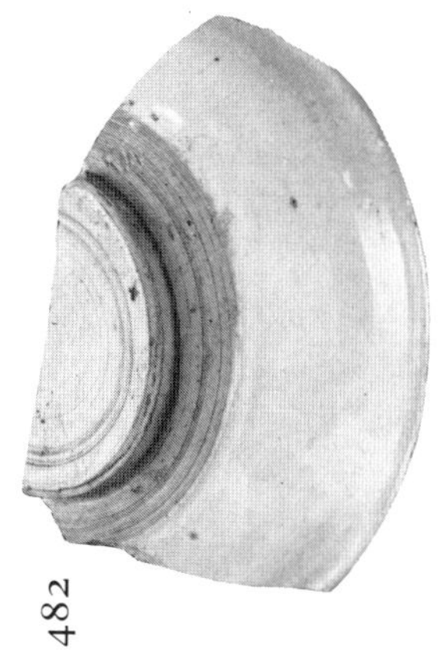

482

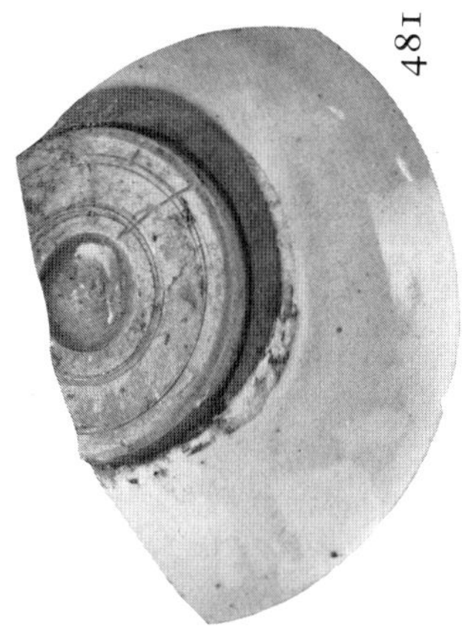

481

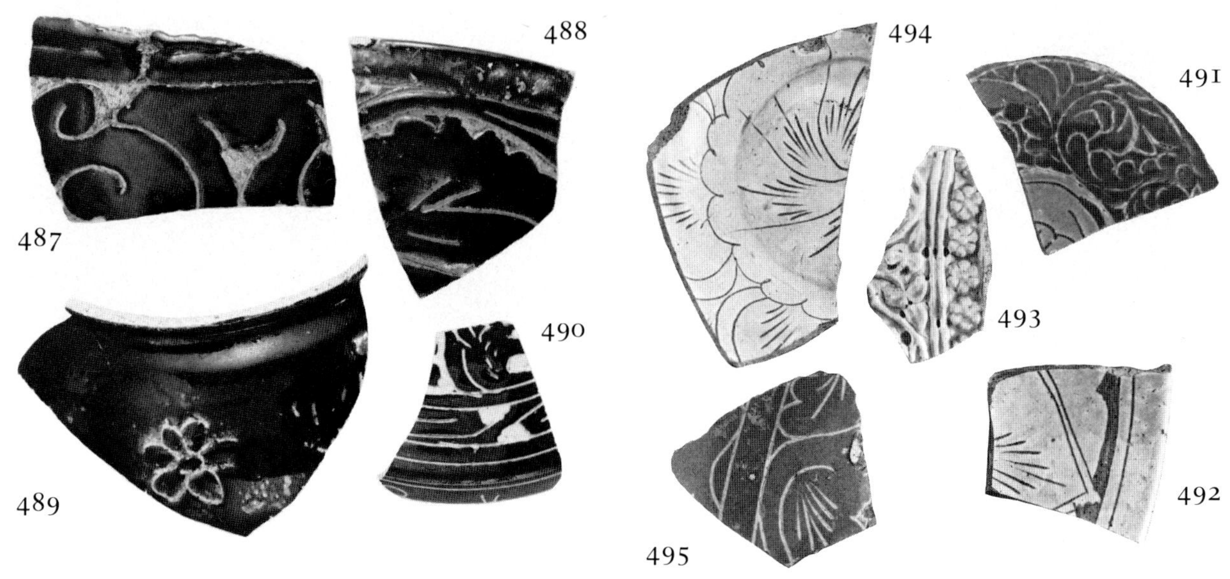

487 488 489 490 491 492 493 494 495 496 497 498 499 500

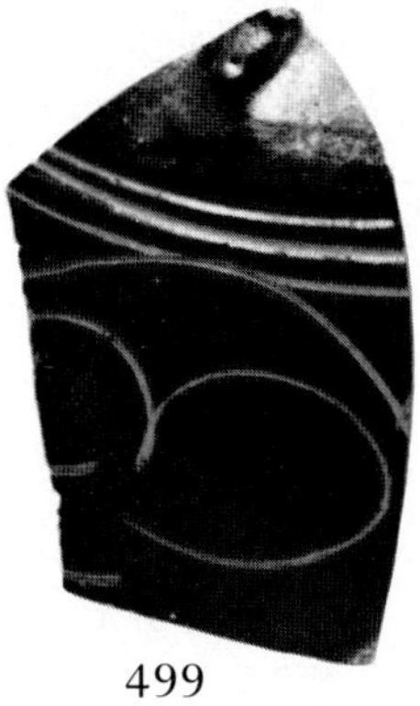

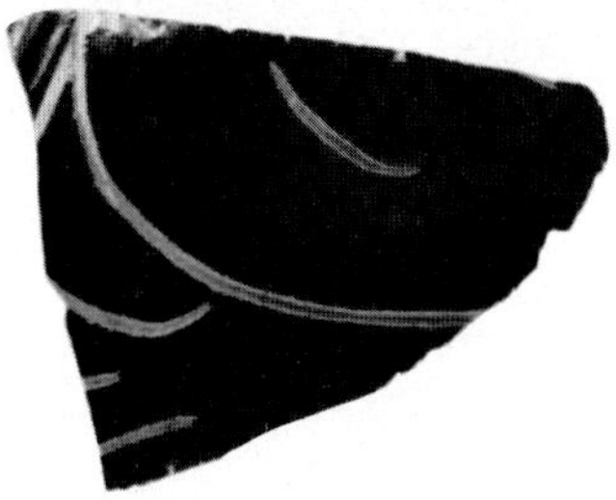

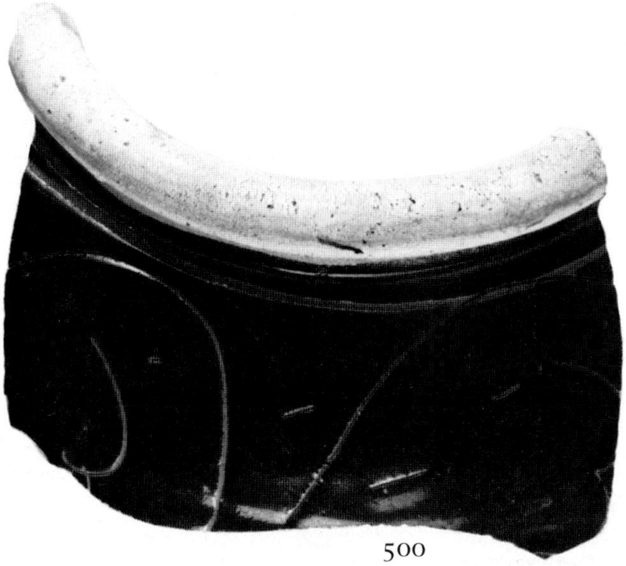

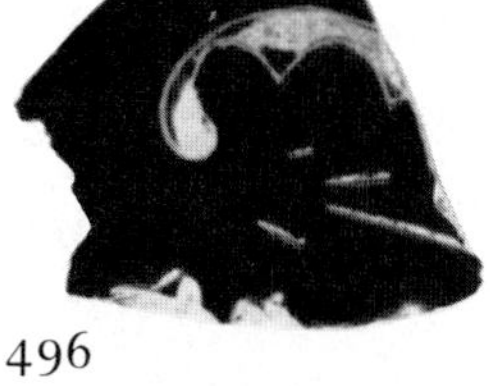

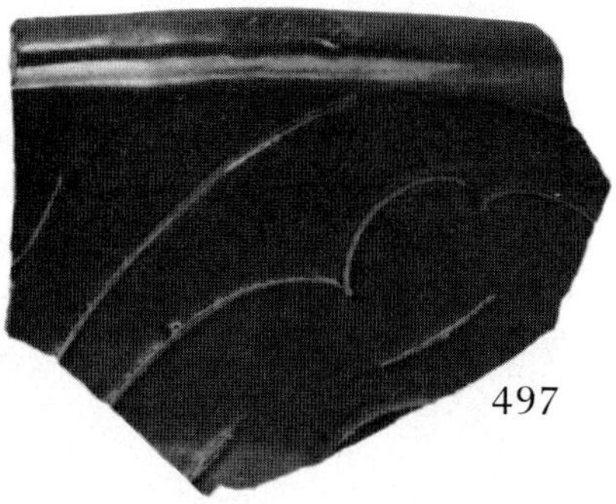